# The Broken Middle

# The Broken Middle

## Out of our Ancient Society

### GILLIAN ROSE

**BLACKWELL**
Oxford UK & Cambridge USA

First published 1992

Blackwell **Publishers**
108 Cowley Road
Oxford OX4 1JF
UK

Three Cambridge Center
Cambridge, Massachusetts 02142
USA

A CIP catalogue record for this book is available from
the British Library.

*Library of Congress Cataloging in Publication Data*

Rose, Gillian.
  The broken middle: out of our ancient society/Gillian Rose.
    p.    cm.
  Includes bibliographical references and index.
  ISBN 0–631–16359–X (alk. paper) – 0–631–18221–7 (pbk)
  1, Philosophy, 2, Law—Philosophy. 3. Ethics.
  4. Philosophy, Modern. 5. Postmodernism. I. Title.
B1649.R73B76   1992
190—dc20                                          91–23667
                                                      CIP

The author and publishers have made every effort to trace those who control
copyright in the chart reproduced here on pages 304–5 from *Community
Architecture* by Nick Wates and Chas Knevitt.

Typeset in 10 on 12pt Bembo
by Graphicraft Typesetters Ltd., Hong Kong
Printed in Great Britain by Billing & Sons Ltd Worcester
This book is printed on acid-free paper.

This book
is dedicated to
Jim Fessenden
and to
Lynn Rose

# Contents

# Acknowledgements

Forbidding as this work may appear at first, it has been my intimate journal and companion over the last few years. It has accompanied me in the move from the University of Sussex to the University of Warwick, and on the journeys made in between — from Jerusalem to Heidelberg to New York and California; and, in between them, on many invisible journeys. And everywhere I go, colleagues and friends and students and family have set me challenges and exploded my horizons.

The germinal chapter of this work arose out of a joint lecture series in the School of European Studies at the University of Sussex in 1985: *Women, State and Revolution*; especial thanks to Sîan Reynolds and Anne Stevens for the original opportunity which, I know, has taken an unconscionably long time to mature. Thanks, too, to Norman Solomon, Alan Udoff and Paul Mendes-Flohr who have opened the international world of Jewish philosophy to me. And to Frank McHugh for introducing me to the intercontinental world of Liberation Theology.

As it ranges across the congregation of the disciplines, the work has continued to be inspired by Tony Thorlby who first invited me to lecture on Kierkegaard within the context of *Modern European Mind* at Sussex. Julius Carlebach, now in Heidelberg, continues to encourage and disagree with me on Judaism and philosophy.

Thanks are due, too, to the ten Ph.d. students who have moved with me from Sussex to Warwick — my itinerant university. Endless discussions with them have sustained this work in its peregrinations.

In the rich environment of Warwick where, across the Departments of Sociology, Law and Philosophy, I find myself among challenging new colleagues and students, many have fast become friends, too numerous to enumerate *in toto*. But special thanks to Joe McCahery for his wit and wisdom; and to Robert Fine, Margaret Archer, David

Wood and Nic Land and Peter Hughes — to each for difficulty and plenitude.

Thanks to Jacqueline Rose, Jim Fessenden, John Milbank and Jay Bernstein for a vigorous foretaste of what may be at stake in the reception of this work — in part or in whole.

Great thanks to Barbara Gray for her ingenuity and expertise in word-processing the manuscript, and for her never-failing fortitude and serenity.

Greg Bright and Howard Caygill suffered and worked the pen-ultimate draft of the text in an act of friendship which assembled grace with law and law with grace. Greg Bright's cover design configures and breaks the middles — utopian and aporetic.

Above all, it is to David Groiser's philosophical imagination that the repeated suspension of the ethical may be traced.

Leamington Spa
April, 1991

# Introduction

## *Diremption of Spirit*

The Owl of Minerva has spread her wings. Not that a shape of life has
grown old, for it has always been already ancient, but we may now be
prepared and readied for comprehension. We may now be prepared and
readied for philosophy's grey in grey; not for the colour on colour of
post-modernity, with its premature celebration of a new epoch for the
coming millennium, even if incipient in the old. For our antiquity has
yet to see the soaring of soft-plumaged Minerva in her nocturnal
figuration.

Philosophy's 'grey in grey' was never intended to damage its endeavour: to keep it quiescent, modestly contemplative, servile or resigned. This subtle array, this grey in grey, would turn hubris not into
humility but into motile configuration. Grey in grey warns against
philosophy's pride of *Sollen*, against any proscription or prescription,
any imposition of ideals, imaginary communities or 'progressive narra-
tions'. Instead the 'idealizations' of philosophy would acknowledge and
recognize actuality and not force or fantasize it. They act as the third,
the middle, their own effectivity at stake between the potentiality and
actuality of the world and engaging at the point where the two come
into a changed relation: not *ex post facto* justification, even less *a priori*
rejuvenation, but reconfiguration, oppositional yet vital – *something
understood*.

The Revolution in the revolutions of 1989 has not 'destroyed' Marxism so much as it has dismantled post-war state-Socialism. We have
been given back the last two hundred years – in life and in letters. All
the debates, all the antinomies of modern state and society addressed
since Hobbes, Smith and Rousseau, have been re-opened as well as the
opportunity to resume examination of the connection between liberalism and Fascism from which post-war state-Socialism has proved such
a dangerous distraction.

In the light of this unforeseen opportunity, the post-modern judgement that has turned against philosophy in order to cultivate a playful Sophistry, replacing knowledge with 'discourses', critique with 'plurality', conceptuality with 'the Other', renouncing in general any association with law or with mediation — may well be mistaken. It may find its hasty celebration of overcome 'Western metaphysics' marred by the fissures of still straining contraries which are neither disbanded nor rendered disarmable by such intellectual velleities. Post-modernity disallows itself any conceptuality or means of comprehension for investigating its own implication and configuration within *the broken middle*. Whereas post-modernity remains dualistic and pits its others against domination, the broken middle is triune. It will investigate the breaks between universal, particular and singular, in individuals and in institutions. Reconfigurations of this trinity, nevertheless, pervade our common sense as oppositions: between inner morality and outer legality, individual autonomy and general heteronomy, active cognition and imposed norm. Made anxious by such inscrutable disjunctions, we invariably attempt to mend them, as will become evident, with *love*, forced or fantasized into the state.

In this work the middle in all its equivocation will appear and reappear as it is found in authorships where it is taken out of the concept and named 'Violence', which is then repeated and represented as ancient — in place of the political history which would come to know why love forced into the state has become ancient. The phenomenological reconstruction of these deconceptualizations and displacements as they appear is attempted here.

The current reaction against philosophy re-enacts the earlier reaction, coterminous with the founding of modernity, according to which philosophy after Kant was 'superseded' by social theory. This supersession was a response to the fourfold differentiation of the meaning of law in Kant — between 'the laws' of necessity and 'the laws' of freedom, and between 'the realm' of legality and 'the realm' of morality. It resulted in the fateful diremption between the conceiving of law as regularity, as positive, and the conceiving of ethics, the ought and the good. The social theory and the philosophy which emerge from this diremption always attempt a forced reconciliation of that which they have made residual by their exclusive accentuation: Comte's positivist law would found a Church, while Nietzsche's Zarathustra would invent New Law Tables.

This diremption between law and ethics — modernity's ancient predicament — is always 'recently' repeated: philosophy is always and hence currently being revalued. Over-unified under some title, such as, 'onto-theology' or 'presence', 'totalization' or 'closure', philosophy is then indicted for this traditionalist pretension, and, once again, it is turned into social theory: 'truth' is revealed to be a value among values; 'rationality', 'justice' and 'freedom' to be types of domination; the faculties of the soul to serve the administration of bodies; while reflexivity and conceptuality are said to be posited by 'discourses', so that meaning is merely the mark of arbitrary, differential signalizations; philosophy of history is seen to be continuous, narratological confection of paralogical discontinuities.

These 'moves', which characterize post-modern thinking, would mend the diremption of law and ethics by turning the struggle between universality, particularity and singularity into a general sociology of control. Yet the security of this new spectatorship is undermined by the tension of freedom and unfreedom which it cannot acknowledge for it has disqualified the actuality of any oppositions which might initiate process and pain − any risk of coming to know. Instead the tension between the contraries of subjective freedom and objective unfreedom appears as unconceptualized aporia − Event of Being, Incursion of the Singular − as a singularity without its contraries of universal and particular. This, as we will see, for all its anti-Utopia and anarchy, will turn into triumphant ecclesiology, as the sociology of the over-controlled secular is inverted into the sociality of saints. Again and again, the diremption of law and ethics will emerge in these configurations.

Even when philosophy and social theory retain their relatively distinct identities, this pattern of the diremption of law and ethics paradoxically keeps philosophy and social theory close, because it appears *within* philosophy and *within* social theory as well as between them: Kierkegaard claims to capture existentially the ethical high ground from the juridical teleology attributed to Hegel; while Durkheim attributes the breakdown in 'social cohesion', i.e. ethical solidarity, in societies based on contract and administrative law, to anomie (*a-nomos*: without a law), in contrast to Weber's attribution of modern 'disenchantment' to the prevalence of the type of formal legal-rational domination separated from the value rationality of the original Protestant ethic.

Since the most 'recent' opposition to philosophy secularizes itself as a sociology of the domination of 'the tradition', while simultaneously rediscovering ineluctable Revelation − as singularity, Event, difference, whether in a gnostic or a negative or, as will be argued, in a positive theology − this work begins by re-examining the original moment of  the modern opposition between holistic comprehension and existential, ethical, Christian Revelation. However, the exposition developed here does not employ the terms now conventional in the opposition between Hegelian-Marxist 'dialectic' and existential 'repetition', with which all

the other oppositions also taken from opposing Kierkegaard or Nietzsche to Hegel and Marx are invariably associated: 'dialectic' implying
objective and absolute truth, philosophy of history, priority of practical
reason or will, identity of thought and being, categorial panlogism;
'repetition' implying interested truth or perspectivism, absence of
historical telos, priority of topography of the body, non-identity of
thought and being, metaphorical elision. This work begins instead by
exploring the diremption of law and ethics as it appears not between
but *within* the conceptuality of Hegel *and* Kierkegaard.

If this is to declare 'with what' the work begins, how can this work
begin? Only with a crisis of communication. For if the diremption of
law and ethics is to appear in the conceptuality of these authorships,
then the form and drama of their works must be shown to yield a
reflexivity which knows that it is bound to resound with the law and
ethics whose diremption is to be witnessed and investigated. This work
begins, therefore, with an essay on the difficulty of beginning, in which
the debate between Hegel and Kierkegaard is restaged through this
predicament of the formal and substantial arrogation of legal and ethical
authority in their authorships – and in mine. Each chapter embraces
the same formal and substantial predicament: on the one hand, it must
presuppose the conceptuality which it would address; on the other
hand, it concentrates on one item of the conceptuality in question. As
the work proceeds, these presuppositions are consecutively and gradually accrued to the exposition, elaborated to their conceptuality, and
then returned to their dynamic in the developing dramaturgy.

For these reasons, the stages and transitions of this conceptual drama
cannot be previewed here; and it follows that, even though names of
authors appear in the titles of the chapters, these chapters are inter-
dependent, and do not provide guides to any of the authors named.

This book develops the work of *Hegel contra Sociology* and *Dialectic of
Nihilism* by pursuing the diremption of law and ethics, expounded, in
the earlier work, as the ideal law which Hegel was unable to obtain,
and, in the later work, as the post-Kantian 'antinomy of law' which
resurfaces in latter-day nihilism. For if in *Hegel contra Sociology* it was
argued that Hegel could not expound a law which is not posited, for
'Antigone's law had no concept, and positing, modern law, has no
intuition';[1] in *Dialectic of Nihilism* the declared antinomianism of post-
structuralism was expounded as a series of regresses to identifiable types
or epochs of legal form, and this paradox was discovered to be continuous with the difficulty in the conceiving of law since Kant. What I
there called 'the antinomy of law' appears here as the dual implication

---

[1] Rose, *Hegel contra Sociology*, p. 199.

of law and ethics. There it appeared as regularity and rule, or as generality and force; or, better, the 'juridical' and the 'litigious' in law, for both of these terms carry impositional and ethical connotations.[2] If *Dialectic of Nihilism* argued that post–structuralist nihilism completes itself as law – unreflected but always historically identifiable – this work argues that post–modern antinomianism completes itself as political theology, as new ecclesiology, mending the diremption of law and ethics. In *Dialectic of Nihilism*, Nietzsche was reclaimed from antinomian nihilism, here Kierkegaard is reclaimed from antinomian repetition: their putative opposition to law turns out to be as misapprehended as their putative opposition to 'knowledge' – whether cognition, critique or comprehension. Similarly, the vulnerability of their ardent students – post–structuralism and post–modernism – to the inversion of their antinomianism into recognizable legal forms or mended ecclesiology, is deeply allied to their disqualification of any complementary comprehension. Not that comprehension completes or closes, but that it returns diremption to where it cannot be overcome in exclusive thought or in partial action – as long as its political history persists. The complementarity of comprehension to diremption involves reflection on what may be ventured – without mending diremption in heaven or on earth.

[2] Rose, *Dialectic of Nihilism*, pp. 2, 17 n. 30.

*Part One*

# From the Middle in the Beginning

# 1

# Personae of the System

## *Kierkegaard, Hegel and Blanchot*

*Unscientific Beginning*

Preliminary
One must just begin, not waste time on doubting.
It is no easy matter.[1]

One must not spend too much time.
One must just begin, and then it would turn out all right.
One should embrace the eternal philosophy.[2]

The tradition of the new, which understands itself to be 'modern' and hence without tradition, has contrived an ironic stance towards the System and its philosopher – Hegel, The Philosopher for modernity as Aristotle became simply The Philosopher to the Middle Ages. As a result of this all-pervasive irony, the most self-proclaimed, unsystematic, fragmentary, contingent, singular, pained and painful beginnings – even Rosenzweig's beginning with death (beginning, that is, with the ending)[3] – in short, the most unscientific beginnings, begin scientifically.

Blanchot summarizes and ostensibly concludes this epoch of the Hegelian vortex-ring:

One cannot 'read' Hegel, except by not reading him. To read, not to read him – to understand, to misunderstand him, to reject him

---

[1] Kierkegaard, *Philosophical Fragments* (HVH-EHH), Supplement, p. 249.
[2] Ibid., p. 248.
[3] Rosenzweig, *The Star of Redemption*, p. 3 tr. p. 5, begins 'Vom Tode, von der Furcht des Todes, hebt alles Erkennen des All an'.

— all this falls under the authority of Hegel or doesn't take place at all. Only the intensity of this nonoccurrence, in the impossibility that there be such a thing, prepares us for a death — the death of reading, the death of writing — which leaves Hegel living: the living travesty of completed Meaning. (Hegel the impostor: this is what makes him invincible, mad with his seriousness, counterfeiter of Truth: 'putting one over' to the point of becoming, all unbeknownst to him, master of irony . . . )[4]

Since Kierkegaard proclaimed already in 1841 that 'irony . . . met its master in Hegel',[5] such mastery — itself conceded here ironically, in verbose and laconic mode, respectively — would appear to operate both retrospectively and prospectively.

What exceeds the system is the impossibility of its failure, and likewise the impossibility of its success. Ultimately nothing can be said of it, and there is a way of keeping still (the lacunary silence of writing), that halts the system, leaving it idle, delivered to the seriousness of irony.[6]

While dual-directional temporality is attributed to *Meister* Hegel, the System is then sketched as an eternally arrested movement, equally an idling stasis. *Mut zur Lücke*, courage for the gaps, the sole residual opposition, can only be yielded by the System itself. The System thereby incorporates and unifies even its own lacks. This is the seriousness of irony; the facetiousness of irony is spent on Hegel — 'the impostor'. System and silence 'deliver' and are 'delivered' by each other, and this mutual qualifying issues in their double disqualification. Can such an effusive and undermining *laudatio* for a philosophy of history have any equal in the history of philosophy?

The correct criticism of the System does not consist (as is most often, complacently, supposed) in finding fault with it, or in interpreting it insufficiently (which even Heidegger sometimes does), but rather in rendering it invincible, invulnerable to criticism or, as they say, inevitable. Then, since nothing escapes it because of its omnipresent unity and the perfect cohesion of everything, there remains no place for fragmentary writing unless it comes into focus as the impossible necessary: as that which is

---

[4] Blanchot, *The Writing of the Disaster*, p. 79, tr. pp. 46–7, citing Sylviane Agacinski.
[5] Kierkegaard, *The Concept of Irony*, p. 260.
[6] Blanchot, *The Writing of the Disaster*, pp. 79–80, tr. p. 47

written in the time outside time, in the sheer suspense which without restraint breaks the seal of unity by, precisely, not breaking it, but by leaving it aside without this ever being able to be known.[7]

This 'correct criticism' coming into and out of focus as 'the impossible necessary' is both more honest and more dishonest than many: it acknowledges that standard refutations of the System in the name of an exceeding moment – contingency (Pannenberg), finitude (Taminiaux),[8] non-identity (Adorno), *differance* (Derrida), *l'Autre/Autrui* (Levinas), pain (Blanchot), death (Rosenzweig) – are strategic: ways of beginning. It also acknowledges that these gestures or 'moves' against the System affirm one, 'Hegel', as Master of those who, by their panironic reversals, themselves reinstate the 'authority' of the very System. They find a way of saying 'of it' by, apparently, saying against it – proclaiming their abandonment loudly to shroud their purloining with silence.

But, here, in this case, the additional ploy of celebrating the only consistent abandonment as *the* one that cannot be known in terms of the omnipresent System cleverly distracts, by drawing attention ostentatiously yet preciously to such modesty 'without restraint', from this most predictable 'move' in which it is once again engaging. The legal title of the beached System is made to signal the immodest, u-topian, fragment, which by virtue of such attention becomes more focused and better known than any laborious, comprehensive thinking.

One thing is clear: *we* cannot now begin with 'Hegel', nor with the 'System', nor, *a fortiori*, with 'Kierkegaard'. Perhaps we may begin by asking why the tradition sets up – in order to worship and to denigrate – the idol of the 'System', and the imperial sovereignty of 'Hegel': authority and author.[9] And, then, why it does the same with 'Kierkegaard', who, pseudonymously, made the paradoxical relation between author, authority, actor and truth, the route of thinking and existing.[10]

---

[7]  Ibid., pp. 100–1, tr. p. 61 amended.

[8]  Taminiaux, *Dialectic and Difference: Finitude in Modern Thought*.

[9]  Derrida attempts to assimilate the 'strange' name 'Hegel' to the eagle, *aigle*, and hence to 'imperial or historic power' in the third paragraph of *Glas*, p. 7, tr. p. 1.

[10]  Thulstrup in *Kierkegaard's Relation to Hegel* defines the relationship empirically not conceptually and only covers up to 1846. Hannay in *Kierkegaard* takes Hegel's 'unhappy consciousness' initially to organize his investigation but does not follow through the rest of the *Phenomenology of Spirit* or the *Logic*. Taylor in *Journeys to Selfhood: Hegel and Kierkegaard* rectifies these limitations by sustaining his contrast and comparison as two *Heilsgeschichte* in the form of *Bildungsgeschichte* beyond the aesthetic and the ethical to logic and philosophy of religion. However, he presupposes and hypostatizes 'selfhood' as a final goal; and, above all, he attributes each and every position to 'Hegel' or to 'Kierkegaard' *simpliciter*, without negotiating phenomenology, system or pseudonym.

Why has the tradition not trusted itself to think without such towering 'authorities' and 'masters', without attributing the content and matter of the tradition to the writing of genii — instead of learning from it what thinking might be and how individuality, whether outstanding or not, is to be identified? To follow Hegel's or Kierkegaard's 'authority' consistently would involve not delineating authorities: to follow the counsel from the *Preface* to the *Phenomenology of Spirit* to proceed without 'pistols'; from the *Concluding Unscientific Postscript* to proceed from the relationship to one's 'own author' and not from the pseudonymous one.

Perhaps it is necessary to begin in more than one way — which is not to propose a plural beginning but to propose another carriageway, without the 'System' and without irony to beginning: to begin again by developing the beginning.

In his seminal essay 'Hermeneutic and Universal History' (1959), Pannenberg makes a shrewd comment on Gadamer's relation to Hegel:

> It is a peculiar spectacle to see how an incisive and penetrating author has his hands full trying to keep his thoughts from going in the direction they inherently want to go. Gadamer's book [*Truth and Method*] offers this kind of spectacle when he strives to avoid the Hegelian total mediation of the truth of the present by means of history.[11]

Pannenberg's subsequent attempt to conceive 'the unity of history' with deference to and independence from both Gadamer and Hegel provides a less guileful but no less difficult and, it turns out, self-concluding beginning. The whole work of Gadamer's is said to be engaged in 'a partly open, partly tacit debate with Hegel'[12] over, precisely, openness: 'With the form of Hegel's philosophy of spirit in mind, he [Gadamer] regards such an undertaking as claiming "to perform a total mediation of history and the present". Against this, Gadamer insists on the "openness . . . in which experience is acquired".'[13] How open, then, can Gadamer's emphasis on the 'openness of experience' be if tacitness is the precondition of its eminence? Fully aware that the author and his thoughts are not to be equated, Pannenberg seems, nevertheless, only half-aware that ruse is needed to pit 'openness' against 'the System'.

He seems even less aware of his own cunning. For while the system of the absolute idea is said to 'overleap' the 'irreducible finitude of

[11] Pannenberg, *Basic Questions in Theology*, p. 129.
[12] Ibid., p. 121 n. 55.
[13] Ibid., p. 121.

experience', to close a future which would continuously bring forth 'surprising experiences', and further to fail 'to *recognize* the impossibility of taking account of the contingent and the individual by means of the universal [emphasis added]',[14] in 'Redemptive Event and History' (1963), the ground of the unity of contingency and continuity is expounded as the origin of events *and* of history:

> The God who by the transcendence of his freedom is the origin of contingency in the world, is also the ground of the unity which comprises the contingencies as history. It seems that only the origin of the contingency of events can, by virtue of its unity, also be the origin of its continuity without injuring its contingency. However, the unity of history does not consist merely in its transcendent origin. Events are not only contingent in relation to each other, but they also cohere among each other. This indwelling connection between them is grounded in the transcendent unity of God, which manifests itself as faithfulness. If, however, the connection of events is grounded in the faithfulness of the free God, then we do not have to conceive a continuity of something enduring from the past into the future: after the manner, say, of a development. Rather, we have to think of events which are in themselves contingent, as being at the same time linked backward and referred to what has happened. By means of such backward linking the continuity of history is constantly re-established. This is the way in which the faithfulness of God expresses itself. Only in this way, as a backward-reaching incorporation of the contingently new into what has been, but not the reverse, as a predetermining mastery and its effects, can the primary connection of history be conceived without losing its contingency.[15]

The attempt to present the origin of continuity *and* contingency without 'a predetermining mastery' and without 'development' can only be stated by the long shots evident in this passage which simply posits and prescribes the perpetual 'incorporation' of contraries. This admitted 'incorporation' which is yet no 'mastery' may be traced to the implicit, yet astonishing, assumption that any 'development' could occur without stumbling blocks or 'surprises' — that development does not presuppose *aporia* but excludes it. 'Finitude' or 'experience', surprising or banal, is only addressed at this level of generality — which greatly exceeds the universality under indictment. The result here, as

---

[14]  Ibid., p. 134.
[15]  Ibid., pp. 74–6.

Pannenberg discovered to a lesser extent in the work of Gadamer, is a Hegelianism rigidified in its efforts to prevent its own self-perfecting, and which falls into such programmatic statements because it fixes its own beginning.

This striving to begin and end in the same paragraph arises from trying to think together the lessons of 'Hegel' and 'Kierkegaard' without the former's so-called 'determinism', and without the latter's oblique, non-homogeneous Incursions into 'the universal correlative connections of human history' at scandalous moments of paradox. Without recognizing what it recognizes so well in its predecessor (Gadamer), however, namely the tacit straining of its own impulse to go beyond these one-dimensional presentations of adversaries, such thinking nevertheless suffers from the repeated inhibiting of its intrinsic 'development': it keeps arresting its own beginning.

Adorno, by limiting his beginning to the 'Construction of the Aesthetic', the subtitle of his book on 'Kierkegaard', keeps ending before he has begun:

> Kierkegaard's doctrine or teaching [*Lehre*] of existing may be called realism without actuality. It contests the identity of thinking and being, without, however, seeking Being anywhere except in the sphere of thinking itself. But here, precisely, it [Being] refuses itself to thinking as answer: the being of the self becomes functional, defined as 'relation' whose movement is to be pledged to an ontological 'meaning' − without *Dasein* thereby becoming transparent. As a result, ontological meaning and the substrate of the self as well as what is predicted of these − the structure of the qualities of inwardness as their 'reality' − become intrinsically antinomical. Kierkegaard's full philosophy of existence is nothing other than the attempt to master the antinomy of *Dasein* in thought, and to justify its truth content. And to do this in systematic form. He manages at every point to make Hegel's 'system of *Dasein*' contemptible. Yet by including *Dasein* in consciousness in his own account; by making the subjective act of freedom into the most inward determination of subjectivity; by subordinating the image of humanity to pure determinations of thought, he succumbs to the pressure of the idealistic system.[16]

Adorno discerns *and* overlooks the paradox of authorship at the same time: he points out, quite rightly, the apparent reduction of existential pathos to the realm of thought it purports to transcend; that 'inward-

---

[16]   Adorno, *Kierkegaard*, p. 156, tr. p. 86. All translations from this work are my own.

ness' and 'subjectivity' would seem to echo, in an ahistorical generalization, Hegel's exposition of the 'hypertrophy of inner life'; and,
furthermore, that delineation of 'stages on life's way' presupposes an
irresistible systematic framework. Yet by simply attributing this
'identity of thought and being' in the 'sphere of thinking' to 'Kierkegaard's doctrine of existing', Adorno is hovering precariously on Johannes Climacus' ladder — vainly translating the latter's self-advertising
philosophical-existential eros into a mismanaged Hegelian systematics,
and quite missing the deeper, ironic engagement of Johannes Climacus
with the persistent modern philosophical illusion of pure (Descartes to
Kant) and sullied (Hegel) 'subjectivity'.

Significantly, it is in the prose poem of his own existential pathos,
*Minima Moralia*, that Adorno, with bitter-sweet precision, engages the
issues of Kierkegaard's authorship by scandalous inversions, such as
'The Health unto Death';[17] 'Wrestling club [of intellectuals] . . . bouts
arranged and contested by inwardness' — 'Their lives, put so radically
at stake, have after all a reliable armoury at their disposal, and the ready
use they make of it gives the lie to their struggle with the angel . . . For
the power which steers the conflicts, the ethos of responsibility and
integrity, is always authoritarian, a mask of the State';[18] 'Gold assay' —
'gold and genuineness [Kierkegaard's doctrine of existence (has) made
the ideal of authenticity a centrepiece of metaphysics] precisely express
only the fungibility, the comparability of things'; 'even in the first
conscious experiences of childhood, . . . the impulses . . . are not quite
"genuine". They always contain an element of initiation, play, wanting
to be different.'[19]

These indignant rejections — which are equally appropriations of
Kierkegaard's own lessons — and which accuse him of no mask, of
feigned mask, of authoritarian mask, amount to *determinate* negations
which have the effect of reaffirming the substance to be reconsidered:
author, authority, truth. In *Minima Moralia* the play of System and
fragment revitalizes both their intrinsic connection and the history of
their difference. Yet in his book *Kierkegaard*, Adorno would feign *not* to
know that 'Johannes Climacus' is the mask of systematic illusion. Even
if Adorno is himself masked (the characterization of Kierkegaard as
'realism without an actuality' might so suggest, since this indictment
inverts the existential claim that existence precedes essence, while the
rest of the argument merely assimilates its terms), his overall

---

[17]  Adorno, *Minima Moralia*, p. 68, tr. p. 58.
[18]  Ibid., pp. 133–4, the 'wrestling match' presumably taken from 'The Concluding
Letter' to Kierkegaard, *Repetition* (HVH-EHH), p. 227.
[19]  Ibid., pp. 201, 206n., 202, tr. pp. 152, 154, 153.

affirmation of comprehensive thinking is too quick to gather 'Kierk-egaad' into its fold on the tinsel ground of the 'construction of the aesthetic', instead of following the whole authorship, pseudonymous *and* signatured. This celerity prescinds the concept as much as the authorship; it terminates the beginning before it has begun.

The beginning can no longer be made by presupposing the concept any more than it can be made by denigrating the System, even ironical-ly. We are now — and have been — beginning by coming to recognize the occlusions and stumbling blocks lying across the beginning. Every beginning so far encountered, whether contra or pro the System, appears as a mask: contra-masks of new-born beginning, *restitutio in prisinum*, yet wrested from the System's authority; pro-masks, drawn from hypostatized representations of the System itself, yet intended, perversely, to re-enter its inner process: the latter — illusory mask, the former — masked illusion. However, all this philosophical wit has itself been to school, I venture, in Hegel's *Phenomenology of Spirit* which recapitulates the play of personae — the story of how natural conscious-ness acquired 'personality' — legal, aesthetic, moral — a story itself fitfully comprehended by philosophical consciousness which then pro-ceeds unevenly through the stumbling blocks of personified aporia after personified aporia as each configured concept is mismatched to its object and corrected by a newly configured concept mismatched to its object, again — and then again.

Just as this play of personae is the key to Hegel's authorship without authority, so systematic illusion is the key to Kierkegaard's pseudo-nymity. More illusion, not less, is needed to eject 'the single one' pseudonymously addressed from further refuge in thought. The author must draw on the plenitude of this illusory resource of thinking: phi-losophy; and on the resource of dramatized illusion: the initial, negative self-relation of the potential single one, or 'actress' — for by 'negative self-relation' woman is explicitly defined, and she may, therefore, have the advantage in coming to understand, in making the beginning. The 'author', however engendered, lapses into thought in order for *her*, the actress's, faith to be possible.

So how can she or we begin when we seem to have lost both our faith *and* our concept: our possibility of beginning?

> For that in which all human life is united is passion, and faith is a passion . . .[20]

Thus the beginning is inferred, *de silentio*: *de silentio* is the legal term for inference from omission.

---

[20] Kierkegaard, *Fear and Trembling* (HVH-EHH), p. 67.

## *Dialectical Lyric*

> Now the story of Abraham has the remarkable quality that it will
> always be glorious no matter how impoverished our understand-
> ing of it, but only − for it is true here too − if we are willing to
> 'labour and be heavy laden'. But labour we will not, and yet we
> still want to understand the story.[21]

The labour required to make us fear and tremble over the story of
Abraham has been repeatedly overlooked.

> Here it is no help to have Abraham as one's father, or seventeen
> centuries of noble ancestry; of anyone who will not work here one
> can say what is written about Israel's virgins, he gives birth to
> wind − while the one who works will give birth to his own
> father.[22]

> This man was no learned exegete, he knew no Hebrew; had he
> known Hebrew then perhaps it might have been easy for him to
> understand the story of Abraham.[23]

Even the most astute and engaged commentators, Adorno and Fackenheim, attribute this dialectical lyric to 'Kierkegaard', and indict it,
respectively, for its caricature of Hegel and of Judaism. But it does not
simply represent the views of 'Kierkegaard', and, *a fortiori*, it does not
tell us what he knows or does not know. Furthermore, it plainly and
carefully begs pardon of both Hegel and Judaism, and proceeds by
dramatic means to the confession: 'For my part I can in a way understand Abraham, but I see very well that I lack . . . the courage to act like
Abraham'.[24] In order to reach this insight cast as a self-judgement,
Johannes *de silentio* suspends not only the ethical but Abraham as father
('no help to have Abraham as one's father') and Hebrew as mother-
tongue ('had he known Hebrew', etc.). While the ethical is suspended
in more senses than *de silentio* admits, the labour of retelling the story is
lost by our efforts to follow its twists and turns.

Fackenheim[25] discusses Kant's judgement of the *Akedah* − the binding of Isaac − which he cites from 'The Conflict of the Faculties':

---

[21]  Kierkegaard, *Fear and Trembling* (AH), p. 58 and (HVH-EHH), p. 28; Matt. 3:9.
[22]  Ibid. (AH), p. 57.
[23]  Ibid., p. 44.
[24]  Ibid., p. 143.
[25]  Fackenheim, *Encounters between Judaism and Modern Philosophy*, p. 34.

Abraham should have replied to this putative divine voice: 'That
I may not kill my good son is absolutely certain. But that you
who appear to me are God is not certain and *cannot* become
certain, even though the voice were to sound from the very
heavens' . . . [For] that a voice which one seems to hear cannot be
divine one can be certain of . . . in case what is commanded is
contrary to moral law. However majestic or supernatural it may
appear to be, one must regard it as a deception.[26]

Kant here delivers the precise judgement which *de silentio* claims Hegel
should deliver: '. . . Hegel goes wrong . . . in not protesting loudly and
clearly against the honour and glory enjoyed by Abraham as the father
of faith when he should really be remitted to some lower court for trial
and exposed as a murderer.'[27] It is Kant not Hegel who appears to
defend the kind of ethical universality which *de silentio* would have us
take as true to The Philosopher's position.

By comparing Kant and 'Kierkegaard' on the *Akedah*, Fackenheim
brings out the many other notions of the ethical suspended in the
retelling of the story:

> In short, whereas Kant bids Jewish thought to reject even the
> original Akedah, Kierkegaard demands of Jewish thought the
> eternal perpetuation of its possibility. Whereas Kant will not let
> the Torah rest on Abraham's merit, Kierkegaard would rob us of
> the Torah, which forbids child sacrifice.[28]

For Kant is concerned to justify biblical faith not as a consequence of
apprehending 'the infinite by the senses' — which the example of the
'myth' of the sacrifice of Isaac is made to serve — but as a teaching
which draws 'from the pure spring of universal rational religion dwelling in every ordinary man . . . which has as its basis a book of God's
covenant with Abraham'.[29] Yet 'if God should really speak to man,
man could still never *know* that it was God speaking'.[30] Kant translates
the ethical — here the experience of the covenantal community — into
the moral — the inner voice of individual conscience. Not that there is
no dilemma but that the covenant, the voice of God, is *presupposed* in
the original, biblical version from the initial command to journey to

---

[26] Kant, *The Conflict of the Faculties*, p. 63 and note.
[27] Kierkegaard, *Fear and Trembling* (AH), pp. 83–4.
[28] Fackenheim, *Encounters between Judaism and Modern Philosophy*, p. 63.
[29] Kant, *The Conflict of the Faculties*, pp. 63, 62.
[30] Ibid., p. 63, emphasis in original.

Mount Moriah: God's speech is prior to human speech. Kant works hard simultaneously to affirm and to deny biblical faith.[31]

'For Kierkegaard every believer is a potential Abraham. For the Midrash the sons of the covenant are children of Abraham, by whose merit the covenant both was established and survived.'[32] What Fackenheim formulates here (against 'Kierkegaard's' misapprehension of the *Akedah*) 'as perpetually reenacted and superseded past',[33] the liturgical repetition of the divine call which founds and identifies the holy community — the actualization not the suspension of the ethical — is the original meaning which *de silentio* does acknowledge when he deliberately sets aside sonship and tongueship. Yet by attributing the narrative voice to 'Kierkegaard' *tout court*, as if his authorship were analogous to Kant's (whose authorship, while not pseudonymous, also relies on personae), when it is *de silentio* who recounts, and when the discourse belongs — scandalously perhaps — to the 'aesthetic' stage, Fackenheim inadvertently reveals just how much labour is required to take a biblical tale which *presupposes* divine interlocutor, covenant, Torah, community, witness, and to recast it as a never-before-heard-of confrontation between the single one and his God.

Adorno picks out a different scandal: what he calls Kierkegaard's 'theology of sacrifice [*Opfertheologie*]',[34] taken from *Fear and Trembling*, which he claims determines 'the dialectical structure of his whole work'.[35] 'Sacrifice' is 'the ultimate category of nature ... elevated and expunged' as the sacrifice of spirit itself.[36] Not Isaac but consciousness and intellect are sacrificed in a 'mythical' reconciliation — the logical outcome of voracious idealism which assimilates actuality to its own notion and simultaneously annihilates itself in the idea of paradoxical sacrifice.[37] This is the paradox behind the paradox: consciousness so over-extended, so all-consuming of 'nature', that it cancels its other, and in so doing destroys itself; for consciousness which has no other is consciousness of nothing or not consciousness: 'Spirit itself is the annihilated natural life'.[38]

Sacrifice is 'mythical', Adorno elaborates, in the Greek sense from

---

[31] Buber also stresses that Kierkegaard 'does not take into consideration the fact that the problematics of the decision of faith is preceded by the problematics of hearing itself'; see 'On the Suspension of the Ethical', in *Eclipse of God*, pp. 117–18.

[32] Fackenheim, *Encounters between Judaism and Modern Philosophy*, p. 66.

[33] Ibid., p. 57.

[34] Adorno, *Kierkegaard*, p. 193, tr. p. 108.

[35] Ibid., p. 206, tr. p. 115.

[36] Ibid., p. 192, tr. p. 107.

[37] Ibid., pp. 192–3, 191, tr. pp. 107–8, 107.

[38] Ibid., p. 195, tr. p. 109.

which Kierkegaard is at such pains to distinguish it in *Fear and Trembling*. The silence of the Greek hero subserves blind fate. It does not restore order but either dominates or is dominated 'by the cosmic caesura'.[39] Kierkegaard's 'polemic' against myth turns into mythical doctrine: the proposition that 'Christ came into the world to suffer' is paradoxical but also mythical: for the idea of abolishing suffering amounts to a mythical extirpation of nature.[40] Not only the ethical but life, too, disappears in the abyss of the natural: expiated by the sacrifice of Christ in the moment.[41]

According to Adorno, Kierkegaard produces a heterodoxy − a gnosticism − by overspiritualizing both the God and man as his follower.[42] The very idea of 'paradoxical sacrifice' is the mythical and historical guise which nature, entirely determined by thought, assumes. 'Paradox' thereby acquires a 'total function', because it categorically includes all contrary specific contents: it cannot therefore be corrected or fulfilled.[43] The shuddering mask of sacrifice − which posits subjectivity as truth − reveals paradox to be a mask of the demonic:

> In demonic sacrifice man remains ruler of sinful creation, through sacrifice he asserts his domination and his demony kills the name of God.[44]

This original and challenging exposition of 'Kierkegaard' has its own masks: it nonchalantly attributes the whole authorship to 'Kierkegaard', and deliberately reduces it to an aesthetic category without acknowledging that it is silence (*de silentio*) who speaks. As a result it presents 'paradox' in terms of 'sacrifice', and 'sacrifice' in terms of oppositions and contradictions: nature/spirit; elevating/expunging; dominator/dominated. 'Paradox' becomes the sum of all possible reconciliations and annihilations.

Adorno has so dedicated his own discourse to the *idea* of 'sacrifice' that he utterly misses the point that nothing is sacrificed; and that no sacrifice ever occurs in *Fear and Trembling*. While Adorno proclaims the aesthetic−erotic oppositions of spirit versus nature, fulfilment versus lack, *de silentio* pits story against story, crisis against crisis, to educate the reader by bringing out the difference between 'resignation', which

---

[39]  Ibid., p. 194, tr. p. 109.

[40]  Ibid., pp. 196, 197, tr. p. 110.

[41]  Ibid., p. 198, tr. p. 111.

[42]  Ibid., pp. 201, 203, tr. pp. 112, 113. *Heterodoxie*, p. 112, is translated as 'heresy'.

[43]  Ibid., p. 208, tr. p. 116.

[44]  Ibid., p. 211, tr. p. 118.

accepts the opposed dichotomies of loss and gain, infinite and finite, spirit and nature; and 'faith', which is repetition or plenitude without possession or presence. These *positions* are not *oppositions* — they can be suffered simultaneously. They do not even share the *tertium comparationis* of being 'positions': the former, 'resignation', may be a position — a 'swimming' position: for or against the tide of infinite pain — but the latter, 'faith', is a matter of 'floating': for which *de silentio* admits he is not strong enough. It is Adorno who reconciles and annihilates oppositions: pseudonyms and 'Kierkegaard'; aesthetic, ethical, religious stages to Christian categories and modes; nature and spirit. Adorno's charge that 'Kierkegaard' proposes reconciliation without realization means that he, Adorno, fails to hear *de silentio* or silence, out of which comes the articulated air — that realization or lack of realization is not only not the same as redemption but not even its opposite. These 'nots' imply no negative theology but sacramental passion. Adorno halts at the dialectical 'sacrifice', where the lyric, *Fear and Trembling*, sacralizes.

> As soon as I want to begin . . . everything turns around and I flee back to the pain of resignation. I can swim in life, but for this mysterious floating I am too heavy. To exist in such a way that my opposition to existence expresses itself every instant as the most beautiful and safest harmony, that I cannot do.[45]

*de silentio*'s confessions of failing — always — are 'his' silence, the silence of the text, its apophatic moment, obtained by mediation and illusion and thus made comprehensible. The illusory persona of 'silence' — no 'person' at all, yet the middle and mediator — can only introduce himself and his concerns with humour and facetiousness: how can a poet, moreover, one who is *et eleganter*,[46] initiate us into the anguish of an undesired revelation? How distract us from the further offence that Abraham — whose career began when he smashed the idols in his father's shop (the Koran dwells more lavishly on this than the Bible)[47] — is taken to represent 'the aesthetic'? Worse still: Abraham, patriarch of patriarchs, is made to illustrate *Christian* chivalry, a romance of the rose — 'the Knight' — whether qualified as 'resigned' or as 'faithful'. This remorseless mounting of paradox upon paradox breaks our inherited and inherent concepts against their limit — casting us out of them and so changing them and us as we cautiously resume their burden.

The ruse of this 'dialectical lyric' is not, as *de silentio* rightly protests,

[45]  Kierkegaard, *Fear and Trembling*, (AH), p. 78.
[46]  Ibid., p. 43.
[47]  Koran, Sura 6:70–85, Sura 21:50–70.

to write the System,[48] but to stage a re-enactment of its first, focal, fatal, and fateful wisdom: that life must be risked in order to be gained; that only by discovering the limit of life − death − is 'life' itself discovered, and recalcitrant otherness opens its potentialities and possibilities. Instead of presenting this drama, intrinsic to and negotiated by each individual life − however collectively defined − as the struggle of two adversaries, the outcome of which will be, at one extreme, death, at the other extreme, mutual recognition, but invariably some unstable and reversible relation of lordship and bondage, subsequently internalized by each, *de silentio* would make us risk not our own life but the life of an other yet dearer than our own: Isaac. He begins by taking a risk − suspending, in the simple sense of setting aside, not the ethical, but the erotic, by narrating a collision which cannot be absorbed into our infinite erotic egoism, and yet is elaborated by disanalogous tales of hopeless love such as the young lad and the princess, Agnete and the Merman.[49] Taking a biblical tale we already know and revere, and trying to isolate it from its age-old ethical and holy meaning, *de silentio* runs the further risks of driving us to Hegel or to Judaism or to Greek tragedy − when the orders of Knighthood are the intended qualification.

The willingness to sacrifice Isaac brings Abraham to a crisis which does not return him to him*self*; he does not progress to a new level of self-consciousness, nor does he 'sacrifice' either consciousness or self, as Adorno claims, for he had neither in the first place − except as one who bears the promise of the future of Israel. Abraham is 'incommensurable', which is why *de silentio* is so voluble.[50] Abraham illustrates 'sublime' pathos while *de silentio* narrates in the pathos of representation; the narrative moves from the biblical sublime to erotic loss, and from these 'to express[ing] the sublime in the pedestrian absolutely.'[51] This *modus* of sublimity in which absolute meaning can only be pointed or referred to, but never adequately expressed in a representation, is the point of ultimate affinity between fear and trembling, Hegel's System and Judaism. In Hegel, Judaism is expounded as the religion of the sublime (and it is this   not the Kantian ethical universality attributed to the System − which is relevant) in which God is said to be utterly

---

[48]   Kierkegaard, *Fear and Trembling* (AH), p. 43.
[49]   Ibid., pp. 70f, 120f. *de silentio* calls it an 'interest . . . in which an individual concentrates the whole of life's reality . . . I have chosen falling in love to illustrate the movements because this interest will no doubt be more readily understood', p. 71n.
[50]   Ibid., p. 69.
[51]   Ibid., p. 70.

remote from the 'natural' world. If, as Fackenheim has commented, this remoteness is balanced by covenantal mutuality,[52] which does not 'mediate' but sacralizes everyday life in minute detail, then that for which *de silentio* has 'no strength' is already and fully comprehensible — regardless of whether it has been or can be achieved.

Thus no generation has learnt from another how to love, no generation can begin other than at the beginning, the task of no later generation is shorter than its predecessor's, and if someone, unlike the previous generation, is unwilling to stay with love but wants to go further, then that is simply idle and foolish talk.[53]

*de silentio* begins again — in the 'Epilogue': it is this modern, historically specific need to separate *the lesson of love from the lesson of law* that accounts for the personae, the masks, and for lyrical and speculative beginnings and endings — whether by *de silentio* or by the Owl of Minerva. *de silentio* distinguishes Abraham from the tragic hero who is saved by the middle term, the ethical. Thus: Agamemnon, Jephthah, Brutus — king, judge, consul — whose communities, (respectively) Greek 'nation', Israel, Roman state, are able to understand the killing of their offspring and hence to grieve with them and for them.[54] Abraham's incomparability is flaunted by the question whether their actions would have been comprehensible had any one of them sacrificed daughters and sons 'unbound by any promise that would decide the fate of his people'.[55] Yet, inadvertently, a point of comparison does emerge from this apparent incommensurability: for it is *the shared and known law* that enables the people in each case to participate in their sovereign's loss; and it is communal lamentation that then makes the movement from loss to restoration. This is how everything is 'received back' when, historically, the people have become distinct from their sovereign. *de silentio*'s ahistorical universal or middle term turns out, on examination, to be the historically — and juridically — specific relation in each case of the ethical, or law, to the absolute: early Greek law, Hebraic judgeship, the law of the late Roman Republic. Abraham inspired, and may still inspire, holy terror — the terror later only suffered and uttered by prophets — because he still embodies in himself the holy nomadic community which has not yet even received the written covenant or

---

52  Fackenheim, *Encounters between Judaism and Modern Philosophy*, p. 99f.
53  Kierkegaard, *Fear and Trembling* (AH) p. 145.
54  Ibid., pp. 86−8.
55  Ibid., p. 87.

Torah, and cannot yet be riven by collisions between covenant, king-
ship and people which occur later, once the community settles the land.
*de silentio* has achieved — fictionalized — an inordinate contrast between
collisions within ethical (i.e. juridical) communities and those 'within' a
holy, nomadic community by, as he confesses, plundering the holy[56] —
suspending the history and fate of holiness in the process.

The aim of both 'authorships' — that of Kierkegaard and that of
Hegel — what makes 'authorship' as such problematic to them and to
their work, is how, contra Kant, to bring Revelation into philosophy:
aesthetically, as the incursion of the incomprehensible; philosophically,
as triune or aporetic reason — universal, particular and singular. Against
the Christian tradition, Revelation does not mean that redemption is
realized; against the tradition of Hegel interpretation, revelation makes
it impossible to attribute the equation of thought and being to the
System. In both of these authorships Revelation serves to leave the
ethical open and unresolved. This is why their work — even their logic
— is obsessed with beginning, and why the tradition which reads
philosophy aesthetically, sees only the absurdity of 'receiving everything back' or 'reconciliation' or even 'totalization'.

There is a final and continued 'fear and trembling': 'Abraham cannot
be mediated, which can also be put by saying he cannot speak. The
moment I speak I express the universal, and when I do not no one can
understand me.'[57] Yet Abraham does speak and the 'whole incident
would lack something' if he had not: 'My son, God will provide
himself a lamb for a burnt offering', which is to speak in 'the form of
irony'[58] for what he says protectively to Isaac affirms his willingness to
proceed. This coda is the key to the development of the authorship
which is preoccupied with how to bring another into a relation with the
absolute when the relation of one to another is genetic: the generations
— parent/child; the genders — male/female. The scandal that the
absolute appears as gendered is, at this point, expressed with ironic
absurdity:

> She will then introduce herself into that order of knighthood
> whose members are not admitted by ballot but anyone can join
> who has the courage to admit him- or herself, that order of
> knighthood which proves its immortality by making no distinc-
> tion between man and woman.[59]

[56]  Ibid., pp. 90, 92.
[57]  Ibid., p. 89.
[58]  Ibid., pp. 140, 142.
[59]  Ibid., p. 74.

## *Crisis in the Life of an Actress*

The 'crisis' consists in having to take our bearings from the works and not, as we are prone to do, the works from our bearings – yet the work is determined to abandon its reader and dissolve its author. In *Repetition*, the beginning is recommenced on the theme of the narrative illusions of the third 'Problemata' of *Fear and Trembling*: how to further the passion of *faith* of another whose *erotic* passion one has aroused and attached to oneself. The various retellings of failure in this furthering are themselves rehearsals for the ultimate repetition at stake: how to release the reader whose interpretative and philosophical eros has been aroused by the narrative and its accompanying reflections.

> Repetition and recollection are the same movement, except in opposite directions, for what is recollected has been, is repeated backward, whereas genuine repetition is recollected forward. Repetition, therefore, if it is possible, makes a person happy, whereas recollection makes him unhappy – assuming, of course, that he gives himself time to live and does not promptly at birth find an excuse to sneak out of life again, for example, that he has forgotten something.
>
> Recollection's love, an author has said, is the only happy love. He is perfectly right in that of course, provided one recollects that initially it makes a person unhappy. Repetition's love is in truth the only happy love.[60]

This proposal concerning repetition comes from the first page of Constantin Constantius' 'report' on how both he, as confidant but also as actor, and the young, 'nameless' man whose love affair he relates and whose letters to him – silent friend and confidant – he presents, fail to achieve any such repetition – even though, in the penultimate letters, the young man calls on the spirit of Job, hero not of faith but of ordeal, who still 'received everything double' – 'If I had not had Job!'[61] The text is concluded, however, by a devastating depredation: for an unforeseen repetition does occur. The young girl, whose release proves beyond the vanity of her lover, manages it herself – and marries. A concluding letter from the 'vanishing' Constantin Constantius tries to

---

[60] Kierkegaard, *Repetition*, (HVH-EHH), p. 131. 'Recollection' is used here in the Greek epistemological sense of 'anamnesis', the prenatal acquisition of knowledge of the Forms.
[61] Ibid., pp. 210, 212, 213.

draw out the lesson of the 'poetical' young man, but the reader addressed, fictional but not vanishing, is 'an inquisitive female'.[62]

The structure of this drama, where the natural or naive persona is a young girl, where the observing or reflective persona, the fictional reader, is a mature woman, and the narrative voice is alternately 'silent' or 'nameless', provides the clue to readership and authorship, pseudonymous *and* signed. It may be compared with 'The Crisis and A Crisis in the Life of an Actress, by *Inter et Inter*',[63] which by virtue of the stark allegorizing of actor *qua* 'actress', and author *qua* '*Inter et Inter*', brings out 'a crisis' of representation and address; 'a' crisis in general, and so, by extension, 'the' crisis — singular. The singular crisis cannot be taken as the literary reflection of the existential-biographical one culled from the *Journals and Papers* of 'SK' — as the tradition of Kierkegaard scholarship has done: that is a way of evading the crisis and overlooking the masks.

> Just for that reason, all those who in truth serve the truth uselessly, that is, without putting it to selfish uses, for whom life is a sheer struggle with the sophisms of existence, whose concern is not how they can best profit for themselves, but how they can most serve the truth and in truth benefit mankind: such persons have been well-informed about the use of deception — in order to test mankind.[64]

Here it is the authorship which confesses, not the confession which gives rise to authorship. Whether at the most intimate 'personal' moments in the papers and journals, or strolling insignificantly in the street — precisely when remaining 'what he really is'[65] — the author is masked and middle, always *inter* and *inter*, mediating and vanishing, the reader launched. Or not quite entirely — for while enough indications are shown to instruct the astute and passionate reader that she is beloved and abandoned, we remain endeared to the author who could not quite abandon himself — 'poor poet SK' — just as we ourselves fight through many had repetitions to achieve the maturity of the actress in crisis.

> Therefore the gallery can naturally never get into its head that precisely in order to *portray* Juliet it is essential that an actress possess a distance in age from Juliet.[66]

[62]  Ibid., pp. 225–31.
[63]  Op. cit., in *Crisis in the Life of an Actress and Other Essays on Drama*, published in four parts in *The Fatherland*, 24–27 July 1848.
[64]  Ibid., p. 81.
[65]  Ibid., p. 83.
[66]  Ibid., p. 87.

By reading *Repetition* from the perspective of the one who does achieve a repetition, 'the young girl', we, actresses, who are not young, may yet achieve — if not 'perfectibility, which unfolds itself through the years' — that other 'resistance to the power of the years, and that is potentiation, which precisely becomes manifest through the years'. 'Direct perfectibility' is not, however, of the order of interest of 'the metamorphosis of . . . potentiation, or a more and more intensive return to the original condition'.[67] The passion of the reader, fictional and singular, is at stake.

In *Repetition* both the lover — 'a poet' — and the confidant fail to repeat, while the beloved — the young girl, no poet — succeeds. What happens to the young girl is to be the crisis of the reader *qua* mature actress, singular, not perfect but potentiated. It is not, however, the crisis of the young girl herself, because she proceeds — and eventually repeats — in a way that is unnarratable; she is silent and drops out of the story quite early on, only reintruding herself to conclude it by her unforeseen repetition. It is the evolving self-consciousness of those who are unable to repeat and so become increasingly 'self'-conscious that is narratable.

A young girl acquires a wholehearted lover whose 'gait', 'movement', 'gestures' are all 'eloquent and glowing with love', and who respects his beloved so discreetly that he will not sit all day with her and become a nuisance.[68] A few days later, however, in spite of maintaining such respectful distance, he becomes melancholy and recollective: 'He was essentially through with the entire relationship.'[69] In itself this is 'the sign of genuine erotic love'; but he is not able to develop 'the vital force to slay this death and transform it into life', which would be to love her and not merely to long for her.[70]

At this point the beloved is unaware of the change in her lover: that she has become merely his ideal and an abandoned one at that. With the reported decision that to let her know what has happened would hurt her too deeply, she becomes, in effect, irrelevant to the narrative: 'she would become his grieving widow'.[71] Under the guise of saving her self-regard, the two narrators repeatedly attempt to effect aberration of her possibility of mourning and recovering; and the rest of the tale relates their disingenuousness towards themselves and her — until she seizes the initiative. So the lover, first, 'pampered [her] with his pain', and thus remains fascinatingly melancholic, arousing an even deeper

---

[67] Ibid., pp. 90–1.
[68] Kierkegaard, *Repetition* (HVH-EHH), p. 135.
[69] Ibid., p. 136.
[70] Ibid., p. 137.
[71] Ibid., p. 138.

affection from the beloved.[72] Instead, as the confidant devises, to save
her pride and gain his release, the lover must become tactless, shallow
and contemptible, so that she may judge him worthless and reject him
on her own account: he must 'show a certain cloying *quasi* love that is
neither indifference nor desire',[73] not profound enough to interest or
wound her in a comprehensible way. Now a mature woman would
object that such cloying and careless untruth is not so deviously controlled, and is, moreover, contemptible of her, not of him; but maturity, however gendered, is not under discussion — for it has already
'slayed' this poetry.

The young girl, in this immature case, fails to notice that love has
changed to longing and again to stickiness: had she responded it might
have been the prelude to actual not ideal love between the two, a way
of disencumbering the lovers of the initial 'poetic confusion'.[74] The
lover, in fact, fails to adopt the stratagem of unpoetic demeanour, as his
need for and resentment of his confidant indicates. The two male
parties remain convinced, however, that simply coming clean 'would
thereby have cut off the possibility for her to exist autonomously'.[75]
Neither seems to suspect the truth — and this is not stated — that she
loves singularly not ideally; and they assume that she is absorbed in
finding her lover interesting. For if she loves singularly then she always
repeats and she would give her lover his freedom, but, of course, he
does not really want that. Nor does the narrator want that, as he reveals
by relating his own failed attempt at repetition in a subplot, which
demonstrates that, although no poet, he, nevertheless, only knows
repetition theatrically and philosophically, and which explains why,
pedantically, he needs to insist that repetition is not Hegelian mediation
— but only extends the contrast to Greek anamnesis — recollection.[76]
Both young men remain in the realm of erotic possibility, 'wandering
about... discovering now one possibility, now another', absorbed in
seeing each possibility configured in its double — on stage, at the
theatre, 'an audible shadow'.[77]

Repetition, although it makes 'something new', is not an embrace of
sheer infinite possibility: 'for that which is repeated has been'.[78] There is
one point in the text where it seems, *prima facie*, that a repetition is
achieved, and its pathos representable and represented:

[72]  Ibid., p. 140.
[73]  Ibid., p. 142.
[74]  Ibid., p. 145.
[75]  Ibid.
[76]  Ibid., pp. 148−9.
[77]  Ibid., p. 155; compare the description of the character Schildknapp as 'a roué of the
potentialities' in Thomas Mann, *Doctor Faustus*, p. 213.
[78]  Kierkegaard, *Repetition*, p. 149.

My being was transparent... Every mood rested in my soul...
Every thought volunteered itself...jubilantly, the most foolish
whim as well as the richest idea. I had a presentiment of every
impression before it arrived and awakened within me. All existence seemed to have fallen in love with me, and everything
quivered in fateful rapport with my being.[79]

Yet it is bathos not pathos which brings out the moral of this: an
irritation in the eye transfigures the mood of perfect prescience into
utter despair, and the incipient narcissism of 'everything in love with
me' reveals the ecstatic to have no more equanimity or self-possession
than the two-year-old empress in a baby carriage he had been admiring
a moment earlier.[80] This avenue, from melancholic lover to infinitely
beloved, is not the one that leads to repetition. Repetition would be the
passage from beloved, loveableness, to love-ableness: from knowing
oneself loved, 'loveable', to finding oneself graced with a plentitude of
being-able-to-love, and thus to risk loving again and again, regardless
of any particular outcome – disastrous or successful. To be love-able:
to love singularly, to forgive, to release, and hence to love again and
again, is the one thing the work can barely speak.[81] For such grace needs
no words in its passion-action, and the two men cannot even imagine
it. The confidant's philosophical discourses on repetition and the history of erotic collision remain unconnected and unconsummated:

The whole thing is a wrestling match in which the universal
breaks with the exception, wrestles with him in conflict and
strengthens him through this wrestling... The legitimate exception is reconciled in the universal...[82]

'She is married'[83] – the repetition this token is made to provide for her
former lover resounds hollowly up to this concluding philosophical
reflection addressed to the reader. Mournfully, the two men want to be
remembered by her – to tarnish her repetition with retrospection.
Since she has achieved perfect memory not perfect prescience, they
cannot touch or taint her, for 'Repetition – that is actuality and the
earnestness of existence. The person who wills repetition is mature in

---

[79]    Ibid., p. 173.
[80]    Ibid., p. 172.
[81]    Compare the 'grammar of desire' developed by Moore in *Let This Mind Be in You*,
ch. 13 and *passim*.
[82]    Kierkegaard, *Repetition*, p. 227.
[83]    Ibid., p. 220.

earnestness.'[84] She has grown, as it were, beyond the work, with its poetical young people, who, with the 'exception' of her, still wrestle with the universal.

The passion of scholarship, itself tutored by this maturation, can only signal the meaningfulness of the work's silence – lest this meaning be disqualified when it would be repeated.


## Code and Commentary

Among the papers of 'SK' may be found a commentary on the concluding letter to the reader of *Repetition* in which the story is decoded philosophically 'in the sphere of individual freedom'.[85] In response to the criticism of the Danish 'Hegelian', Professor Heiberg, who argued that repetition is a category of nature rather than finite spirit, contemplation rather than existence, world-spirit rather than individual spirit, this apologia protests that, thus understood, repetition would be indistinguishable from mediation, and thereby would make 'the transcendence of movement illusory'.[86]

The translation of the story into terms designed to oppose Heiberg's charges inevitably involves mediation: 'When applied in the sphere of individual freedom, the concept of repetition has a history, inasmuch as freedom passes through several stages in order to attain itself.'[87] However, since the so-called 'Hegelianism' of Heiberg bears no relation to Hegel's *Phenomenology of Spirit*, a unique opportunity arises for a contrast between existential and phenomenological repetition. 'Phenomenological repetition' means the philosophical reconstruction and education of risk – where 'philosophy' traces the developmental and changing configuration of concept and object, and where 'risk' means the 'crisis' or 'transcendence' of each transition. 'Here again, this means that when happiness ceases, when the crisis comes, freedom must press forward, not retreat.'[88] This future-oriented formulation does not do justice to the distinction between affirming the future as sheer infinite possibility, and repetition as the movement forward which affirms 'what has been'. It is only by the latter movement that the former opens out. In this source, however, the four stages serve to clarify the development at stake: they are uncannily analogous to the development

---

[84]  Ibid., p. 133.
[85]  Ibid., p. 301.
[86]  Ibid., p. 308.
[87]  Ibid., p. 301.
[88]  Ibid., p. 317.

expounded in the *Phenomenology of Spirit*. Both works keep – and reveal – the 'secret piece of intelligence' from a readership whose
formal philosophical and religious education is taken for granted;
namely, 'how repetition progresses along this path until it signifies
atonement'.[89]

At the first stage of freedom as repetition, pleasure falls into despair;
in the *Phenomenology*, pleasure becomes coupled with necessity: the
issue is despair. At the second stage, sagacity amounts to merely
instrumental shrewdness; phenomenologically, acknowledgement of
others is revealed as interested, as a 'spiritual animal kingdom': the issue
is despair. At the third stage, a Stoic retreat seems to be achieved, 'I
myself play the Stoic',[90] yet remains utterly vulnerable; phenomenologically, Stoicism is haunted by all that it rescinds. At the fourth stage,
repetition is readiness for anxiety;[91] phenomenologically, knowledge
and risk continue colliding at the individual and at the world-historical
level. In what follows, the *Phenomenology* almost elaborates the 'stages
of freedom'.

At the first stage of individual freedom –

Freedom is first qualified as desire [or pleasure] or as being in
desire. What it now fears is repetition, for it seems as if repetition
has a magic power to keep freedom captive once it has tricked it
into its power. But despite all of desire's ingenuity, repetition
appears. Freedom in desire despairs.[92]

Phenomenologically –

The world is experienced as the 'negative' when self-
consciousness makes 'pleasure' its particular goal. The other is
only recognised as something to be consumed and enjoyed, not as
productive activity, nor as universal law, nor as ethical life. Hence
the transitoriness of consumption, the intrinsic and contingent
impossibility of continually satisfying the desire for pleasure, is
experienced as an utterly alien and an incomprehensible law
or necessity . . . experienced as a blind fate . . . whose work is the
destruction of individuality, for it thwarts its only goal, that of
pleasure . . .

---

89   Ibid., p. 313.
90   Ibid., p. 303.
91   Cf. (HVH-EHH) 'concerned freedom', p. 302 with (WL) 'anxious freedom', p. 13.
92   Compare (HVH-EHH), p. 301 and (WL), pp. 11–12.

[Instead of plunging into enjoying life, a life of pleasure, con-
sciousness] has really only plunged into consciousness of its own
lifelessness and has as its lot only empty and alien necessity, a *dead*
actuality.[93]

At this first stage of individual freedom and at this configuration
of self-consciousness, the priority given to desire or pleasure and its
realization amounts to a fear of all change, of everything else in the
world and all other relations to other things. As a result, even pleasure
itself is lost.

At the second stage –

Simultaneously freedom appears in a higher form . . . qualified as
sagacity [shrewdness] . . . has only a finite relation to its object and
is qualified only aesthetically ambiguously. Repetition is assumed
to exist, but freedom's task in [shrewdness] is continually to gain
a new aspect of repetition . . . [everything is transformed into a
'matter of business' . . . that is, it is seen in terms of whether it is a
limitation or not for ones's own ends.] People who in freedom do
not stand in any higher relation to the idea usually embellish this
standpoint as the highest wisdom. But since freedom qualified as
[shrewdness] is only finitely qualified, repetition must appear
again, namely, repetition of the trickery by which [shrewdness]
wants to fool repetition and make it into something else.
[Shrewdness] despairs.[94]

Phenomenologically, at the second stage, when self-consciousness
appears to acknowledge or recognize others and productive activity as
participation in a common universal, yet, in effect, understands everything – work and other people – solely in terms of its own particular
interests, it becomes a 'spiritual animal kingdom': 'spiritual' because it
appears to be in an ethical relation to others; 'animal' because the other
is really treated as a means to an interested end.[95] At the second stage of
individual freedom, and at this configuration of self-consciousness, an
instrumental relation to others, or relative ethical life, is given the
priority of an absolute wisdom, and, therefore, remains vulnerable to
everything outside the narrow confines of self-interest.

At the third stage of individual freedom –

<hr/>

[93]   Hegel, *Phenomenology of Spirit*, Miller paras. 361−3 and Rose, *Hegel contra Sociology*,
p. 168.
[94]   Kierkegaard, *Repetition* (HVH-EHH), p. 301; (WL), p. 12 plus passage interpolated
from 'The Rotation of Crops', *Either/Or* (DFS-LMS), vol. I as indicated, p. 285.
[95]   Hegel, *Phenomenology of Spirit*, Miller para. 405; Rose, *Hegel contra Sociology*,
pp. 176−7.

Now freedom breaks forth in its highest form, in which it is qualified in relation to itself. Here everything is reversed and the very opposite of the first standpoint appears. Now freedom's supreme interest is precisely to bring about repetition, and its only fear is that variation [change] would have the power to disturb its eternal nature. Here emerges the issue: *Is repetition possible?* Freedom itself is now the repetition. If it were the case that freedom in the individuality related to the surrounding world could become so immersed, so to speak, in the result that it cannot take itself back again (repeat itself), then everything is lost. Consequently, what freedom fears here is not repetition but variation; what it wants is not variation but repetition. If this will to repetition is stoicism, then it contradicts itself and thereby ends in destroying itself in order to affirm repetition in that way, which is the same as throwing a thing away in order to hide it most securely.[96]

Phenomenologically, self-consciousness becomes Stoical as a tentative at self-determination: it does not explicitly reject the 'world' — the vicissitudes of fortune — but tries to neutralize the world by disdaining fortune, both good and bad; whether master or slave, 'on the throne or in chains, in the utter dependence of its individual existence, its aim is to be free, and maintain that lifeless indifference which steadfastly withdraws from the bustle of existence, alike from being active as from being passive, into the simple essentiality of thought'.[97] Stoicism, passing on through Scepticism, becomes 'the unhappy consciousness'.

Stoicism displays the same features in both expositions: its ambition is to evade the world, now understood not as the relative-ethical but cosmically, as fortune. The aim is to remain unmoved by the revolutions of the world — its variations or vicissitudes — to avoid the agony of any more education. This pose lacks poise: it empties repetition of its content and represents a flight into thought.

The fourth stage of individual freedom occurs when Stoicism 'has stepped aside', from its Pyrrhic victory over the world. Instead of warding off the threat of uncontrolled change it is prepared to face the future anxiously 'and with the passionate eloquence of concerned freedom proclaims its presence in the conflict'.[98]

Since the *Phenomenology of Spirit* is historical, genealogical and futural, once the flight into thought has occurred the conflict can never be unmediated again. The 'secret' of the *Phenomenology*, corresponding to

[96] Kierkegaard, *Repetition*, (HVH-EHH), p. 302; (WL), p. 12.
[97] Hegel, *Phenomenology of Spirit*, Miller para.199; Rose, *Hegel contra Sociology*, pp. 160–1.
[98] Kierkegaard, *Repetition* (HVH-EHH), p. 302; (WL), pp. 12–13.

the fourth stage, lies in the challenge of expounding its own flights into thought — thereby risking further flight, yet taking that risk for the sake of provoking instead renewed negotiation of thought and its others — 'the world'. This very process, as 'SK' would then say, 'proclaims its presence in the conflict'.

Outside the *Journal and Papers*, which thus amount to the philosophical workshop of the authorship, and which demonstrate, unwittingly, its deep affinities with Hegel's *Phenomenology*, the philosophical persona wears the borrowed mask of 'Johannes Climacus' in order to carry out this project which was summarized as early as *The Concept of Irony*:

> Irony is like the negative way, not the truth but the way. Everyone who has a result merely as such does not possess it, for he has not the way . . . though not the way whereby one who imagines himself to have a result comes to possess it, but the way whereby the result forsakes him.[99]

If the story of *Repetition* amounts to the forsaking, the philosophical versions back up this dereliction by turning contemporaneous philosophical truth into 'a result' — hypostatizing it as the System; and, even more deviously, by impersonating it precisely as *a* way, but not, by implication, *the* way.

> Add to this that the task of our age must surely *be seen to be* that of translating the results of philosophy into the personal life, personally to appropriate these results.[100]

Three philosophical works are attributed to 'Johannes Climacus', and one psychological work to Anti-Climacus, an assumed but not an invented name.[101] *Climax*, the Greek for ladder, was the name accorded to the author of *The Ladder of Divine Ascent*, *scala paradisi*, a classic of eastern Christian monasticism, written in the sixth to seventh century. John Climacus lived in the Sinai desert at the foot of Mount Musa where he developed the notion of *hesychia*, inner silence and solitary prayer, versus *polylogia*, talkative prayer. There are thirty ascetic steps on the ladder which calibrate the ascent towards and presuppose 'in-

---

[99] Kierkegaard, *The Concept of Irony*, p. 340.
[100] Ibid., emphasis added.
[101] 'Johannes Climacus' is the pseudonym for *Philosophical Fragments, Concluding Unscientific Postscript to the Philosophical Fragments*, while S. Kierkegaard is 'responsible for publication'; *The Sickness Unto Death* is by Anti-Climacus and edited by S. Kierkegaard; *Johannes Climacus*, not published by Kierkegaard, is a philosophical biography of Climacus.

augurated' or 'realized' eschatology.[102] To adopt this symbolism in the construction of the philosophical authorship is to invoke the erotic religiosity of aspiration and yearning. It condenses Greek orthodox Christian mysticism with classic Greek philosophy: God as the divine object of human love, the unitary love beyond all diverse earthly ones; and the *psyche* or soul recalling or recollecting the archetype in its desire for a particular image. 'Climacus' is another polylogic pseudonym culled from silence − *hesychia*; while the idea and image of *ascending* the ladder deliberately draws attention away from the function of a ladder (*die Leiter*) in the *Phenomenology* which involves *descent* as well as ascent.[103] The philosophy of 'Climacus' will be concerned exclusively with ascent.

> Hegel is a Johannes *Climacus* who does not storm the heavens as do the giants − by setting mountain upon mountain − but *climbs up* to them by means of his syllogisms.[104]

However, the use of this particular assumed name is intended to alert the reader to the limitations of the philosophical authorship and its arguments: '... do me the favour to cite the name of the respective pseudonymous author'.[105] Yet commentators persist in attributing the views expressed in the philosophical works to 'Kierkegaard' *tout court*, instead of understanding the works presented under the name 'Climacus' as a translation of philosophical result into 'way', a translation, moreover, which is intended '*to be seen to be*' in order to demonstrate further that even this way is not *the* way and so to effect the forsaking of the reader, 'the educative effect of companionship with an ideality which imposes distance'.[106] The way is destroyed by being made available vicariously, by being represented, yet the unavoidability of representation is acknowledged as a predicament.

## Duplexity and Duplicity

> Thus as soon as I want to express immediacy in language contradiction is present, for language is ideal.

[102]   See Ware, 'Introduction', John Climacus, *Ladder of Divine Ascent*, p. 30.
[103]   See Hegel, *Phenomenology of Spirit*, p. 28 tr. Miller para. 26. Compare St John of the Cross, *Ascent of Mount Carmel*.
[104]   Kierkegaard, *Johannes Climacus*, (HVH-EHH), p. 231.
[105]   Kierkegaard, *Concluding Unscientific Postscript*; this imploration occurs in 'A First and Last Declaration', appended in the name of S. Kierkegaard, p. 558, after the initials 'JC' at the end of 550pp (pp. not numbered between 551 and 558).
[106]   Ibid., p. 553.

As soon as I state the immediate the statement is first and fore-
most untrue, for I cannot state anything immediately, but only
mediately.[107]

Even the animals are not shut out from this wisdom but, on the
contrary, show themselves to be most profoundly initiated into it;
for they do not just stand idly in front of sensuous things as if
these possessed intrinsic being, but, despairing of their reality, and
completely assured of their nothingness, they fall to without cere-
mony and eat them up. And all Nature, like the animals, celebrates these open Mysteries which teach the truth about sensuous
things.[108]

While the third passage, which is from the *Phenomenology*, is whimsical,
humorous and 'existential' by comparison with the first two from the
*Journals and Papers*, all three register that ideality is involved in express-
ing or negotiating immediacy. The resulting duplexity inside and outside language demands a countervailing duplicity to overcome the
doubt engendered by the remove of ideality. In the unfinished and
unpublished work, *Johannes Climacus, or De omnibus dubitandum est − A
Narrative*,[109] the consequences of this predicament are followed along a
path subsequently dissembled in the works 'by' Johannes Climacus.

While the subtitle and superscript from Spinoza lead one to suspect
an essay on Cartesian doubt, what follows is another essay on the
beginning, which itself begins, and repeats its beginning, with biographical confession and with difficulty − with the difficulty of beginning and with the beginning of difficulty: the entanglement of aporia
with itself.

The introduction is cast as a biography related by one who has the
most intimate knowledge of the experience and thoughts of another,
Johannes Climacus. The poignant intensity of Climacus' relationship
with his strange father, who takes him on imaginary walks indoors, has
two consequences relevant to his subsequent attempts to begin to philosophize. It gives him an extraordinarily entwined sense of omnipotence
and impotence in the same personality: for 'his father combined an
irresistible dialectic with an omnipotent imagination' together with a
proneness to self-deprecation, 'I am good for nothing; I cannot do a

---

[107] Kierkegaard, *Johannes Climacus*, (HVH-EHH), pp. 251, 252.
[108] Hegel, *Phenomenology of Spirit*, Miller para. 109.
[109] See Kierkegaard, *Johannes Climacus* (HVH-EHH) Manuscript first page, pp. 228−9
(not numbered); probably written before *Fear and Trembling* and *Repetition*, after
*Either/Or*.

thing...'[110] etc. – intellectual virtuosity matched by utter worldlessness. It also gives him an enduring femininity: he identifies with his
father and 'quickly learnt his father's magic art', but remains 'such an
innocent young person that he might have been taken for a girl instead
of a man.'[111] It is not innocence, however, but eros that qualifies his
personality profoundly: as 'woman's whole life is love ... his whole life
was thinking'.[112] By the end of the 'Introduction', Johannes Climacus
has two abiding qualities: an insatiable intellectual eros, 'his delight to
begin with a single thought and then, by way of coherent thinking, to
climb step by step to a higher one, because to him coherent thinking
was a *scala paradisi*';[113] and, when coherence breaks down and he becomes despondent, a relish for difficulty: 'he then had an ever higher
goal: with his will to press his way through the windings of the
difficulty.'[114]

'With quiet solemnity, it was decreed that he should begin' to become a philosopher. This Climacus proceeds to do by juxtaposing the
venerable and venerated thesis 'Everything must be doubted' with three
different versions of it:

1   philosophy begins with doubt;
2   in order to philosophize, one must have doubted;
3   modern philosophy begins with doubt.[115]

He proceeds to consider these theses in the order 3:1:2.

The third thesis 'modern philosophy begins with doubt', seems, at
first, to be a 'historical report'. It turns out, however, to involve a
distinction between modern and pre-modern philosophy, but such a
distinction can itself only be justified or grounded philosophically as an
essential and necessary yet historically specific transformation. In this
case the third thesis becomes comparable to the first, but, instead of
beginning with doubt, the beginning now seems to evoke 'presentiment', indescribable difficulty and self-awareness:

> Thus the individual *must become conscious of himself and in this
> consciousness of himself also becomes conscious of his significance as a
> moment in modern philosophy; in turn modern philosophy must become*

---

[110]   Ibid., pp. 121, 124.
[111]   Ibid., pp. 120, 156.
[112]   Ibid., p. 123.
[113]   Ibid., p. 118.
[114]   Ibid., p. 124.
[115]   Ibid., pp. 131, 132.

*conscious of itself as an element in a prior philosophy, which in turn must become conscious of itself as an element in the historical unfolding of the eternal philosophy.*[116]

Instead of shouldering this eternal-historical burden of philosophical self-consciousness, cast here as a perfected Hegelianism, Climacus prefers to lose all consciousness: *'he fainted!'*[117] For it to 'be possible for every single moment to become aware of its eternal validity as a moment in the whole that, after all, would require that the individual be omniscient and that the world be finished'.[118] The alternative to this philosophical hubris, 'which would mean slaying the present with the thought of eternity and yet preserving its fresh life ... wanting to know the future as a present and yet simultaneously as a future'[119] is 'to prophesy': 'just as one could have an intimation of a necessity in the past, was it not also conceivable that one could have an intimation of a necessity in the future.'[120] Prophecy, unlike philosophy, is 'precarious'; it presupposes neither omniscience nor world-at-an-end. The concept of prophecy is not pursued further in the work because it is in effect enacted by Johannes Climacus, who is still too precarious to begin to philosophize — as terrified by the commands of the philosophical tradition as the prophets on hearing the voice of God.

The first thesis, 'philosophy begins with doubt', appears, contrary to the third, to be philosophical, but it turns out to be historical: 'doubt' is a category of reflection, whereas 'wonder' is an 'immediate category' and involves no reflection:

> When a later philosopher said: Philosophy begins with wonder —
> he was straightway in continuity with the Greeks ... But every
> time a later philosopher repeats or says these words: Philosophy
> begins with doubt — the continuity is broken, for doubt is pre-
> cisely a polemic against what went before.[121]

This leads to a 'new difficulty', for if the continuity is broken how can the instruction 'to doubt' itself be passed on?[122] The new difficulty also turns out to be a version of the one already encountered: how can the individual thinker relate to a thesis which is both eternal and historical

---

[116]   Ibid., p. 140.
[117]   Ibid., p. 141.
[118]   Ibid.
[119]   Ibid., p. 143.
[120]   Ibid., p. 142.
[121]   Ibid., p. 145.
[122]   Ibid., p. 146.

for it too presupposes both a universal and a historically limited truth?[123] Reaffirming that doubt must belong to the 'subjective' beginning – not to the absolute or objective beginning – that is, to individual consciousness, Climacus gives priority to the individual who receives the instruction. A return to the original antinomy ensues: if authority – tradition, philosophy – ordains the doubt, this is tantamount to commanding either the abolition of authority or the abolition of doubt. The first abolition would amount to a submission to slaughter – like, as he says, the Knight who slew the troll with the latter's own bloodthirsty sword. Rather than commit trollicide, as it were, Johannes Climacus finds two refuges: *Aller Anfang ist schwer* – All beginning is difficult; while 'smiles and tears . . . lie close to one another' in this girlish temperament.[124]

Finally, the second thesis, 'in order to philosophize, one must have doubted', recapitulates this long-winded initiation process which begins – not with doubt – but with many aporetic starts and stops. By embracing the awefulness of beginning, which binds and looses, continuous and new:

> Come what may, whether it leads to everything or to nothing, makes me wise or mad, I shall stake everything but shall not let go of the thought.[125]

The beginning is made – with aporia, with wonder, with prophecy, with repetition, but not with doubt.

The second, incomplete, part of *Johannes Climacus* opens with an apparently new resolve by Climacus to think under his own auspices by bidding farewell to philosophy.[126] This apparently new attitude is bogus: it retains an aesthetic-erotic impulse, 'the sweet joys and sorrows of a first love affair',[127] beset by anxious recollection until it adopts the method of making everything 'as simple as possible', announcing, archly, that the beginning is to be engaged yet again.[128]

The purity of this beginning is assailed yet again by its transcendental form: 'What must the nature of existence be in order for doubt to be possible?' The deduction of *'doubt's ideal possibility in consciousness'*[129] rests on the observation that for truth (and therefore for doubt about

[123]  Ibid., p. 147.
[124]  Ibid., pp. 155–6.
[125]  Ibid., p. 159.
[126]  Ibid., pp. 163, 165.
[127]  Ibid., p. 163.
[128]  Ibid., p. 165.
[129]  Ibid., p. 166, emphasis in original.

the truth) to become an issue for consciousness it must take an interested relation to its object, and must find itself, consequently, in
contradiction with itself: 'immediacy is reality', but '[t]he moment I
make a statement about reality contradiction is present, for what I say is
ideality [or mediate]'. This accounts for the possibility of doubt: it 'lies
in consciousness, whose nature is a contradiction that is produced by
duplexity and that itself produces a duplexity'.[130] According to this
exposition, it is the collision of reality with ideality that gives rise to
consciousness, and hence to doubt. Doubt presupposes this triad — no
term of which exists without the other two: 'the categories of consciousness, however, are *trichotomous*'.[131] The categories of reflection
are, by contrast, 'always dichotonomous' and 'disinterested', the sheer
'possibility of relation' without an interested consciousness bringing
them into relation for the sake of truth and so risking doubt.

However, it has to be admitted 'that language seems to conflict with
this, for in most languages ... the term "to doubt" is etymologically
related to the word "two" [*dubito (duo) zweifeln (zwei) tvivle (tve)
σκέπτειν (to doubt)] ... Yet ... as soon as I as mind become two, I
am *eo ipso* three.'[132] This truism is attributed to the birth of consciousness as truth-concerned. Yet the text speaks against this conclusion in
several senses: the argument develops as a rumination in Climacus' head
— hence as a reflection. Within the argument, reflection *and* consciousness are opposed as two to three, as retrogressive knowledge versus
highest form of existence, as presupposition versus act. However, by
defining reflection as two, as *contraries*, and consciousness as *contradiction*, Climacus' philosophizing *belies its own developing reflection*, which
recognizes doubt as doubt in relation to *its* presuppositions: reflection in
the narrower sense of two contraries, and consciousness as the trichotomy which falters at the point where mind enters the picture. Reflection has in effect developed one trichotomy into a new one with the
same structure as that ascribed to the original impasse of consciousness,
a dichotomy and a relation to that dichotomy, now resumed as the
dichotomy of consciousness and reflection, and a further reflection on
that dichotomy which may indeed provoke further doubt.

The reversing of this virtual development of thinking is built into the
original dichotomy of immediacy and mediacy posited as 'reality' and
'ideality'. For if '[i]n the question of truth, consciousness is brought

---

[130]   Ibid., p. 168.
[131]   Ibid., p. 169.
[132]   Ibid., p. 169 and 'Supplement', p. 258, Pap. IV B 13:2 n.d., 1842–3; and see p. 344
n. 38.

into a relation with something else',[133] then consciousness is essentially mediation and only thus does the illusion of immediacy arise: for consciousness presupposes that the object to which it relates is independent of it — is 'reality'. Yet Climacus proceeds to define immediacy 'as reality itself', and not as *illusory* reality even though he has nevertheless shown that 'immediacy' is posited by consciousness and by the word or language which intends it or is interested in it. 'Immediacy' is said to be 'reality itself' although it will be transformed by the contradiction which results from attributing an illusory independence to 'reality' when the other which exceeds any such positing always remains to be negotiated. This transformation is the pain of existing, and its dynamic conceptual exposition is equally concerned with such pain as the view which gives static priority to trichotomous doubting consciousness.

The second part, and, indeed, the whole work, breaks off in the midst of further reflecting on consciousness' discovery of its contradiction. The argument that the collision emerges from consciousness' essential relating activity is restated in terms of repetition: 'Immediately there is no collision, but mediately it is present. As soon as the question of a *repetition* arises, the collision is present, for only a repetition of what has been before is conceivable.'[134] This 'what has been before' is taken up as the question of how 'what is' is repeated, that is, whether something in the world 'was the same one I had seen before'. The question of sameness or repetition (identity) only arises when ideality and reality 'touch each other', when 'something in the moment is explained by ideality as a repetition'. This 'redoubling' of what is (reality) as what is (ideality) cannot occur in time (reality) nor in eternity (ideality) but only in consciousness. The contradiction that 'that which is, is also in another mode' is only now designated 'recollection' and said to involve 'the same contradiction': recollection 'is not ideality; it is ideality that has been. It is not reality; it is reality that has been . . . '.[135] The contradiction is not the same, however, because it can only be stated in relation to temporality — formerly dismissed as uncrucial. The contradiction, single or redoubled, between what 'is' apprehended as what 'has been' — displays the structure of what it is to recognize something as the same thing, as repeated. The exposition concentrates on the repetition and contradiction, but in effect,

---

[133] Ibid., p. 167.
[134] Ibid., p. 171.
[135] At the end of the sentence which sets out this 'double contradiction' the text breaks off: ibid., pp. 171–2.

expounds how something comes to be recognized or judged to be the same thing. It reveals, however, that this occurs when 'what is' is recognized as 'what has been' – a perfect and past tense which captures the unity and difference of being and essence or illusory being. (The German *Wesen*, and the Latin *essence* are past participles of the verb 'to be', the latter invented for philosophy.)

The exposition breaks off at the point where the dichotomy of ideality/reality and the concomitant assimilation of language and word to the ideal pole breaks down. 'Word' and 'language' are themselves precipitates of the trichotomous act of judgement and its further reflection: they partake of the illusion that they constitute a realm independent of the collision, and that as 'ideality' they belong to the initial dichotomous reflection, whereas in fact they belong to the reflection subsequent to the collision, which is dissembled in this philosophical biography as the coy and ingenuous beginning of philosophizing on the part of the boy-girl Climacus. It is this logic of illusion in which originally dichotomous contraries show a trichotomous identity and non-identity as a result of developing reflection on the beginning that henceforth was more successfully disguised in works 'by' Climacus. So much so that its speculative perfecting has not previously been attempted.

### Illusory Fragments

The title page of *Philosophical Fragments or A Fragment of Philosophy*, by Johannes Climacus, edited by S. Kierkegaard, asks 'Can a historical point of departure be given for an eternal consciousness; how can such a point of departure be of more than historical interest; can an eternal happiness be built on historical knowledge?'[136] In this work the drama of philosophy and existence is staged in the coulisses of the logic of essence and the logic of being: being or existence will prevail over essence – but only in thought. Victory from a position which thus separates thought and being restores the position refuted, only the identity and non-identity of thought and being, or illusory being, could present existential pathos without self-disqualification. Climacus, knowingly, falls again to his own mask.

### PROBLEMATA
Is the past more necessary than the future?
This can be significant with respect to the solution of the

---

[136]  Kierkegaard, *Philosophical Fragments* (HVH-EHH), p. 1 (not numbered).

problem of possibility — how does Hegel answer it? In the *Logic*, in the doctrine of essence. Here we get the explanation that the possible is the actual, the actual is the possible. It is simple enough in a science, at the conclusion of which one has arrived at possibility. It is then a tautology.

This is important in connection with the doctrine of the relation between the future and God's foreknowledge.

The old thesis that knowledge neither takes away nor adds.

See Boethius, pp. 126–7, later used by Leibniz.[137]

This juxtaposition of Hegel with Boethius and Leibniz becomes assimilation in the course of the text: so that the logic of essence is read in terms of pre-Kantian notions of possibility, actuality and necessity, in terms, that is, of the logic of being. Lamentably, Climacus' philosophical sleight-of-hand, ironic and masked, has come to found a whole, anti-philosophical culture, now *de rigueur*, which, sometimes masked but often unmasked, perpetuates an erstwhile ruse as an assault on the history of philosophy. While this interpreting of the logic of essence in pre-Kantian terms is explicitly developed in the 'Interlude' between chapters 4 and 5, between 'contemporary following' and 'following at second hand', its ethos prevails over the whole work. The ultimate irony is that Climacus presents a weak argument metaphysically for 'the historical point of departure for an eternal consciousness', when there is a much stronger one in the logic with which he ostensibly engages but cleverly evades.

The malpractice in Hegel is easily pointed out. The absolute method explains all world history; the science that is to explain the single human being is ethics. On the one hand, this is quite neglected in Hegel, and insofar as he explains anything, it is usually in such a way that no living being can exist accordingly, and if he were to exist according to the few better things to be found there, then he would instantly explode the absolute method. Hegel can manage much better with the dead, for they are silent.[138]

While Climacus' ambition is to wrest history and existence from the clutches of the absolute method, the sentiment expressed in this passage determines him to proceed with a phenomenological consistency itself learnt from the Master of irony. In a response to a review of the *Fragments* he explains

---

137  Ibid., 'Supplement', p. 182.
138  Ibid., 'Supplement', p. 207.

the book is written for people in the know, whose trouble is they know too much ... sensible communication consist[s] ... in taking his knowledge away from him ... the changed form would indeed take something away from him, and yet this taking away is precisely communication.[139]

This confiscating of what is known bears comparison with the declaration from the 'Preface' to the *Phenomenology of Spirit* that it is familiarity which inhibits recognition.[140] Climacus proceeds to invert the normal meaning of communication: it 'does not aim at making the difficulty even easier ... the difficulty is invested with a new form and thus actually made difficult'.[141] This reaffirmation of the quest to find a *form* by which to reinsinuate the aporia, 'the difficulty', into over-educated minds, will be the impulse which finally absolves the work from its unconsummated confrontation with its imaginary adversary.

In the section of the *Concluding Unscientific Postscript* on the *Philosophical Fragments* Climacus claims that he did not deal in the latter work with how 'an eternal happiness is decided in time through the relationship to something historical' by mediating Christianity with speculative thought.[142] But he does not admit what form he does employ: a deductive conceptuality which lapses periodically into self-deprecating facetiousness. This deduction starts on pagan ground – as he protests – but only to draw out the contrary categories by opposition.

The initial 'thought-project' uses the notion of learning the truth, and hence of teacher, learner, truth, as *tertium comparationis* to distinguish the Socratic difficulty that 'any point of departure in time is *eo ipso* something accidental, a vanishing point, an occasion', because, in recollecting the truth, 'self-knowledge is God-knowledge', and the teacher dispensable;[143] from '*the fullness of time*', when the teacher 'provides the condition' of truth, the learner exists as created, as untruth, through his own fault, but with no possibility of recollecting the truth.[144] 'Let us call it *sin*' and 'Let us call ... such a teacher ... saviour ... deliverer ... reconciler'.[145] Let us call this learner 'the follower' ... this change 'conversion', this sorrow 'repentance'.[146] The moment now has

---

[139] Ibid., cited in 'Historical Introduction' to *Philosophical Fragments*, pp. xxi–xxii from *Concluding Unscientific Postscript*.
[140] Hegel, *Phenomenology of Spirit*, p. 35, tr. Miller para. 31.
[141] Kierkegaard, *Philosophical Fragments* (HVH-EHH), p. xxii.
[142] Kierkegaard, *Concluding Unscientific Postscript*, pp. 330, 338.
[143] Kierkegaard, *Philosophical Fragments* (HVH-EHH), p. 11.
[144] Ibid., p. 18.
[145] Ibid., pp. 13–17.
[146] Ibid., pp. 18–19.

decisive significance — for, whereas by Socratic midwifery the person gives birth to himself

> and in so doing forgot everything else in the world and in a more profound sense owed no human being anything, so too the one who is born again owes no human being anything, but owes the divine teacher everything . . . and must . . . forget himself.[147]

The succinctness and clarity of these conceptual distinctions produce an intellectual embarrassment which leads Climacus to an existential one: thinking this rebirth, the transition from 'not to be' to 'to be', can only be done by one who is reborn; otherwise it would be 'unreasonable', 'ludicrous', for prior to the moment of birth the person is in a state of non-existence. At this point Climacus' modesty is disingenuous since he is not non—existent at all — he is in the Greek pathos of recollection which the work overall intrigues to assimilate to the pathos of the moment — and then it collapses under the weight of its own argument, for Climacus, even as *hesychast*, cannot himself 'provide the condition'. The thought-project bows itself out in facetious discomfort as 'the most ludicrous of all project-cranks'.[148]

Climacus does not, indeed, mediate Christianity with speculative thought — for that would call for the expounding of the truth and untruth of Christianity world-historically. Instead he deduces and posits a set of concepts — of 'the god', 'the saviour', 'repentance', and 'rebirth' by contrast with a posited exemplar of Greek philosophical pathos. He then retreats fervently from this travesty of Christian singularities (Christ, becoming a Christian) as a final bid to restore — *via negativa* — the concepts he would prefer not to expound yet whose exposition will henceforth be presupposed.

For the following chapter, 'The God as Teacher and Saviour (A Poetical Venture)', amounts to an aesthetic rewriting of this unrepresentable 'rebirth', the transition from 'not to be' to 'to be',[149] recasting it this time by contrast not with Greek recollection but with the characters of Socratic eros. Even though the analogy of human love with divine love will prove imperfect, the analogy itself must first be distinguished from the confusion of sexual and intellectual eros, of who is lover and who beloved, from which Socrates had to extricate himself. Socrates, having aroused it, nevertheless refuses the desire of the learner — Plato, Alcibiades — for the sake of the learner's love of the divine

147 Ibid., p. 19.
148 Ibid., p. 21.
149 Ibid., pp. 20, 30f.

towards which the learner has merely stumbled in his progress.[150] By contrast 'the god' 'moves himself... there... is no need that moves him'.[151] His love does not presuppose lack. The learner, now conceived as the beloved, shares the characteristics of the former: 'is in untruth – indeed is there through his own fault – and yet he is the object of the god's love.'[152] The difficulty now is that 'only in love is the difference made equal, and only in equality or in unity is there understanding'. Unhappiness ensues, 'the result not of the lovers' being unable to have each other but of their being unable to understand one another'; for such understanding may 'destroy what is different'.[153]

As soon as this analogy between divine and human love is developed poetically it breaks down: a king loves a maiden of lowly station in life who does not suspect his identity.[154] When the possibility of a unity accomplished by the maiden's 'ascent' is explored, the analogy breaks down even in terms of an imaginary human love: 'not to disclose itself [the King] is the death of love; to disclose itself is the death of the beloved.'[155] When the possibility of a unity brought about by descent is explored the poetry as well as the analogy dissolves. The analogy is explicitly transgressed: 'Between one human being and another, to be of assistance is supreme, but to beget is reserved for the god, whose love is *procreative* but [lest this 'procreative' resound with Socratic analogy] not that procreative love of which Socrates knew'.[156] Once descent is the key-note: that it is the 'boundlessness of love' which is to be revealed, then the idea of revelation is exceeded, for to reveal something depends on boundaries and delineations – unless it is specific, divine Revelation and that would put us in the context of Scriptural Revelations whereas we are engrossed in poetic philosophizing. And now the poetry disintegrates for

> Look, there he stands – the god. Where? There. Can you not see him? He is the god, and yet he has no place where he can lay his head, and he does not dare turn to any person lest that person be offended at him.[157]

No place in letters any more than in life: for all attempts to mask this saviour as suffering servant fall prey to extraneous significations. While

---

[150]   Ibid., pp. 24–5.
[151]   Ibid., p. 24.
[152]   Ibid., p. 28.
[153]   Ibid., p. 25.
[154]   Ibid., p. 26.
[155]   Ibid., p. 30.
[156]   Ibid., p. 31.
[157]   Ibid., p. 32.

it seems as if social status has been reversed from the previous analogy
of ascent — now the lover not the beloved is of lowly station in life —
all dialectic of master and servant is truncated: power and servitude
cannot be changed or educated for the god is simultaneously omnipotent and ineffective.[158] In short, in this analogy, the teacher/saviour is
not a mask: 'the form of a servant was not something put on'. This
proposition, reiterated three times,[159] to guard in vain against the
delusions of representation which, culminating with feminine analogies
of 'repentant prostitute', 'purest of women', and 'mother's sorrow', can
only lead to the dismissal of the poet: 'Thus speaks the poet', and a bare
restatement of the theme which eludes poetry as it eludes philosophy:
'this becoming — how difficult it really is, and how like a difficult
birth.'[160]

Back on the familiar ground of the aporia of the beginning, now
advanced as a 'rebirth', Climacus is seized by panic. This time the
poetic venture retreats from the border of Revelation where it would
seem to usurp Scripture, 'the shabbiest plagiarism'.[161] Philosophy suddenly appears to offer a comparatively safe refuge, and so, to avoid the
implicit sacrilege that the god has need of these poetic lucubrations,
the birth is at the last minute turned into the birth of philosophy in
wonder. 'This thought did not arise in my heart', cites 1 Corinthians 2
to insist that the divine is not reduced to human wisdom, 'and [he,
adoringly] finds it to be the most wondrously beautiful thought'. The
'wonder' overtakes the thought: 'we both are now standing before this
wonder'; the poem was 'no poem at all but *the wonder*'.[162]

Projecting and venturing, thinking and poetry, continue to delimit
themselves from their difference — but only conceptually and poetically. This very limitation – that difference is transfigured by the medium
that strives to acknowledge it — is made to yield absolute difference:
this is 'the absolute paradox'. And once again this procedure reveals a
conceptual structure, and is assimilated into the poetic mission.

The repeated collapse and self-effacement of what has been so far
ventured and projected is now proclaimed as the education of 'the
understanding', the ultimate passion of which is to 'will the collision
which is its own downfall'.[163] The erotic analogy is redeployed to
imply that the passion of the understanding is to lose itself in another;
here to overreach its own capabilities in seeking to know the unknow-

---

[158] Ibid., pp. 32, 33.
[159] Ibid., pp. 31, 32, 33.
[160] Ibid., pp. 34.
[161] Ibid., p. 35.
[162] Ibid., p. 36, emphasis in original.
[163] Ibid., p. 37.

able: '[L]et us call this unknown *the god*'.[164] The inevitable translating of being into essence or ideality which attends all attempts to demonstrate or prove the existence of the god — Spinoza's explaining *perfectio* by *realitas, esse*, is assimilated to Leibniz' 'If God is possible, he is *eo ipso* necessary' — is reaffirmed.[165] This doomed project is of a secondary order by comparison with what it reveals existentially:

> By beginning, then, I have presupposed the ideality, have presupposed that I will succeed in accomplishing it, but what else is that but presupposing that the god exists and actually beginning with trust in him.[166]

At last, it seems, the failure of the beginning reveals that we have already begun: already staked — a trust.

In this intellectualist way, though, Climacus is developing a further challenge — perhaps the most painful of the whole work — and which the remainder will dwell on and develop. For if '[t]he paradoxical passion of the understanding is, then, continually colliding with this unknown, which certainly does exist but is also unknown and to that extent does not exist',[167] then everything will turn on how this frontier is negotiated: whether the understanding will accept that the unknown is unknowable — that this difference at the very point of disclosure will never be disclosed — and whether it will take on this absolute difference by taking on as its own untruth that truth which exceeds it as 'consciousness of sin'; or whether the understanding will try to make the unknown knowable by dispersing this difference of differences into fantastical fabrications in which 'paganism has been adequately luxuriant'[168] — and, by implication, not only paganism.

Climacus delineates here the 'terrible' dilemma — 'the absolute paradox' — that faces humanity, individually and collectively: either willingness to suffer the pain of this limitation again and again or to take flight into idolatry. Climacus can only present the absolute paradox, make it 'conceivable', by employing a trope from his 'story': that the god 'wants' to teach this difference which remains unassimilable to the understanding, and hence not only contrary to any implication that the god should 'want', but also beyond even 'proclamation':[169] only accessible to the understanding in the moment of passion when it is as

---

164   Ibid., p. 39.
165   Ibid., pp. 41–2n.
166   Ibid., p. 42.
167   Ibid., p. 44.
168   Ibid., p. 45.
169   Ibid., p. 47.

willing to cease knowing itself as it is to cease trying to know the unknowable.[170] Even this would be bad politics – idolatry – if the unknowable is finite not infinite; almost unbearable pain if the other is 'the god'.

> Thus the paradox becomes even more terrible, or the same paradox has the duplexity by which it manifests itself as the absolute – negatively, by bringing into prominence the absolute difference of sin and, positively, by wanting to annul this absolute difference in the absolute equality.[171]

This attempt to mediate sin and faith by the metaphysical categories of 'absolute difference' and 'absolute equality', covered by the flippant title 'caprice', must now be rescued from the 'acoustical illusion' that the understanding has itself 'discovered' the offence of the paradox. While the understanding may be offended 'at' the paradox, it has not originated either the paradox or the offence: 'No, the offense *comes into existence* with the paradox; if it *comes into existence*...we have the moment, around which everything revolves.'[172] But, to borrow Climacus' own approach, does the moment 'come into existence' accidentally or essentially? The answer must be 'essentially', for otherwise we go back to Socrates and make the understanding the measure and the learner himself the truth. Metaphysics, it seems, is far less capricious than Climacus has bargained for: he must defend 'coming into existence' in order to introduce 'the moment' on which the explication of sin, untruth and their transfiguration depends, yet 'coming into existence' must be essential – otherwise we return to a Socratic vanishing moment which 'does not exist, has not been, and will not come', and absolute difference will vanish too.[173]

Predictably, the 'Appendix' concludes self-deprecatingly: with the charge that the discourse of offence has been plundered from others who speak as if offended, yet who 'hold firm' to the priority of the paradox.[174] The metaphysical crux that 'coming-into-existence' is 'essential', that the superlative affirmation of being turns into the ideal, is – for the moment – postponed.[175]

The labour of translating the three original historical questions into

---

[170]  Ibid., pp. 47, 39.
[171]  Ibid., p. 47.
[172]  Ibid., p. 51.
[173]  Ibid., pp. 51–2.
[174]  Ibid., pp. 53–4.
[175]  I hyphenate the phrase 'coming-into-existence' (and its variations) to bring out its metaphysical peculiarity.

logical questions continues 'with our poem': 'The Situation of the Contemporary Follower'.[176] The servant form is not 'put on', but this is 'loose talk', belonging to a narrative that must undermine itself since the god 'cannot be envisioned, and that was the very reason he was in the form of the servant'.[177] For the 'historical' in the more concrete sense, which covers finite signification as such, 'is inconsequential'.[178]

At this stage, poetizing the god, always precarious, is only intelligible from the perspective of what is to be demonstrated: that 'contemporaneity' is defined by the encounter between understanding and the paradox in faith, which can only occur when the eternal provides the condition in the moment.[179] 'Contemporaneity' is not defined by witnessing an historical event in itself, nor by any historical event providing a vanishing occasion for the eternal. The eternal becomes itself the condition which is received in the moment. In this way 'the god in the form of servant', 'contemporaneity,' and 'follower', lose all signification not culled from the paradox. Furthermore, a 'follower at second hand' becomes a distinction without a difference.

The discussion deliberately defies intelligibility by simultaneously drawing on and disqualifying connotations: the eternal and historical apart from each other may provide the occasion but not the condition: 'only in that happy passion which we call faith ['the third something ... in which this occurs'], the object of which is the paradox − but the paradox specifically unites the contradictions, is the eternalizing of the historical and the historicizing of the eternal'.[180]

Poetry, which has 'the god walking about in the city', and knowledge, which is either exclusively eternal or exclusively temporal and historical, are middles or thirds distinguished, *e contrario*, from this third which is 'faith'. The moment, which provides the condition for faith, has been reaffirmed as an inconceivable temporality whilst it is deprived of its customary place.

> [N]o knowledge can have as its object this absurdity that the eternal is the historical.[181]

The charge of 'absurdity' belongs, however, to the aesthetic authorship. Climacus, who ostensibly treats 'knowledge' as solely the province of a 'Socrates', has now climbed the ladder to the *Logic* of his

176  Ibid., p. 55.
177  Ibid., p. 63.
178  Ibid., p. 59.
179  Ibid., pp. 58, 59.
180  Ibid., pp. 61, 59.
181  Ibid., p. 62.

immediate predecessor — Hegel — which rethinks reason for the sake of Revelation.

The encounter between the logic of being and the logic of essence is staged on the ground of illusory being: the 'Interlude', introduced with exquisite facetiousness, assumes in 'earnestness and jest' that 1,843 years have elapsed since the death of the teacher. This then accurate but illusory, in any case insignificant, amount of time/date, provokes profuse apologies from Climacus whose prolixity stresses the lengthy allowance of time 'for the sake of the illusion'[182] — the illusion which is no illusion but is his immediacy and yet is an illusion (and not only because 1,992 years have elapsed).

The 'Interlude' poses two questions: 'Is the Past More Necessary than the Future? Or Has the Possible by having Become Actual Become More Necessary than It Was?' The argument falls under the headings

1  Coming into Existence
2  The Historical
3  The Past
4  The Apprehension of the Past
5  Appendix: Application[183]

Since Climacus takes off the Socratic mask and argues explicitly with the history of philosophy, mentioning Aristotle, the Stoics, Descartes, Leibniz, Spinoza,[184] and Hegel, by name, and thus from within the philosophy of history, his close reasoning may be matched accordingly.

How is that changed which comes into existence or what is the change (κινησις) of coming into existence?[185]

Coming-into-existence is a general process of 'change': *kinesis*.

Not so with coming into existence, for if that which comes into existence does not in itself remain unchanged in the change of coming into existence, then the coming into existence is not *this* coming into existence . . .

All other change . . . presupposes the existence of that in which change is taking place . . .[186]

[182]  Ibid., pp. 72−88.
[183]  Ibid., p. 72.
[184]  Ibid., the last two discussed in the note to ibid., pp. 41−2; see p. 42 n. 165 *supra*.
[185]  Ibid., p. 73.
[186]  Ibid.

The fourfold negative of the first of these propositions (Not...
not ... unchanged ... not) distracts from the fact that they both assert
the same thing: that for change to be identified something must remain
the same. The first proposition concerns not a changing thing but the
change of coming-into-existence itself, which must therefore provide
'in itself' – in the very changing – something unchanged. For it
cannot provide, as can all other change, something unchanged 'in
which' the change occurs. Ergo: 'This change, then, is not in essence
but in being and is from not existing to existing.'[187]

So far, 'change' or 'transition' is at stake: from non-being to being, or
becoming. Once some *thing* comes into existence, it/we would be in the
realm of possibility and actuality, or essence. But Climacus argues for
'coming-into-existence', so that 'non-being' itself bears the weight of
the constant which makes the idea that 'this' has changed meaningful:

> But this non-being that is abandoned by that which comes into
> existence must also exist, for otherwise 'that which comes into
> existence would not remain unchanged in the coming into exis-
> tence' ... [188]

Climacus here *insinuates the logic of essence into the logic of being or
existence*, instead of distinguishing 'change' or 'transition' between one
in relation to another (which characterizes determinations in the sphere
of being or existence) from the *movement* of one in *negative* self-relation
to itself (which characterizes determinations in the sphere of essence).[189]

> [S]uch a being that nevertheless is a non-being is possibility, and a
> being that is being is indeed actual being or actuality, and the
> change of coming into existence is the transition from possibility
> to actuality.[190]

This passage expounds the *transition* of coming-into-existence from
non-being to being under the terminology of possibility and actuality. It
leads to the demonstration that necessity cannot be 'a unity of possibility and actuality', because 'the essence of necessity is to be': 'necessity'
obliterates the suffering of coming-into-existence which the assimilation of possibility and actuality to non-being and being, respectively,

---

[187] Ibid.
[188] Ibid., p. 73 citing the repeated proposition from the same paragraph.
[189] Compare Hegel, *Science of Logic* II, p. 5, tr. p. 390.
[190] Kierkegaard, *Philosophical Fragments*, p. 74.

has rendered illogical.[191] For coming-into-existence implies a 'double uncertainty: the nothingness of non-being and the annihilated possibility' − and that in a double sense, too, annihilation of possibilities excluded, and annihilation of the possibility of the one accepted.[192]

By arguing that 'the essence of necessity is to be', so that if possibility and actuality add up to necessity, then possibility and actuality pertain to essence not being, and coming-into-being is foreclosed, Climacus overlooks the 'being' of necessity, possibility and actuality which he concedes is essential. He undermines and exploits the logic of essence.

For necessity is the 'blind' unity of being and essence,[193] or as Climacus puts it, 'the necessary is always related to itself and is related to itself in the same way'.[194] It can always be stated in this formal or absolute way: recognizing no other or 'light-shy' (*das Lichtscheue*).[195] But when relative necessity, or real actuality and possibility are considered, then the movement (not the transition) from possibility to actuality is a negation (not an annihilation), 'a going together with itself [*Zusammengehen mit sich selbst*]'. Possibility is not 'annihilated' by actuality but 'pregnant' with it (*inhaltsvolle Ansichsein*), and 'when all the conditions of something are completely present it enters into actuality'.[196]

Climacus − simply but with great prolixity − reduces the logic of essence to the logic of being. Furthermore his conclusion that

> the change of coming into existence is actuality; the transition takes place in freedom ... not by way of necessity ... but ... by way of ... a freely acting cause.[197]

posits − without prolixity − a third logic, 'the freely acting cause'. From the perspective of the absolute relation or subjective logic − this ultimate, 'free' cause − Climacus has expounded actuality, the movement of essence, as the logic of being, the transition of coming-into-existence from non-being to being.

Everything that has come into existence is *eo ipso* historical.[198]

---

[191] Ibid.
[192] Ibid., p. 81 compare *Sickness Unto Death*, (HVH-EHH), p. 36 when the argument is developed without philosophical mask.
[193] Hegel, *Science of Logic* II, p. 183, tr. p. 552.
[194] Kierkegaard, *Philosophical Fragments*, p. 74.
[195] Hegel, *Science of Logic* II, p. 183, tr. p. 553.
[196] Ibid., II p. 178, pp. 547−8, 'this negation' is 'not a transition but a going-together-with-itself', a 'movement of self-sublating real possibility'.
[197] Kierkegaard, *Philosophical Fragments*, p. 75.
[198] Ibid., p. 75.

In this sense, nature is also 'historical' although it comes-into-existence 'simultaneously', that is, as space.[199] To be distinguished from nature, 'historical' coming-into-existence must be 'past', 'a redoubling', that is, it must retain the 'possibility of coming into existence within its own coming into existence'.[200] In order to introduce this further idea of coming-into-existence as historical yet still possible, Climacus continues to expound the logic of essence, 'the historical', that is, what *has been* (*Wesen*), with the logic of being, arresting the argument with a sublime prophetic pointing:

> The more special historical coming into existence comes into existence by way of a relatively freely acting cause, which in turn definitively points to an absolutely freely acting cause.[201]

Pointing cannot be 'definitive': it conjures up the urgent finger of the Forerunner occupying a different kind of space from the Crucified.[202] This moment signals the perfect faith but imperfect confidence of prophecy, the uncertainty of which Climacus wishes to claim for the historical, and which subsequently he denies to prophecy, characterizing it as the future necessary tense, corresponding, *tout court*, to philosophy's past necessary which he seeks to discredit.[203]

The 'redoubled' historical or 'the past' which has come-into-existence but cannot subsequently be changed, is the focus of Climacus' concern. This unchangeableness is not the unchangeableness of necessity, because by virtue of 'having occurred, it demonstrated that it was not necessary'. Its actuality, its 'thus and so, cannot become different', but from this it does not follow that its possibility, 'its how, could not have been different'.[204] Climacus can only let himself down at this point: for the real or essential possibility of 'the special historical' could no more be different than its actuality, while to stress that its formal possibility could have been different, would make the occurrence, as he would himself express it, into a different 'this'. Far from attributing blind necessity to everything that has occurred or denying contingency, this distinction illustrates that logic is nuanced richly enough to differentiate 'coming-into-existence' from 'came-into-existence' – logic which relates being and essence: past, unchangeable, but which *has* moved or developed, and which retains these determinations in its expression.

---

[199]   Ibid., pp. 75–6.
[200]   Ibid., p. 76.
[201]   Ibid.
[202]   I allude here to the Grünewald altarpiece, *Unter den Linden*, Colmar.
[203]   Ibid., p. 78n.
[204]   Ibid., p. 77.

With the fourth heading 'Apprehension of the Past' these reflections on general logic begin to betray peculiar features: they seek to marry two things quite outside logic. On the one, objective hand, 'a special historical case' turns out to be the specific (i.e. unique) concept of Christ; on the other, subjective hand, the uncertainty without which that 'event' *qua* advent cannot offer the occasion for faith must be secured.

By inquiring into how knowledge of the past is acquired, Climacus demonstrates that its basis is always belief. For once any immediately perceived object, for example, a star, is reflected upon as having come into existence, as historical, then belief is requisite for that certitude which retains the uncertainties of non-being and annihilated possibilities.[205] Knowledge as such — and not only of the past — depends on the 'illusiveness' of these transitions from non-being and from multiple possibility.[206] For all judging of cause and effect involves a transition from immediate sensation to a reflected conclusion, a suspension of immediate presence and hence an opening up of doubt, resolvable only by belief: 'a sense for coming into existence', 'an act of will'.[207]

Not 'illusive' but elusive and elliptical, this argument draws on unavowed conceptuality while claiming Greek Scepticism as its predecessor.[208] To believe that the star (to take that choice example) has come-into-existence involves a belief in creation as opposed to belief in the eternity of the universe: a specific 'belief' called forth by the availability of alternative accounts. The star is to serve, not only for any cause and effect, but also as analogy for 'Christ', a concept which involves belief because it has the peculiar feature of singularity, of having only one instance, and faith, because it calls for personal encounter. The doubt/belief involved in ordinary judgement of cause and effect is strikingly irrelevant to these two exceptions. This general but irrelevant 'illusiveness' is what Climacus prefers not to call illusion: that 'what has been' has both entered duration, 'occurred', and is past, 'timelessly past' or 'unchangeable', a unifying or coming together of being and essence that is blindly, unmoveably necessary.[209]

We shall now return to our poem and to our assumption that the god *has* been.[210]

---

[205] Ibid., pp. 83−4.
[206] Ibid., p. 81.
[207] Ibid., pp. 84, 82.
[208] Ibid., pp. 82−3, 84−5.
[209] 'Timelessly past being' is Hegel's description of essence or 'what has been', *gewesen*; see *Science of Logic* II, p. 3, tr. p. 389.
[210] Kierkegaard, *Philosophical Fragments*, pp. 86−7.

Confident that lack of confidence is now safe on the ground that this historical 'has been' of the god 'pertains not to essence but to being',[211] to faith not recollection, the call goes out for 'assent' not truth or knowledge. 'Assent' to what?

> to the god's having come into existence, whereby the god's eternal essence is inflected into the dialectical qualifications of coming into existence.[212]

Since Climacus appears to think that this is the only basis on which he can dissolve the idea of the immediate contemporary, and, *a fortiori*, of the follower at second hand, this admission of inflecting essence into coming-into-existence is instructive in relation to what, logically, has occurred. For 'inflection' pertains to verbs and Climacus has inflected his verbs so as to deflect essence into existence and logic into assent. He has, in effect, expounded *kenosis*, the self-'emptying' or renunciation of the divine nature, in part, in the Incarnation, not *kinesis*, change or transition, and this − as he warned at the outset − by taking something away. All this labour to take us out of the concept and to dissolve therewith the idea of there being an assent at 'second hand' when the good news has never been received at second hand, but at third hand − via the Holy Spirit.

It is this unspoken third that has been sententiously released by demonstrating that there is no faith without concept and no concept without faith, for neither 'Climacus' nor the *Science of Logic* would expound the incarnation in either the logic of being or the logic of essence. This explains why Climacus' conclusion is both festive and solemn.[213] Once again he answers the question concerning 'a historical point of departure' by removing it from myth, from history, from philosophy; and, with familiar, fervent apologies, the last sentence repeats the old question: 'how shall we ever manage to begin?'[214]

---

211 Ibid., p. 87.
212 Ibid.
213 See ibid., p. 107f.
214 Ibid., p. 110.

# 2

# Regina and Felice —
# In Repetition of Her

## Kierkegaard and Kafka

### Confession and Authority

The sexual is the expression for the prodigious contradiction that the immortal spirit is determined as *genus*.[1]

Had I had faith, I should have remained with Regina.[2]

He [Kafka] said to me [Brod], 'What I have to do, I can do only alone. Become clear about the ultimate things. The Western Jew is not clear about them, and therefore has no right to marry'.[3]

With what do these passages begin? With the erotic? With the ethical? With 'the religious'? With the absurd? With the attempt to transform the erotic-aesthetic into the ethical under the signature of 'the religious'? Disembellishing of this kind is conventionally conceived as a flight

---

[1]  *The Concept of Anxiety* (RT), p. 69, 'contradiction' in German in the original and in translation.

[2]  *The Journals of Kierkegaard* (Dru), Berlin, 17 May, 1843, pp. 86–7.

[3]  Brod, *Franz Kafka, A Biography*, tr. p. 166, cited in German in Robertson, *Kafka*, pp. 187–8. This chapter as a whole, while it refers critically at several points to Brod's biography of Kafka, attempts to take up the challenge implied but not followed through by both Eric Heller and Walter Benjamin when they judge Brod's 'religious' interpretation of Kafka to be naive in itself, and to provide evidence, more generally, of our progressive deprivation 'of all sureness of religious discrimination' (Heller, 'The World of Franz Kafka', pp. 60–1). The comparison with Kierkegaard, developed in this chapter *without* prejudging the *tertuim quid*, attempts to begin to rectify this lack of discrimination, and to make more precise Benjamin's command 'not to lose sight of the purity and beauty of a failure' ('Max Brod's Book on Kafka', p. 148), and to account for the oscillations he mentions in his essay on Kafka between the — in his view, equally mistaken — psychoanalytical and theological interpretations ('Franz Kafka', p. 127).

from fear of the father to an absolute without law – as repression and projection. These successive and simultaneous 'stages' of existence – the aesthetic, the ethical and the religious – are taken from the *Concluding Unscientific Postscript*. 'The aesthetic' is the sphere of desire; 'the ethical' is the sphere of responsibility, family and law; 'religiousness A' is edifying religion, and 'religiousness B', the paradox. These 'stages' appear arbitrary if they are taken as demarcations of content. But, what emerges, as illustrated in the opening passages, if the stages themselves begin with their very form? Question, proposition, judgement, pluperfect, conditional perfect: each vehicle of confessional inquiry into precisely the call to confess – into authority, author, actor, truth?

'Confession' is not the sum of admissions, nor content as such, but Janus-faced form: it probes the recesses to reveal whatever both shuns release and also yearns to be released; yet ambivalent revelations of this kind depend on a prior Revelation which calls them forth. Just as we forget the other face of confession because it so deeply forms us, but has now sloughed off its original Christianity; so, too, we forget the Janus-faces of the original Greek philosophical myth of the origin of our genders.

The 'Speech of Aristophanes' in Plato's *Symposium* posits three kinds of human beings: male, female and 'man-woman', the last of these born of the moon; each with 'one head to two faces, which looked opposite ways'. All three are subsequently sliced in two and their face and half-neck are turned to the section side. Human gender is thus generated by Zeus to thwart humankind's pretensions 'to mount high heaven' and 'assault the gods in fight' – a strategy which issues in an ambiguity of loss and gain comparable to the confusing of tongues with which the building and ascent of the tower of Babel is thwarted. Two sexes result from the Greek godly zeal but three kinds of inclination: woman for woman; man for man; woman for man and vice versa. 'Each of us, then, is but a tally of a man . . . for our sins we are all dispersed.' The craving for and pursuit of our former entirety is called 'Love'.[4]

The addition by scholars of 'confessional' journals, papers and correspondence to the *oeuvre* of Kierkegaard and of Kafka, reduces the Janus of confession to the Janus of gender. The gender-Janus is then read in terms of personal limitations and their progressive or regressive overcoming. This approach, confident that it possesses knowledge before engaging the sources, cannot hear what the vulnerability behind the voluble voices of confession would tell: the imperfect welcome accorded to the call, both absolute *and* relative. For the hypertrophy of confessed meaning is the inverse indicator of the shying from the other face.

[4] *Symposium*, 189c–193.

Author, reader and commentator share the same dilemma: how to transfer the beginning from one countenance to the other — confession to its authority, while still suffering and acting out of the unfinished and unfinishable need to speak? And so we encounter these 'author-ships' at a life-crisis: breaking off their engagements yet writing incessantly to or about their fiancées, they defamiliarize the customary transition from the erotic to the ethical. The mix of modes, apparently more and less fictional, circling around the crisis, gives us the idea of authorship-difficulty in the first place. The challenge is to continue reading this *failing towards form* in its two aspects: from the aesthetic to the ethical to the absolute, as the inability to marry; from the absolute to the ethical to the aesthetic, as the inability to write without arrogating illegitimate authority. If this dual-directional approach is sustainable and sustained, a 'third' will emerge: the law revealed and concealed in the absence of *gravitas* — no marriage — and in the absence of grace — no silence — only 'poetry'. The one thing needful is to bear this suspense — this anxiety — of beginning.

Brod, Buber and Blanchot seem to be sources for the conventional wisdom concerning Kafka and Kierkegaard: that while Kafka himself judged their fate to be similar, 'Kierkegaard's' suspension of the ethical was not an option he, Kafka, could take:

> Kafka's story and the story of Kierkegaard's engagement have been compared, by Kafka himself among others. But the conflict is different. Kierkegaard can renounce Regina; he can renounce the ethical level. Access to the religious level is not thereby compromised; rather it is made possible. But Kafka, if he abandons the earthly happiness of a normal life, also abandons the steadiness of a just life. He makes himself an outlaw, deprives himself of the ground and the foundation he needs in order to be and, in a way, deprives the law of this ground.[5]

[5] Blanchot, 'The Work's Space and Its Demand', in *The Space of Literature*, p. 61. Compare Brod, 'He was reading a Kierkegaard anthology, "The Book of the Judge": The similarity between Kierkegaard's fate and his own became clear to him', which is confirmed by the *Diary* entry for 21 August 1913, p. 232, tr. p. 230. Compare, too, Brod: 'It is obvious that Kafka was not at all striving after a paradox, an ideal in principle unachievable — like Kierkegaard, like the "theology of crisis", but — and this is the decisive factor — that he wanted an intelligently fulfilled, good and proper life, that he stood more perhaps on the side of Martin Buber, who, in rejecting Kierkegaard, the solitary, from principle, says of living with a wife, "Marriage is the exemplary bond, as no other bond does, it carries us into the great bondage and only as bondsmen can we enter into the freedom of the children of God ..." citing Buber, 'The Question for the Individual [*sic*]', *Between Man and Man* (Brod, *Franz Kafka*, pp. 144, 198). See, too, Kafka's letter to Brod where he discusses Kierkegaard, March 1918 and April 1918, (*Letters to Friends, Family and Editors*, pp. 234–40, tr. pp. 199–203.) Robertson also compares Kafka and Kierkegaard on Abraham, *Kafka*, pp. 191–6.

The travesty contained in the implication that throughout Kierkegaard's authorship the ethical is either 'suspended' or 'either/or', is here compounded with the memory of 'Kierkegaard' as solitary and asocial into the imaginary heritage of a 'story' (aesthetic) which may simply be predicated of its author/main character. That the ethical is richly equivocal in Kierkegaard's authorship, even in aesthetic terms: 'suspended', 'either/or', 'simultaneous' stage, will be secondary to the argument to be developed here: that Kierkegaard is the less equivocal 'ethical' author than Kafka, in spite of the latter's Judaism.

> His [Kafka's] is Abraham's eternal dilemma. What is demanded of Abraham is not only that he sacrifice his son, but God himself. The son is God's future on earth, for it is time which is truly the Promised Land – the true, the only dwelling place of the chosen people and of God in his people. Yet Abraham, by sacrificing his only son, must sacrifice time, and time sacrificed will certainly not be given back in the eternal beyond. The beyond is nothing other than the future, the future of God in time. The beyond is Isaac.[6]

Blanchot here justifies his judgement of the difference between Kierkegaard and Kafka by developing this Abrahamic analogy. Kafka cannot renounce the ethical for the sake of the absolute because the ethical is the appearance of the absolute in time – not in the Hegelian sense of the realization of the rational, but in the Hebraic sense of succeeding generations. With this extended expatiation Blanchot takes back the relation to law that he has conceded differentiates Kafka from Kierkegaard in the first place: Kafka needs the law, but, without becoming a father, there can be no appearance of God. Isaac, however, is only the 'beyond' under the condition that Abraham is in the pre-legal relation of promise to God; even so, the commandment to sacrifice Isaac overrides the futural 'beyond' and calls for an unconditioned response to the eternal 'beyond'. Kafka, however, is a Jew living within the law, which persists regardless of his marital or progenitorial status: his dilemma is within God's omniabsence, the law's omnipresence. The difficulty is how to be a modern Jew without marriage or family (a problem compounded if one is a woman). It is as a Jew on the periphery of the law that Kafka hears Abraham's story – the law is given: his relation to it is equivocal.[7]

---

[6]  Blanchot, 'The Works Space and Its Demand', p. 61.
[7]  Compare Rosenzweig, 'All of us to whom Judaism, to whom being a Jew, has again become the pivot of our lives ... we all know that in being Jews we must not give up anything, not renounce anything, but lead everything back to Judaism. From the periphery back to the center; from the outside, in'; *Franz Rosenzweig, His Life and Thought*, presented by N. N. Glatzer, p. 231.

The assumption of unproblematic access to two contrasted stories of the renunciation of the ethical also seems to imply that the law is not already present in the very form in which these admissions of failure are offered up. It normalizes and personifies 'Kierkegaard' and 'Kafka' when the notions of actor, author, authority and truth are at stake: for what are these if not ethical notions?

Is it possible to ask why Kierkegaard and Kafka broke off their engagements, and what relation their not marrying has to their authorships, without denying the anxiety of beginning? If 'not marrying' is taken as perpetually posed or poised at the frontier between the other and the Other, where otherness becomes blurred – both relative or gendered, and absolute or God – so that the ethical law, the middle, is the most ambivalent and equivocal of all, then the relation to gendered otherness and thus to self-relation – woman to woman, man to man, woman to man, and vice versa – can be raised without reduction of authorship to psychology, theology, or sociology. This is to remain both with the anxiety of beginning and with the equivocation of the middle, manifest in the manifold *failing towards form*. The very authorship-difficulty itself may be seen to arise not only in memory of her,[8] but in repetition of her: not only the movement backward of recollection and restoration but resurging forward under the sign of reconfiguring gender difference – from anxiety to celebration and celebration of anxiety around the Janus-faces of our failing.

Regina and Felice: 'Queen' and 'Happiness'. The rhythm and symbolism of these two names would seem to announce what their affianced, in each case, had to refuse.[9] Yet these breached relationships may be made to broach radically different accounts depending upon from which face we take our bearings: from the intimacy of confession, or from – let us call it – the 'paradox'. If we work sedulously both ways, the third, implicit in this split-directionality, may emerge.

First, let us confess: both Kierkegaard and Kafka died young. Kierkegaard lived from May 1813 to November 1855, Kafka from 3 July 1883 to 3 June 1924. They lived, therefore forty-two and almost forty-one years, respectively. Both Kierkegaard and Kafka wrote of their fathers as overbearing in their struggle for identity and in their consequent strengths and weaknesses. Kafka, in his unsent 'Letter to his Father', re-enacts his resentment at his dependency on his overwhelming parent;[10] Kierkegaard in his *Journals* laments the 'sin' of his father, who,

---

[8]   See Elisabeth Schüssler-Fiorenza, *In Memory of Her: A Feminist Theological Reconstruction of Christian Origins.*
[9]   See Lowrie, 'Regina – September 1840 to October 1841', in *A Short Life of Kierkegaard*, pp. 135–143.
[10]   In *Wedding Preparations in the Country*, pp. 119–62, tr. pp. 157–217.

as a young man in bleak conditions, cursed God on Jutland Heath, and, somehow, felt that this had led to the death of his wife and five of his seven children before they reached the age of thirty-four.[11] Both Kierkegaard and Kafka became engaged and broke off their engagements – Kafka twice. In letters, journals and diaries both offered irremediable melancholy in order to account for breaking the engagement; and both also created fictions or narratives concerning the difficulty in marrying: *inter alia*, Kierkegaard's pseudonymous *Repetition*, 'Quidam's Diary' in *Stages on Life's Way*; Kafka's *Wedding Preparations in the Country*.

Now let us witness the paradox: both address the relation between not marrying, authorship, authority, actor/actress and truth: Kierkegaard 'Guilty?/Not Guilty?' in *Stages on Life's Way*, *Concluding Unscientific Postscript*; Kafka, *Letters to Felice*, '109 Aphorisms'. When confessions and fictions, fictional confessions ('The Diary of a Seducer') and 'true' confession which requires the composing of fiction (*Dichtung*), are read from the face of the paradox, Kierkegaard and Kafka are scrupulously consistent with respect to gender. In the tradition of Aristophanes' founding myth, the lover/ seducer and beloved/seduced swap gender places. In the realm of the aesthetic, dramatized as the erotic, woman and man collide, alternatively, as sexual subject and as sexual object.

From the paradox: 'the prodigious contradiction that the immortal spirit is determined as genus'.[12] When the immortal spirit is determined, that is, incarnate, as 'mortal' – being born and dying, generated, gendered, generating, belonging to a generation, that is, as 'genus' – this 'contradiction' of immortal and mortal is 'prodigious': it produces all the works of the erotic-aesthetic, familial-ethical. This 'contradiction', origin of anxiety, is equally the anxiety of beginning, precisely because all such works or 'stages' are simultaneous, even while existence concentrates, intermittently, on one or the other.

Genus or gender begins in Kierkegaard and in Kafka as woman and as man, as erotic subject and as erotic object: 'her' point of view is dramatized as much as 'his'.[13] From the face of the paradox, 'immortal spirit', s/he is single'. The felicitous coincidence that the English translation of Kierkegaard's 'single one' falls into the contrary of single/ married enriches the issue. The contrast is not between the 'individual' and 'the social' ('the individual' is the social category, *par excellence*, in any case: *in-dividuum*, or that which cannot be *further* sub-divided,

[11]  See Lowrie, 'Background', *A Short Life*, pp. 3–30.
[12]  *The Concept of Anxiety* (RT), p. 69, see n. 1, *supra*.
[13]  For 'point of view', see Kierkegaard, *The Point of View for My Work as An Author: A Report to History*.

which presupposes prior division),[14] but between the relative other, mortal and gendered, and the absolute Other, immortal and ungendered – which runs the gamut from the erotic to religiousness 'A' and 'B', and which is, in every instance, social. The single one – married or not, 'workman or judge', woman or man – emerges from the face of the paradox; not that social statuses are overlooked or treated indifferently, but that they, middles, may yet afford different beginnings, prodigiously animated and adversarial, which arise from the 'contradiction' of mortal and immortal. 'Contradiction' becomes itself a prodigious mode of expression for the paradox.

Kafka, from the erotic face: 'Wedding Preparations in the Country'. The journey towards the country and the preparations for marriage are presented as increasingly 'more disagreeable and difficult': 'Oh beautiful city and beautiful the way home', expostulates the bridegroom, Raban, in a disturbing reversal of modern disturbance, where the country is most often seen as the simple, beautiful home destroyed by the city.[15] Kafka from the paradox: in the letters to Felice, Kafka presents a different sentiment – not only fear of his desire for Felice and of its maturation into the ethical, but also concern that their marriage should enhance the singleness of each equally.

> 29th December 1913, evening
> You misunderstand if you imagine that what keeps me from marrying is the thought that in winning you I would gain less than I would lose by giving up my solitary existence. I know you think this; orally you expressed yourself in this way, and I contradicted, but, as I see, not vehemently enough. For me it was not a matter of giving something up, for even after marriage I would go on being the very same person I am, and this precisely – if you so choose – is the serious problem that would confront you. What prevents me was the imagined feeling that complete isolation meant an obligation for me, not a gain, not a pleasure, (at least not in the sense you imagine), but duty and suffering. I don't believe it any more, it was a pure fabrication (perhaps this knowledge will help me to go on), and is most easily disproved by the fact that I cannot live without you. Just you, just as you are, including that terrible paragraph in your letter, that's the way I want you. And yet not for the sake of finding solace, not for my

---

[14] Compare Nietzsche, 'In morality man treats himself not as *individuum* but as *dividuum*', *Human All Too Human*, Schlechta, I, p. 491, tr. p. 42.

[15] *Wedding Preparations in the Country*, p. 24, tr. p. 30.

own gratification, but so that you should live with me here as an independent human being.[16]

> 1st January 1914, Midnight
>
> ... it is not possible to get married provided and so long as you are aware of and able to foresee the losses with as much perspicacity as one may conclude from your letter. To enter upon marriage with a conscious sense of loss – this I admit is not possible, and I would not allow it to happen even if you wanted it, because in the only kind of marriage I want, husband and wife, in the very essence of their being, must be equals in order to exist independently within this unit – which in that case would be impossible.[17]

Ambivalence and equivocation are here reversed – the latter profounder than the former. For if ambivalence reveals the desire for and fear of loss or gain of freedom in erotic and ethical commitment to another, equivocation – much harder to express – reveals the questioning of the conditions under which marrying (not marriage, not the ethical as such) would enhance the singleness of each.

From the erotic face: in one place in his *Journals*, Kierkegaard presents his own melancholy as the reason for breaking the engagement in 1841:

> How great is womanly devotion – but the curse which rests upon me is never to be allowed to let anyone deeply and inwardly join themselves to me ... My relationship to her may, I truly believe, be called unhappy love – I love her – I own her – her only wish is to remain with me – her family implore me – it is my greatest wish and I have to say 'no'. In order to make it easier for her I will, if possible, make her believe that I simply deceived her, that I am a frivolous man, so as, if possible, to make her hate me; for I believe that it will always be more difficult for her if she suspected that the cause was melancholy – how alike are melancholy and frivolity.[18]

Here ambivalence, his and hers, seeks expiation by the concern to restore her erotic possibility, her singleness in the simple sense. The verb tenses of the journal 'confessions' speak the turn to the face of the paradox:

> Had I had faith, I should have remained with Regina.[19]

[16]  *Letters to Felice*, pp. 483–4, tr. pp. 462–3.
[17]  Ibid., p. 487, tr. pp. 465–6.
[18]  *The Journals of Kierkegaard* (Dru), p. 76.
[19]  Ibid., p. 86.

Failing from faith elicits the failing towards form and this is why the ethical is equivocal: it may be faith or it may be falsehood.

> Had I not honoured her above myself, as my future wife, had I not been prouder of her honour than of mine, then I should have remained silent and have fulfilled her wish and mine and have been married to her — there are so many marriages that conceal their little tale. That I did not want; in that way she would have become my concubine; I would rather have murdered her.[20]

'Honour', eminently social category, is here calibrated on the invisible scales of singleness where fully single and fully ethical would equal each other. To force a justification of his retreat would be to require a relapse into recollection: 'But if I had had to explain myself then I would have had to initiate her into terrible things: my relation to my father, his melancholy, the eternal darkness that broods deep within, my going astray, pleasures and excesses which in the eyes of God are not perhaps so terrible...'[21] The verb tenses here, form of the paradox, speak the truth — terrible things attending terrible tenses.

Kierkegaard, like Kafka, would not marry for gratification, for solace; while Kafka emphasizes that neither he nor Felice were single enough to marry, here Kierkegaard stresses that he would not and could not marry because *he* was not single enough.

> But would it be possible now for someone who has believed the forgiveness of his sins to become young enough erotically to fall in love [sic].[22]

The 'no' implicitly called for is undermined and completed by the 'had I had faith I would have', both converging implicitly on ethical resolution. 'Marriage' is the way in which 'young' eros and maturer 'forgiveness' may be lived together; and in this answering affirmation of the ethical as marriage, family, most quiet, most difficult enclave within civil society, might be discerned a deeply Judaic sentiment.

However, the verb tense of this restless question belies even its own beatitude and brings the shifting faces of the paradox back into focus. From the confessional face, the ambivalent erotic countenance predominates: 'I cannot marry Regina/Felice because I/my father am too sinful'; from the paradox: 'Regina/Felice and I do not marry because of the forgiveness of sins'. Form fails in both cases: the first, not marrying;

---

[20] Ibid., p. 87.
[21] Ibid.
[22] *Journals and Papers*, Vol. 2, p. 48, no question mark.

the second, reduction of existence to an exclusive forgiveness – the ethical refused in each position. Yet the subject–object relationship changes: 'she', the object initially, becomes, subsequently, joint subject, 'we'. Only the verb tense of the joint confession 'Had *we* had faith . . .' would join the single ones and preserve their singleness – hypothetically. The 'ethical' is the prodigious expression, the third, for these failings towards form which always find themselves back in the agony of erotic middle and anxious beginning, back in the equivocation of the tenses: 'had I had . . .'.

> It is in fact just as you [Brod] say: the problem of arriving at a true marriage is his [Kierkegaard's] principal concern, the concern that is forever rising into his consciousness.

And, further on in the same letter to Brod, from March 1918, Kafka comments: 'And *Either/Or* and *The Instant* are certainly two very different lenses through which one can examine this life forwards or backwards and of course in both directions at the same time.'[23]

This perpetual reversing of authorship and authority emerges with especial clarity in the first of the 'Three Discourses on Imagined Occasions', published separately to accompany *Stages on Life's Way*. Entitled 'On the Occasion of a Confession' it explores 'what it means to seek after God'. In the course of this seeking the seeker becomes the one who is sought.[24] Such confessing, one might say, is precipitated by the tension which holds off this interchange of action and passion by imagining its occasion.

### From the True Antagonist

> [O]nly the lack of perfect love makes A incapable of perfect marriage with B. I still cannot read the first book of Either/Or without repugnance.[25]

> My Friend,
> The lines upon which your eye first falls were written last.[26]

With what does the ethical begin? With the difficulty that cannot rest with either perfection or repugnance – with the 'scandal' of the ethical,

23  *Letters to Friends*, p. 235, tr. pp. 199–200.
24  Op. cit. (WL), pp. 457–65.
25  Kafka, Zürau, March 1918, *Letters to Friends*, p. 236, tr. p. 200.
26  Kierkegaard, *Either/Or* (WL), Vol. II, p. 5.

as Kafka's response so aptly evinces it here. Not with 'suspension', nor with exclusive 'either/or':

> So marriage is threatened from two sides: if the individual has not put himself in a relationship of faith to God as spirit, paganism haunts his brain as a fantastic reminiscence, and then he cannot enter into any marriage; or, on the other hand, he has become entirely spiritual, and so neither in this case can he marry. Even if both the former and the latter of these were wed, such a love affair and such a wedding is not marriage.[27]

The ethical begins and ends with the classical modes: with Plato's *Symposium* and with Aristotle's *Ethics*: with the friends carousing and devising myths to analyse eros in 'The Banquet', with which *Stages on Life's Way* begins; with friendship, apparently dealt with last in *Either/Or*.[28] Yet the whole of Part II of *Either/Or* addresses 'My Friend'. If eros and friendship are quintessentially Greek, confession quintessentially Christian, then here the ethical takes the form of the letters and pages of 'B' confessing to a friend, 'A', about the ethical validity of marriage. The minimalism of these masks, 'A' and 'B', proves no defence against the rhetoric or reality of gender for the two male correspondents. While the stages are lived simultaneously, they are indicated by the temporality of gender: erotic momentariness of the genders; ethical eternity of the generations; finite/infinite of the approaches to religiousness 'A' and 'B'. Keys to the pathos of personality: the compression of universality and temporality, expressed comically, tragically, humorously or silently, are given in the *Concluding Unscientific Postscript*.

The ethical begins with beginners, with young people, and with the beginning of philosophy, with a banquet-symposium, with eros, with the myth retold so that lover-beloved appears as seducer-seduced, young man and young woman − which aroused Kafka's 'repugnance'. The ethical proceeds with the maturation of the young, with the beginning of tragedy, ancient and modern − with Antigone, Margarete, Elvira, with the 'bringing up' of eros, or, how the beloved, the 'seduced' one, becomes the lover (this has affinities with Kafka's insight into failing towards perfection).

The fifth speaker at the Banquet, Johannes − soubriquet: 'the seducer' − retells Aristophanes' myth of the birth of eros, claiming to speak 'in praise of woman', but not, however, in praise of love. He proposes

---

[27] 'Observations about Marriage', *Stages* (WL), p. 106.
[28] See *Either/Or* (WL), Vol. II, p. 321; (HVH-EHH), Part II, pp. 316−17.

that 'the resolution of desire is the gist of living', but his myth illustrates the deliberate cultivating of arousal so as to avoid the resolution
of desire at all costs.[29]

The gods, jealous of their own creation: man, sole sex, 'so the Greeks
report' (the Greeks 'report' three original sexes, as we noted above), yet
not able to revoke him, seek a power to take him captive, a power
'weaker than his own' and yet stronger, 'strong enough to compel'.[30]
'This power was woman', able to do more than the gods themselves:

> Thus the gods fashioned her, delicate and ethereal as the mists of
> a summer's night and yet plump like a ripened fruit, light as a bird
> in spite of the fact that she carried a world of craving, light
> because the play of forces is unified at the invisible center of a
> negative relationship in which she is related to herself...[31]

This 'negative relationship in which she is related to herself' is the
correlate of his negative self-relation: 'man upon catching sight of her
should be amazed as one who gets a sight of himself in the glass, and
yet again as if he were familiar with this sight, amazed as one who sees
himself reflected in perfection'.[32]

Thus speaks Johannes, the seducer. He comments philosophically on
this myth in the midst of introducing it:

> I leave for a moment the myth. The concept of man corresponds
> exactly to the idea of man. One therefore can think of a single'
> man existing and nothing more than that. On the other hand, the
> idea of woman is a generality which is not exhaustively exem-
> plified in any single woman. She is not *ebenbürtig* with man but is
> later, is a part of man, and yet more complete than him. Whether
> it be that the gods took a part of him while he slept, ... or that
> they divided him in equal parts so that woman is a half – in any
> case it is man that was divided ... She is a deception, but that she
> is only in her second phase, and for him who is deceived. She is
> finiteness but in her first phase is raised to the highest power in
> the delusive infinity of all divine and human illusions'.[33]

The erotic, the seducer, is not deceived by the second phase – after
all, it is he who proposes these phases. He recognizes that 'she is a

[29] 'The Banquet', *Stages* (WL), p. 82.
[30] Ibid., p. 83.
[31] Ibid., p. 85.
[32] Ibid.
[33] Ibid., pp. 84–5.

collective term, to say one woman means many women', that 'she' is the projection of *his* own disowned possibilities. '[F]or her idea is only a workshop of possibilities' — 'possibilities' for the erotic or seducer, that is, not for she, herself.[34] This is to say nothing about the possibilities of 'woman', collectively or singly. For this myth posits her only in the 'ignorance of innocence', only complicitly as 'longing' for this idea of herself and its seducer, which she, herself, nevertheless, is not.[35] The idea, the seduced woman, may marry, be faithful and die, 'volatilized and resolved again into the inexplicable element from which the gods formed her...'[36] Don Giovanni's Elvira matches this 'immediate stage of the erotic' in the first part of *Either/Or*, and the aptness of the ambiguous genitive in this case shows how tendentious it is to refer to 'Kafka's Felice' or to 'Kafka's Milena'.

To experience oneself as this negative self-relation can be formative if explored beyond the parameters of the initial myth. It may also be an initiation into a reflexive power of infinite potentiality, this time on the part of the one who is seduced and abandoned, not the seducer. Margarete, borrowed from Goethe's *Faust*, is the mask of this reflection and here the difference from the Greek is significant. According to 'The Speech of Socrates', which comes after the speech of Aristophanes in the *Symposium*, Diotima explains that the loveable, *the beloved*, is 'truly beautiful, tender, perfect, and heaven blest', while Love, son of Resource and Poverty, is 'far from tender or beautiful'. In short, the lovable is not Love whose Resources always ebb away.[37] In the pseudonymous retelling or extending of Faust, Margarete, initially the beloved, the loveable, becomes love — impossible to the Greeks, for here love-able-ness, ability to love, learnt from loss, becomes a steady not an ebbing resource. She lost a singularity not a generality: beloved herself as a generality, she herself loved a unique and singular being, and she suffers the pain of loss and resolution. She cannot pass like the seducer to another instant of the generality, nor like one who is deceived by the idea, to the negative repetition of despair. She was unconditionally deceived and laments:

'Can I forget him? Can the brook, then, however far it continues to flow, forget the spring, forget its source... Then it must cease to flow... Can I become another being, can I be born again of another mother who is not my mother? Can I forget him? Then I must cease to be!'

---

[34] Ibid., p. 85.
[35] Ibid., p. 86.
[36] Ibid., p. 87.
[37] *Symposium*, 203c–204d.

'Can I remember him? Can my memory call him forth, now that he is vanished, I who am myself only a memory of him? . . .'[38]

Among these discarded possibilities the forward repetition she raises but refuses: 'Can I become another being . . . born again of a mother who is not my mother?' indicates that her lament is imperfect: she remains a 'silhouette', in the unhappiness of recollection. The perspicacious idea that a woman might become her own mother contrasts with the ideality of disowning her own powers by bestowing them on to the lover who has destructively projected and disowned his own.

However, although Margarete develops beyond the mythical and is able to love, she was nothing at first in herself – except what her innocence meant to Faust, and she remains overwhelmed by his doubt. While her love is unconditional and therefore singular, it 'must end by shattering her soul'.[39]

The third of 'these three women betrothed to sorrow'[40] *is* something in herself, and she matures to become 'the unhappiest one'. Her not being able to marry arises as the 'workshop' of her own possibilities, and shows her as tragic in her own right. Yet by dramatizing modern Antigone as her own mother (as it were), Greek Antigone's ethical life is effaced.

Modern Antigone is the only one to know that her father, Oedipus, now dead, was her mother's child and that she is the child of their union.[41] As in Hegel's *Phenomenology* and in Freud, selective retelling of the Theban tragedies stands for the crux of the collision of the ethical with itself to reveal its hidden nature: 'Her life does not unfold like the Greek Antigone's; it is turned inward, not outward. The stage is inside, not outside; it is a spiritual stage'.[42] The Greek stage is just as spiritual, it may be protested: the collision is explicit in the Greek, hidden in the modern. In the Greek, Antigone continues the pathos of Oedipus' tragedy into her defiance of the King, and it is this totality of the family's fate that 'makes the spectator's sorrow so very profound'.[43] In the modern version, Antigone herself provides the occasion for Oedipus' tragedy. Proud and energetic, she guards the honour and glory of

[38] 'Shadowgraphs', *Either/Or* (DFS-LMS), Vol. I, p. 211; cf. (HVH-EHH), Part I, pp. 212–13.
[39] 'Silhouettes', in ibid. (HVH-EHH), Part I, pp. 209–10.
[40] Ibid., p. 214.
[41] 'The Tragic in Ancient Drama', in ibid., pp. 153–64, p. 227; (DFS-LMS). Vol. I, pp. 152–62, 225.
[42] Ibid. (HVH-EHH), Part I, p. 157.
[43] Ibid., p. 156.

her lineage by cherishing her secret knowledge at the cost of not marrying so as not to burden another with the guilt of it. This initially Greek sentiment is modernized by the restlessness induced by her pain, containable while her father was alive through her uncertainty concerning his knowledge, but potentially explosive now he is dead, and she vulnerable to other collisions. First collision: she falls in love; with the pain of her unrevealable secret as her dowry, she is torn between her love for her father and for herself. Second collision: her sympathetic love for her beloved − whose ardour is only increased by her evident affection − is countered by some intense but unarticulated difficulty. Since the alternatives are to live in grief with the secret or to die if deprived of it, 'At whose hand does she fall, then? At the hand of the living or the dead?' At the hand of the dead − the recollection of her father; at the hand of the living, 'in as much as her unhappy love is the occasion for the recollection to slay her'.[44]

This rewriting of *The Antigone* brings out a seminal element relevant to Freud's account of Oedipus, even while it destroys Hegel's exposition of *The Antigone*. The guilt incurred by Oedipus in his desire for his parent must be that for Queen Merope, his foster-mother, who brought him up, and from whom he fled on hearing the prediction that he would kill his father and marry his mother, because he believed *her* to be his mother. He subsequently desires Jocasta not because she is his mother, but because it never occurs to him that she might be his mother. Only the spectators' participating by projecting their desire for the person they *know to be* their mother on to their dramatic-ironic knowledge of the true relationship between Jocasta and Oedipus illustrates the psychoanalytic myth which proves its point by presupposing the profundity of the spectators' dilemma.

In the modern version, neither Oedipus and Jocasta nor anyone else come to know they are related and, quite consistently, they live happily ever after. They live happily 'ever after', but Antigone comes to know, and, protecting all except herself, she remains true in the guilty implication of her passion for her father and 'half'-brother.

This pathos of recollection makes her into 'the unhappiest one', who slips out of life alleging − and it is true − that she has forgotten, that is, that she fixedly remembers − something. 'She remembers that for which she ought to hope so that what she hopes for lies behind her and what she remembers lies before.'[45]

*The Antigone* in modern dress is concluded by a chorus of facetious irony:

---

44 Ibid., p. 164.
45 'The Unhappiest One', in ibid., p. 225.

Look over there, what a beautiful union! The one generation
offers a hand to the other! Is it an invitation to blessing, to faithful
solidarity, to a happy dance? . . . She's provided for; the grief of a
family is enough for a human life. She has turned her back on
hope; she has exchanged its fickleness for the faithfulness of recollection. Stay happy, then, dear Antigone! We wish you a long
life, as meaningful as a deep sigh. May no forgetfulness rob you
of anything! May the daily bitterness of sorrow be offered to you
abundantly![46]

    This pseudonymous modern Antigone, like the pseudonymous mod-
ern Abraham and Isaac, robs us of the original ethical and holy meanings yet also relies on them to tell the tale anew. By making *The
Antigone* the site of Oedipus' tragedy, *The Antigone* is set back in a
generation where the family is the state, and not on the territory of the
generation of *The Antigone* where families compete for the state.
Tragedy results because the universal of the state is both separate from
and not separate from family-honour. In the modern Antigone, Greek
shame or sorrow – guilt – becomes secret pain. Yet this modern
'amphiboly in her pain'[47] is only comprehensible against the ethical
contexts of lineage-honour and the chorus of religious horror which – it
is implied but never stated – would irrupt on revelation of the truth.
    Modern Antigone holds off the expiation which is implicit in her
hidden pain as it is explicit to the original Antigone: 'Because we suffer
we acknowledge we have erred'.[48] Her modernity, only too comprehensible, is that she may fail to take the risk that would save all parties.
She is not epically Greek nor tragically modern: she displays that
terrible 'autonomy': that independence from contemporaries that sustains itself by utter dependence on the preceding generation, and, in
turn, generates nothing – will result in no succeeding generation. This
erotic stage is mediated: it has these negative implications so that reflection on the remorse, repentance, repetition, impossible within its terms,
nevertheless is called by them into witness.
    'With a husband who becomes temporal, and he through her.'[49]
*Concluding Unscientific Postscript* gives the key to the temporality of
gender and the pathos of personality narrated in the aesthetic mode in
*Either/Or*: 'Johannes the Seducer ends with the proposition that *woman
is only the moment* . . . Where Johannes the Seducer ends, there the Judge

---

[46]  Ibid., p. 227.
[47]  'The Tragic in Ancient Drama', in ibid., p. 161.
[48]  *Antigone*, v. 926, cited by Hegel, *Phenomenology*, Miller para. 470.
[49]  'The Banquet', *Stages* (WL), p. 88.

begins: that *woman's beauty increases with the years*', time has no power over her.[50] In the first case, time is 'accentuated' aesthetically, in the second case, it is 'accentuated' ethically. The impersonation of man in woman and woman in man is the way the significance attached to time is traced for every standpoint up to that of the paradox, 'which paradoxically accentuates time'.[51]

Who marries? The judge and his conscience, the other sex, 'which is both the more religious and the more aesthetic'. Marriage valorizes the mature woman. She gains weight and is no longer aesthetically light and ethereal. Scrupulously sexist, this is narrated from the perspective of his sin: 'woman is man's conscience'.[52] Entry into the ethical, into marriage, also has the 'aesthetic validity' of liberating the husband from the sordidness of the master-slave reversals to which he would be reduced if he had to rely on the canniness of servants:

It is marriage therefore which first gives a man his positive freedom, because this relationship is of a sort that extends over his whole life, over the least things as well as the greatest . . . It . . . liberates him from people precisely by the fact that it binds him to one person. I have often noticed that unmarried people toil exactly like slaves. First of all they are slaves to their whims: they can indulge them freely without rendering and accounting to anybody; but then they become dependent, indeed, slaves, to other people . . . a servant, a housekeeper . . . In them the master's whims and proclivities are impersonated and expressed in clock-time. They know at what time the master gets up, or rather how early he's to be called, or rather how long in advance his study must be warmed before they call him. They know how . . . to close the windows when he goes out, to put out the boot-jacks and slippers for him when he comes home, etc., etc. All this the servants, especially if they are a bit shrewd, know very well how to do. In spite, then, of the fact that all this is done punctiliously, such unmarried persons are often not satisfied. They are able, in fact, to purchase for themselves the satisfaction of every wish. Once in a while they are ill-tempered and peevish, then weak and good-natured. A few dollars makes it all right. The servant promptly learns to take advantage of this: it is enough if, at suitable intervals, he does something a bit wrong, lets the master rage, then he is in despair, and thereupon receives a *douceur*. So the

50   'A *Contemporary Effort*', *Concluding Unscientific Postscript* (DFS-WL), p. 265.
51   Ibid.
52   'Esthetic Validity of Marriage', *Either/Or* (HVH-EHH), Part II, pp. 66–7.

master is captivated by such a personality, he doesn't know whether he ought to wonder most at his punctuality or at the sincere repentance he shows when he has done something amiss. Thus such a personality becomes indispensable to the master and is a perfect despot.[53]

This impersonation of oneself in another as clock-time would seem to eroticize the inequality of the master–servant relationship. Marriage liberates from this mechanical time and introduces melodic tempo:

It brings melody into a man's eccentric movement; it gives strength and meaning to the woman's quiet life, but only insofar as she seeks this in the man and thus this strength does not become an unfeminine masculinity. His proud ebullience is dampened by his constant returning to her; her weakness is strengthened by her leaning on him.[54]

She is 'man's disciplinarian', yet such strength is emphatically not to acquire an 'unfeminine masculinity'. These conflicting qualities reveal that the time of melodic mutual impersonation is as inherently unstable and full of potential reversals as the previous clock-time. Melodic marriage has itself to be shored up by the implicit *Sollen* its exposition requires. The ethical, albeit in its 'aesthetic validity', may lapse into the mechanical time of the new disciplinarian – while the life of one of its parties may acquire a strength and meaning with as yet no specified time pathos.

'This is not my invention, this sketch; it is yours.'[55] With a series of such arch apostrophes the silent Friend/reader is led through the trauma of marrying, resisting and succumbing to the transformation of love from the aesthetic to the ethical, unsure whether his marriage will be melodic or mechanical.

While the prospect of equilibrium of the aesthetic and the ethical in the development of personality is held out in the second half of the second part of *Either/Or*, it is not as an equilibrium between husband and wife (which, indeed, achieves new reaches of instability), but the balance between two 'arranged' marriages: that of the judge-narrator himself and the one he arranges for his 'hero'. While the newly arranged marriage acts out the ethical from the Janus of gender – deepening the dependence of each – the mature marriage of the judge-narrator puts on and off the masks of impersonations:

---

[53] Ibid. (WL), Vol. II, p. 68n., cf. (HVH-EHH), Part II, p. 67n.
[54] Ibid., Part II, p. 67.
[55] Ibid., p. 100.

I am a married man, and you know that I have the most profound respect for this relationship, and I know that I humble myself in total love under it, but yet I know that in another sense I am higher than this relationship. But I also know that in entirely the same sense this is the case with my wife, and that is why I would not, as you know, love that young girl, because she would not have this point of view.[56]

The criterion for this position, which moves in and out of impersonation, and knows and respects that the gendered other does so too, is the 'inner or immanent teleology' which opens each single one to a concretion 'whose characteristic is to intervene actively in the world . . . a movement from himself through the world to himself'. The movement returns because the single one is both implicated in the other, the impersonation, 'the world', and also lets her go, acknowledging, equally, that he is impersonated in her and is her impersonation:

If this is the way things really are, then in a certain sense the individual comes to stand higher than every relationship, but from this it in no way follows that he is not in that relationship; nor does this mean that any despotism is implied here, since the same thing holds true for every individual.[57]

In order to persuade the Friend that the ethical is truly an advance on the aesthetic-erotic the judge-narrator arranges a marriage for his imaginary 'hero' − heroic in displaying the courage to do the ordinary − 'if I have him marry, I'll quietly manage to get him off my hands and happily hand him over to his wife'.[58] Our hero, who 'lives by his work', is gradually won over to the ethical view, the universal, which does not show how a pair of *extraordinary* people may become happy but how *every* married couple can become so. 'It sees the relationship as " . . . absolute and does not take the differences as guarantees but understands them as tasks"'.[59]

These taskful differences emerge from the 'secret rapport' which the wife, about the same age as her husband, has with time. Time outside his work has no meaning for the husband who relapses into melancholy once left to his own resources. Her resources, her tasks, restore time to him: sitting desolate and lost, he watches her, participates in, without comprehending, her activities, 'and in the end I find myself within time

---

[56] 'Balance between Esthetic and Ethical', in ibid., p. 275.
[57] Ibid., pp. 274−5; cf. (WL), Vol. II, p. 279.
[58] Ibid., p. 298.
[59] Ibid., p. 305; cf. (WL), Vol. II, p. 310.

again'.[60] Here the judge speaks on his own and his hero's behalf; both husbands in this scenario are in the relationship but are not higher than it, fully impersonated in the 'virtuosity' of their wives.

Confessing his utter dependence on her abilities which cater to his need for time-shortening, his 'temporal' needs, and without which he is comic and tragic, on the verge of the anxiety of doubt and the agony of despair, he topples over into an angry diatribe against the emancipation of women for fear of what he — perpetually — stands to lose:

> I cannot tell you with what pain the thought can pierce my soul, nor what passionate indignation, what hate, I harbour toward anyone who dares to express such ideas.[61]

The implication that makes him feel most insecure is to be found among the torrent of abuse forthcoming:

> Could there really be one woman simple and vain and pitiable enough to believe that within the definition of man she would become more perfect than man, not to perceive that her loss would be irreparable?[62]

Her irreparable 'loss', predictably, is left to our imagination, while his loss continues to be lavishly explored: 'without her he is an unstable spirit, an unhappy creature who cannot find rest, has no abode . . . on the whole she is to me a symbol of the congregation . . . because to the extent she bestows the finite on him, she is stronger than he'.[63] This qualified and dubious superiority justifies the apparently revolutionary argument that congregations should be represented by clergywomen. Since this proposal seems to bypass the relation to the eternal it is not so much offensive as irrelevant to any less symbolic notion of clergy and congregation. But no; both more aesthetic and more religious, the glimmer of her singleness — when she is not immediately finite and impersonating what is impossible to him, but has faith, not 'within the definition of man', far beyond any definitions, any aesthetic — is here only definable as a fuller resignation: 'Women's prayer is much more substantial, her resignation different'.[64] He prays for the strength to renounce his wish or for another to be able to do so; her prayer is

60   Ibid., p. 307.
61   Ibid., p. 311.
62   Ibid., p. 312.
63   Ibid., p. 313.
64   Ibid., p. 315.

intercessory — she prays for the fulfilment of wishes regardless of the consequences to herself:

> In a certain sense, then, woman has more faith than man, because woman believes that for God all things are possible; man believes that for God something is impossible.[65]

Having pulled her faith back to the aesthetic 'beauty of an intercessory prayer',[66] the married judge-narrator turns his attention directly to his hero and his observer — both addressed now as 'friend', the quintessence of the ethical for Aristotle, but not as 'valid' as marriage for this 'deposition'. So the judge, too, confesses, dismisses his Scribes, and relays his wife's judgement: 'my wife is fond of you . . . She sees very well that you lack a certain degree of womanliness. You are too proud to be able to devote yourself'.[67] Her criticism of the Friend is the only note of discord in her otherwise studiously complaisant and complacent life.

Doubt, despair, pride, and injustice to others, on the part of the man, may be exchanged for the judge-narrator's 'love of life', dependent still on her constant ministrations. The other way, in but not of the relationship, is summed up in conclusion with apparent neutrality: 'the genuinely extraordinary person is the genuinely ordinary person' seeking to express the universal but encountering difficulties, and

> he will come to the aid of the particular and give it meaning as the universal. If he then detects that the experiment is a failure, he will have arranged everything so that what wounds him is not the particular but the universal . . . he will not allow himself to be distracted by the curious misunderstanding that the particular has a greater friend in him than it has in itself.[68]

Without the ethical impersonations of gender-relations this theme can only be restated in the philosophical terms of universal and particular. For no terms as such suffice — man, perched perilously on the aesthetic-ethical border of anxiety; woman, ever intercessory yet impeccably composed; particular transmuted into universal. The first set of terms are too personal, the second set too impersonal; the first, sacralizes the finite, the second, sacralizes the infinite capacity; both fail towards

---

[65] Ibid.
[66] Ibid., p. 316.
[67] Ibid., p. 326.
[68] Ibid., pp. 329–30.

love-able-ness, 'in' but not 'of' the relationship that is replenished whatever its fate – Friendship of friendships, broken or fulfilled. The final word, 'Ultimatum', confessing prayer –

> by always joyfully thanking you as we gladly confess that in relation to you we are always in the wrong.[69]

Once again the middle is in the beginning: in-personation; and the beginning is in the middle: faith.

### Commandment or Curse?

Loquacious in letters written to Brod in January to March 1918, over his adoption and subsequent loss of identification with *Kierkegaard's Relationship to 'Her'* and over his repugnance from the first part of *Either/Or*,[70] Kafka greeted his reading of Kierkegaard's *Instant*, a polemical Christian work, in his notebook entry for the same period, 7 February 1918, with the dual signal of silence – 'Christ, moment' – preceded by a commentary in the form of an interrogation in which the two faces epiphanize as four voices:

> I should welcome eternity, and when I do find it I am sad. I should find myself perfect by virtue of eternity – and feel myself depressed?

> You say: I should – feel. In saying this do you express a commandment that is within yourself?

> That is what I mean.

> Now it is impossible that only a commandment is implanted in you, in such a way that you only hear that commandment and that nothing more happens. Is it a continual or only an occasional commandment?

> As to that I cannot be sure. I believe, however, it is a continual commandment, but that I hear it only occasionally.

> From what do you draw that conclusion?

---

[69]  '*Ultimatum* [A Final Word]', in ibid., p. 341.
[70]  *Letters to Friends*, middle or end January 1918, pp. 224–5, tr. p. 190; beginning March 1918, p. 235, tr. pp. 199–200.

From the fact that I hear it, as it were, even when I do not hear it, in such a way that, although it is not audible itself, it muffles or embitters the voice bidding me to do the other thing: that is to say the voice that makes me ill at ease with eternity.

And do you hear the other voice [*Gegenstimme*] in a similar way when the commandment of eternity [*Ewigkeitsgebot*] is speaking?

Yes, then too, indeed sometimes I believe that I hear nothing but the opposed voice and then the voice from eternity seems to be only a dream and it is as though I were just letting the dream go on talking at random.

Why do you compare the inner commandment to a dream? Does it seem senseless as a dream, incoherent, inevitable, unique, making you happy or frightening you equally without cause, not wholly communicable but demanding to be communicated?

All that — senseless; for only if I do not obey it can I maintain myself here; incoherent, for I don't know whose command it is and what he is aiming at; inevitable, for it finds me unprepared, descending upon me surprisingly as dreams descend upon the sleeper, who, after all, since he lay down to sleep, must have been prepared for dreams. It is unique or at least seems to be so, for I cannot obey it, it does not mingle with reality, and so it keeps its immaculate uniqueness; it makes me happy, or frightens me, both without cause, though admittedly it does the first much more rarely than the second; it is not communicable, because it is not intelligible, and for the same reason it demands to be communicated.[71]

Not 'Christ' — but commandment; not 'moment' or the paradox of an eternal happiness built upon historical knowledge — but the curse of continual commandment grating against the temporal demands of the opposed and embittered voice. Not silence — but an inner climate fraught with a muffled voice; not the single one as possibility or power — but an individual, overpowered and underpowered. Vacillating between the command of eternity and the opposed voice, and, equally, between the interrogating voice and the sad, obsessively communicating voice, the first person reports on a haunting *impasse*, but does not come to welcome it – which would be to transfigure *aporia* into *euporia*.

---

[71]  7 February 1918, 'The Eight Octavo Notebooks', *Wedding Preparations*, pp. 81–2, tr. pp. 105–6.

This 'commandment or curse' interrogation presents a gender-anonymous one in the throes of anxiety of the middle – not confronting the true antagonist, which would be to be always in the wrong, nor the untrue antagonist, the gendered other, but staying at the point of irruption of anxiety. The non-intelligible inner commandment which nevertheless insists on being communicated is, in effect, imperative but not comprehendable – which is precisely what Kant calls the 'intelligibility' of the categorical imperative, the *Sollen*, the forceful inner voice of conscience, which cannot be known, but which makes practical judgement possible, that is, 'communicable' in the sense of there being a form for making a maxim of the will universal, a procedure, as it were, for action. Here the demand to be communicated makes practical judgement impossible. Since in Judaism the commandment has content as well as form and is communally contestable, the Janus masks assumed here seem to cherish the priority of a Kantian formal, negative self-relation, while refusing to act. This is equally evident in the order of argument of the well-known 'How can I relate to Judaism when I cannot relate to myself?',[72] for, traditionally, participation in Judaism would foreclose this anxiety of self-relating.

On these face values it would seem, *pace* Blanchot, that Kafka is *less* qualified than Kierkegaard to relate the absolute – in the sense of the *Akedah* – to the ethical – marriage, law, etc. However, in Kafka, as in Kierkegaard, the value of the middle is only fully assessable after the confrontation with sin and evil in the 109 'Zürau Aphorisms' – not because they represent self-controlled meditations in contrast to the surrender to the angels and demons of his narratives, letters and diaries, as Brod argues;[73] nor because they witness the passage from *Verantwortung* as guilt-laden individual accountability of the early fiction, to *Verantwortung* as responsibility for the communal preserving of individual 'spiritual integrity', as Robertson argues;[74] but simply because the aphorisms dwell on the anxiety of the middle, held on and off, resented here.

In the interrogation, the first person admits to being sad, and this suggests that Kafka's authorship corresponds to Kierkegaard's designation of 'the unhappiest one', a suggestion which has a further possible source in Brod's oft-quoted exchange between himself and Kafka from 28 February, 1920:

He [Kafka]: 'We are nihilistic thoughts that came into God's head.' I [Brod] quoted in support the doctrine of the Gnostics

---

[72]  *The Diaries of Franz Kafka*, 8 January 1914, p. 255, tr. p. 252.
[73]  Brod, *Kafka*, p. 243.
[74]  Robertson, *Kafka*, pp. 134–5, 190–1.

concerning the Demiurge, the evil creator of the world, the doctrine of the world as a sin of God's. 'No', said Kafka, 'I believe
that we are not such a radical relapse of God's, only one of his bad
moods. He had a bad day.' 'So there would be hope outside our
world?' He smiled: 'Plenty of hope – for God –no end of hope –
only not for us.'[75]

On first blush this exchange seems to illustrate Kierkegaard's intensification of Hegel's 'unhappy consciousness' into the unhappiest. The
unhappy one 'has his ideal, the substance of his life, the plenitude of his
consciousness, his essential nature, outside himself.'[76] The unhappiest
one is absent to himself not only in memory but also in hope, because
even hope is no longer an anticipated or postponed future but also
already past and gone, 'because it has already been experienced or
should have been experienced and thus has passed over into
recollection.'[77] Kafka adds further turns of the screw: there is 'plenty of
hope' – God possesses our hope, as it were; we are not only absent to
ourselves in hope, but even this hope is absent to us. Cruelty of
creation: we, creatures, malcreated in the first place, are then denied
refuge in any alleviation of the present in hope, and left with no future
and no present. Denied the dignity of even gnostic acosmos, this state is
flippantly attributed to the contingency of the creator's fit of spleen. Yet
Brod did not overlook how this remorseless account is delivered with
the smile of the ironist: it confirms 'his dream-poetical and his paradox-
humoristic turns of expression'.[78]
More precisely, the meaning of this exchange depends on both the
ironic-smile *and* the humour-paradox: irony, the incognito at the aesthetic border of the ethical; humour-paradox, the incognito at the
ethical border of the religious.[79] Irony sets 'differences together (like the
idea of God with an outing in the Deer Park)'. Here, the idea of God
with His transient moodiness, with the arbitrariness of the finite, set
against the infinite ethical requirement, in such a way that the ethical
passion of the ironist is both accentuated and passes unnoticed into the
cultural infinity, here human hopelessness, accentuated at the same
time. The smile is all that remains of this contradiction which seems
otherwise flatly to deny the ethical by insisting on human hopelessness,
and which brings finiteness into God himself.[80] The dispassionate

75  Brod, *Kafka*, p. 75.
76  Kierkegaard, 'The Unhappiest One', *Either/Or* (HVH-EHH), Part I, p. 222; (DFS-
LMS) Vol. I, p. 220.
77  Ibid., p. 225; Vol. I, p. 223.
78  Brod, *Kafka*, p. 75.
79  *Concluding Unscientific Postscript* (DFS-WL), p. 448.
80  Ibid., pp. 448–9.

sacrilege of God's bad humour reveals the second, 'maturer' incognito of the humorist, his absolute religious passion, which sets up a screen between itself and others in order to safeguard and insure the inwardness of suffering and the God-relationship.[81] The God-idea is set into disjunction with other things, in this case, with itself, in order to cherish the inner, ethical uncertainty 'which is the mark and form of faith'.[82] God's bad humour coupled with human hopelessness – dispassionately delivered – conceal and reveal, ironically, the passionate good humour of the utterer and the utterance, beyond hope or hopelessness.

'The fact that there is nothing but a spiritual world deprives us of hope and gives us certainty.'[83] The form of the aphorism is thus ethical: the condensed appearance of the pathos and anxiety of the utterer. The mix of personifications with the impersonal tone of irony and humour are themselves compressions of the equivocation of the middle: irony at the border of the aesthetic and the religious; humour at the border of the ethical and the religious.

The 'commandment or curse' interrogation concerns a sad one who vainly explores the ethical complaint of being both overpowered and underpowered. In a further exchange with Brod, at the end of March 1918, Kafka himself makes Kierkegaard provide a Talmudic commentary on powerlessness and hopelessness:

> And the following passage is not from the Talmud: 'As soon as a man comes along who has something primitive about him, so that he does not say: One must take the world as it is (this sign that one is a stickleback and therefore not worth catching), but who says: However the world is, I shall stay with my original nature, which I am not about to change to suit what the world regards as good. The moment this word is pronounced, a metamorphosis takes place in the whole of existence. As when the word is spoken in the fairy tale and the palace that has been enchanted for a hundred years opens its gates and everything comes to life: the whole of existence becomes sheer attentiveness. The angels have work to do and look on curiously to see what will happen, for this interests them. On the other side, dark, uncanny demons, who have long sat idle, gnawing their fingers, leap up and stretch their limbs; for, so they say, here there is something for us, for which we have long waited, etc.'[84]

---

[81]  Ibid., p. 452.
[82]  Ibid., p. 453.
[83]  Numbered but not entitled, 'Reflections on Sin, Suffering, Hope and the True Way', pp. 30–40, tr. pp. 38–53, *Wedding Preparations*. Cited here by number: Aphorism 62.
[84]  *Letters to Friends*, p. 239, tr. p. 203; Brod, *Kafka*, pp. 170–4.

In the 'commandment or curse' interrogation the opposition between the voice of eternity and the voice of the world is not overcome; here, by uttering and acting on the original, untried word, the split between two dogmatically opposed worlds is transformed. The temporal world in its warring integrity is compelled to attend, and, only then, is the struggle between its good and its evil joined. Risking out into the world opens up both good and evil forces which may be then 'overpowered' — by contrast with the disconcerting commandment which is held off and thereby reinforces the enchantment of the oppositions instead of engaging and overcoming them. The 'primitive' one who begins by proclaiming he will not change, finds himself at that very moment metamorphosed into the anxiety of the middle — the angels and demons now have their chance. The 'sad' one who will not begin, the stickleback, but with a glancing conscience, remains in the groove of not beginning; the primitive one always ready for the anxiety of the middle — ready for the ethical; the sad one never ready for the anxiety of beginning — never ready for the ethical; the first — commanded and commanding; the second — cursed.

From the anxiety of the middle, the transparent words yet enigmatic meaning of the 109 'Zürau Aphorisms' — some more explicitly in the face of the gender-Janus, others facing faith directly — may be read as the compressing of the aesthetic and the religious into the ethical passion which reveals itself in these failings towards form.[85]

'From the true antagonist illimitable courage is transmitted to you.'[86] This sets the counterweight, the measure, in spite of its enigma, to all the other struggles with which the aphorisms are as full as the rest of Kafka's authorship. Here the difference is that the antagonist appears in the guise, the mask, of 'evil'. But what is evil? 'Evil is a radiation of the human consciousness in certain transitional positions . . .'[87] The aphorisms cover the territory of the interrogation and of the 'Talmudic'-Kierkegaard letter of Kafka to Brod: the temptation of the world when the commandment is refused is contrasted with the temptation of the world when the commandment is heard and the world risked, the battle with angels and demons joined. Kierkegaard distinguishes between these two kinds of temptation:

> In temptation, it is the lower that tempts, in *Anfechtung* it is the higher . . . and when he is now about to relate himself absolutely to the absolute, he [the individual] discovers the limit, and the conflict of *Anfechtung* becomes an expression for this limit. / As

[85] Cf. 'Granted, the religious relationship wishes to reveal itself, but cannot do so in this world . . .', *Letters to Friends*, p. 239, tr. p. 203.
[86] Aphorism 23.
[87] Aphorism 85.

soon as we leave out the relationship to an absolute *telos* and let this exhaust itself in relative ends, *Anfechtung* ceases to exist.[88]

This higher temptation, 'from the true antagonist', may be compressed into the expression of the relative Janus, masked as gender: 'One of the most effective means of seduction that evil has is the challenge to struggle. It is like the struggle with women, which ends in bed.'[89] The banality of this analogy is perhaps alleviated by 11 and 12:

> Differences in the view one can have of things, for instance of an apple: the view of a little boy who has to crane his neck in order to glimpse the apple on the table, and the view of the master of the house, who takes the apple and freely hands it to the person sitting at the table with him.[90]

Apple, prime symbol of forbidden fruit and temptation of the relative kind, expounded here as the middle but beyond temptation. The apple is the Janus-face: one way glimpsed yet out of reach to the little one in opposition to the master; the other way handed out by the master within the community of adults; craned neck or assured gesture; boy glimpsing: master disposing. To the little one, apparently, the command would exclude participation. And yet, 'since you are scrambling up a cliff, about as steep as you yourself are if seen from below, the regression [i.e. declivity] can only be caused by the nature of the ground, and you must not despair.'[91] Despair set on this incline may venture its own hand: 'As firmly as the hand grips the stone. But it grips it firmly only in order to fling it away all the further. But the way leads into those distances too.'[92]

At Aphorism 23 the true antagonist appears and the prospect of illimitable courage 'transmitted to you', that is, mediated, placed in the middle of middles – of all other struggles. The illimitable prospect arises precisely when one faces, discovers, the limit – the true antagonist who by being 'true' is absolute not relative. Yet there is still *agon* in

---

[88] Kierkegaard, *Concluding Unscientific Postscript* (DFS-WL), pp. 410, 411, 410. The Danish word is *Anfaegtelese* which is translated into its German equivalent, *Anfechtung*, temptation, from *anfechten*, to trouble, *fechten* to fence or to fight. *Versuchung* means temptation in the usual sense, from *versuchen*, to try, attempt, experiment. The translators suggest that the difference is between 'repellent' temptation and 'enticing' temptation (p. 569).

[89] Aphorisms 7 and 8.

[90] Aphorisms 11 and 12.

[91] Aphorism 14.

[92] Aphorism 21.

relating to this *Anfechtung*, 'the nemesis upon the strong moment [not the weak] in the absolute relationship . . . without continuity . . . with the individual's ethical habitus . . . the opposition of the absolute itself'.[93] Facing this awe-ful way will provide the courage for facing all the other ways.

> Expulsion from Paradise is in its main aspect eternal: that is to say, although expulsion from Paradise is final, and life in the world unavoidable, the eternity of the process (or, expressed in temporal terms, the eternal repetition of the process) nevertheless makes it possible not only that we might remain in Paradise permanently, but that we may in fact be there permanently, no matter whether we know it here or not.[94]

Permanently dispersed into the oppositions of the gender-Janus, yet the very repetition of that fate makes the other fate possible too – makes possibility itself, repetition forward, possible too – whether we know it or not. Aphorisms 70 and 71 turn to that ungendered face: 'The indestructible is one: it is each individual human being and at the same time it is common to all, hence the incomparably indivisible union exists between human beings'. Indivis-ibles not in-dividuals, an unexpected 'we' emerges – momentarily. The union dissolves: 'Association with human beings lures one into self-observation.'[95] The gender-Janus leads out of self-observation and back again: 'Sensual love deceives one as to the nature of heavenly love; it could not do so alone, but since it unconsciously has the element of heavenly love within it, it can do so.'[96] Is it not the lover who is deceived, and the love-able one who learns? The author tires of these masks and confesses the intrigue of truth: 'Truth is indivisible, hence it cannot recognize itself; anyone who wants to recognize it has to be a lie.'[97]

In the fifth, penultimate, place, a summary: 'This world's method of seduction and the token of the guarantee that this world is only a transition are one and the same'[98] – the lower 'seduction' and the higher temptation meet at the Janus-face: 'Rightly so, for only in this way can the world seduce us, and it is in keeping within the truth.' Otherwise we remain sad, cursed with commandment, instead of seeing temptation itself as the way through and beyond the world. 'The worst thing, however, is that after the seduction has been successful we

---

[93] Kierkegaard, *Concluding Unscientific Postscript*, p. 411.
[94] Aphorisms 64, 65.
[95] Aphorism 77.
[96] Aphorism 79.
[97] Aphorism 80.
[98] Aphorism 105.

forget the guarantee and thus actually the Good has lured us into Evil, the woman's glance into her bed.' This is to remain at the gender-face and not to make the transition – definition of evil, and of world, discussed above.[99] The feeble coda, 'the woman's glance into her bed', reaffirms the point – it makes an absolute telos relative, and so trails the argument off without clinching it. It illustrates what is precisely warned against: projecting an absolute struggle on to gendered otherness.

The ethical passion which informs these aphorisms cannot reach an ethical expression. The command to love one's neighbour as oneself is inverted:

> Humility provides everyone, even him who despairs in solitude, with the strongest relationship to his fellow man, and this immediately, though, of course, only in the case of complete and permanent humility. It can do this because it is the true language of prayer, at once adoration and the firmest of unions. The relationship to one's fellow man is the relationship of prayer, the relationship to oneself is the relationship of striving; it is from prayer that one draws the strength for one's striving.[100]

If humility mounts to supplicatory prayer: to be able to accept that God loves one's fellow as one is loved, to be released from usurping God's place in possessive love, then atonement cannot be coerced by striving, striving is glanced by grace. Instead of striving to be able to love the neighbour, to pray, one must pray in order to strive.

> There is no need for you to leave the house. Stay at your table and listen. Don't even listen, just wait. Don't even wait, be completely quiet and alone. The world will offer itself to you unasked, it can't do otherwise, in raptures it will writhe before you.[101]

There must be apples on that table.

This communality of the fruitful table versus the solitary attending, sublated as reinitiation into the 'world', is more diffusely equivocal than Kierkegaard's pseudonymous 'positions' against world renunciation and embrace: 'This inhumanity towards man is at the same time presumption towards God.'[102] And Kierkegaard's pseudonymous gender-facetiousness also takes a different tone from Kafka and a more explicit contradictoriness: the hypothesis of 'woman's weakness' as part precondition for the civic, holy, poetic and troubled plea for marriage is

---

[99]   Compare Aphorisms 105 and 85 (see discussion of Aphorism 23 (n. 86) *supra*).
[100]  Aphorism 106.
[101]  Coda to the Aphorisms.
[102]  *Stages* (WL), p. 169.

castigated within a few pages by the same remonstrating voice as a fiction.[103] For the ethical 'is a transitional sphere which however one does not pass through once for all'.[104]

Read from the Janus of this middle, the Kafka-dramas are restive, the Kierkegaard-dramas restless: the Kafka-dramas are ill at ease with their very desire to refuse the law; the Kierkegaard-dramas are consistently positioned in relation to the law, which, thereby, both retains and suspends its authority. Far from judging, therefore, as did the initial interlocutors, Brod, Buber and Blanchot, that Kafka fails towards the law while Kierkegaard fails away from it, we are called to witness the discomforts of 'Kafka's authorship crisis *around* the law, 'Kierkegaard's' crisis *within* the law.

For does not the former authorship 'truly' confess:

> It is not inertia, ill will, awkwardness . . . that cause me to fail, or not even to get near failings: family life, friendship, marriage, profession, literature. It is not that, but the lack of ground under-foot, of air, of the commandment. It is my task to create these . . . I have not been guided into life by the hand of Christianity — admittedly now slack and failing — as Kierkegaard was, and have not caught the hem of the Jewish prayer-mantle — now flying away from us — as the Zionists have. I am an end or a beginning.[105]

## Failing towards Form

With what, then, does the ethical end? — in repetition of her who, by means of humour, breaches the border at which gender-impersonation ceases.

Betrayed as beloved she could have become the lover of lovers:

> That the girl assists to get him out upon the deep there can be no doubt . . . If the girl had been characterized by spirit and less by feminine loveliness, if she had been very magnanimous, she would have said to him as he sat pursuing his deceit . . . I perceive that thou must have thy freedom . . . So take it, without any reproaches, without anger between us, without thanks on thy

---

[103] Ibid., pp. 121, 145.

[104] *Stages*, p. 430 — brackets omitted.

[105] 25 February 1918, 'The Eight Octavo Notebooks', *Wedding Preparations*, p. 89, tr. pp. 113–14. Compare Stéphane Mosès, 'Zur Frage des Gesetzes: Gershom Scholems Kafka–Bild', in *Kafka und das Judentum*, pp. 13–34.

part, but with the consciousness on my part that I have done the best I could.

Her imputed maturity would, however, be his ruin:

> If this had come to pass, he would have been crushed, he would have sunk to the ground in shame, for with his passion he can endure all evil treatment when he knows he is the better one, but he would not have been able to forget that he was the debtor to such magnanimity, the greatness of which he would discover with demoniac keenness of sight.

It would be as if she had crossed the border from potentiality to omnipotence: 'an injustice to him, for from his standpoint he too had meant well. In the experiment he is not humbled by a human hand but by God.'[106]

For only an infinite power can make another free without corrupting itself:

> The greatest good which can be done to any being, greater than any end to which it can be created, is to make it free. In order to be able to do that omnipotence is necessary. That will sound curious, since of all things omnipotence, so at least it would seem, should make things dependent. But if we rightly consider omnipotence, then clearly it must have the quality of so taking itself back in the very manifestation of its all-powerfulness that the results of this act of the omnipotent can be independent. This is why one man cannot make another man quite free, because the one who has the power is imprisoned in it and consequently always has a false relation to him who he wishes to be free. That is why there is a finite self-love in all finite power ... It is only a miserable and worldly picture of the dialectic of power to say that it becomes greater in proportion as it can compel and make things dependent. Socrates knew better; the art of using power is 'to make free'. But between men that can never happen, though it may always be necessary to stress that this is the greatest good; only omnipotence can do so in truth.[107]

This theoretical experiment relies on an extended analogy between infinite and finite power to express an unknowable and unstateable

---

[106] Kierkegaard, *Stages*, p. 427.
[107] *The Journals of Kierkegaard* (Dru), pp. 113–14; also elaborated and included in *Christian Discourses* (WL), p. 187n.; discussed by Haecker in *Kierkegaard*, pp. 18–20.

existential truth. As existential pathos, 'woman' provides the expression at every stage — coming into sight as the initial or aesthetic pathos of 'myth', coming into judgement as the ethical pathos of 'conscience', and leading off stage at the decisive religious border with the pathos of humour; momentary, eternal and transtemporal, respectively.[108]

'He' may not be able to survive her magnanimity, for his despair is defined by her myth; but God can celebrate her maturation:

> Religiosity with humour as its incognito is therefore a synthesis of absolute religious passion ... with a maturity of spirit, which withdraws the religiosity away from all externality back into inwardness, where again it is absolute religious passion.[109]

'Humour' is a mode of reconciliation to pain, not as a comic preserving of despair, which 'knows no way out', but as the border line for the religiousness of hidden inwardness which comprehends guilt-consciousness as a totality. Humour revokes this profundity in jest, but, 'inasmuch as in the eternal recollection [s]he is constantly related to an eternal happiness', the comic revocation is itself 'constantly evanescent'.[110]

She is the expert in this stage of repetition:

> But because humour is always a concealed pain, it is an instance of sympathy. In irony there is no sympathy, there is self-assurance, and therefore its sympathy is sympathetic in an entirely indirect way, not with any man in particular, but with the idea of self-assurance as the possibility of every man. Hence in woman one often finds humour but never irony. If an essay is made at it, it ill becomes her, and a purely womanly nature would regard irony as a kind of cruelty.[111]

This 'purely womanly nature' is posited at the border where the humorous perspective exceeds both the 'nature' and the 'gender difference' it appears to affirm, for humour 'discovers the comic' precisely 'by putting the total guilt together with the relativity as between man and man',[112] and, by extension, with the relativity between man and woman, woman and woman. 'In repetition of her' is a humorous acknowledgement that this repetition renders the difference of 'her'

---

[108] *Concluding Unscientific Postscript*, Part 2, ch. IV sec. 11 A1–3.
[109] Ibid., p. 452.
[110] Ibid., pp. 465, 464, 493.
[111] Ibid., p. 491.
[112] Ibid., p. 493.

negligible — alas, we women are now cruelly ironic, nay — facetious — too.

To return to the difference: humour to greet the eternal recollection of guilt is not despair, 'for despair is always the infinite, the eternal, the total, at the instant of impatience; and all despair is a kind of bad temper'.[113] Kafka dramatizes this 'bad temper' in *The Trial* — the trial of despair — and comments on it in the *Aphorisms*. Kierkegaard has Frater Taciturnus delineate the fault-lines of despair in the *Stages* and provides the philosophical commentary in the *Concluding Unscientific Postscript* which has a 'Conclusion' — followed by a 'Revocation': 'to the effect that everything is to be understood that it is understood to be revoked'.[114]

With what does the ethical end? With this humorous revocation which returns us to the equivocation of the middle. Writing from faith not despair, from possibility not gender difference, yet not making 'faith' or 'possibility' — any more than despair or gender ambivalence — into an unanxious beginning, these authorships, failing towards and away from form, repeat the difficulty of and with the law. 'Law', not synonymous with any of the 'stages' with which this chapter began, emerges as the predicament which elicits form out of the equivocation of the ethical and anxiety of beginning. 'Law' emerges as the agon of these authorships.

[113]   Ibid., p. 492.
[114]   Ibid., p. 547.

# 3

# Anxiety of Beginning

## *Kierkegaard, Freud and Lacan*

### *Beginning of Anxiety*

Moreover the law entered, that the offence might abound. But where sin abounded, grace did much more abound.[1]

If the equivocation of the middle — the Janus-faces of our failing — makes us flee, existentially, or in commentary and criticism, in one way or another to the beginning — pagan or erotic, spiritual or religious — this choice and chosen anxiety of beginning may now appear as the beginning of anxiety — the law helplessly held at the middle by such a flight. Thus the beginning, too, is Janus-faced: looking both to the anxiety of beginning and to the beginning of anxiety since the law is always already begun.

No forgiveness of sin is possible in the pseudonymous, aesthetic authorship because we do not yet know what 'sin' is. So the facetious masks of gender are evident even at the border of humour and religiousness — up to and including the concluding 'Revocation', when all the labour of marriage, clockwork and melodic, is preserved and abolished. The more deeply we look into beginning — anxiety of beginning and beginning of anxiety — the more we will be returned to the middle.

For this anxiety of beginning which is equally beginning of anxiety, Kierkegaard's authorship offers the 'system' to Freud. The movement of repetition backwards and forwards pivots around the equivocal middle and yields a persistently ethical reflection. Reflection in both authorships is dedicated to releasing for risk: 'this infinite recklessness is

[1] Rom. 5:20.

authority';[2] but it is only the pseudonymous one who returns risk explicitly to its ethical counterpart.

When both authorships are read from the pivot of anxiety, of repetition backwards and forwards, then the opposition between Kierkegaard as a 'religious' author and Freud as an anti-religious author is no longer informative. Instead of Freud providing a psychoanalytic mathesis for Kierkegaard, it is the latter's authorship which deals systematically with all three of the ego's severe masters — the external world, the super-ego and the id[3] — and relates anxiety explicitly to law and ethics. In both cases — anxiety of beginning and beginning of anxiety — the Janus-faces of guilt and freedom are the pivot of authorship as such. How to proceed, how to begin, when law precedes desire and intelligibility: desire and intelligibility do not precede law; when anxiety defines sin, not sin anxiety; when will to power as risk or *ressentiment* lords over will to life, mere self-preservation; in short, when existence is always already invested — conceptual and commanded.

Without law, no sin: without sin, no grace; this epigrammatic reduction of Pauline preaching is reformed in the structure of Kierkegaard's psychological authorship. Dogmatics can only be expounded in psychological terms by the deployment of two ecologies of facetiousness. However, as with the *Philosophical Fragments*, it will be demonstrated that these works suffer and act the coinciding of the epitome of existence at the epitome of the concept.

> The power which is given to a man (in possibility) is altogether dialectical, and the only true expression for a true understanding of himself in possibility is precisely that he has the power to destroy himself, because even though he be stronger than the entire world, he nevertheless is not stronger than himself.[4]

No human being can make another free: 'omnipotence alone' can do so, 'because omnipotence is always taking itself back', and is therefore without the self-love, the self-corruption, infecting the analogous human act, which consequently always has a false relation to him whom he wishes to free'.[5] If one cannot be more powerful than oneself, and if no other human being can have the uncorrupted power to bind and loose another — for, in both cases, 'the one who has the power is

[2]  Kierkegaard, *Journals* (HVH-EHH), vol. I, 183, p. 73.
[3]  Freud, 'Dissection of the Personality', *New Introductory Lectures on Psychoanalysis*, PFL, vol. 2, pp. 110, 117.
[4]  Kierkegaard, *Journals* (HVH-EHH), 46, p. 19.
[5]  Kierkegaard, *Journals* (Dru), p. 113.

imprisoned in it' — then how can there be an 'art of power' which escapes this dialectic?[6]

Only if the idea of creation *ex nihilo* can be established: the creating of something out of nothing — a creature which endures independently of its creator, and therefore does not persist by virtue of diminution of the creator's powers, nor by dependence of the creature, nor by means of any relation as such on the part of the creator, one who can 'give' or 'bring forth' without 'giving away', and by 'taking itself back'. 'Between men that can never happen, though it may always be necessary to stress that it is the greatest good.'[7] Out of this negative theology of creation — 'and that is what is inconceivable'[8] — emerge ethics and evil.

> [I]f a person does not first use all the power given him against himself, thereby destroying himself, he is either a dolt or a coward in spite of all his courage.[9]

Very power against himself is very powerlessness against this power: 'the most radical expression of this powerlessness is sin'.[10] What can the 'art of using power' be, when the theory of its praxis yields the inconceivable — creation *ex nihilo*? It involves the denial of power as 'capacity', 'faculty', '*a priori* possibility', and the acknowledgement of power as *what there is* — as actuality itself — and again and again. In this sense of power as repeated act there is 'possibility' — in spite of its antagonistic duality — for and against oneself, and others.

Omnipotence, in its freedom and in its power to make free, may not be 'conceivable', but the seemingly non-committal reference to the 'givenness' of power, that it has been aroused and is not the arouser, has unexplored implications. 'Given' means 'gift'; *charis*, Greek for 'gift', comes from the verb meaning 'to grow'. It is law which arouses power — sympathetic and antipathetic; law which binds and looses, to which power responds against itself or for itself. Law is abundant and abounding: it is not the contrary of grace, which tempers its letter with mercy and equity.

The Kierkegaard authorship is ethical because of its premise that law is always already given. Anxiety, therefore, has an origin, a beginning: 'being given'; and it is always already there or posited: 'law'. The art of power is 'freedom': how to be always all-ready for anxiety. Creation *ex*

---

6   Ibid.
7   Ibid.
8   Ibid.
9   Kierkegaard, *Journals* (HVH-EHH), 46, p. 19.
10   Ibid.

*nihilo* may be inconceivable, but destruction *ex nihilo* is the beginning, the onset of all intelligibility.

When attention is focused *at the beginning* of a work on discrediting the System, its historicism, its closure, etc., in the name of existential 'freedom' or the released 'other', this, in effect, proudly obsoletes 'freedom' and otherness — political or existential. Such apparent house-clearing amounts to a recollection which is itself a refusal, an unreadiness, for anxiety. It awards itself a certainty while claiming to breed no certainties.

Active exercise of will to power called out by birthing into law is the Janus-face of anxiety: between recollection and repetition, movement backwards and movement forwards — eternally, which is equally at every instant, poised between guilt and freedom:

> Recollection and repetition are the same movement, only in opposite directions; for what is recollected has been, is repeated backwards, whereas repetition properly so called is recollected forwards. Therefore repetition, if it is possible, makes a man happy, whereas recollection makes him unhappy — provided, that is, he gives himself time to live and does not at once, in the very moment of birth, try to find a pretext for stealing out of life, alleging, for example, that he has forgotten something.[11]

Relationship to time emerges in both authorships as the medium or middle which indicates movement backwards or forwards, anxiety staved off or embraced. Time stands — or passes — therefore, as the register of the law. Yet the exposition of time has to be couched either in aesthetic terms — as 'repetition', or in terms of philosophical commentary, for example, as four 'stages' — pleasure, shrewdness, Stoicism, 'anxious readiness'.[12]

In both authorships — and this is staged in Nietzsche's *Thus Spoke Zarathustra* as in Heidegger's *Being and Time* — 'anxiety' charts the oscillation between self-destruction and risking one's life — between destruction and creation. This oscillation in anxiety is the education of existence which, therefore, is not prior to concept, institution or ethic, but is the existential failing towards and away from the middle itself, for 'education' is the *experience* of concept, institution, law.

Without the prejudice of modernism, which labels the Kierkegaard authorship *exclusively* 'existential', the Freudian 'psychoanalytic', the Heideggerian 'phenomenological', the Nietzschean 'Dionysian', the

---

[11] Kierkegaard, *Repetition* (WL), p. 33; ch. 1, p. 19 *supra*.
[12] See ch. 1, pp. 24–7, *supra*.

modernity at issue in each case would emerge as ethical. Yet, at the same time, ethical initiative is ruined – dirempted into morality and legality, autonomy and heteronomy, inner and outer, independence and dependence, existence and 'law'.

## *It is Sown a Natural Body*[13]

> But too often it has been overlooked that the opposite of sin is not *virtue*, not by any manner of means. This is in part a pagan view which is content with a merely human measure, and properly does not know what *sin* is, that all sin is before God. No, *the opposite of sin is faith*, as is affirmed in Romans 14.23, 'Whatsoever is not of faith is sin'. And for the whole of Christianity it is one of the most decisive definitions that the opposite of sin is not virtue but faith.[14]

'Vigilius Haufniensis' – Watchman of Copenhagen, respectfully signs the 'Preface' to *The Concept of Anxiety* and declares his equal willingness to assume the Latin name 'Christen Madsen'.[15] 'Anti-Climacus' signs *The Sickness Unto Death* with 'S. Kierkegaard' as editor. A journal entry seems to admit that Kierkegaard regarded himself as 'higher than Johannes Climacus, lower than Anti-Climacus', but the tone of this apparently straightforward confession is coloured by the facetious preceding comparison of the two Climacuses: Johannes Climacus 'even says himself he is not a Christian', while 'one seems to be able to detect' that Anti-Climacus 'regards himself to be a Christian on an extraordinary high level'.[16]

The name 'Watchman' implies the censor and the law; the name 'Anti-Climacus' implies the contrary to the erotic religiosity of 'Climacus', the one who ascends the ladder: it implies the descent of grace. The contrast and complementarity of these two names, in effect, law and grace, and the movement they jointly imply from censorship to agapic descent, correspond to the respective logic and ethic of the two works. Together they describe a cycle which runs from law to anxiety and from despair to grace. 'Sin' is the shared middle term which covers anxiety and despair, and, because the opposite of sin is faith *not* virtue, or, because it is confidence *not* courage, the second movement of faith

---

[13] 1 Cor. 15:44.
[14] Kierkegaard, *Sickness Unto Death* (WL), p. 213.
[15] Kierkegaard, *Concept of Anxiety* (RT), pp. 7–8, 221.
[16] Kierkegaard, *Sickness Unto Death* (HVH-EHH), pp. xii, 139.

emerging beyond despair effects a return to the *ethical* categories of
virtue and courage, to the law, which set the cycle in motion, without
the initial ambivalence of the ethical middle but with the deeper
equivocation of this movement. This return to law with the actuality of
sin within its scope is entitled the 'new' or 'second' ethics.[17]

The beginning of *The Concept of Anxiety* is made by addressing the
double difficulty of this particular reflection: how to begin a work
about the beginning, or, the anxiety of beginning here meets the beginning of anxiety:

> 'Mediation' is equivocal, for it suggests simultaneously the rela-
> tion between the two and the result of the relation, that in which
> the two relate themselves to each other as well as the two that
> related themselves to each other.[18]

In lieu of complacently positing 'mediation', its movement and repose are to be subjected to 'a more profound dialectical test'.[19] At the
same time as Hegel's *Science of Logic* is cited, precisely on the logic and
meaning of essence (*Wesen* as 'timelessly past being' from the past of
*sein*, *gewesen*), and the test of mediation announced (and subsequently
followed through to the exposition of the 'self' as the relation of the
relation, or the third), strange pixies and goblins, 'busy clerks' of
Hegelian logic, and facetious attributions of 'brilliance'[20] are deployed
to distinguish 'the transition of logic into becoming' from the coming
forth of existence and actuality.[21] The beginning is, in this way, made
anxious, which is to sow confusion deliberately, since anxiety is to be
the beginning.

'Anxiety', a psychological concept, is to be explored in relation to
'the dogma of hereditary sin', but sin cannot be explored psychologically, aesthetically, metaphysically or ethically, nor by any scientific reflection, for it is not a state, '*de potentia*', according to possibility, 'but *de
actu* or *in actu* [according to actuality or in actuality] it is again and
again'.[22]

As a science by its very nature translates acts into their precondition or
possibility, psychology can only deal with sin anxiously, 'while again
and again it is in anxiety over the portrayal that it itself brings forth'.[23]

---

[17]   Kierkegaard, *Concept of Anxiety* (RT), pp. 20, 23.
[18]   Ibid., p. 11.
[19]   Ibid., p. 11, 12n.
[20]   Ibid.
[21]   Ibid., p. 13.
[22]   Ibid., p. 15.
[23]   Ibid.

How even more anxious is this exposition which relies on the metaphysical distinction of 'possibility' and 'actuality' to convey the 'mood' of 'a discovering anxiety' — 'discovering' is used adjectivally to convey a mode of anxiety.[24]

The 'earnestness' of so much subterfuge is the intention to initiate the reader into a 'secret': the secret of conversing, 'in which the single individual speaks as the single individual to the single individual', according to which criterion true sermonizing is pitted against the disdainful preaching of contemporary pastors, and Socratic conversing is pitted against Sophistical speechifying.[25]

How to bring the insinuated actuality of sin into conversing through this indirectly confessed anxiety implicitly preoccupies the resumed discussion of ethics — the uncompromising ideality of which usually prompts the deployment of metaphysical, aesthetic or psychological categories to 'reach' actuality.[26] Put metaphysically, sin is 'actuality' to ethics' 'ideality'; put 'earnestly', or 'singular to singular', ethics is 'shipwrecked with the aid of repentance' — a presupposition that goes beyond the individual, and a scepticism that negates the realization of virtue.[27] 'New' ethics or 'second' ethics, which has the actuality of sin within its scopes, would not presuppose ideality but sets it as a task, 'not by a movement from above and downward but from below and upward'.[28] It is indeed the two sciences here disparaged as first ethics — Hegel's logic of essence and Aristotle's *Nicomachean Ethics* — that will be recombined, on the basis of psychological investigation into the 'real possibility' of sin to yield the 'second' ethics.

For psychology, the doctrine of subjective spirit, 'when it comes to the issue of sin, must first pass over into the doctrine of absolute spirit', here called 'dogmatics'. It is this 'dogmatics' which the second ethics completes and so avoids the metaphysics of the first. In spite of this specious facility with which the terms of the System may be translated into the terms of the 'task' or drama of the 'Introduction', it follows that 'the introduction may be correct, while the deliberation itself concerning the concept of anxiety may be entirely incorrect'.[29] And, as has emerged, the 'Introduction' or beginning introduced the 'mood' of anxiety which cannot be spoken except metaphysically and facetiously, and a reflection on anxiety. This shows that the beginning is ironically systematic — consistent with the unrepresentability of its concept.

---

[24] Ibid., p. 15.
[25] Ibid., p. 16.
[26] Ibid., pp. 16–17.
[27] Ibid., pp. 17–18, 19.
[28] Ibid., p. 20.
[29] Ibid., p. 24.

The beginning or first task of 'discovering anxiety' is to dethrone two customary beginnings: 'the concept of hereditary sin' and 'the first sin, Adam's sin', which, preceding the history of the human race, would give it 'a fantastic beginning'.[30] If 'Adam' means that the individual is 'simultaneously himself and the whole race', then the movement of this contradiction implies that both the individual and the race have a history, and it does not make Adam into something 'outside' the race, nor does it make his sin different from the present or the sinfulness of any individual.[31]

The concept of the first sin, '[t]hrough the first sin, sin came into the world', will not usurp the beginning if '[p]recisely in the same way it is true of every subsequent man's first sin, that, through it, sin comes into the world'.[32] This preserves and conceptualizes the quantitative history of the race, and the qualitative participation of the individual: 'the race does not begin anew with each individual, in which case that would be no race at all, but every individual begins anew with the race'.[33]

Nor is the idea of Adam's 'innocence' and its loss to convey a beginning of guilt fantastically specific to him: 'every man loses innocence essentially in the same way that Adam lost it'.[34] The voice of 'discovering anxiety' becomes increasingly irritable as the strain of contesting beginnings in this way mounts up — whether logical, immediate or ethical innocence. For all such beginnings are already annulled or transcended, but there is, as yet, no argument that will demonstrate the 'entirely different' approach which comes out of the ethical qualification.[35]

Adam's 'innocence' does not provide the beginning yet 'innocence is ignorance'.[36] The beginning is not, however, the end of innocence understood as initiation into knowledge. The fall or beginning involves initiation into prohibition: 'it was the prohibition itself not to eat of the tree of knowledge that gave birth to the sin of Adam'.[37] It is the encounter with the normative as such which has repercussions for cognitive status: 'somehow the prohibition only predisposes that which breaks forth in Adam's qualitative leap'.[38] The explanation of this leap from norm to knowledge requires psychology — the psychology of

---

[30] Ibid., p. 25.
[31] Ibid., pp. 26–9 — this argument, it is insisted, is not Pelagian, Socinian, nor 'philanthropic singular', p. 28.
[32] Ibid., p. 31.
[33] Ibid., pp. 33–4.
[34] Ibid., p. 36.
[35] Ibid., pp. 38–41.
[36] Ibid., p. 38.
[37] Ibid., p. 39.
[38] Ibid., emphasis added.

anxiety. Even the psychological explanation, however, will retain an 'elastic ambiguity'[39] so as not to substitute explanation for event, nor, *a fortiori*, the poetry of this vigilant pseudonym for the pathos of anxiety.

'Innocence is ignorance', but not immediately, not at the beginning. Innocence is not ignorance until it enters into the opposition of ignorance and knowledge. Before that encounter, innocence is already anxious, but in a diffuse, unfocused way. It expresses itself as *a sympathetic antipathy* and *an antipathetic sympathy*': the discovering anxiety of the child, 'a seeking for the adventurous, the monstrous, and the enigmatic'; a pleasing, captivating, not a troublesome anxiety.[40]

This guiltless anxiety — like guilty anxiety yet to come — does not refer to anything definite, but 'is freedom's actuality as the possibility of possibility'.[41] It is the encounter with a third which will make the difference and effect the passage to the contraries of ignorance and knowledge. But this 'hostile' third power is ambiguous: it is both alien *and* what qualifies man as spirit. For 'man is a synthesis of the psychical and the physical; however a synthesis is unthinkable if the two are not united in a third', or, rather, if the two are not *disunified* in the third — which opens up the opposition between soul and body in the first place.[42] 'Anxiety' is the term for this relating of a relation for it captures the ambiguity of the 'source'.

Even the metaphysics of this third, referred to as the relation of 'spirit', presupposes the dénouement: 'Innocence still is, but only a word is required and then ignorance is concentrated.'[43] The 'word' turns out to be *the commandment*: 'Only from the tree of the knowledge of good and evil you must not eat.' The word is enigmatic: it is not understood. Before eating of the 'forbidden' tree there can be no comprehension. The prohibition does not awaken desire, for there is still no knowledge, but it does induce anxiety, for the prohibition awakens freedom's possibility, 'the anxious possibility of *being able*'.[44]

The word of judgement follows the word of prohibition: 'You shall certainly die'. While this deterrent is as incomprehensible as desire, the terror of anxiety is yet intensified, for the judgement conveys that infinite possibility anticipated by the prohibition as imminent possibility. This metaphysical commentary on the biblical narrative has now brought innocence 'to its uttermost'.[45] In conclusion, 'discovering an-

---

[39] Ibid., p. 41.
[40] Ibid., p. 42.
[41] Ibid., p. 42.
[42] Ibid., p. 43.
[43] Ibid., p. 44.
[44] Ibid.
[45] Ibid., p. 45.

xiety' concedes that the hearing and the voice are within Adam himself, for in language innocence 'possesses the expression for everything spiritual'.[46] This 'internal' speaking to itself of innocence does not imply that it possesses the knowledge or comprehension of good and evil which, as the exposition has sought to show, comes or '*is* only for freedom [Vigilius Haufniensis' emphasis]'.[47]

The beginning is speculative for the beginning is the word — the enigmatic commandment — which is always already presupposed. The beginning can only be made by the middle — *qua* the word — in its enigmatic power *and* in its meaning, 'the difference between good or evil' which is known *and* left aside. Instead, the copula bears the 'elastic' ambiguity of this circularity. 'Innocence is ignorance' is repeated: 'Innocence is . . .'; 'Innocence still is . . .'; 'Innocence is ignorance . . .'; and also introduces exquisite qualification: 'is concentrated . . .'; 'is brought to its uttermost . . .'. Only in this way can the exorbitant mix of metaphysical categorization and facetious pseudonymity be accounted for. It is the determination of reflection which speaks in these anxious tones — for it has lost its confidence and its faith in philosophical reflection. Here — as everywhere in Kierkegaard's authorship — we have *the logic of illusion in the facetious style.*

This ambiguous notion of 'spirit' — the hostile yet internal power which opens up the self as the relation taken to the relation of soul and body — will do further duty: as the unknown third, the enigmatic Word or Commandment, 'spirit' gives rise to anxiety, 'the consequence is a double one, that sin came into the world and that sexuality was posited; the one is to be inseparable from the other'.[48] Gender is posited equally with sexuality, where a human being is 'a synthesis that reposes in a third', a synthesis of soul and body. 'Synthesis' does not mean unifying the distinction between soul and body, but the incursion of differentiation which posits a human as animal at the very moment s/he becomes wo/man. The natural, sexual body is posited by the spiritual body: 'man can attain this ultimate point only in the moment the spirit becomes actual. Before that time he is not animal, but neither is he really man.'[49]

What is called the actuality of 'spirit' here, was attributed earlier in the argument to 'the enigmatic word' or to commandment and prohibition, and to language as such: the law, equally inner and outer, opens up the contraries of soul and body, the negotiating or living of which

---

[46]   Ibid.
[47]   Ibid., p. 46.
[48]   Ibid., p. 48.
[49]   Ibid., p. 49.

gives each individual the task which becomes his or her history: 'sinfulness is by no means sensuousness, but without sin there is no sexuality, and without sexuality, no history ... an angel has no history'.[50] The contraries of soul and body posited as the 'contradiction' of gender and generation, or sexuality, is 'the actuality that is preceded by freedom's possibility'. Not the choosing of good and evil but possibility, 'to *be able*', gives rise to anxiety, the 'intermediate' psychological term for this passing of possibility over into actuality which is not logical nor ethical, but existential, 'entangled freedom', where freedom is entangled in itself.[51]

'The more profound the anxiety, the more profound the culture';[52] anxiety belongs to woman 'more than to man'.[53] Is anxiety then, and by implication 'woman', a sign of perfection? 'There remains the serpent.'[54] Eve, not the serpent, brings out the meaning of temptation: 'that every man is tempted by himself', not from without.[55] Here 'man' includes woman in the sense that it clarifies what a *human* being is – both individual and the 'race' or generation. 'Eve is a derived creature', yet 'it is the fact of being derived that predisposes the particular individual, yet without making *him* guilty'.[56] Her derivation clarifies his.

Sensuousness is not sinfulness, but since sin was posited and continues to be posited, it makes sensuousness sinfulness.[57] Eating the fruit of the tree of knowledge brings the distinction between good and evil into the world and also sexual difference as 'drive'. Both presuppose 'freedom's showing–itself–for–itself in the anxiety of possibility', the synthesis of soul and body reposing in a third, an anxiety without an object, qualitative and original to each single one, distinguished from anxiety with an object, accumulated quantity, which pertains to the race or generation, or the individual under one of these classes.[58]

'Woman is more sensuous than man and has more anxiety.'[59] As each 'more' reveals, the difference may be merely quantitative. 'Eve outwardly prefigures the consequence of the relationship of generation.'[60] 'The greatness of anxiety is a prophecy of the greatness of perfection.' 'Greatness' is here a quality for it presupposes that the quantitative

---

[50]  Ibid.
[51]  Ibid.
[52]  Ibid., p. 42.
[53]  Ibid., p. 47n.
[54]  Ibid., p. 48.
[55]  Ibid.
[56]  Ibid., p. 47, emphasis added.
[57]  Ibid., pp. 76, 79; cf. 'The sexual as such is not the sinful' (p. 68).
[58]  Ibid., pp. 76–7, 63.
[59]  Ibid., p. 64.
[60]  Ibid. p. 63.

'more' of sensuousness deepens the cleft of spirit: the 'synthesis' of body and soul. That 'woman is more sensuous than man' is not justifiable or significant, meaningful or arguable in itself: expounded historically, it involves reference, in ironic, aesthetic terms, to Greek plasticity of beauty; in facetious, ethical terms, to procreation and marriage.[61] That 'woman is more anxious than man',[62] on the other hand, is a qualitative proposition pertaining to the depth and task of the synthesis. Even so, the exposition is punctuated by aesthetic, quantitative examples: a young woman whom we are commanded to 'picture', will become more anxious when a man fastens his desiring glance on her, whereas, in the reverse situation, he — subjected to her desirous glance — will experience 'disgust mingled with modesty, precisely because he is more qualified as spirit'.[63] This example is to serve an investigation 'always conceived in the direction of freedom'.[64] 'In spirit there is no difference between man and woman'[65] — yet she is judged 'more' anxious; he 'more' spirit. What is illustrated, therefore, is anxiety with an object, and spirit as a quantity; what is conceptualized is the relation to the third, anxiety, without object and without repose.

The discussion struggles to express the presupposition of sexual difference, prior to desire, knowledge and ignorance: to capture innocence which is, even so, the beginning of knowledge 'that has ignorance as its first qualification'. This is called 'modesty' and defined as 'anxiety, because spirit is found at the extreme point of the difference of the synthesis in such a way that spirit is not merely qualified as body but as body with a generic difference. Nevertheless, modesty is a knowledge of the generic difference, but not as a relation to a generic difference, which is to say, the sexual urge as such is not present.'[66] This difference between knowledge of, and relation to, generic difference captures the meaning of the synthesis of body and soul, or, rather, it shows how the idea of 'synthesis', opened up by the relation to the third as possibility or 'being able', without an object, is originally conceivable as extreme lack of synthesis: 'Therefore the anxiety found in modesty is prodigiously ambiguous.' It involves 'no trace of sensuous lust' and feels ashamed — of nothing.[67] A second example is the anxiety of childbirth in which spirit is present, 'because it is spirit which establishes the synthesis',[68] yet also redundant. Similarly, even in conjugal relations

[61]  Ibid., pp. 64–6.
[62]  Ibid., p. 66.
[63]  Ibid., p. 67.
[64]  Ibid., p. 66.
[65]  Ibid., p. 70.
[66]  Ibid., p. 68.
[67]  Ibid.
[68]  Ibid., p. 71.

this anxiety of modesty may be present. These examples, critical and ethical, draw out the prevalence of the anxiety of possibility in situations where there is already a relation to generic difference and knowledge of good and evil. Anxiety precedes the erotic and succeeds its culminations – marriage, childbirth.

'At the furthest point of one extreme of the synthesis . . . the spirit trembles, for in this moment it does not have its task, it is as if it were suspended.'[69] The qualitative 'more' of anxiety and sensuousness for the procreated individual in relation to the original one is here distinguished from the 'more' (or less) of one particular individual in relation to another particular one. The qualitative 'more' that makes a human being an individual or self by the means of the idea of 'synthesis', and the evident lack of synthesis, may be approached now that its quality is apparent; 'spirit's anxiety in assuming responsibility for sensuousness becomes a greater anxiety.'[70] 'Sin' does not mean any particular innate characteristic, but 'the ambiguity in which the individual becomes both guilty and innocent'.[71]

While the reflection continues to examine 'the dreadful fact that *anxiety about sin produces sin*'[72] there is no further elaboration of the meaning of 'spirit', of its 'synthesizing' responsibility, of being simultaneously guilty and innocent. No further elaboration, that is, of the prohibition and judgement, the commandment, the 'enigmatic' word, which, prior to any knowledge or understanding, opened up possibility, 'being able', the synthesis of mind and body, by 'reposing' it in 'a third'. 'Anxiety' indicates that there is no repose and no synthesis for the 'spirit' which is born of such a trichotomy: always hearing the commandment itself behind the form of prohibition and the judgement – prior, that is, to understanding what any specific prohibition enjoins. Yet here is the beginning: the commandment is always being heard haunting the middle: in the middle of specific prohibition and judgement echoes the daunting beginning.

The elaboration of the 'third', the 'synthesis' of psyche and body – never achieved – which leads to the discomfort of anxiety and offers no repose, is resumed and restated as 'a *synthesis of the temporal and the eternal*'.[73] Although the term 'spirit' begs the question concerning the posited 'synthesis' of body and soul while testifying to the predicament of anxiety, it at least holds the position of the third term which preconditions the apparently initial dichotomy. The second 'synthesis' has only two poles – the temporal and the eternal.

[69] Ibid., p. 72.
[70] Ibid., p. 73.
[71] Ibid.
[72] Ibid, emphasis in original.
[73] Ibid., p. 85, emphasis in original.

Yet, once again, the search for the third — which must be there because it is presupposed — takes a metaphysical turn when, generated out of the distinction of time and eternity, *in effect* but not explicitly, it inscribes the commandment. 'Time' *qua* infinite succession — *qua* past, present and future — is a passing-by without a present moment.[74] From this perspective, a moment which is present can only be thought as annulled succession, or be represented as 'contentless' vanishing as opposed to 'contentful' present.[75] For the 'eternal' — expressed as a 'contrary' — 'the eternal' ... is the present'.[76] 'Is' bears the burden of fullness and is distinguished by a positing voice from the 'is' that is contained in 'time *is* infinite succession', or, not present. The 'moment', substantive to capture this fullness, is 'figurative', liable to be conceived abstractly, in terms of time — which it *is* not.[77] Nor is this fullness 'sensuousness', for sensuousness — from the previous statement of the synthesis of body and soul — is here the analogue of successive, passing temporality. All similar attempts to co-opt Latin or Greek terms lapse into temporal or spatial abstractions connoting merely vanishing time: 'the moment is not properly an atom of time but an atom of eternity'.[78]

This inevitable tendency for the attempt to state the third to end up couched in the very terms to which it is the third is no longer resisted in an admission which embraces the circularity by re-setting the task:

> The synthesis of the temporal and eternal is not another synthesis
> but is the expression for the first synthesis, according to which
> man is a synthesis of psyche and body that is sustained by spirit.
> As soon as spirit is posited, the moment is present ... Nature
> does not lie in the moment.[79]

But it is the notion of spirit that the second synthesis was to elucidate. Now 'spirit' and 'moment' are simply posited jointly and opposed to 'nature'; while the concept of 'temporality' is appropriated to term 'that ambiguity in which time and eternity touch each other ... time constantly intersects eternity and eternity constantly pervades time'.[80]

This fabulating loquaciousness is here not only the voice of pseudonymous, philosophical reflection at the level of positing understanding — which it also certainly is — engaged in yet another facetious

---

[74]  Ibid.
[75]  Ibid., p. 86.
[76]  Ibid.
[77]  Ibid., p. 87.
[78]  Ibid., p. 88.
[79]  Ibid., pp. 88–9.
[80]  Ibid., p. 89.

failure of philosophy to conceptualize either the journey or impasses of faith — but also index of the limitation of philosophy *and* of faith in conceiving the law, which opens up both conceptuality and anxiety in their mutual implication and dependence. For these expositions of the synthesis-which-is-none can be simply retraced to its underdeveloped initiator — prohibition and judgement — 'enigmatic word', or commandment. The reposing and uncomfortable third is the commandment which when perfectly heard (which implies both the imperative and its comprehension), whether 'Thou shalt' or 'Thou shalt not', gives 'the moment'; when imperfectly heard, coercive and unfulfilled, gives rise to the experience of time as successive — past, present, future.

Reflection on the commandment, set by the initial consideration of the biblical prohibition and judgement yet deflected subsequently into the unexplicated 'third' or 'spirit', re-emerges in the admission that, in spite of the distinction between eternity and place or position in time as past, present, and future, 'the future is the incognito in which the eternal, even though it is incommensurable with time, nevertheless preserves its association with time'.[81] Contrasted with Platonic 'recollection', the metaphysical equivalent of 'Greek life', this emphasis on the eminence of futurity at the interaction of eternity and time in effect opposes law and philosophy: the commandment, heard and fulfilled without coercion, moves forwards, while philosophical apprehension concerns the shape of life grown old. The perficient, proleptic commandment, anticipation of Kingdom and Messiah, rehearses as a collective possibility what the aesthetic opposition between recollection, or movement backwards, and repetition, or movement forwards, rehearses as individual possibility. The absence of any conceptual or existential development of the substitution of 'spirit' for 'commandment', means that distinctions and relations between collective and individual possibility, between anxiety and law, between commandment and apprehension, that is, between existence and law and between command and concept, remain at the level of insinuation.

That these are the issues is confirmed under the heading 'Anxiety Defined Dialectically As Guilt': 'It is usually said that Judaism is the standpoint of the law. However, this could also be expressed by stating that Judaism lies in anxiety.'[82] This furnishes indirect evidence that anxiety presupposes law. Yet, immediately, it becomes essential to distinguish the way anxiety over 'being able' is cancelled through guilt and repentance in Judaism and in Christianity. The Jew's 'recourse to the sacrifice' is said to be 'the profound tragedy of Judaism', for sac-

---

[81] Ibid.
[82] Ibid., p. 103.

rifice can only be repeated again and again without helping him, 'for that which would properly help him would be the cancellation of the relation of anxiety to guilt and the positing of an actual relation'.[83] 'Sin' is this actual relation and 'only with sin is atonement posited, and its sacrifice is not repeated'.[84] It is not the 'outward perfection of the sacrifice' which alleviates guilt, but, 'on the contrary, the perfection of the sacrifice corresponds to the fact that the actual relation of sin is posited'.[85]

This anachronistic pitting of sacrifice against law so that 'Judaism' is characterized both as a living religion of the law and at the same time as an ancient culture of temple sacrifice comparable to ancient Greek culture: 'To the oracle in paganism corresponds the sacrifice in Judaism',[86] is made to serve a deeper distinguishing of Judaism from Christianity which speciously rededuces the Christian judgement that Judaism is a religion of empty, external observance, and reproduces the Christian conflation of the biblical Hebrews with post-biblical Rabbinic Judaism. By doing so in this context, attention is distracted again from the pivot of the law. The Jew is represented as seeking to assuage the guilt learnt from law without achieving the repentance and atonement that comes from the positing of the actuality of sin. It is this actuality that may cancel the anxiety of possibility, but the Jew remains with 'the anxiety of guilt'.

The economy of sin 'posited' in Christianity does duty here for the absence of any sustained reflection on the economy of law. The anomalous insertion of 'atonement', a term from dogmatics, into a psychological and pseudonymous text indicates further inconsistency of method − and not only is 'sin' posited here, but, surprisingly, 'Christianity', too. For law in Judaism itself offers precisely the experience claimed exclusively for the cancelling of 'anxious possibility' by the actuality of sin. Always already within the law, the commandment in Judaism is known both in its existence and in its content which is negotiable and negotiated. There is therefore no anxiety of beginning or beginning of anxiety: the 'guilt' of being able is not an anxiety of possibility but always the actuality of the individual, because the law is 'actual' − collective, inclusive, contentful; on the one hand, 613 commands, on the other, perpetual negotiation of their meaning. The Day of Atonement, Yom Kippur, was developed *after* the fall of the Second Temple and the end of priestly sacrifice. Sacrifice is replaced, as it were, by guilt and atonement − the contrary of the Night Watchman's account. The

[83]   Ibid., p. 104.
[84]   Ibid.
[85]   Ibid.
[86]   Ibid.

Jew is inside the law, the Christian outside: for the Jew, within the command, atonement is actual and annually renewable; for the Christian, within the anxiety of uncomprehended prohibition, the law is external, salvation only posited with sin.

Anxiety for Judaism and for the individual Jew begins when the law he is always within meets the law without — the law of pagan Roman or Christian state and civil society. To the extent that post-biblical Judaism *as a religion* presupposes encounter with imperial law, Judaism will be anxious: just as historical Christianity, formulated to safeguard its good news against Roman legality, is anxious, but, ironically, attributes to Judaism, the religion and people of the living law, the externality of law learnt from *pax Romana*.

## It is Raised a Spiritual Body[87]

> It was not the repression that created the anxiety; the anxiety was there earlier; it was the anxiety that made the repression.[88]

This inversion of causation in the aetiology of anxiety summarizes the change between Freud's early and mature understanding of anxiety; it witnesses an anxiety of beginning as well as variations in the beginning of anxiety. The beginning of anxiety is first said to be birth itself, then internal libidinal danger, and, finally, external danger-situation.[89] The anxiety of beginning the investigation, and of reporting its findings, evident in each discussion, indicates a difficulty with repetition — with both the psychological concept of 'the compulsion to repeat' and with its Janus-face, a 'freely mobile ego' with perfect memory.[90] This difficulty turns out to be the pivot of the question of authority in Freud, where anxiety of beginning indicates the equivocation of the ethical and yields the agon and limit of his authorship.

In the thinking of Kierkegaard and of Freud, 'anxiety' is a Janus-faced concept which looks back to the aetiology of guilt and forwards to freedom. Pseudonymously, anxiety creates sin: sin does not create anxiety; psychoanalytically, anxiety creates repression: repression does not create anxiety. Anxiety is the pivot of movement backwards and movement forwards, of recollection and repetition, of loss and possibility, because it holds the middle — the 'third' or spirit or commandment

---

[87]  1 Cor. 15:44.
[88]  Freud, 'Anxiety and Instinctual Life', PFL, vol. 2, p. 118.
[89]  Ibid., pp. 113–44.
[90]  Compare 'Beyond the Pleasure Principle', PFL, vol. 11, p. 307 with 'Inhibitions, Symptoms and Anxiety', PFL, vol. 10, p. 312.

to body and soul, pseudonymously; the third to internal, 'neurotic' and external, 'real' danger, psychoanalytically.

It would be equally wrong to claim that psychoanalysis uncovers the repression arising from the pseudonymous account of sin, as it would be wrong, conversely, to assimilate pseudonymous aesthetic repetition forwards to psychoanalytic compulsion to repeat or to fixation on a screen memory shielding a repressed prototype. The law, whether Anti-Climacus' 'enigmatic word' or Lacan's 'symbolic order', could then only be conceived mono-dimensionally as being 'absolutely condemned to reproduce the mistakes of my father'.[91]

In the second book of his *Seminar*, Lacan argues that 'sin' is 'the third term' which disrupts pagan, Platonic, dyadic recognition and consequent reminiscence of man's natural object.[92] The 'new order' of sin sets repetition as the path for human advance. This is said to be illustrated by Kierkegaard's (*sic*) return to Berlin, recounted in *Repetition*, to repeat an experience of recollected, infinite pleasure. The 'total failure' of this experiment furnishes evidence of the 'path of a tenacious repetition' essential to human advance.[93]

This 'need' for repetition, 'man's' need, arises from the 'intrusion of the symbolic register' which separates objects in their 'radical function as symbols', from natural objects where there is a 'harmony between man and his world of objects'. This harmony is said by Lacan 'with Kierkegaard [*sic*]' to involve *ancient* reminiscence (= recollection), recognition. The symbolic object, on the contrary, has to be rediscovered by generating substitutive objects, 'to find the object again, to repeat the object'.[94] Freud's account of the compulsion to repeat is represented here as 'the conquest, the structuration of the world through the effort of labour, along the path of repetition'.[95]

This assimilation of *soi-disant* 'Kierkegaardian' repetition to Freud's 'compulsion to repeat' does justice to neither. 'Sin' is not 'the third term' which interferes in the otherwise harmonious cognition of familiar objects — subsequently searched symbolically to regain infinite initial pleasure by means of substitutions or repetitions. 'Sin' is here itself substituted for 'anxiety', while the use of repetition as 'substitution' refuses even the flexibility of the knight of resignation. 'Recognition' is made into immediate cognition; 'repetition' into desire for the missing object; while 'resignation' — taking a relation to loss and gain by cultivating the stance of infinite pain, but not the search for substitute infinite pleasure — is not countenanced. For it is, indeed, resignation to

[91]  See Lacan, 'The Circuit', *Seminar*, Bk II, p. 89.
[92]  Ibid., p. 87.
[93]  Ibid., p. 88.
[94]  Ibid., 'Introduction to the *Entwurf*', p. 100.
[95]  Ibid.

loss which is recollection or 'movement backwards' and which has repetition or 'movement forwards' as its contrary. Repetition returns the knight of faith to the finite; s/he 'receives everything back'. After passing through the movement of resignation, the realm of loss and gain, there is no 'substitution': 'to receive everything back' is an aesthetic expression for experiencing the finite as new, as an *emergent* harmony, inconceivable either as the *initial* harmony or as the endless attempt at symbolic substitution in Lacan.

Even in the aesthetic authorship 'repetition' is outside the prudence of loss or gain.* In the psychological pseudonymous authorship, 'anxiety' is the ambiguous midpoint between sin and faith: 'anxiety is freedom's possibility';[96] 'sin' is not posited as this third between 'reminiscence' and recollection. To place 'sin' in this position robs anxiety of its creativity, and it reduces the account of the commandment or law presupposed by anxiety from 'enigmatic word' to closed 'circuit in which I am integrated'.[97] Instead of raising the question of whether and how the law is heard: 'I am absolutely condemned to reproduce', 'in its aberrant form', 'the chain of discourse' bequeathed by the 'mistakes' of my father so that 'the problem of a situation of life or death' which 'I have to put to someone else' leads those to whom I transmit the chain to be 'just as likely' to 'falter'.[98] According to Lacan, this small circuit of the symbolic order — in which collectivities as well as individuals are caught, 'an entire nation or half the world' — can only be circumvented in Freud by positing a biology of life and death so that partaking of the death instinct itself opens this perspective on the symbolic decomposition of life.[99] The 'absolute' symbolic order which introduces 'the need for repetition' is 'beyond all the biological mechanisms of equilibration, of harmonisation and of agreement'.[100] However, the pseudonymous commandment — enigmatic, ambiguous and anxious — has a prodigiousness of possibility, inconceivable in these anthropological terms of 'man's need for repetition'.[101]

Equally, this assimilating of 'Kierkegaardian' repetition to Freudian 'compulsion to repeat' obfuscates repetition forwards in Freud. The three alternative accounts of the beginning of anxiety and of instinctual repetition[102] in his writings amount to that ambiguousness of anxiety

---

* In Lacan as in Adorno (compare p. 15 *supra*) there is no place to be like Phlebas the Phoenician who forgot 'the deep sea swell/And the profit and loss' (Eliot, *The Wasteland*, ll. 313–14).

[96]  Kierkegaard, *Concept of Anxiety* (RT), p. 155.
[97]  Lacan, 'The Circuit', p. 89.
[98]  Ibid., pp. 88–9.
[99]  Ibid., p. 90.
[100]  Ibid.
[101]  Ibid., p. 88.
[102]  See Freud, 'Beyond the Pleasure Principle', PFL, vol. 11, pp. 310–12, 326.

which marks an anxiety of beginning. It is the showing of a dissembling: how the difficulty of possibility is linked to authorship and authority, or where *the author and the authority make way for repetition forwards.*

'In analysis, the person is dead after the analysis is over.'[103] H. D., pen name of Hilda Doolittle, the American poet briefly analysed by Freud in the early 1930s in Vienna, reports this rare evocation of a successful analysis. '"Which person?" He said, "It would not matter if I were seventy-seven or forty-seven." I now remember that I will be forty-seven on my next birthday. "In analysis, the person is dead after the analysis is over — as dead as your father."'[104] Death, like repetition, has two meanings for Freud: negatively, death is linked to the compulsion to repeat, which retards analysis or makes it fail — the passive relation to death; positively, it is linked to risking one's life, daring death, the active relation to death; or, negatively, repetition backwards, blocked memory, or recollection fixated on a screen type; and positively, repetition forwards, 'perfect memory' or a 'freely mobile ego'.

The beginning of anxiety was first seen as 'a consequence of the event of birth'. It began, as it were, with the beginning of human life, the effect of anxiety arising subsequently as 'a repetition of the situation then experienced'.[105] This position was modified so that it provided merely the means for making a distinction between realistic and neurotic anxiety in situations of external danger. Anxiety is generated 'realistically' when the reaction to the danger adapts itself to the new situation adequately for dealing with it, 'neurotically' when the original situation dominates the new and results in inexpedient paralysis. 'Anxiety' here means repetition of the original trauma, or 'unpleasure', which cannot be discharged, now understood, not as the event of birth, but as internal libidinal danger. The 'quota of libido' attached to a repressed idea becomes unemployable and changes into anxiety,[106] which arises from the repressed instinctual impulses.

'We no longer feel able to say that.'[107] Instead, the ego is now 'the sole seat of anxiety'; it 'alone can produce and feel anxiety', because 'the internal instinctual danger . . . turn[s] out to be a determinant and preparation for an external, real, situation of danger'.[108] The material out of which the anxiety is made is less important in explaining its generation

103   H. D., *Tribute to Freud*, p. 141.
104   Ibid.; Freud was 77 years old at the time.
105   Freud, 'Inhibitions, Symptoms and Anxiety', PFL, vol. 10, p. 321.
106   Freud, 'Anxiety and Instinctual Life', PFL, vol. 2, p. 115.
107   Ibid., p. 124.
108   Ibid., pp. 117–18.

than the new order of explanation: 'it was not the repression that created the anxiety; the anxiety was there earlier; it was the anxiety that made the repression'.[109] Anxiety is thus realistic: there is 'a particular determinant of anxiety (that is, situation of danger) . . . allotted to every stage of development as being appropriate to it'.[110] Anxiety as a reaction to external danger on the part of the ego results in — not from — repression: the ego excludes the repressed from its 'great organization' so that even when the danger situation changes, the now-restricted ego cannot undo the earlier repression, and 'the new impulse has no choice but to obey the compulsion to repeat'.[111]

This apparent reversal of causal order from repression causing anxiety to anxiety causing repression, which is equally from internal danger to external danger, and from material to process of anxiety, from 'id' to 'ego', is not as 'new' or 'stable' as it is proclaimed.[112] Clear priority is now given to the ego's anticipated unpleasure in 'well-remembered situations of danger',[113] and the repression of the associated impulse, but the connection of the three main species of anxiety — realistic, neurotic and moral — with the ego's three dependent relations — to the external world, to the id and to the super-ego — is hardly 'simplified'.[114] While the pivot of the ego, implied even in the original formulation that attributed agency to 'repression' and posited anxiety as the *consequent* of repression, is unequivocal in the revised formulation, which posits 'anxiety' as the cause of repression, still the relation between the ego's 'three tyrannical masters' — the external world, the super-ego and the id — remains as set out in the immediately preceding lecture. There they are presented as three species of potentially conflictual command, not as material versus mechanism: the ego 'feels hemmed in on three sides, threatened by three kinds of danger, to which, if it is hard pressed, it reacts by generating anxiety'.[115] The beginning of anxiety is, in this way, returned to or restated at its middle, immersed in its multiple dangers — internal and external: 'real', neurotic and moral. This middle — the conflicting words of command — is equally the anxiety of beginning — not only an account of 'the compulsion to repeat', but an inducement of repetition forwards which cannot take place as the result of any authorial authority.

---

109  Ibid., p. 118.
110  Ibid., p. 120.
111  Freud, 'Inhibitions, Symptoms and Anxiety', PFL, vol. 10, p. 312.
112  Freud, 'Anxiety and Instinctual Life', PFL, vol. 2, p. 117.
113  Ibid., p. 121.
114  Ibid., pp. 117–18.
115  Freud, 'Dissection of the Personality', PFL, vol. 2, p. 110.

> The ego is the actual seat of anxiety ... What it is that the ego
> fears from the external and from the libidinal danger cannot be
> specified; we know that the fear is of being over-whelmed or
> annihilated, but it cannot be grasped analytically.[116]

The anxiety of beginning is discernible whenever the account of the
beginning of anxiety returns to its middle, the ego, 'a frontier creature',
which 'tries to mediate between the world and the id';[117] and when the
theoretical or metapsychological accounts of the repetition of the life
and death instincts, with all their adverted and admitted insufficiencies,
meet the practical accounts of the five resistance repetitions which make
for or against a successful analysis. In the first kind of account, the
author acknowledges the limits of his authorship; in the second, the
analyst confronts both the interference of his own authority − transference resistance, and the supervenient authority of the super-ego −
super-ego resistance, which limits the authority of both analyst and
analysand. Out of these theoretical-metapsychological and practical-
analytical-existential accounts of repetition backwards − of the compulsion to repeat, death instincts and anxiety − can be drawn guidelines,
explicit and implicit, on repetition forwards.

The argument in 'Beyond the Pleasure Principle' is informative in its
tortuousness − for 'instincts' in general and in particular are defined in
terms of repetition. In general, they are traced to the need '*to restore an
earlier state of things*'.[118] In particular, the self-preservation instinct is
explicated both in terms of how it ensures that the organism 'dies only
in its own fashion';[119] and, in oppositional terms, between those 'germ-
cells' which repeat a mode of existence as the species-mode of dying,
versus those 'germ-cells' which repeat the *beginning* of the process
of development, 'a fresh start' which prolongs the journey.[120] Repetition abolishes tensions in the first instance; the fresh '*vital differences*'
must be 'lived off', in the second.[121] The idea of 'the compulsion to
repeat' is itself repeated: as a psychoanalytical explanation of anxiety
and of analysis resistance, *qua* the repetition of unpleasure, and then in a
reflexion on the child's inherent tendency to repeat both pleasurable
*and* unpleasurable experiences. It re-emerges as a metapsychological
notion applicable to 'instincts', to 'germ-cells', to metapsychological

---

[116]  Freud, 'The Ego and the Id', PFL, vol. 11, p. 399.
[117]  Ibid., p. 398.
[118]  Op. cit., PFL, vol. 11, p. 308, emphasis in original.
[119]  Ibid., p. 312.
[120]  Ibid., pp. 312, 313.
[121]  Ibid., p. 329, emphasis in original.

concepts and, 'unwittingly', steers 'into the harbour of Schopenhauer's philosophy'.[122]

The dualism of life and death instincts is re-established once it gains the topographical clarification that a portion of ego or self-preservation instincts are life or sexual instincts, that not *all* 'guardians of life' are 'the myrmidons of death', or not immediately, for some are libidinal and lead to new life.[123] Yet the 'compulsion to repeat' is installed as the *tertium comparationis* of life and death: for all living – *mere* living or self-preservation, and *more* living or conjugation – is, metapsychologically, repetition forwards, 'the aim of all life is death', when, psychoanalytically, the compulsion means repetition backwards. Now, metapsychologically, repetition moves forwards by moving backwards: preservation or persistence, 'life', is retrograde; it restores 'an earlier state of affairs', precisely because it 'presses ever forward unsubdued';[124] new life repeats the same course, as a prolongation of this journey to death.

'Beyond the Pleasure Principle' introduces a deep ambiguity into the meaning of 'the compulsion to repeat', between the metapsychological and the analytical meanings: this divergence of forwards and backwards evinces the anxiety of beginning – the delineation of an untheorizable, existential repetition forwards, which emerges from the consideration of what repetition means in 'anxiety', in 'life', and in 'death'.

If analysis seeks to restore 'perfect memory' to blocked memory or recollection, the movement backwards, that may itself be fixated on a screen memory, then the five psychoanalytic meanings of resistance-repetition can themselves be seen to yield the meaning of this perfecting, this repetition forwards: three ego-resistances – knowledge resistance, transference resistance and the gain from illness – id resistance, and super-ego resistance.[125] Knowledge resistance, the easiest to overcome, implies that repetition forwards is not a question of knowledge: one may come to know of a repression without thereby overcoming it; and, nevertheless, still repeat it backwards. Transference resistance means repeating the repression in the relation to the analyst, acting it out symptomatically instead of overcoming it. The authority of the analyst is paradoxical: essential to moving the analysand beyond repetition backwards, yet potentially dangerous in that the authority may reinforce repetition backwards so that relation to an external authority is again

---

[122]   Ibid., p. 322.
[123]   Ibid., p. 312, revised, pp. 325–6.
[124]   Ibid., p. 315 citing Goethe's Mephistopheles.
[125]   The following account is taken from 'Addenda XI', 'Inhibitions, Symptoms and Anxiety', PFL, vol. 10, pp. 318–20.

substituted for taking a relation to one's own authority. The problem of authorship occurs not only in the role of the analyst but also in the response of the analysand. The third ego-resistance is 'the gain from illness', by which the symptom is assimilated into the ego, and results in unwillingness to renounce the satisfaction or the substitute relief which the symptom affords. This symptom repetition is also repetition backwards — the consolation of the unhappiness of recollection or resignation.

The id-resistance follows after the ego has decided to relinquish its resistance but 'still has difficulty in undoing the repressions', because 'the power of the compulsion to repeat — the attraction exerted by the unconscious prototype upon the repressed instinctual process — has still to be overcome.' The 'period of strenuous effort' required to achieve this is called 'working-through'. 'Working-through' is the pivot which decides whether the analysis is successful or unsuccessful, whether it overcomes the repetition backwards, the repressed prototype, and issues in a 'freely mobile ego', repetition forwards.

The fifth resistance, 'the last to be discovered', comes from the super-ego and also inhibits successful analysis, set out in the idea of 'working-through', because of the need for guilt and the desire for punishment. Elsewhere Freud admits 'there is often no counteracting force of a similar order of strength which the treatment can oppose to it'.[126]

The guilt, the 'moral' factor, may be unconscious and it may require an alternative ego ideal — 'prophet, saviour and redeemer'[127] which analysis does not permit the analyst to provide. The religious terminology indicates Freud's linking of this destructive need with religious projections: 'the general character of harshness and cruelty exhibited by the ideal — its dictatorial "Thou shalt"',[128] and implies a critique of paternalistic religion — the erotic religiosity of desire and its refusal — which prevents a repetition forwards. It is this critique, which, *prima facie*, might seem most at odds with a 'religious' authorship, that most coincides with it. For Freud admits that psychoanalysis — whether as science or as analysis — cannot delineate the saviour, redeemer, or prophet; that, by implication, the analysand will have to provide for herself; and, moreover, one that would make possible the repetition forwards that this negative theology of resistances seeks to insinuate. The points at which analysis can do no more: when it demurs at the description of what anxiety fears, and when it falters at what repetition

126  Freud, 'The Ego and the Id', PFL, vol. 11, p. 391 n. 1.
127  Ibid.
128  Ibid., p. 396.

forwards might mean in the face of the super-ego — the cultural or religious ideal which lacks a 'countervailing force', *an ethic* — these points at which it ends or declines to recommend are the points at which repetition forwards would, if it could, begin. These *Leerstellen* evince the anxiety of beginning.

As H. D. reports: '"In analysis the person is dead after the analysis is over". Which person?'[129] And how dead is dead? In the essay 'Our Attitude to Death' Freud elaborates this idea of death as beyond the 'person', as the beginning, or repetition forwards, to mean risking one's own life and encouraging others to risk theirs, by contrast with the denial of death, the negative attitude, betrayed by our 'effort to reduce death from a necessity to a chance event'.[130]

> But this attitude of ours towards death has a powerful effect on our lives. Life is impoverished, it loses its interest when the highest stake in the game of living, life itself, may not be risked. It becomes shallow and empty as, let us say, an American flirtation, in which it is understood from the first that nothing is to happen, as contrasted with a Continental love affair in which both partners must constantly bear its serious consequences in mind. Our emotional ties, the unbearable intensity of our grief, make us disinclined to court danger for ourselves and for those who belong to us. We dare not contemplate a great many undertakings which are dangerous, but in fact indispensable... We are paralyzed by the thought of who is to take [our place in our family relationships] if a disaster should occur. Thus the tendency to exclude death from our calculations in life brings in its train many other renunciations and exclusions. Yet the motto of the Hanseatic League ran: '*Navigare necesse est, vivere non necesse*'. ('It is necessary to sail the seas, it is not necessary to live')[131]

Is it not even implied here that repetition forwards may involve risking the lives of those 'who belong to us' — that everyone may aspire to the temptation of Abraham over Isaac?

The beginning of anxiety is overshadowed by the integrity of authorial anxiety of beginning which seeks to deliver authorship over to the authority of the addressee. Yet in both authorships, Freud's and Kierkegaard's, authority persists in the middle between authorship and authority in the species of command: the three 'severe masters' and the

---

[129]  H.D., *Tribute to Freud*, p. 141.
[130]  Freud, 'Our Attitude Towards Death', PFL, vol. 12, p. 78.
[131]  Ibid., pp. 78–9.

'enigmatic word'. Possibility or 'being able' — that simultaneous innocence and guilt — *anxiety*, that may be disposed backwards or risked
forwards, debouches into the unknowables — law and existence. The
*command* to navigate beyond life, beyond death, beyond the person,
does not issue beyond the concept nor beyond the ethical.

## Ruin of Ethical Life

> Socrates, Socrates, Socrates! Yes, we may well call your name
> three times; it would not be too much to call it ten times, if it
> would be of any help. Popular opinion maintains that the world
> needs a republic, needs a new social order and a new religion —
> but no-one considers that what the world, confused simply by too
> much knowledge, needs is a Socrates.[132]

As the cycle — anxiety to sin; sin to despair; despair to grace —
returns to the ethical, the tone of facetiousness surfaces again. The
anxiety of beginning is manifest in the elaboration of the *psychology* of
despair which seeks to demonstrate that 'not to be in despair must
signify the destroyed possibility of being able to be in despair; if a
person is truly not to be in despair, he must at every moment destroy
the possibility'.[133] This universal and never-ending, always-beginning,
predicament implies that there exist many forms of unconscious despair; the psychological exposition teases them out. In the *dogmatics* of
despair, 'sin' is posited as '*before God, or with the conception of God, in
despair not to will to be oneself, or in despair to will to be oneself*'; psychologically, this is the difference between weakness and defiance.[134] The
exposition of 'the most dialectical frontier between despair and sin' is
no longer psychological, but verges back on the aesthetic and the
religious: the suffering is now that of a 'poet-existence' which has
'something in common with the despair of resignation' — the knight of
resignation of *Fear and Trembling* leaps to mind — 'except that the
concept of God is present'.[135] Although these propositions from
dogmatics are intrinsically incapable of being represented, the exposition relies on the poetical analogy of God as lovelorn consolation, when
anguish is preferred to faith by the one who despairs.

'And now, what of Christianity!'[136] Unanswerable question, punctu-

---

132  Kierkegaard, *Sickness Unto Death*, p. 92.
133  Ibid., p. 15.
134  Ibid., p. 77, emphasis in original.
135  Ibid.
136  Ibid., p. 85.

ated as expostulation, for grace is not only unrepresentable but unspeakable, and can only be presented as — offence: 'Truly, if there is anything to lose one's mind over, this is it! ... because his mind cannot grasp it, because he cannot attain bold confidence in the face of it and therefore must get rid of it, pass it off as a bagatelle, nonsense and folly, for it seems as if it would choke him'.[137] In this *via negativa*, faith is dramatized as the passion and imagination to be offended — with its arsenal of illustrative analogies and anecdotes.

The argument that the willingness *to be offended* is the condition of potential faith, and the subsequent concession that 'the Jews had a perfect right to be offended by Christ because he claimed to forgive sins',[138] implies the exceptional qualification of the Jews in the stakes of faith. Yet the return to the ethical Janus is effected by discussion of Socrates and the Greeks, not by discussion of *Talmud Torah* of Rabbinic Judaism; and, once again, the pivot of the law is displaced on to the pivot of Greek knowledge and ignorance. From knowledge and ignorance as defining the ironic-ethical Janus, the exposition 'teaches' about sin as 'a little further back'.[139] Yet this teaching of the offence is 'the suit that the divine as the prosecutor ventures to bring against man'.[140] The 'enigmatic word' is, at it were, found on both sides: ethical *and* dogmatic, facetious *and* posited — the anxiety of beginning still evident in the concluding of Anti-Climacus.

While the Greek view that to know right is to do right is too intellectual, lacking the Christian account of wilful defiance — knowingly not doing good or knowingly doing wrong — nevertheless, it affords the ironic-ethical correction:[141] that when a vaunted claim to know right is mismatched with action, then the claim to know right is manifestly discredited. The Greek view can pick out hypocrisy and error — Christian or Greek — but it cannot pick out defiance and sin, that is, despair — a corruption of willing, not of knowing. Yet this Christian addition to the conception of the human being is intended to reinforce the ethical task *for the age* — 'Christendom' needs the Socratic ethical-ironic distinction between intellectual understanding and practical 'understanding', to replace its excessive knowledge with a Socratic ignorance 'not as a conclusion that ultimately assists men in their deepest misery, since that annuls precisely the difference between understanding and understanding, but as the ethical conception of

---

[137]   Ibid., pp. 85—6.
[138]   Ibid., p. 116.
[139]   Ibid., p. 95.
[140]   Ibid.
[141]   Ibid., p. 90.

everyday life'.[142] This ruin of ethical life, disjointed here between the 'deepest misery' of the individual and the ethical 'everyday' of the age, the collective fate of the culture of Christendom, bears the scar of that 'enigmatic word' which stands for the resignation and consolation of Anti-Climacus' attempts at 'faith'.

[142]   Ibid., p. 92.

# Part Two

# From the Beginning
# in the Middle

# 4

# Repetition in the Feast
## Mann and Girard

### Myth out of the Hands of the Fascists

In this book [*Joseph and his Brothers*], the myth has been taken out
of Fascist hands and humanized down to the last recess of its
language ... In the idea of humanity, the human idea, the sense
for the past and that for the future, tradition and revolution form
a strange and, to my mind, infinitely attractive mixture.[1]

What kind of feast is this repetition? Not the marriage feast for which
we are too young or too old;[2] not Johannes Climacus' 'festive room'
dedicated to 'the jungle growth of difficulty'.[3] *Joseph and his Brothers*
celebrates a feast of the gods, the third humanism of 'the union of the
beast-god with the God-man'.[4] How can the retelling of the biblical
Joseph story be a feast of the *gods* when it is announced as a 'rabbinical
Midrash' on the Torah and thus on its sole and singular God?[5]

The telling is the key to the meaning of the feast and to the meaning
of the repetition: the paradoxes of author, authority and actor are fully
integrated into the metaphysic of this monument to — what Lukács

---

[1] Mann, *The Theme of the Joseph Novels*, p. 21. *Joseph and his Brothers*, originally
published as four books, 1933–43; edition used, Fischer 1, 2, 3; trans. Penguin, 1978.
Compare Gabriel Josipovici's criticism of *Joseph* as myth, which includes a comparison
with Kierkegaard's *Fear and Trembling*, in the 'The Man in the Field', ch. xiv, *The Book of
God*, pp. 276–94.
[2] See ch. 2, *supra*, pp. 59–60 and nn. 22, 27.
[3] Kierkegaard, *Journals* (Dru), pp. 82–3.
[4] For 'the third humanism', see Mann, 'Freud and the Future', pp. 190–1, tr. p. 427, and
'Zum Problem des Antisemitismus', p. 37; for the 'beast-god' see 'Goethe and Tolstoy',
p. 168, tr. p. 175.
[5] Mann, *The Theme of the Joseph Novels*, pp. 14–15.

argued the novel could only fail towards[6] — the reuniting of time and history; an attempt to reveal things hidden since the foundation of the world,[7] and thereby to found the world anew; but — and this will be the pivot of the argument — only facetiously.

'Once upon a time', the childlike beginning of the story-teller is marshalled to monitor repetition backwards and forwards: 'What concerns us here is not calculable time. Rather it is time's abrogation [*Aufhebung*] and dissolution in the alternation of tradition and prophecy, which lends to the phrase "once upon a time" its double sense of past and future and therewith its burden of potential present.'[8] This does not express nostalgia for 'presence', but celebration of the contemporaneity of the past, a way of acknowledging its meaning, both hidden and revealed, so that it becomes a burden of potentiality, a difficult 'present', that may have a future. The proclamation exalts the childlike teller of the beginning — 'once upon a time' — into the wise teller of the middle — 'tradition' — and then into the reckless teller of the end — 'prophecy'.

Repetition, movement backwards and forwards, celebration of contemporaneity, new beginning, 'the abrogation [*die Aufhebung*] of the difference between "was" and "is"',[9] is matched by the acknowledgement of old beginnings, figured by the tropes of 'above' and 'below', for the equal 'celebration of the meeting between poetry and analysis',[10] meeting in the ethical of the 'lower world, the unconscious, the id',[11] 'blessing from the depths beneath', with simultaneous 'blessing from heaven above'.[12] Simultaneity of 'above' and 'below' in each individual; contemporaneity of 'was' and 'is' — and thus 'will be' — in the collectivity; these two repetitions are gathered in the third — the telling. The telling becomes epic uttering, prophetic performing, blessing — what is told: 'myth'; the telling: 'temple masque':

> The original story to be sure long ago played itself out to the end and what we here relate is only a repetition in the feast, a temple masque, as it were.[13]

[6]   Lukács, *The Theory of the Novel*, pp. 74–5, 80–1, 124–5.
[7]   Girard, *Things Hidden Since the Foundation of the World*, is discussed below, pp. 116–42.
[8]   *Joseph*, Bd 1 p. 22, tr. p. 18.
[9]   Ibid., Bd 2 p. 935, tr. p. 825.
[10]  'Freud and the Future', p. 190, tr. p. 427.
[11]  Ibid.
[12]  *Joseph*, Bd 1 p. 39, tr. p. 33.
[13]  Ibid., Bd 2 p. 935, tr. p. 825.

For it *is*, always *is*, however much we say It was. Thus speaks the myth, which is only the garment of the mystery . . . the holiday garment of the mystery is the feast.[14]

While Mann would no more claim to be a prophet than Kierkegaard would allow himself to be credited an apostle, the master of ceremonies at the poetic feast would bring the author and the reader to the brink:

What we here relate is only a repetition in the feast . . . Otherwise, out of sheer anxiety and concern, then sweat might be standing on our brows![15]

Crossing the border between 'witness at first or second hand' and genuine contemporaneity, willing to be scandalized, which is insinuated here while apparently denied, captures the impulse of Kierkegaard's pseudonymity:[16]

The very maximum of what one human being can do for another in relation to that wherein each man has to do solely with himself, is to inspire him with concern and unrest.[17]

By alternating unequivocal positing with facetious disowning of meaning, and by alternating comparative commentary on ancient world-religions which are assimilated into one single myth with litany-like blessing, conferred from heaven above and from the depths beneath, Mann transfigures the poet into gnostic seer where Kierkegaard transfigures Christian gnosis into poetry.

Gnostic cosmology of 'the ensouling of man by his unauthorized creators'[18] is mobilized by Mann to demonstrate the shared dilemma of author and actor so that the crisis of Joseph's identity is homologous with the crisis of authorial identity which can therefore be conceived and represented.

For I am and am not just because *I* am I . . . For the pattern and the traditional come from the depths which lie beneath and are

---

[14]   Ibid., Bd 1 pp. 38–9, tr. p. 33. Compare the opening of Mann, *The Holy Sinner*, 'Who Rings?', pp. 1–6.
[15]   *Joseph*, Bd 2 p. 935, tr. p. 825.
[16]   See ch. 1, *supra*.
[17]   Kierkegaard, *Concluding Unscientific Postscript*, p. 346.
[18]   Hans Jonas, *The Gnostic Religion*, pp. 62–5.

what binds us, whereas the I is from God and is of the spirit, which is free.[19]

What Joseph says here to Pharaoh has been prepared by the 'Prelude' to the work, where the battle over the middle term, the 'soul', not evident in the parameters paraded here, was joined. For Kierkegaard there is no conceivable or representable cosmology that would ease the disrelation of author to authority; as a result, author and actor always skirt the danger that their relation to authority may become aesthetic instead of existential:

> The pathos of the poet is therefore essentially imaginative pathos ... Aesthetic pathos expresses itself in words, and may in its truth indicate that the individual leaves his real self in order to lose himself in the Idea: while existential pathos is present whenever the Idea is brought into relation with the existence of the individual so as to transform it. If in relating itself to the individual's existence the absolute *telos* fails to transform it absolutely, the relationship is not one of existential pathos, but of aesthetic pathos.[20]

*Joseph and his Brothers* begins with a 'Prelude' subtitled 'Descent into Hell', descent which turns into an elegiac descant on the recession and repetition of 'time-coulisses':[21] 'time' as the theatrical wings, off-stage, receding one by one into a 'bottomless' past; and 'time' behind the scenes, or, eternity. The work begins both at the 'origin' of time, 'from the days of Set',[22] the day of the founding fratricide; and it begins in eternity − with a Gnostic prehistory of the soul.[23] It begins with the anxiety of beginning and with the beginning of anxiety: with the anxiety of beginning, for the descent is a descent into 'hell'; with the beginning of anxiety, the timeless nature of unconscious motifs. It begins, that is, before the middle − with bald expositions and statements of repetitions to be encountered ethically in the body of the 'Tales'. repetition of the founding fratricide, from Set to Joseph, elaborated as the mythical repetition of time; and 'the doctrine and romance of the soul', elaborated as the cosmological repetition of eternity.[24]

[19]  *Joseph*, Bd 3 pp. 1061–2, tr. p. 937, 'I' not emphasized in translation.
[20]  Kierkegaard, *Concluding Unscientific Postscript*, p. 347.
[21]  *Joseph*, Bd 1 p. 13, tr. pp. 10–11.
[22]  Ibid., Bd 1 p. 15, tr. p. 12.
[23]  Ibid., Bd 1 pp. 27–32, tr. pp. 23–7.
[24]  Ibid., Bd 1 p. 30 tr. p. 25.

While the compound mythology 'mingles' Hebraic, Babylonian, Egyptian and Greek traditions,[25] the compound Gnosticism mingles elements incorporated into Avesta, Islam, Manichæanism, Gnosticism and Hellenism,[26] to produce a heterodox pre-cosmic history which will disestablish anthropological and authorial ambition.

Primal man, 'God's chosen champion in the struggle against that evil which penetrated into the new creation',[27] was formed before the creation of the world, a body made of pure light with no soul. Sparks from 'this human light essence' are fettered by the seven Archons, or demiurges, spiritually malevolent yet powerful creators, who ensoul the holy spark with its seven appetites; or, alternatively, the pre-cosmic spirit becomes enamoured of its reflection in matter and in this way acquires a soul.[28] The world or cosmos is brought into being only at this point by the true Deity to alleviate the passion of the fallen soul. Deity not demiurge then dispatches a 'second emissary' of the spirit to rouse the soul to leave the world of matter and return to its divine source.[29] This second spirit seeks to enlighten the soul about its divine spark and fateful cosmic history, for, in spite of the language of 'fall' or 'capture', the soul is not sinful but ignorant of its prehistory and possibility.

This second emissary, 'second descent of the divine',[30] potential saviour of the soul, corresponds to the Gnostic 'Alien' or 'Stranger' to the world, but he 'does not come just once into the world but . . . from the beginning of time he wanders in different forms through history, himself exiled in the world, and revealing himself ever anew until, with his gathering-in complete, he can be released from his cosmic mission'.[31]

It is this tragic and redemptive mask which is ambushed by our author who confesses that he has thereby appropriated a further agonizing predicament. Commissioned to retrieve the world from its relation to matter, when, freed from pain and desire, 'straightway the end of the world is come, death done away and matter restored to her ancient freedom',[32] the ambassador becomes troubled in the role of 'slayer' and 'grave-digger' of the world, and takes on something of the 'colour' of the soul. Instead of dismissing 'death out of the world, it finds itself on

---

[25]  *The Theme of the Joseph Novels*, p. 15.
[26]  *Joseph*, Bd 1 p. 27, tr. p. 23.
[27]  Ibid.
[28]  Ibid., Bd 1 p. 28, tr. pp. 23–4; compare Jonas, *The Gnostic Religion*, pp. 53, 63–4.
[29]  *Joseph*, Bd 1 p. 29, tr. pp. 24–5.
[30]  See Jonas, *The Gnostic Religion*, p. 76.
[31]  Ibid., p. 79.
[32]  *Joseph*, Bd 1 p. 30, tr. p. 26.

the contrary regarded as the deathly principle, as that which brings death into the world'.[33] Spirit, sent to recall the spark to its origin so that it may cast off its psychic envelope, comes to realize that this blissful reunion of the spark with its origin is literally psychic death, the destruction of the soul as well as the destruction of the world, the cessation of eros. 'Comes to realize' is the allegorical *Bildung* of this interpolated authorship-difficulty.

For this faltering 'spirit' represents the human story-teller, allegorically reincarnated, who confides here how he compromises before this restoration which would mean annihilation of soul, world and intercessorial 'spirit' itself:

> The spirit is of its nature and essentially the principle of the future, and represents the It will be, It is to be; whereas the goodness of the form-bound soul has reference to the past and the holy It was. It remains controversial, which life and which death; since both, the world involved with nature and the spirit detached from the world, the principle of the past and the principle of the future, claim, each in its own way, to be the water of life, and each accuses the other of dealings with death.[34]

This 'origin' of the author/story-teller in acosmic hubris and repeated world-wandering humility is equally the origin of the facetious tone of the work, fashioned exactly to cloak this philosophy. 'Facetious' in three ways which develop from each other: first, in the sense of 'faceted', many faces — the many guises of the reincarnated narrator-saviour who sees his role reflected in other saviours, assimilated to this Gnostic acosmology, partaking thereby in the gnostic pseudonym 'Christ', who becomes a self-consciously mythic saviour.[35] 'Facetious' in the second, dominant sense taken from *facetiae*, old books of a humorous or erotic character, where 'facetious' means addicted to erotic humour. For if spirit retains some soul it retains the erotic in spite of knowledge of the divine — and this lends the work a mocking tone which is both abrasive and gentle. With its mix of sensuous and liturgical prose, supercilious and comic, compelling and discomforting, this style appears ill-suited to its overall meaning, for that meaning is at odds with itself. Unsure whether to enlighten the world about its cosmic history and divine nature, or to relieve its unconscious, its sexual history, the 'Prelude' opts for a balance:

---

[33]  Ibid., Bd 1 p. 31, tr. p. 26.
[34]  Ibid., Bd 1 p. 34, tr. p. 29.
[35]  'Freud and the Future', p. 188, tr. pp. 424–5.

But the mystery, and the unexpressed hope of God, lie in their union, in the genuine penetration of spirit into the world of the soul, in the inter-penetration of both principles, in a hallowing of the one through the other which should bring about a present humanity blessed with blessings from heaven above and from the depths beneath.[36]

Even if this were conceivable and consistent with the cosmology of such a compromise, the enlightened but immured soul dwells in a narration resounding with the Gnostic laughter of its would-be re-deemer. Unsure himself if he heralds life or death, he cannot join in the feast where 'life and death meet and know each other'.[37] Facetiousness does not feast – it dissembles its dirge.

Finally, facetiousness, honest to its own failing, will spoil two other feasts. Positing a 'present humanity' – even while preluding on its difficulty – the facetious style undermines both the concocted revolutionary politics and the planned 'meeting' between 'psychoanalysis and poetry' which the *Joseph* stories are made to stage. For only anxiety – not partial enlightenment – would relieve the tone and set the table. Facetiousness, not repetition, is the truth of this text, *Doctor Faustus* will be its expiation – 'myth out of the hands of the fascists'.

The soul as 'giver of the given' – yes, my friends, I am well aware that in the novel this conception reaches an ironic pitch which is not authorized either in Oriental wisdom or in the analytical view.[38]

This 'pitch' of irony in *Joseph* which would settle the soul between matter and spirit, and between tradition and prophecy, will be expounded here as 'facetiousness' in order to distinguish it from the equally specific 'pitches' of irony in earlier and subsequent works. *Joseph* is vaunted as 'the first public meeting' of literature and psychoanalysis yet poetic licence is closely guarded: 'Indeed it would be too much to say that I came to psychoanalysis. It came to me.'[39] The indigestion of story-teller and story at the *Joseph* feast is one decipherable stage in the evolution of Mann's authorship: for the ironic masks of authority derive at every other stage, too, from the anxiety of beginning and the beginning of anxiety.

[36] *Joseph*, Bd 1 pp. 34–5, tr. p. 29.
[37] Ibid., Bd 1 p. 39, tr. p. 33.
[38] 'Freud and the Future', p. 183, tr. p. 421, corrected.
[39] Ibid., Bd 1 pp. 174, 176–7, tr. p. 412 corrected, p. 414.

The 'pitch' of irony registers the infinite erotic oscillation of the soul in the *Reflections of a Non-Political Man* (1918)[40] which reappears in *Joseph* as the young Joseph's secret dedication to the moon cult. Irony appears as the 'pathos of the middle' in the estimation of the genius of Goethe, 'divine animal', forerunner of a new religiosity in 'Goethe and Tolstoy' (1922).[41] In *Joseph*, 'repetition in the feast', the new humanism to incorporate the insight of Freud − 'knight of the unconscious' − should be *beyond* irony, but instead it reaches an 'unauthorized' pitch. Irony turns subsequently from the Gnostic vainglory of *Joseph* to the history of *Doctor Faustus* − from myth *posited* as 'out of the hands of the fascists' in *Joseph*, to the artistic and political history of Germany recursively *exposited* from within the hands of the Fascists in *Doctor Faustus*: from the short-lived revolution of Akhenaton (or Ikhnaton) in Egypt, to the illusory 'documentation' of Germany set in 1943; from the 'romance and doctrine' of the Gnostic soul to the prosaic soul of Serenus Zeitblom ('serene bloom of time') chronicling the lamentations of the faustian soul; from blessings raining from all directions yet deflected by facetiousness in *Joseph*, to the consummate facetiousness which, by dramatized representation of Germany's pact, 'signed with her blood', would exploit such collusion by − in the last sentence of all − folding the hands and *begging* a blessing. 'A lonely man folds his hands and speaks: "God be merciful to thy poor soul, my friend, my Fatherland!"'[42]

In a letter of 4 July 1920, Mann refers Karl Maria Weber to the exposition of erotic irony included in his 'non-political man' − 'an unexpected context':

> The relationship of life and mind . . . is an extremely delicate, difficult, agitating, painful relationship charged *with irony and eroticism* . . . For yearning passes back and forth between life and mind. Life, too, longs for mind. Two worlds whose relation is erotic *without clarification of the sexual polarity*, without the one representing the male and the other the female principle: such are life and mind. *Therefore there is no union between them but only the brief, inebriating illusion of union and understanding, an eternal tension without resolution is the problem of beauty* that the mind feels life and life feels mind as 'beautiful' . . . The mind that loves is not fanatical; it is ingenious, political: it woos, and its wooing is erotic irony . . . [43]

---

[40]  See ch. 12, 'Irony and Radicalism', pp. 419–35.
[41]  Translation in *Essays of Three Decades*, pp. 93–175.
[42]  *Doctor Faustus*, p. 510, tr. p. 490.
[43]  *Letters*, p. 96, citing *Reflections of a Non-Political Man*, pp. 419–20, emphases in original.

The 'problem of eroticism, indeed the problem of beauty' appears here as a 'covert yearning' between life and mind which gives rise to infinite oscillations between them.[44] This kind of irony is the servant of erotic love that suffers its painful predicament and yet enjoys its own resources and devices, thriving on the 'eternal tension without resolution'. 'Difficult' and ingenious, such irony translates the beginning of anxiety, 'delicate' and 'agitating', into the anxiety of beginning − into 'politics', erotic and riskful. Here 'wooing' rehearses the ethical middle − 'without clarification of the sexual polarity'. 'Erotic irony' qualifies the relation of authorship and authority as well as any representation, any 'beauty', within these parameters of unsettled perpetuity: 'the truly philosophical and poetical relationship'.[45]

'Irony' as this yawning rent of yearning, passing to and fro between interchangeable poles − evident throughout the authorship − is transformed two years later into the sober statement of 'irony' as 'the pathos of the middle . . . its moral too, its ethos'.[46]

I have been told that in Hebrew the words for knowing and insight have the same stem as the word for between.[47]

The famous essay 'Goethe and Tolstoy' (1922) in which the genii of Goethe and Tolstoy are compared with Dostoyevsky and Schiller, but also in the most central and sustained way with each other, itself exercises irony as 'playful reserve'. This kind of irony is no longer tension without resolution, but the harmony of eternal contraries carried by 'infinite irony' − 'as the sustained note carries the resolution'.[48] The 'and' of the title, conjunctive middle, 'plays slyly and irresponsibly' with the contrasted figures of Goethe and Tolstoy for the sake of a greater responsibility, a 'reserve' which refuses the aesthetic − 'beautiful is resolution' − and produces a politics.[49] The 'pathos of the middle . . . its moral too, its ethos', yield the 'playful reserve' of 'Folk and humanity', national and universal ethic, clearly opposed to Fascist, chauvinistic 'feasts of the solstice', and reclaiming for Germany, by expounding the greatness of Goethe, the vocation of 'bourgeois world-middle', national yet cosmopolitan culture.[50]

Out of grief at the loss of this politics of the middle, the anxiety of

44   *Letters*, ibid.
45   Ibid.
46   'Goethe and Tolstoy', p. 167, tr. p. 173.
47   Ibid., p. 167, tr. p. 174. The stem 'bin', beth-yod-nun, found in *mevin* − 'understanding' and in *havanah* − 'knowing'.
48   'Goethe and Tolstoy', p. 167, tr. p. 173.
49   Ibid., p. 166, tr. pp. 173−4.
50   Ibid., pp. 166−9, tr. pp. 173−5.

beginning is transmuted into the beginning of anxiety by delineation of 'the slowly mounting dawn of a new religious sense . . . the union of the beast-god with the god–man that will some day bring about the redemption of the race of mankind'.[51] Evidence for this 'dawn' is culled from the life and works of the four authors, considered in each case, in Goethe's phrase, as 'fragments of one great confession',[52] out of which Goethe emerges – unequivocally, in spite of all 'ironic reserve' – as the beginning towards the middle of 'the pure idea of man himself'.[53]

Goethe's plastic creativity is contrasted with Tolstoy's tendency towards idealization, two modes of 'synthesis of art and nature',[54] in terms of the legend of the giant Antaeus 'who was unconquerable because full strength streamed into him whenever he touched his mother earth'.[55] Constantly renewing contact with this source, Goethe's tactility, '*Ich bin ein Plastiker*',[56] seems the key to what 'earth', or 'nature' might mean here, and to his superior credentials as 'source', 'mother', 'dawn' – in short, beginning. Metaphorically, the giant bends majestically yet tenderly down to earth; metaphysically, Mann develops an ontology of 'origin'.

As opposed to 'critique' with its 'idealism, moralization, rhetoric', organic creativity 'is the preoccupation of the children of God and nature'.[57] This Spinozism, based on the idea 'of the perfectitude and necessity of all being, on the idea of a world free from final ends and final causes, in which evil has its rights like good',[58] amounts to a 'humility of nature' which will be 'in conflict with the disproportionate, favoured, and dogmatic presumption of spirit',[59] and with 'the profoundest concern with the salvation of one's *own soul*'.[60]

Ironic reserve wears the masks at this point of these unabashed epistemological adversaries and extends their animosity without reserve into the realm of politics, where no middle seems evident either:

> All national character belongs to the natural spirit, and all tendency towards the cosmopolitan to the spiritual. The word 'ethnic'

---

51  Ibid., pp. 168–9, tr. p. 175.
52  Ibid., p. 74, tr. p. 100.
53  Ibid., p. 168, tr. p. 174.
54  Ibid., p. 135, tr. p. 149.
55  Ibid., p. 95, tr. p. 117.
56  Ibid., p. 91, tr. p. 113.
57  Ibid., pp. 91–2, 91, tr. pp. 114, 113.
58  Ibid., p. 92, tr. p. 114.
59  Ibid., p. 97, tr. p. 118.
60  Ibid., p. 92, tr. p. 114, emphasis in German.

brings together two conceptions which we do not ordinarily connect, paganism and nationalism, thus by implication, and conversely, every super-national and human point of view is classified in our mind as Christian in spirit.[61]

While racial or national loyalty is 'aristocratic', Christianity, humanity, and civilization 'all represent the conflicting principle of the spirit of democracy, and the process of spiritualization is at the same time one of democratization'.[62] Out of these further irreconcilables, 'the pathos of renunciation' − in love, in work, in 'destiny' − emerges as Goethe's 'majestic work of spiritualization', which, unlike Tolstoy's unsuccessful struggles 'to throw off nature's yoke', amounts to a 'mandate' to civilize (*sittigende Sendung*) the national, and so create an ethos, a middle, out of such deep suffering.[63] Expounding this ethos as pedagogy, alluding to it as the new religious sense, the essayist only just avoids positing or imposing what is implied as a new political ideal 'doctrinaire and theoretic [*Konstruktives*]',[64] and reserves himself ironically on the new dawn of the 'divine animal' − beast-god/god-man − whose 'soul-economy' is posited − but with the evident irony of its evasion:

The main thing is that nothing should come too easy. Effortless nature − that is crude. Effortless spirit is without root − or substance. A lofty encounter of nature and spirit as they mutually yearn towards each other − that is man.[65]

Erotic irony of 'yearning' is here included within 'playful' ironic reserve, which will itself be sublated in the unreserved − whole-hearted and whole-bodied − 'play', or rather 'performance' of 'repetition in the feast'. At the same time, the new religiosity emerging from this confrontation with the 'dark side' of Goethe will be sublated in the 'new humanism' emerging from the subsequent confrontation with Freud − 'man and gallant knight . . . between Death and the Devil'.[66] While irony marks the border between the aesthetic-erotic and the ethical, humour − slow and sour − marks the border of the ethical and the religious or 'mythical' − both religiousness 'A' in its edification, and religiousness 'B', the paradox but only in the facetious style.

---

[61]  Ibid., pp. 121–2, tr. p. 137.
[62]  Ibid., p. 126, tr. p. 141.
[63]  Ibid., pp. 125, 124, tr. pp. 141, 140.
[64]  Ibid., p. 132, tr. p. 146, against which Goethe himself rebelled.
[65]  Ibid., p. 138, tr. p. 151.
[66]  'Freud and the Future', p. 175, tr. p. 413.

I told about beginnings, where everything came into being for the
first time.[67]

Confessed as 'the clandestine tendency of the Joseph story' in relation
to which ambition the author, 'as usual, had at the outset been quite
innocent', Mann, no longer so bashful, explicitly supplements the
story-telling by reading Freud in his own name and in the name of
'myth'. In two essays on Freud (1929 and 1936),[68] in an essay entitled
'The Theme of the Joseph Novels' (1942),[69] and in an essay 'On the
Problem of Anti-Semitism' (1937),[70] Freud is discussed in the light of
the Joseph work: the Joseph work is not discussed in the light of Freud.
The discovery of the 'unconscious' and the original feast may be posited
as the beginning only because this beginning is perennial, repeated
continually. It is this idea of repetition as a collective pattern of 'myth'
reappearing in each generation and in each individual which colours
Mann's appropriation of Freud's concepts of 'unconscious', 'id' and
'ego', so that he transforms them into a phylogenetic logos. The revelation that the feast commemorates the killing of the father and the
founding of the ethical order is secondary to its 'deeply conservative
nature', common to all 'reformations'.[71]

This feasting of Freud on his eightieth birthday and at the fount of
Mann's myth — 'making as it does the light of psychology play on
myth'[72] — concludes with a toast to a new 'humanism of the future':

> It will be a humanism standing in a different relation to the
> powers of the lower world, the unconscious, the id: a relation
> bolder, freer, blither . . .[73]

Embarrassed at this momentarily uninhibited vision of the 'poet's utopia', Mann masters his inebriation at Freud's feast and concedes that the
truth of that other feast — the feast of humanity, his hope for the future
— cannot be posited, it can only be artistically ironized. In this case, 'the

---

[67] *The Theme of the Joseph Novels*, p. 16.
[68] Mann sent the first essay to Freud who corrected it; 'Die Stellung Freuds in der modernen Geistesgeschichte', pp. 256–80; 'Freud und die Zukunft', *Essays*, Bd 3, pp. 73–92.
[69] An address delivered at the Library of Congress, 1942.
[70] This appears in *Sieben Manifeste zur 'Jüdischen Fragen', 1936–1940*.
[71] 'Die Stellung Freuds in der modernen Geistesgeschichte', p. 260.
[72] 'Freud and the Future', p. 190, tr. p. 427.
[73] Ibid., pp. 190–1, tr. p. 427; cf. 'Zum Problem des Antisemitismus', p. 37 which suggests three humanisms to the two of the Freud essay; see, too, *The Theme of the Joseph Novels*, p. 8.

Joseph of the novel' is credited with the same artistry, the same irony, the same festive facetiousness in the face of the myth as the author unguardedly exhibits himself.[74]

The 'birth of the Ego out of the mythical collective' makes the individual self-conscious that he embodies the myth, an awareness which is equally subjective conceit and substantial surrender.[75] Whether Abraham or Jacob, 'weighty with stories', dedication to God demands the 'proud assertion of the ego' which 'loftily feels itself the subject and hero of its stories'.[76] Joseph is the epitome of this conceit: in him the balance tips further towards emancipation and away from participation in the collective myth. 'The ego ... soon becomes an artistic ego .../one who, it is true, still participates in the collective and mythical, but in a banteringly spiritual and playful, purposefully conscious manner'.[77] The pathos of the Joseph ego — the stations at which its 'dominant originality' becomes repetition — depends on how the ego 'flows back from arrogant absoluteness into the collective, common'.[78]

This 'thematic' treatment of the education of Joseph places exclusive emphasis on the ego. In 'Freud and the Future', the genesis of the *Joseph* work is developed in terms of the topography of the id: 'the unconscious, the id, is primitive and irrational, is pure dynamic. It knows no values, no good or evil, no morality. It even knows no time, no temporal flow, nor any effect of time upon its psychic process.'[79] The ego, on this account, leads a 'nervous and anguished existence', hemmed in between the unconscious, the outer world and the super-ego.[80] This 'pathetic' and 'alarming' situation of the ego is, however, set aside for the general and topographically less determinate implication that 'it is our own will that unconsciously appears as inexorable objective destiny', the soul's 'own destiny', the soul's 'own contriving'.[81] Instead of highlighting the inexorable and painful conflict between the three masters of the ego, the emphasis on the timeless id leads to the agreement with Angelus Silesius' collateral that 'Abraham is in a sense the father of God' — not that God may be in the place of the father — and to the confluence in each individual of 'the typical and the individual', not to the conflict of irreconcilable identifications.[82]

---

74  'Freud and the Future', pp. 189, 190, tr. pp. 426, 427.
75  *The Theme of the Joseph Novels*, p. 17.
76  Ibid.
77  Ibid., p. 18.
78  Ibid., pp. 17, 18.
79  'Freud and the Future', pp. 178–9, tr. p. 416.
80  Ibid., pp. 179–80, tr. p. 417.
81  Ibid., pp. 180–1, tr. p. 418.
82  Ibid., pp. 183–4, tr. pp. 420–1.

Set in Hebraic and Egyptian antiquity, the ego of this mythical id is different from our own: 'less exclusive, less sharply defined. It was, as it were, open behind; it received much from the past and by repeating it gave it presentness again.'[83] Without resistances, this 'active' ego 'proudly and darkly' enjoys its mythical knowledge, 'its recurrence and its typicality'. This celebration is shared with the mythically oriented artist who respects the artistry of his characters, themselves elaborations of historical, biblical and mythological figures.

'The life in the myth, life as a sacred repetition, is a historical form of life, for the man of ancient times lived thus.'[84] In 'Freud and the Future' Mann demonstrates the novel as a kind of epic performance by deducing the homology and 'presentness' of past and future; of author, actor, reader; of ego and id. At the feast of stories and of the story — of Joseph, 'celebrant of life', enacting anew 'the story of the mangled, buried and arisen God', one 'participant', the Story-Teller of story-tellers, presents these narrated events both as 'hocus-pocus' and as 'solemn';[85] passing, as it were, from the severe style of these commentaries on *Joseph* to the facetious style of the work itself.

If the severe style of these commentaries posits the beginning and toasts the utopia of the end, the facetious style of the text suffers the anxiety of beginning by setting out the beginning of anxiety in the Gnostic 'Prelude': 'Descent into Hell'. The stories in the main body of the work then present the paradox from the ethical middle, with quasi-liturgical insistence that each personification of the middle — the mediator or story-teller — is indiscernible from and identical with the first, the beginning: Eliezer, steward and first servant from Abraham to Jacob, is '*the* Eliezer altogether' who reappears in each generation, his ego 'opened at the back'.[86] This 'lunar syntax [*Mondgrammatik*]'[87] must halt its repetitions in order to tell its tales: it becomes ironic when it represents the aesthetic-erotic elements of the *Tales*, movement *backwards* of recollection; it becomes humorous when it represents the ethical-religious elements, movement *forwards* of recollection.

'Lunar syntax' of the promiscuous moon — female to the sun, male to the earth — which, from the opening pages, symbolizes Joseph's androgyny,[88] becomes exquisitely facetious when it represents move-

---

[83] Ibid., p. 187, tr. p. 424.
[84] Ibid., p. 186, tr. p. 423.
[85] Ibid., pp. 188–9, pp. 425–6.
[86] *Joseph*, Bd 1 pp. 89–90, tr. pp. 77–8. Compare 'all the Eliezers of the past gather to shape the Eliezer of the present, so that he speaks in the first person of that Eliezer who was Abram's servant, though he was far from being the same man', 'Freud and the Future', p. 184, tr. p. 422.
[87] Title of a section, *Joseph*, Bd 1 pp. 89–90, tr. pp. 77–8.
[88] Ibid., Bd 1 pp. 43–8, tr. pp. 36–40.

ment backwards and forwards at once: in the form and figure of
Potiphar. Erotic irony resurfaces in the portrayal of Joseph as self-
consciously desirable in a way that is both masculine and feminine. This
emphasis may have been taken from Sufi literature in which the highest
compliment to a woman is 'she seems a Joseph'.[89] Overarching and
over-awing the sexual ambidexterity of Joseph is Potiphar, the eunuch,
a blubber of sexless flesh, yet in the position of authority, of the father.
The temptation of Joseph by Mut, Potiphar's wife, is overshadowed by
the law of this inarticulate hulk.

Joseph is first taken up by Potiphar when, working as his gardener,
he discourses to his master about the hermaphroditism of trees. 'Is that
a male or female tree behind you?' asks Potiphar:

> It is a fruit-bearing one, my lord, it will bear. But whether one
> should call that male or female is uncertain . . . is their power male
> or female, begetting or bearing, which produces their works? We
> can not tell, for the power is of both kinds, and the tree of life
> must have been hermaphrodite, two-sexed, as trees mostly
> are . . . the whole world is divided in twain, and we speak of male
> and female and cannot even agree in distinguishing between them,
> discussing whether the fruitful tree is male or the barren . . ./or the
> fruit-bearing nuts female and male the unfruitful which only bear
> pollen and are barren/ But the bottom of the world and the tree of
> life are neither male nor female, rather both in one. And what
> does that mean? It means they are neither. Virgin are they, like the
> bearded goddess, and are father and mother at once to the thing
> they beget, for they are above sex and their power of giving has
> nothing to do with being torn in twain.[90]

This idea is gratifying to the omnipotent and impotent Potiphar and
leads Joseph to promotion in his household. When the narration facetiously enumerates the seven reasons for Joseph rejecting the blandish-
ments of Mut, Potiphar's wife, and for preserving the 'blithe, even
supercilious chastity' of his 'brideship with God',[91] the first and fore-
most reason is that Joseph sees Potiphar not only in terms of his father
but in terms of his betrothal to the God of his own father: 'Joseph's

---

[89]   Compare the passage which introduces the story of the princess who loved a slave,
from *The Conference of the Birds*, Farid Ud-Din Attar's mystical Sufi poem: 'A great king
had a daughter whose fair face / Was like the full moon in its radiant grace. / She seemed
a Joseph, and her dimpled chin / The well that lovely youth was hidden in.' Farid Ud-Din
Attar, *The Conference of the Birds*, p. 197.

[90]   *Joseph*, Bd 2 pp. 666–7, tr. pp. 595–6.

[91]   Ibid., Bd 2 p. 845, tr. p. 751.

fantasy actually did no less than see, in the obese aristocratic person of
Mut's honorary husband the courtier of the sun, and in his melancholy
egotism, the earthly counterpart and fleshly reproduction of the wife-
less and childless, lonely and jealous God of his father, with whom he
was bent on keeping loving human faith.'[92] This potential usurpation
by the son of the rights of the father mocks the psychoanalytic meaning
of 'father' by conjuring up a risible picture of God as the castrated
father, the eunuch God. Incorporated into Joseph's phantasy, this hermeneutic irreverence is also facetious: as divine prohibition, movement
backwards, representing the erotic irony of the soul in the ethical; and
as unrepresentable Godhead, movement forwards, representing the
humour of the ethical–religious 'spirit'. The resulting facetious image of
God as eunuch is also allied to the metaphor of hermaphroditic trees.
Resourcefully delivered by Joseph to insinuate himself into Potiphar's
favour, the discourse on trees also insinuates the idea of a creative being
prior to any differentiation into male and female. With this remorseless
facetiousness, spirit – or the silence of the paradox – is made to speak
out of irony and humour, without necessarily settling the direction of
its gnostic salvation – worldwards or worldless.

The patterned psychology of *Joseph* is matched by its posited politics.
Liturgical repetition of the idea of the feast alternates with the telling of
the tales which circulate from descent into hell to re-emerge to blessings
from heaven above and from the earth beneath. The intoned insistence
on the pattern necessitates the facetious representation of any ostensibly
unprecedented experience, any relating of 'unique' events. It makes
individual suffering into a pre-established harmony of hubris and
humility, secondary to the individual's self-conscious artistry which
turns 'character' into actor, and actor into co-author of the myth s/he
embodies.

*Joseph in Egypt* is improbably set in the historical time of the short-
lived revolution of Amenhotep of the Eighteenth Dynasty. Ascending
the throne as a youth, he changed his name to Ikhnaton and his capital
city from Karnak to On in order to inaugurate a religious reformation,
which Mann – like Freud, who speculates in *Moses and Monotheism*
that Moses may have been an Egyptian adherent or inheritor of this
fleeting cult[93] – presents as a monotheistic prototype of Hebraic and
Christian 'myth'.[94] While this epoch is seen historically as the attempt

---

[92]   Ibid., Bd 2 p. 849, tr. p. 752.
[93]   Op. cit., PFL vol. 13 pp. 257–62. Mann may have been adapting Freud's argument,
although I know of no corroborative evidence of this.
[94]   *The Theme of the Joseph Novels*, pp. 12–13; *Joseph*, Bd 2 p. 700, tr. p. 624, Bd 3
pp. 1079, 1019, tr. pp. 953, 900. See Käte Hamburger, *Thomas Manns Biblisches Werk*, pp.
61–6.

to strengthen and centralize the court of Amenhotep by means of a universalizing, cosmopolitan enlightenment against the old powerful and conservative priesthood serving the traditional cult, it serves – in the cult of this authorship – to forge the link between Amenhotep's enlightenment and the non-enlightened tradition, with its ancient pantheon, its deifications of sexuality and death, subsequently mobilized by Gnosticism to represent the world as the underworld.

The names of the competing gods assumed by the succeeding Pharaohs stake out the claims of the new politics: both Amun-Re and Atum-Re are called 'Sun in his Bark', yet Amun-Re is 'rigid and strict', hostile to every sort of wide-ranging speculation, averse to foreign influence, abiding by unarguable custom and the sacred tradition; while Atum-Re is 'flexible and blithe', god of universal sunship and the going-down of the sun, assimilated when pronounced as 'Aton' to the 'youth mangled by the boar and bewailed by the flutes in Asia's gorges and groves'.[95] In this way, enlightenment and tradition, sunship and depthship, above and below, are combined in this vibrant, universal god.

The preciousness of the boy-king, 'hypersensitive and tender youth', consort of Nefertiti, founds a conceit comparable to Joseph: the former's mix of assertive sovereignty with intrinsic frailty contrasting with the latter's mix of intrinsic predominance with contingent vulnerability. Aestheticizing politics, Mann romances about this royal reformer, 'searcher of God, like Joseph's forefathers, and enamoured of a dreamy religion of love',[96] while Freud follows through what this reformation suppressed as well as the new doctrines that it posited: confiscation of the property belonging to the old temple and persecution of the popular propensity towards the old god.[97] While Mann's account of this epoch, conflating the historical with the biblical, culminates in the description of vast sums pouring into Pharaoh's coffers, riches resulting from the measures taken as a result of Joseph's interpretation of Pharaoh's dreams, and in the report of grain distributed with largesse to the people,[98] it then subsides into the tearful finale of Jacob's final blessings and death, overshadowing a passing reference – at odds, of course, with the wisdom and happy outcome of Pharaoh's actions in the biblical source – to the growing estrangement of Pharaoh from his people, who '[i]n his anguished zeal for his own revelation', suppressed the old revelation and now reaps a bitter harvest of 'hopeless strife' between the old and new deities, isolation from the hostile people, suspicious even

---

95   *Joseph*, Bd 3 p. 700, tr. p. 624.
96   *The Theme of the Joseph Novels*, p. 13.
97   'Moses and Monotheism', pp. 261-2.
98   *Joseph*, Bd 3 p. 1316, tr. p. 1165.

of his own courtiers.[99] Freud informs us fully of the political outcome of the historical source. The 'mood of fanatical vindictiveness' among priesthood and people provoked by measures taken against them, found 'free expression after the King's death'.[100] A short period of shadowy successors was followed by a period of anarchy until 'a general, Haremhab, succeeded in restoring order'.[101] Thus ended '[t]he glorious Eighteenth Dynasty' — its empire lost, the ancient religion and the ancient politics restored: 'The Aten religion was abolished, Akenaten's royal city was destroyed and plundered and his memory proscribed as that of a criminal.'[102]

This outcome, the seed of which is sown but not grown in *Joseph in Egypt* and *Joseph the Provider*, clarifies the inconsistencies and evasions which arise when the ethical is posited as unequivocal, as new beginning, symbolized by the politics of this religious reformation, to clear the stage for the psychological patterning, the repetition of the myth. Poet's pseudo-Platonic utopia — parallel pre-patterning of politics and psychology — produces an aestheticized middle which refuses equally equivocation of the ethical and anxiety of beginning. Gnostic prevarication presides as the residual integrity over this transparent medium which, darkly hinted, is a glass obscured.

The eschatological promise of repetition in the feast — a 'present' humanity; 'present' not as recollection or nostalgia for lost plenitude, but as acknowledgement of difficulty that will release the burden of potential future — is narrated or 'performed' in *Joseph* as the education of his existence. Education of existence without anxiety of existence — neither Kierkegaardian, nor Freudian 'repression resistance' — dilutes the unconscious into the untroubled, blithe artistry of a confidence-man. Psychologically, the feast is turned into a tea party,[103] while, politically, it turns into a bloodbath instead of a ritual — a simultaneous acknowledgement and containment of human destructiveness and human creativity.

[99]  Ibid., Bd 3 p. 1355, tr. pp. 1200–1, six pages before the end of the work in translation, seven and a half in German.
[100]  'Moses and Monotheism', p. 261.
[101]  Ibid.
[102]  Ibid., p. 262.
[103]  A tea party takes place in *Joseph*, in which the twelfth *Sura* of the Koran is elaborated. Zukeika (the Islamic name of Potiphar's wife) holds a party to demonstrate to her women friends how irresistible Joseph is. In Mann's version, Mut has fruit served with delicate fruit knives and she carefully times Joseph's first appearance. As he appears, all the matrons accidentally cut themselves with the knives, which is taken as evidence of Joseph's great sexual power; see 'The Ladies' Party', Bd. 2 pp. 902–16, tr. pp. 797–809.

Repetition is no longer a *cultus* but a barbarism of pure culture − a repetition in a third, additional sense to the two familiar ones of movement backwards and movement forwards: new, futural, open at the front, but only finitely 'whole', as partial in its zeal as the self-consciousness separated from ethical life out of which it arose. This repetition creates new possibilities, effects change from old gods, old institutions, the old law, but such change, when it settles, reinforces and accentuates the old oppositions. Unroutinized charisma delegitimized, the old domination returns, all the more precipitately when the posited yet 'dreamy' charisma of the king sleeps away the dialectic of customary institutions deliberately overthrown. This substitution of an overly rationalized 'ethical' for the equivocation of the middle brings both the psychology and the politics into discredit. Not heeding the warning evident in his own authorial facetiousness, the author of *Joseph* would continue, blithe and artful, in the mask of the actor − thereby abrogating the burden of his authority. The confession from the 'Prologue' to his 'non-political' reflections remains relevant to this attempt to take myth out of the hands of the Fascists:

> An artist's work, an artist's writing: a person speaks here who
> . . . is not accustomed to speak but rather to have others, people
> and things, speak, and who therefore 'has' others speak even
> when he seems to be, *and thinks* he is, speaking directly himself. A
> trace of the actor, the lawyer, of play, artistry, detachment, of
> lack of conviction and of that poetic sophistry . . . It is not for me
> to solve the paradox of this mixture of dialectics and genuine
> honestly striving will to truth . . .[104]

Let it not be solved but let it be noted that, in the case of *Joseph*, it is possible to pretend to too little authority as well as too much. Blithe actor couples with facetious author.

## *Tradition and Prophecy in the Severe and in the Facetious Style*

There was not one kind of Eris alone, but all over the earth there are two . . . one fosters evil war and battle, being cruel . . . the other, elder daughter of dark night . . . set in the roots of the earth . . . stirs up even the shiftless to toil; for a man grows eager to work when he considers his neighbour . . . this Eris is whole-

---

[104] Mann, *Reflections of a Non-Political Man*, p. 3.

some for men. And potter is angry with potter, and craftsman with craftsman, and beggar is jealous of beggar and minstrel of minstrel.[105]

Hesiod opens *Works and Days*, the poem on agriculture, by distinguishing between two goddesses both named 'Eris' — one goddess of destructive envy, the other goddess of creative emulation, goad to excel. Nietzsche, in one place, would seem to deduce the actuality of these two modes of 'envy' which Hesiod merely places side by side:

> Where equality really has prevailed and been permanently established there arises that tendency which is on the whole accounted immoral and can hardly be conceived of in a state of nature: *envy*. The envious man is conscious of every respect in which the man he envies exceeds the common measure and desires to push him down to it — or to raise himself up to the height of the other: out of which there arise two different modes of action which Hesiod designated as the evil and the good Eris.[106]

This apparently unrelenting perspicacity concerning the rivalry of equals, symbolized by the goddess-doubles, 'Eris', will turn out to be one tone in Nietzsche's finely nuanced appreciation of the centrality of *agon* — organized competition and contest — to Greek ethics: in Homer, in gymnastics, in the *Symposium* — birth and banquet of philosophy itself.[107] Formalized displaying of reverence and respect for the adversary becomes the basis for his idea in the *Genealogy of Morals* of 'nobility', with its love for the enemy; an account of Greek *paideia* in which violence is acknowledged by its perpetrators as the education of existence, as *Bildung*, but without, *mirabile dictu*, any hint of sacrifice.[108]

Now it could be argued that the account of Thomas Mann's *Joseph and his Brothers* developed so far as 'performance' and as facetious authorship has proceeded like Hamlet without the Prince, for it has resolutely overlooked the centrality of sacrifice — the founding fratricide — to Mann's recasting of a non-mythical biblical source as 'myth'. The

---

[105] Hesiod's *Works and Days*, lines 11–24, pp. 3–5, tr. amended.
[106] Nietzsche, 'The Wanderer and his Shadow', *Human All Too Human*, Bk 2, para. 29, *Werke* I, p. 891, tr. p. 315.
[107] See 'Homers Wettkampf', *Werke* III, pp. 292–5; 'Expeditions of an Untimely Man', *Twilight of the Idols*, para. 23, *Werke* III, pp. 449–50, tr. pp. 80–1, 'Philosophy in the manner of Plato should rather be defined as an erotic contest and inward intensification of the old agonal gymnastics and their *presuppositions*'.
[108] See *On the Genealogy of Morals*, first essay, para. 10, *Werke* III, pp. 230–1, p. 39.

weak and selective assimilation of Freud's account of the feast – totem of the murdered father, taboo of incest – to Mann's mythic playfulness, it would follow, indicates a graver *gestus*: murder of the brother, founding fratricide, act of sacrificial violence against an arbitrary victim, repeated in ritual, which stills the crisis of the reciprocal violence of equals and re-establishes the differences of social harmony. Authorship then, *contra* Kierkegaard, becomes apostleship, for, apart from Christ – according to René Girard – it is the definitive vocation of the novel, but not of the romance, to reveal mimetic violence and its effects:

> Novelistic conversion calls to mind the *analusis* of the Greek and Christian rebirth. In this final movement the novelist reaches the heights of Western literature; he merges with the great religious ethics and the most elevated forms of humanism, those which have chosen the least accessible part of man.[109]

In his ambition to take myth out of the hands of the Fascists and to develop a new, 'difficult' humanism, Mann would concur with the idea of authorship proclaimed here. In the further implication that this ethical insight justifies reworking any literary source – including the biblical – in terms of its 'mythical' presuppositions, Mann and Girard would seem to have been to school together.

> From the perspective of unanimous victimage finally revealed, even the more archaic biblical texts look like reinterpretations of earlier myths powerful enough to undermine the mythical products of victimage *because* they side with the scapegoat and turn back this demonic figure into an innocent victim. Behind the story told by the eleven brothers to Joseph's father, Jacob, there is the vengeful consensus of this violent community and later on, in Egypt, this vengeful consensus reappears once more when Joseph is imprisoned.[110]

While Sandor Goodhart has developed further this reading of the biblical 'I am Joseph',[111] Thomas Mann would seem, like René Girard, to thematize metabiblical myth itself, and to extend Girard's attribution

---

[109]   Girard, *Deceit, Desire and the Novel*, p. 308.
[110]   'An Interview with René Girard', '*To Double Business Bound*', p. 226.
[111]   Sandor Goodhart, '"I am Joseph": René Girard and the Prophetic Law', in *Violence and Truth*, pp. 53–74.

of demythologization from biblical writers and the great novelists, now including himself, to biblical 'characters' themselves.

'From the days of Set', the Egyptian refrain 'relished' by Joseph, punctuates the 'Prelude' to *Joseph and his Brothers*, offering a mythic elaboration of the story-teller's 'once upon a time', as original time.[112] For the time is that of 'the sacrifice, murder and dismemberment' of Osiris and Set for the sake of the succession, 'so that Osiris, the Sacrifice, now ruled as lord of the dead and everlasting king of the lower world'.[113] From the essay on the 'Theme' of the novel it would appear, too, that the stress on original time serves to reveal the foundations of the world:

> the attractive novelty ... of this kind of fable telling [was] that everything was there for the first time, that one foundation took place after the other, the foundation of love, of envy, of hatred, of murder, and of much else.[114]

If 'myth' also means for Mann, as he tirelessly repeats, making the 'past', that is, these foundations, timelessly present, then, on this Girardian reading, Joseph acquires the status of a ritual to end all rituals. Mann's revealing of the connection of the Hebraic story with other ancient 'timeless mythologies', the Babylonian, the Egyptian and the Greek, which are 'mingled' and 'made transparent' by each other, and his insisting that Joseph 'enacts in his own person' the Adonis and the Tammuz−Osiris myth, each 'mangled, buried and arisen' gods (with the additional scandal that Joseph knows and celebrates this coincidence of revelations more with mirthful intelligence than with understated wisdom),[115] would confirm Girard's argument that an act of unanimous, murderous sacrifice forms the foundation of the social order, its effectiveness depending − outside fiction − on the participants' ignorance of the arbitrary nature of their choice of victim.[116] This could also explain the facetious and blithe tone of Mann's work. For by enacting, and by making Joseph himself enjoy a conscious disenchantment of original violence, Mann must, according to this account, be aware of the risk that he cannot control the possible effect of this revelation − the outbreak of more violence. Depriving humankind of its hitherto blissful ignorance of the unanimous sacrificial solution to social crisis,

---

[112]  *Joseph*, Bd 1 p. 15, tr. p. 12.
[113]  Ibid., Bd 1 pp. 15, 14, tr. pp. 12, 11.
[114]  *The Theme of the Joseph Novels*, pp. 16–17.
[115]  'Freud and the Future', p. 189, tr. p. 426. *Joseph*, Bd 1 p. 18, tr. p. 15.
[116]  Girard, *Things Hidden Since the Foundation of the World*, BK 1, Chs 1 and 2, pp. 3–83.

such novelistic 'enacting' runs the risk of perpetuating the reciprocal violence it thereby reveals. Intellectual and artistic disenchantment of original violence may itself unleash further violence; for it amounts to sacrificial — that is, unanimous — rejection of unanimous sacrifice.[117] The only alternative, in Girard's terms, to 'the arrival of the ultimate emergency', would be a non-sacrificial love, which cannot be commanded but only revealed as in the great novels and the Christian Gospels.[118]

Sacrifice, on this reading, has its origin in mimetic rivalry, its effectiveness in the 'arbitrary' victim, whose selection will, nevertheless, be provided with rationalizing justifications, its result in re-establishing social harmony. The oldest stories of the Old Testament including the Joseph stories are covered by the Girardian hypothesis that assimilates biblical 'myths' to World Mythology under the sign of the scapegoat, and also identifies in them the stirrings of a demythologizing impulse which culminates in the Gospels.[119]

Three 'great moments' are summarized in this hypothesis that religion 'is organized around a more or less violent disavowal of human violence':[120]

1  Dissolution in conflict, removal of the differences and hierarchies which constitute the community in its wholeness;
2  the *all against one* of collective violence;
3  the development of interdictions and rituals.[121]

To the first moment belongs the theme of warring brothers; to the second moment belongs the resort to violence — the expulsion of one of the brothers which resolves the crisis and restores 'differentiation'; to the third moment, the establishment of interdiction and sacrifice, belongs, in the case of the Joseph story, the deifying of the victim in Egypt after his 'sacrifice', and the blood on the tunic as remnant of the hidden sacrifice.[122] However, there is a dialectic of concealment and

---

[117] *Violence and the Sacred*, pp. 24–5; 'In fact, demystification leads to constantly increasing violence, a violence perhaps less "hypocritical" than the violence it seeks to expose, but more energetic, more virulent, and the harbinger of something far worse — a violence that knows no bounds'.

[118] '*To Double Business Bound*', p. 227; *Things Hidden Since the Foundation of the World*, pp. 127–8, and Bk 2, ch. 2, and pp. 276–80, pp. 180–223; see, too, J. P. Dupuy, 'Totalization and Misrecognition', in *Violence and Truth*, p. 79.

[119] See *Things Hidden Since the Foundation of the World*, Bk 11, ch. 1, pp. 141–79.

[120] Ibid., p. 166.

[121] Ibid., p. 142.

[122] Ibid., pp. 142, 149–52.

revelation in this story. From a strictly 'mythological' perspective, 'the eleven brothers would appear first of all as the passive objects of the violence' of their favouritized brother.[123] An original pre-biblical myth would have sanctioned the charge of hubris against Joseph, malevolent hero.[124] However, each of the two combined biblical sources seeks to rehabilitate Joseph at the expense of his brothers 'even if each is also concerned with partially exempting one of the brothers from blame' — Reuben and Judah.[125] More explicitly, the accusation of Potiphar's wife against Joseph — with its incestuous undertones — is not mythically corroborated but undermined.[126] As a result, the rehabilitation of Joseph at the end of the story has a desacralizing not a deifying effect, and the Joseph story belongs to the Judaeo-Christian progressive scriptural demystification of mythic sacrifice which brings the victim to light. This prefigures the Gospel revelation of the founding murder.[127]

The evident counter-intuitive aspects of this account of a pre-biblical myth, repeated and undermined in the biblical version, appear to be uncannily confirmed by Mann's novelistic 'enacting' — whether justified as a deduction of the biblical text or not. Mann's mythic retelling emphasizes both poles — the mythic patterning and the progressive demythologization.

First, Joseph is absorbed, egoistically and collectively, in the myth of Set — 'sacrificed' by a brother — foundation of all myth; yet Joseph's story is also distanced from any actual sacrifice or murder and contrasted with a primitive epoch of child sacrifice — with Laban's clumsiness in not listening to God and behaving 'according to outworn custom' in slaughtering his son and burying him in the foundation of his house.[128] Girard places the old saw on new foundations: the Law and the Prophets constitute a *praefiguratio Christi*, 'a first step outside the sacrificial system, and the first gradual withering of sacrificial resources'.[129]

Second, the mimetic rivalry of the brothers, which causes increasing violence among them until the sacrificial crisis leads to their unification against an arbitrary victim who is subsequently sacralized, is presented both mimetically *and* knowingly by Joseph himself under the mythic heading 'The Grove of Adonis', assimilated to the founding fratricide of

[123]  Ibid., pp. 151–2.
[124]  Ibid., p. 152.
[125]  Ibid.
[126]  Ibid.
[127]  Ibid., pp. 153, 154, 158.
[128]  *The Theme of the Joseph Novels*, pp. 19–20; *Joseph*, Bd 1 p. 354, tr. p. 317.
[129]  *Things Hidden Since the Foundation of the World*, pp. 205–6; pp. 154, 268.

Tammuz.[130] From the beginning of the story, the 'mimetic' rivalry of doubles predominates over 'acquisitive' rivalry, for the privilege and blessing of first-born sonship is bestowed on Joseph, who is not first born, by Jacob, 'with the most arbitrary exercise of authority'.[131] The nominal nature of this right provokes the mimetic crisis among the brothers, rivals and doubles of each other. In the 'Grove of Adonis' Joseph initiates Benjamin into the meaning of the myth — inadvertently displaying his own investment in its violence, while apparently leading them both beyond violence. Surrounded by miniature seed boxes, symbols of the funeral feast of Adonis, Joseph envinces great irritation when Benjamin attempts to imitate his myrtle wreath. This irascibility is discerned by the younger brother to arise from the jealous guarding of the blessing of 'first-bornship', bestowed but not inherited. In this subtle way, Joseph himself reveals mimetic unease, prey to rivalry with the brother who is closest, most qualified as double. When, subsequently, he initiates Benjamin into the mystery of sacrifice, his telling of the meaning of the myth poignantly displays knowledge and ignorance: knowledge of the violence assuaged by the sacrifice, ignorance of his own tendency towards it; knowing himself as victim-to-be, not knowing himself as roused to the same violence. In this way, Joseph's telling the tale of his own deification as victim implicates himself, and the innocence passes from the all-too-omniscient victim to the child-witness, Benjamin, who registers his older brother's aggression and vulnerability, but does not speak it back. Benjamin, disquieted, yet intent on hearing the secret dissolved in Joseph's tale of sacrifice — collective lamentation, and resurrection — applauds Joseph knowingly when, at its concluding, the older brother places the sacrificial garland on his own head.[132]

Third, by revealing the ill-will of Joseph, victim but also mimetic double, this apparently embellishing yet, in effect, critical episode confirms and inverts the Girardian idea of the mythic malevolence of the hero which always covers up the arbitrary choice and innocence of the victim. For here Joseph is revealed to be 'malevolent', to be as invested in mimetic rivalry and violence as his brothers, and, from the Adonis episode on, his mix of hubris and humility in knowing the pattern he enacts is overshadowed by his further, fundamental ignorance of his stake in it. Thus his restoration to his brothers is not sacralized as a resurrection; instead it is presented as a learning experi-

---

[130]  *Joseph*, Bd 1 pp. 328–42, tr. pp. 293–306.
[131]  Ibid., Bd 1 p. 61, tr. p. 52.
[132]  Ibid., Bd 1 pp. 330–1, tr. p. 295.

ence for all the parties involved: the psychology of what each knows
and does not want to know is transcended by mutual acknowledgement
of violence, which includes the violence of Jacob's arbitrariness and the
brothers' reciprocal mimesis — 'God has forgiven us'.[133] The work ends
with Jacob's new hierarchy of blessings for the future in which differences are re-established, with Joseph's sons, Ephraim and Manasseh,
who are included, but with Joseph, alone among the brothers,
excluded.[134] No mythic exclusion, nor, simply, atemporal repetition in
the feast, but a beginning of exoneration which will last only as long as
collective and individual implication in both violence and peace continue to be acknowledged.

Fourth and finally, the Girardian hypothesis of the scapegoat could
cover the utopia, the un-placeability, of the Gnostic spirit of story-
telling as presented in the 'Prelude': unsure whether it should aid the
death of the world by drawing *psyche* back to its unfallen origin, or
advance the life of the world by encouraging the adventures of *eros*.
This nice ambiguity of life and death — that to enlighten life or the soul
could result in the death of the 'world' — may indicate that to abolish
death, that is, 'sacrifice', would be to arrest what has passed for 'life' —
reciprocal violence assuaged by founding violence — which Gnosticism
of all religious soteriologies has explicitly and uninhibitedly attributed
to the violence of demiurgic God or aeons and emissaries. Perhaps (God
forbid!) the Gnostic story-teller anticipates that he may provoke another
vaticide — murder of the prophet — if his revelation of the meaning of
the tradition should suffer the same fate and achieve the same status as
the original Scriptures: 'immolation' of the seer, and perpetuation of the
sacrificial principle at the basis of Western culture.[135]

The very speciousness of this Girardian reading of Mann's *Joseph* has,
nevertheless, hinted at the dialectic restrained in its key terms: 'violence', 'law', 'love'. To make this account of *Joseph* as an absolute
beginning hold, Mann's ethical middle has to bear the repressed
equivocation in its facetious style; whereas Kierkegaard, pseudonymous, aesthetic and witty, 'suspends' the ethical; Girard expatiates in
the implacable 'severe style'.

In the morphogenetic account of 'hominization' deduced in *Things
Hidden Since the Foundation of the World* and presented pre-critically as a
'fundamental anthropology', Girard insists that law, conceived solely as
prohibition, has the transhistorical *function* of curbing pre-existing,

---

[133]   Ibid., Bd 3 p. 1302, tr. p. 1152.
[134]   Ibid., Bd 3 p. 1333, tr. p. 1180.
[135]   *Things Hidden Since the Foundation of the World*, p. 249.

originative, imitative violence; he does not consider that it might be the changing *form* by which domination, 'violence', is configured in each historical jurisdiction.[136] Yet this positing of mimesis and murder as the secret precondition of law is betrayed almost as soon as it is proposed:

> Primitive societies have never shared our conception of violence. For us, violence has a conceptual autonomy, a specificity that is utterly unknown to primitive societies. We tend to focus on the individual act, whereas primitive societies attach only limited importance to it and have essentially pragmatic reasons for refusing to isolate such an act from its context. This context is one of violence. What permits us to conceive abstractly of an act of violence and to view it as an isolated crime is the power of a juridicial institution that transcends all antagonists.[137]

The circularity imbedded in this 'extending' of the abstract idea of the individual 'violent' act to its concrete context, also denoted and described as 'violent', indicates the historical context and precondition of the theory in a way which is not intended. The isolating of violence from law is here revealed — but not conceded — to belong to a phenomenology of historical and juridical experience. The stages of this phenomenology — which belies his own explicit reasoning — may be assembled from Girard's main works: the legal preconditions of violence in primitive societies from *Violence and the Sacred*; the political history of violence in the nineteenth century from *Deceit, Desire and the Novel*; while in *Things Hidden Since the Foundation of the World*, law can be discerned in the exposition of the New Testament as revealing violence and counterposing and teaching 'non-differentiated love',[138] which is meant, however, to be located as far beyond prohibition as violence is meant to precede it. In short, throughout the Girardian *corpus*: *ubi* violence — *ibi ius*: wherever 'violence' is posited or abolished, there law is presupposed and may be extricated.

The absence of irony — or its dramatic cognates, humour or facetiousness — in the presentation of a theory which itself argues the necessity of assuming what it has to explain, is striking. The 'invisibility' of the founding murder means that mimetic rivalry and violence can only be discerned in the presence of the law and order they originate. The style is severe in spite of this discursive circularity because 'societies' with a judicial system are compared with 'societies' of direct

---

[136] Ibid., Bk 1, ch. 1, pp. 3–47.
[137] Ibid., pp. 11–12.
[138] Ibid., p. 270.

revenge — which is to presuppose the concept of ordered relationships, or 'society'. By relating 'all prohibition and ritual', that is, what is forbidden and what is celebrated in controlled repetition, to mimetic conflict, the negative and ecstatic connotations of social and legal order are exhibited, while the positive connotations of social and legal order are smuggled into the exposition of the blood-feud from which the ideas of violence and of justice as vengeance are fundamentally derived.[139]

Since the idea of a violent act and also of 'violence' as such is abstract, conceivable only by virtue of a judicial system 'that transcends all antagonists', that isolates individual acts and classifies them, a violent 'context' is, admittedly, presupposed — not as a lapse but as an always lurking presence — even in the most advanced judicial system.[140] This 'context' is the blood-feud, explicit in primitive 'societies', incipient in all. The blood-feud, described as the cycle of vengeance, its motivation 'the vengeful imitation of the preceding murder', can only be stopped by 'sacrifice', that is, by a death that 'does not automatically entail a [further] act of vengeance.'[141] All religious and judicial or legal institutions are seen as 'curative' methods designed 'to deflect this mode of vengeance.'[142] The main distinction between a religious and a judicial method is that an independent legal authority frees people 'from the terrible obligations of vengeance'. The presence of such a 'restraining force' in 'policed' societies reduces the constant tensions of primitive societies so that 'the relationships between individuals, including total strangers, is characterized by an extraordinary air of informality, flexibility, and even audacity'.[143]

In this objectified historical and juridical phenomenology, all social institutions are conceived equally as repetition backwards. Law, order and justice are presupposed and undermined at the same time. For even the primitive 'society' of the blood-feud implies formal and ritualized justice in a way which Girard denies applies to any society, primitive or advanced:

> The idea of justice as a balanced scale, an exercise in exquisite impartiality, is utterly foreign to this theory, which sees the roots of justice in differences among men and the demise of justice in the elimination of these differences.[144]

---

[139]  Ibid., pp. 12, 21; *Violence and the Sacred*, chs 1 and 2, pp. 1–67, *passim*.
[140]  *Things Hidden Since the Foundation of the World*, p. 12; *Violence and the Sacred*, p. 17.
[141]  *Things Hidden Since the Foundation of the World*, ibid.; *Violence and the Sacred*, p. 13.
[142]  *Violence and the Sacred*, pp. 15, 21–2.
[143]  Ibid., p. 20.
[144]  Ibid., p. 51.

However, the distinction between two kinds of justice drawn here is without a difference. For the classic definition of justice is purely formal: that fairness consists in treating like cases alike. It implies that justice has always meant what Girard wants to contrast it with — the re-establishing of differences judged to be just. 'Like' cases treated alike implies the identification of relevant differences which justify differential treatment. It follows that the demise of justice could equally well be described as the elimination of differences without compromising the idea of impartial justice. The blood-feud exemplifies such judgement as much as any other restorative institution. However, Girard has defined the blood-feud as depending exclusively on subsumptive judgement and reserves the form of discriminative judgement to contrast with it.

While retributive or commutative justice can therefore be literally seen as a form of *justice*, retributive justice is usually contrasted with distributive justice: tribal law with the law of the city. But Girard will not bring justice into the city. It is therefore not justice he demystifies but democracy. For Athena to have her right next to the Furies involves the recognition that there are different *kinds* of law — without any one kind having priority over any other. Girard's distinction between primitive and advanced 'societies' reveals that he does implicitly conceptualize this. For this distinction presupposes the social or law not as prohibition but as form — a form of order, 'society', which will also be a form of violence. If Girard were to expound the *Oresteia* instead of concentrating on Oedipus and Dionysus,[145] the transition from kin vengeance to democracy would emerge. Both constitute forms of justice, and the sacrifice under each regime is never simply of a 'victim' or 'scapegoat'; it is the witnessing by the transgressor, together with chorus and audience, of having 'injured in himself the same life that he has injured'.[146]

Although Girard has claimed that in his early work *Deceit, Desire and the Novel* (more accurately entitled in the original: *Mensonge romantique et vérité romanesque*, which might be translated as *Romantic Mendacity and Novelistic Truth*) he had not yet fully uncovered the unanimous victimage mechanism,[147] he develops there an account of 'metaphysical desire' which shows the 'victim' to be fully implicated in a dialectic with its other; and which contextualizes their contest not in a vicious circle of violence but in the political history of modernity, independently defined.

---

[145]   Ibid., 'Oedipus and the Surrogate Victim' and 'Dionysus', chs. 3 and 5, pp. 68–88, 119–42.
[146]   Hegel, 'The Spirit of Christianity and its Fate', in *Early Theological Writings*, p. 445, tr. p. 232.
[147]   'Interview', '*To Double Business Bound*', pp. 199–200.

The thesis that desire is mimetic and 'metaphysical' is argued on two fronts: it is intended to puncture the vanity of romantic, modern man who believes that his desires are spontaneous and autonomous; and to refuse the 'Hegelian' idea that conflict or struggle is dialectical, that it inaugurates 'the reign of spirit', or in other terms, that negation is determinate.[148] 'Metaphysical' desire is not physical — not desire for an object — but desire for what the other, the 'mediator', desires, so that, secretly revered as model, he becomes a rival and obstacle.[149] This mediation becomes increasingly 'internal' as the contact between the mediator and the subject becomes increasingly close, that is, it will emerge, as there is more social equality between the two.[150]

'Victimage' is here understood as the contagion of the internal mediation of desire: that one catches one's desires, as it were, from one's neighbour, who may well have caught them from oneself in the first place. Desire is thereby redoubled by being shared, and this 'double' or reciprocal or negative mediation of imitation defines modern society.[151] Awareness of this mimetic nature of desire produces a master—slave relationship where rapid role-reversals of master and slave may be deliberately engineered by dissembling one's own desire and provoking the desire of the rivalrous, enslaved other by pretending to a desire one does not feel:

> The struggle ends when one of the partners admits his desire and humbles his pride. Henceforth no reversal of imitation is possible, for the *slave's* admitted desire destroys that of the *master* and ensures his genuine indifference.[152]

Staking one's freedom against the other's is reduced here to this stasis of the slave's violent desire met with the violence of the master's vain indifference.[153] Spuriously distinguished from Hegel's dialectic of master and slave, which is projected back into a pre-bourgeois violent past, Girard claims that 'we all have a vague feeling' that 'only a synthesis' of this dialectic with 'the unhappy consciousness' will suffice. Vagueness becomes the exact claim that such a synthesis is 'precisely [*sic*] what the novelistic dialectic permits us to glimpse'.[154] By claiming that the

---

[148]   *Deceit, Desire and the Novel*, pp. 16, 110.
[149]   Ibid., p. 13.
[150]   Ibid., p. 9.
[151]   Ibid., pp. 99–101.
[152]   Ibid., p. 109.
[153]   Ibid.
[154]   Ibid., pp. 111–12.

Hegelian dialectic rests on fear, defined as 'physical courage', which alone determines who is master and who slave, Girard is able to claim as his own the exposition of unhappy consciousness as the master–slave struggle internalized and removed from any physical correlates, thereby detracting from the pivot of work, which mediates and relieves the slave's fear and makes the master dependent on the slave in Hegel's account. This creativity in work is then disowned and projected on to the supernatural actuality of the unhappy consciousness, which does not, therefore, as Girard would have it, relive 'the primordial struggle' by staking his freedom on the least of his desires.[155]

It is this denial that subjectivity has any substance — whether ethical or work-ethical — that makes Girard's account of mimetic desire 'metaphysical' in a sense he does not admit: *a priori* and posited. When he sets 'metaphysical' violence in the 'modern' rather than the primitive, Greek or biblical context, he merely reproduces its symptoms, although the account reveals, in effect, a causation it cannot concede.

'The unhappiness of modernity', as evident in the novels of Stendhal and Balzac, is attributed solely to the increase in 'internal mediation' and the rivalry of equals. This is related to change in political organization, which displaces class and social relations, but not to the separation of the state from civil society which it indicates. The changing configuration of social violence which goes together with the development of civil or bourgeois law is conceptualized as pre-legal nature:

> The revolutionaries thought they would be destroying vanity when they destroyed the privileges of the noble ... Who is there left to imitate after the 'tyrant'? Henceforth men shall copy each other; idolatry of one person is replaced by hatred of a hundred thousand rivals.[156]

This is summed up in the cynical slogan: '*Men will become gods for each other*'.[157] The resulting political conflict under a constitutional monarchy is traced, following Stendhal, to the replacement of 'gay' vanity by the 'sad' vanity of the aristocracy, fallen to an ignoble, hence bourgeois, defence of privilege. 'Principles no longer cause rivalry; it is a metaphysical rivalry, which slips into contrary principles.'[158] This is taken to confirm the durability of 'internal mediation' — rivalry induced by a

---

[155]  Ibid., p. 112.
[156]  Ibid., p. 119.
[157]  Ibid., emphasis in original.
[158]  Ibid., p. 131.

socially close and equal model – regardless of historical specificity and political possibilities. The symptoms of social and political life are posited as the underlying structure of motivation because the perspective of metaphysical desire and metaphysical rivalry is unable to comprehend what it presupposes. There is no 'internal mediation' in Girard's account but only a focus on '[h]istoric and psychic evolution'[159] – on an account of the anxiety of honour which develops when the bourgeoisie inherits the social norms of aristocracy.[160] The perspective of 'mediation' would, by contrast, unravel how abstract individual rights are internalized so that each individual becomes unequal to him or herself, and would show how this social insecurity of identity inhibits participation in the state and in politics. It would show how political antagonisms are mediated by social relations; and how crises of individual and class identity are mediated by political impossibilities. It would show how mutual violence arises from specific legal forms, not how violence, distinguishable solely in terms of 'increasing' quantity, 'functions' transhistorically, across principles.

Girard concludes that what nineteenth-century writers saw as the evolution of republicanism or democracy would be seen today as the 'evolution' of totalitarianism:

> As the mediator comes nearer the concrete differences between men grow smaller, abstract opposition plays an even larger role in individual and collective existence . . . every human force is braced in a struggle that is as relentless as it is senseless, since no concrete difference or positive value is involved. Totalitarianism is precisely this. The social and political aspects of this phenomenon cannot be distinguished from its personal and private aspects.[161]

Tradition and prophecy *in the severe style* leads to this cynicism. Positing its own authority as unproblematic, it ends up positing a *finis* – an absolute end: all desires mobilized 'in the service of nothingness', from which only the novelist, who gives up being an eternal victim and gives up seeing his beloved as a monstrous divinity, may convert.[162] Tradition and prophecy *in the facetious style* – Mann's relentless attention to the authority of authorship – keeps undermining its absolute beginning, and returns, unwittingly, to the equivocation of the middle.

[159]  Ibid., p. 129.
[160]  See Elias, *The Civilizing Process*, Vols 1 and 2.
[161]  *Deceit, Desire and the Novel*, pp. 137–8.
[162]  Ibid., pp. 138, 299.

## *Violence-in-Love*

In both cases, Mann's and Girard's, the feast is spoiled: Mann's repetition in the feast of a new, difficult humanism; Girard's re-affirmation of *agape*, the original Christian love-feast, love without violence. This sect mentality becomes the only refuge for humankind's invincible enslavement to violence, and even this is dangerous to proclaim.[163] The repeatedly posited beginning in Mann and the repeatedly posited end in Girard, display the same lack of faith in the violence to be found in love, the love to be found in violence – the law to be found in both. Gnosticism, explicit in Mann, implicit in Girard, results from the attempt of each to abolish the ethical instead of suspending and releasing it. Ambitious to evade both the anxiety of beginning and the equivocation of the middle, these authorships, nevertheless, reveal the political histories they presuppose. This comparison of Mann's masked Gnostic authorship with Girard's unmasked Gnostic authorship brings out the politics of anxiety and the anxiety of politics in Kierkegaard's pseudonymous and signed Christian authorship. And it is the latter who also turns out to have the most knowing and most loving relationship to violence, murder – 'sacrifice'.

If Mann admits a Gnostic soteriology, Girard evinces a Gnostic sociology: creation is evil and the creator God is a malevolent demiurge demanding violent sacrifice, while the Godhead is the god of love; humanity is not sinful but unenlightened – its fate hitherto depending on ignorance, its future on whether it can take on the truth; human society is not founded on order but on chaos[164] – the chaos of undifferentiated mimesis, alleviated, spasmodically, by sacrifice, prohibition and ritual; Girard's 'spirit', like Mann's, is unsure whether it brings life or death – for the prophecy may provoke another vaticide. Acosmology coupled with the doctrine and romance of the soul characterize equally Mann's universal poetry and Girard's new science.[165]

---

[163] Girard refers fleetingly to Nygren's exposition of *agape* to capture the alternative love he is recommending (*Things Hidden Since the Foundation of the World*, pp. 215, 277), even though he admits that his anthropology cannot deal with 'questions of *faith* and *grace*', p. 216. Since, like Nygren (*Agape and Eros*), he keeps agapic love without a *tertium comparationis* to erotic love, I argue he is implicitly affirming a 'sect' as opposed to a 'church' mentality, as that distinction is made by Troeltsch, *The Social Teaching of the Christian Churches*. For further discussion of Nygren, see *infra*, pp. 165, 167–9 and of Troeltsch, *infra*, pp. 179–83.

[164] See Jonas, *The Gnostic Religion*, esp. Part III, 'Gnosticism and the Classical Mind', pp. 239–89.

[165] 'Universal poetry' alludes to German romantic irony and to Hegel's *Aesthetics*; 'New science' to Vico's *New Science*.

To the Christian tradition, the story of Abraham and Isaac is one of sacrifice;[166] to the Jewish tradition, Isaac is bound (*Akedah* means 'the binding' of Isaac); to Johannes *de silentio* of *Fear and Trembling* what happens is 'suspended' — known *and* not known — he aims to transform us from witness at second hand to contemporaneous witness. According to Kierkegaard's authorship, then, the emphasis is on binding not sacrifice: on the witness of Abraham and of the reader not on any act of violence; on the movement of faith not the killing of an innocent victim. The use of a pseudonym within an 'aesthetic' authorship — which represents what cannot be represented by an 'author' who is none – is as intrinsic to the way meaning is suspended as the explicit 'suspension of the ethical'. For it woos a witness at first hand — without the self-refuting 'hypothesis' of capturing a pre-ethical condition of a founding murder. *To posit that the ethical is 'suspended' is to acknowledge that it is always already presupposed.* It grants a momentary licence to hold the ethical fixed and unchanging. But once this is granted, the moment will be imperceptible, for the movement of faith does not take place in time, or, it takes place in every moment of time; whereas, if the ethical is abolished, then a time outside time, or a social reality outside social reality, must, illogically, be posited. Faith cannot speak to justify itself in ethical terms because it is movement not act, so there is nothing to justify, but also because, *contra* Girard, faith *knows* that it is implicated in violence just at the point at which it desists — without this knowing being either the rational pseudo-knowledge which *de silentio* attributes to the Hegelian system, or the mythical knowing of *Joseph*, or the arbitrary orientation which Girardian ignorance dictates.

The silence of the paradox is the witness of participation in the command to love and in the love which commands. It acknowledges the violence in love and the love in violence because the law is in both: the violence in love — Abraham's exclusive, violent love of Isaac; the love in violence — his willingness to bind Isaac with faith not with resignation, not with the prospect of loss, but a free offering, freely given  oblation not sacrifice.[167] It Is *this witness alone* — this always already knowing yet being willing to stake oneself again — that prevents one from becoming an arbitrary perpetrator or an arbitrary victim; that prevents one, actively or passively, from acting with arbitrary violence. Such witnessing is always ready — it is therefore the begin-

---

[166]  See John R. Elliott, Jr, 'The Sacrifice of Isaac as Comedy and Tragedy', in *Medieval English Drama*, eds Jerome Taylor and A. H. Nelson, pp. 157–76.
[167]  See Josef Pieper, *Leisure The Basis of Culture*, pp. 74, 80–1.

ning in the middle: the middle in the beginning — holding itself alert in
the anxiety and equivocation of each.

Not only the ethical but meaning as such is suspended in the
pseudonymous retelling of the *Akedah*. Four distinct senses in which the
ethical is suspended, implicitly as well as explicitly, are discernible:
explicitly, the ethical means the universal or social law which would
classify a sacrifice as 'murder'. This 'suspension' serves to set a beginning without denying the equivocation of the middle. Implicitly, the
holy is suspended, the pre-covenantal community set aside, so that
Abraham may be represented both as an individual in conflict with
himself, and, for the sake of moving towards the idea of the single one,
in conflict with his God. Thirdly, and also implicitly, the structure of
law is suspended: the fact that this story has been preserved in biblical
and rabbinic Judaism as part of its liturgy, repeated in the context of
ritual which returns the congregation to its law — not conceived solely
as prohibition. Fourthly, meaning as such is suspended because the
command returns its recipient to the original innocence and guilt of
becoming 'able', prior to understanding the command. Such mix of
innocence and guilt is itself now knowable as the violence in love and
the love in violence.

There is a short, extraordinarily dense chapter in 'The Tales of Jacob'
in which Mann compresses the methods of the 'Praise' and 'Problemata'
of *Fear and Trembling*, retelling the binding of Isaac from a series of
linked perspectives that tend towards witness and not — as throughout
*Joseph* otherwise — towards myth.[168]

Jacob, in the preceding chapter, has confronted Joseph and admon-
ished him over his voluptuous, pagan, moon homage.[169] Disarmed by
Joseph's glib justification of his idolatry, Jacob is suddenly seized with a
paroxysm of trembling and transported mentally into a repetition of the
*Akedah* with Joseph in the place of Isaac. Instantaneously — for the
movement of faith or lack of it suspends time as the ethical is suspended
— he relates with bitter resignation the outcome of his testing. He failed
to kill — and he is not convinced, even retrospectively, that he might
have relied on the known outcome of the story, urged upon him by
Joseph. In this way, he suspends the ethical — but as an intrigue: to
make Joseph resume it. He draws Joseph further into the agony of
witness, and only when Joseph becomes willing to assume the violence
in love, the love in violence implied in the command, is he released for
a faith without idolatry.

[168]  'The Testing', *Joseph*, Bd 1 pp. 75–8, tr. pp. 64–7.
[169]  'The Monkey Land of Egypt', Bd 1, pp. 70–5, tr. pp. 59–69.

By means of three arguments, Jacob insists that the ethical is suspended, even though the command is only identifiable as repetition of the *Akedah* because it is 'the command and the precept' — that is, it is the law, together with its interpretation.[170] He denies that he, Jacob, is indistinguishable from Abraham — so he cannot rely on the known outcome; such reliance would, in any case, disqualify him as tried and tested — only Abraham would have been called; finally, he persists in lamenting his failure, acknowledging the violence of his love for Joseph which pitted him against the violence of the command to kill him: the violence in love against the love in violence within the law.

Jacob's uncompromising remorse is the beginning of atonement. For Joseph takes over the argument again and returns them both to the law. Scandalously, he interprets Jacob's violence in love as God's violence in love. He claims that Jacob's reluctance to kill is God's wisdom — what God meant to teach: that the commandment to sacrifice the first-born in the Abraham story belongs to idolatry and is replaced by a second overriding command when Isaac is bound — the command not to kill. Jacob's refusal to kill amounts in effect to a fulfilment of the command as it is interpreted in the tradition. His agony registers the violence in his love in opposition to the violence in the command to kill passing over into the violence of the teaching; love in the violence of exposing the violence in love, the latter by this reversal, correlative with the violence in God's zealous love of man. By speaking so, Joseph, too, finds himself back within the law — his wit not as profound as Jacob's wisdom which finds partial relief in Joseph's exposition, but is still sorrowful that he lacked — and may ever lack — perfect confidence: the violence of learning is never complete.

By suspending the ethical in this history explored by his characters, Mann draws in a witnessing which learns the law by confronting the violence in love and the love in violence. While elsewhere in *Joseph*, anxiety and ethics are abolished by blithe mythologizing, betrayed by facetiousness, the ethical is suspended here for the sake of the anxiety of witness by discursive means — a learning developed by reasoning, a *Bildung* with all its agon and incompleteness.

The meaning of 'violence' seems to have changed — from univocal destruction and annihilation to any forming of initially recalcitrant

---

[170] *Joseph*, Bd 1 p. 76, tr. p. 65. Both the law and its interpretation, '*Der Befehl und die Weisung*', were revealed to Moses but only the law was written; thus the revelation is considered to be equally the origin of the oral tradition. In Hebrew the distinction is between *Hukkim* and *Mishpatim*, see Maimonides' 'Introduction to Mishneh Torah', p. 35.

material, human or non-human, to any pitting of the will against opposition or resistance, regardless of the outcome, negative or positive. Girard himself extends the meaning of 'violence', founded on murder and sacrifice recursively, to an account not only of hominization but of humanization: the development of the child who, as disciple to its model, hears its very first 'no' as 'a banishment' and 'is incapable of meeting violence with violence'.[171] Restricted to its utterly negative connotations, 'violence' is here not so much 'hypothesized' as hypostatized.

Kierkegaard's pseudonymous 'suspension of the ethical' avoids this sequestering of 'violence' while exploring the development of individual faith in its violent encounter with love and law. Hegel's phenomenological master—slave dialectic suspends the ethical — *Sittlichkeit* — in order to explore how the violence between two misrecognizing self-consciousnesses will be settled provisionally by death, enslavement, work or unhappiness; this same dialectic of development is then re-explored as *Antigone* in the restored context of 'ethical life'. By initially suspending the ethical, both authors are able to bring a formation, an education (*Bildung*), into representation as a *struggle* — *agon* — in which 'violence' is inseparable from staking oneself, from experience as such — the initial yet yielding recalcitrance of action and passion. Without 'violence', which is not sacrifice but risk, language, labour, love — life — would not live.

'Violence' is not, once again, being posited as prior to law: it is presupposed as the call of law. Yet it has, apparently, turned into an attribute of power — quite the contrary of Hannah Arendt's opposing of 'power' and 'violence' in her book *On Violence*, according to which 'violence' is the resort of the powerless, the breakdown of power.[172] 'Power' is expounded by her not as coercive means but as the condition of political community which makes means—ends thinking and acting possible.[173] While 'power' is functional and in need of legitimation, 'violence' may, sometimes, be justified but is never legitimate.[174] If, however, 'violence' is as intrinsic to the operation of power as to its breakdown — without implying that power is 'disguised force', but that existentially its exercise implies risk — then the difference between power as precondition, whether creative or coercive, and the 'violence' of the powerless becomes a difference between the violence that sustains

[171] *Violence and the Sacred*, p. 175.
[172] Op. cit., pp. 52–6.
[173] Ibid., p. 51.
[174] Ibid., pp. 44–6.

power and the violence that erupts in the resort to force, violence in law and violence out of law, when 'lawful' violence captures the predicament of violence in love and love in violence.

In fine, 'violence' cannot be isolated without being posited as the lowest common denominator of action, whether good or bad; while, if, on the contrary, it is presupposed, then there is no need to theorize it as such. All isolating of 'violence' is therefore suspicious unless the ethical is suspended and its historical and legal precondition recognized. For only then is the agony of witness at stake: the anxiety of beginning and the equivocation of the middle acknowledged and embraced in the authorial predicament. This endeavour transforms 'anxiety' and 'equivocation' from psychological terms into political ones; acknowledgements of the beginning in the middle: the middle in the beginning.[175]

The challenge is to cease this abolition of the ethical and to restore the political history of ethical life: without the cynicism of violence, without the facetiousness of myth, but not without authorial irony – not without the anxiety of beginning and the equivocation of the middle. This irony has been learnt from the pseudonymous one: it is the lesson that the most existential moment of ethical suspension is the most consistent witnessing of the history of ethical and political actuality.[176]

---

[175] Cf. Sheldon Wolin's use of 'anxiety' as a political concept in *Politics and Vision*, in the section 'Liberalism and Anxiety' in ch. 9, 'Liberalism and the Decline of Political Philosophy', pp. 286–351.

[176] Mann may himself have conceded – but only facetiously – that *Joseph*, designed to remove myth from the hands of the Fascists, tended instead, in its effect of removing equivocation, to redeliver it to such hands, when, in *Doctor Faustus*, he represents in the repellent figure of Dr Chaim Breisacher – who Scholem describes as 'a kind of metaphysical super-Nazi' – the scholar Oskar Goldberg, whose theory of the authenticity of ancient magical Hebraism, developed in the latter's *Die Wirklichkeit der Hebräer*, 1925, Scholem claims became the foundation of the first part of Mann's *Joseph*, 'The Tales of Jacob' (see Scholem, *The Story of a Friendship*, pp. 122–6, tr. pp. 95–8). In ch. 28 of *Doctor Faustus*, Breisacher defends the idea of a vital and violent pre-biblical sacrificial cult, which was later destroyed, and even the memory of it suppressed, by biblical individuation. Zeitblom judges these compelling absurdities to be indicative of the extraordinary coincidence of the avant-garde and the reactionary, 'the new world of anti-humanity'. If, indeed, the scholar subsequently dramatized as Breisacher did provide the main source for *Joseph*, this would support the argument developed here that the work depends on a proto-Girardian account of sacrifice and violence which had later to be discarded because of its inability to deal with what are called in this work 'anxiety of beginning' and 'equivocation of the ethical' (see *Doctor Faustus*, pp. 274–85, tr. pp. 269–75).

# 5

# Love and the State

## *Varnhagen, Luxemburg and Arendt*

### *Suspending the Political*

'The single individual' can mean the one and only, and 'the single individual' can mean every [one]. So if one would provoke attention dialectically, one should use the category of 'the individual' with a double lash to it. The pride in the one thought incites some, the humility in the second thought deters others, but the confusion involved in the double meaning provokes attention dialectically . . . But I believe that people have for the most part paid attention only to 'the individual' of the pseudonyms and have confounded me as a matter of course with the pseudonyms − and hence all this talk of my pride and arrogance, a condemnation of me which really amounts only to self-denunciation.[1]

The human being who has lost his place in a community, his political status in the struggle of his time, and the legal personality which makes his actions and part of his destiny a consistent whole, is left with those qualities which usually can become articulate only in the sphere of private life and must remain unqualified, mere existence in all matters of public concern. This mere existence . . . can be adequately dealt with only by the unpredictable hazards of friendship and sympathy, or by the great and incalculable grace of love, which says with Augustine, '*Volo ut sis* (I want you to be),' without being able to give any particular reason for such supreme and unsurpassable affirmation.[2]

---

[1] Kierkegaard, *The Point of View for My Work as An Author: A Report to History*, p. 124.
[2] Arendt, *The Origins of Totalitarianism*, p. 301.

'What a drama!' Isn't it? 'What a bore! Same thing over and over again'. And I, I feel as though I haven't said one tenth of it and not at all what I wanted to say.

> Language is false to the voice,
> the voice is false to thoughts;
> Thoughts fly up from the soul
> before they are caught in words.

Adieu! I almost regret this letter. Perhaps you will be angry? Perhaps you will laugh? Oh, no, do not laugh.

> Pray beloved maiden welcome the ghost
> As in the olden days.[3]

Each author here struggles with what the first of the three, Kierkegaard, finally set out in *The Point of View for My Work as An Author* — the paradox and politics of authorship. The second passage, from the conclusion to Part Two, 'Imperialism', of Hannah Arendt's *The Origins of Totalitarianism*, ('The Decline of the Nation State and the End of the Rights of Man'), and the third passage, from Rosa Luxemburg's letter to Leo Jogiches of 16 July 1897, show these two authors aiming but failing towards the dialectical provocation of attention claimed by the first. Each passage strains to express the politics of metaphysics — the aporia of theoretical reference, everyone and every 'one'; the politics of action — how the individual is to be called into activity, singularly and collectively; and the politics of authorship — that the author herself bears the paradox in her name, which is, therefore, equally a pseudonym, whether explicitly so or not. Each passage embraces these dilemmas, shared by author and actor, this equivocation of the middle, which persists in any exploration of the beginning or the end, and which implies that the ethical can only ever be 'suspended' — neither surrendered on the one hand, nor posited on the other.

Rahel Varnhagen, Rosa Luxemburg and Hannah Arendt display this paradox of authorship in their work and lives which together span three crises of state and civil society in Prussia and Germany — the first, from the late eighteenth-century bureaucratic reform, which represents the transition from aristocratic to bourgeois society; to the second, up to the

---

[3]　Luxemburg, Letter 6, 16 July 1897, to Leo Jogiches, in *Comrade and Lover*, p. 25, and nn. 2 and 3, citing Adam Mickiewicz (1798–1855), *The Forefathers* and *The Ghost*.

defeat of Social Democracy, which represents the transition from bourgeois society to class struggle; and the third, the rise of Fascism, which represents the transition from Social Democracy to totalitarian rule by non-synchronous class elements. As women and as Jews, they are especially qualified witnesses of the equivocation of the middle by virtue of their exclusion from three abstract universalities: as women, excluded from the revolutionary fraternity of man − liberal-bourgeois and socialist; as Jews, excluded from the community of Christian love; and for both reasons excluded from civil status. Without *droits de l'homme* and without *droits de citoyen*, and lacking Christian consolation, the triple deprivations of these three authorships expose the separation of citizenship in the modern legal state from gender, from religion and from 'civil society' itself. They reveal how posited universality of 'rights of man' and 'rights of the citizen' deposits customary statuses within the violence of civil society. Yet this tension of middlewomanship is sustained in all three authorships: they neither opt to abandon political universality, even though it is demonstrably spurious; nor to resolve its inconsistency and antinomy in any ethical immediacy of love: 'community', 'nation', 'race', 'religion' or 'gender'. Remaining within the agon of authorship they cultivate aporetic universalism, restless affirmation and undermining of political form and political action, which never loses sight of the continuing mutual corruption of the state and civil society − whether the state is separated from or united with gender, religion, politics.

This unsettled and unsettling approach, which is not a 'position' because it will not *posit* anything, and refuses any beginning or end, would yet induce repetition forwards − a beginning in the middle. The politics of this 'middle', conceived now as 'social' and as 'civil' in the sense of sociability or civility, and of *gesellschaftlich*, contractual, civil society or civil law, involves indirect communication, not 'ideal-speech situation' or ideal communication. It intrigues with the idea of 'everyone' to reach every 'one' − but without offering any new security, neither individual nor collective.

If, according to Girard, violence results from the rivalry of *equals*, and is terminable only by a victimage mechanism which founds and refounds the social order by instigating difference; for anti-Climacus, doctor of the soul, violence is the result of the *inequality* between everyone and every 'one' − who is stronger, perhaps, than the whole world but not stronger than herself; while for *de silentio*, violence would be the result of forfeiting and not suspending the ethical − for this would be the only way to perceive the 'sacrifice' of Isaac. How to represent the aporia between everyone and every 'one' is the difficulty

− difficulty of the difficulty. For it emerges only by suspending the ethical, or by donning the pseudonymous mask of the psychologist to examine 'the relation of the relation' − whether anxious or demonic, or any other manifestation of violence. Neither the relation of the relation − body and soul or time and eternity − nor the difference within each opposition, for 'difference' would be the metaphysical contrary of 'identity', this difficulty itself, the *aporia*, is what is being staked.

It is under the most precarious signature − 'Kierkegaard' − that the suspension of the ethical is released to the institutions and the meaning of 'the present age', that violence is released to the possibility of politics. If these explorations of the meaning of 1848 are taken together with the exposition of Luther's politics to be found in Kierkegaard's *Journals*, they yield 'the double danger' of what it is to succumb either to worldly or to otherworldly authority, which is followed consistently through the changing relation between religion and politics from the Reformation to the 'present age'. By reconsidering Rousseau, Hegel, Weber and Troeltsch as exponents of this changing relation of religion and politics, the negotiating of *the double danger* in the authorships of Varnhagen, Luxemburg and Arendt may then be explored phenomeno-logically as 'the beautiful soul', 'the culture of terror', and 'the hard heart of hypocritical judgement'.

Changing from author to editor and then again to author, 'S. Kierke-gaard' in the third 'Preface' of *The Book on Adler*, written in the wake of 1848, addresses 'the catastrophe' of the present age, when 'the editor' had been concerned with 'the confusion' of the present age. Under this changeable pseudonym, the author argues, employing facetiously sim-ple illustrations, against the social and political resolution of difficulty in the community of love − whether Pietist or Communist. Even the agapic community, based on recognition of the singularity of each, would amount to an increase in heteronomous authority. This is not to be confused with Kant's critique of heteronomous legality which seeks to justify autonomous morality. From the pseudonymous per-spective, autonomous morality is just another kind of pseudo-authority or authorship. The agapic community would deny the world and be subverted in its development by what it denies. The community as a whole would succumb to the violence of civil society as every member of it would succumb to her violence against herself. Posited communal love translates into social violence of individuals.

Signing and dating his 'interpretation of our age', 'S. Kierkegaard, October 7, 1848', the author, thus declaimed, provides the direct state-ment that the reflection, while it comes from one who is 'something of a poet, who moreover is a thinker', comes from one who is 'without authority' — the oft-repeated warning.[4] However, further resources of facetiousness are needed in order to develop the thesis that while the Reformation *turned religion into politics*, 1848 must *turn politics into 'religion'*. For this implies equally a distance from Protestant inwardness and from Pietistic politics — from any 'undialectical' end of politics[5] which would be equally to end anxiety of beginning and equivocation of the middle — for Protestant inwardness affirms hypocritical individualism while Pietistic politics affirms totalitarian egalitarianism, and both reinstate illegitimate authority, internal and external.

Far from conforming to Marcuse's caricature of existential freedom from Kierkegaard to Sartre — that it affirms absolute freedom regardless of repressive social institutions which simply provide 'the coefficient of adversity' — Kierkegaard returns again and again in his *Journals and Papers* to the argument, which Marcuse also advances in the chapter on Luther and Calvin in his essay 'A Study on Authority', that Luther delivered religion into the hands of the Prince, merely replacing papal authority with secular authority.[6]

Luther altered Christianity by altering martyrdom.[7]

The indictment of Luther's idea of witness from the *Journals and Papers* affords a rare glimpse of the integrity of Kierkegaard's subterfuges, for he speaks directly — that is, in Christian terms — about Luther's lack of indirection, his undialectical affirmation of faith, and the unintended spiritual, social, and political consequences of such affirmation, or, in other words, his affirmation of an end which explicitly abolishes anxiety of beginning, and, inadvertently, becomes servile to the middle — without its equivocation.

Instead of 'arousing restlessness' and making spiritual life 'more strenuous', Luther makes it soothing and reassuring.[8] Transfiguration of anguish, which occurred in Luther's own case after twenty years of fear and trembling and of spiritual and scholarly discipline, is universalized by Protestantism so that it is made available for all — without any 'one' undergoing the intensity of Luther's testing. 'This extremely powerful

---

[4]  *On Authority and Revelation*, p. lxiii.

[5]  For Luther, dialectic and politics, see *Søren Kierkegaard's Journals and Papers*, Vol. 3, L–R, 'Luther', q.v., *passim*, and especially 2469 p. 66, 2514 p. 80, 2521, pp. 83–4, 2524 pp. 85–6.

[6]  'Sartre's Existentialism [1948]', pp. 173, 174, 188–9; and 'A Study on Authority [1936]', pp. 56–78, in *Studies in Critical Philosophy*.

[7]  *Journals and Papers*, Vol. 3, 'Luther', q.v. 2550 p. 100.

[8]  Ibid., 2550 p. 101, 2514 p. 80.

resource and reassurance' becomes the cloak of an inwardness which everyone has the licence to counterfeit.[9]

Although the principle of Protestantism and its consequences are distinguished from the development of Luther's own spirituality and what he preached, their source is implicit in Luther's emphasis — lack of dialectic and lack of paradox in what he proclaimed and in the way in which he proclaimed it. As a reformer, he fought to 'throw off burdens', but, as it were, he threw off too many burdens, or rather, burdens of too many kinds: 'Consequently the proper Christian mark of *double danger* is missing here.'[10] To throw off the burden of papal authority without retaining the anguish and authority of the paradox merely leads from one human to another human authority, to political and social compromise with 'the established order', which takes Luther in vain and nullifies his contribution.[11]

The political consequence of serving the Prince instead of the Pope is matched by the baleful social consequences of stressing faith as the one thing needful, regardless of works, whether meritorious or not. Abolition of the abuse of earning spiritual merit by works results in abolition of charity as such: marriage replaces any responsibility for the poor. To redress the law with the gospel leads to exclusive and excessive demand for 'gospel, gospel'.[12] Faith produces 'the scoundrel' who protests a hidden inwardness which has sacrificed everything, 'while outwardly he reaps profit and cuts quite a figure in society'.[13] By one's works, on the other hand, without ever earning merit, one may be 'incessantly halted and checked on the way to eternity'.[14] The alternative is to sanctify unlicensed imagination of inwardness which sits, apparently comfortable and unperturbed, while outwardly it continues to live for any prescribed secular goals.[15] It is far harder and far rarer, 'stupendously high', 'infinitely high',[16] to be able to retain and acquire the world and also not to possess it — to pass, as it were, straight to faith, without resignation, without works, without law, than to pass with them. The mistake is that such detached faith begins with the end, while the principle of works 'begins with the beginning, and begins with what is common to us',[17] that is, with what is in the middle. No

[9]   Ibid., 2544 p. 96.
[10]  Ibid., 2514 p. 80, emphasis added.
[11]  Ibid., 2528 p. 87, 2514 p. 80.
[12]  Ibid., 2527 p. 87.
[13]  Ibid., 2543 p. 93.
[14]  Ibid., 2543 p. 95.
[15]  Ibid., 2543 pp. 93–5.
[16]  Ibid., 2543 p. 94.
[17]  Ibid., 2543 p. 93.

earnest of merit, the principle of works prevents anyone from becoming 'a hero' of his own inwardness while outwardly living with no responsibility at all.[18]

If this contrast of faith and works were the last — or, indeed the first — word, it would, of course, be as undialectical as Luther's position. It would risk the abuse of works, which, even uncrowned with merit, could equally well alleviate the double danger; and it would condemn to impossibility (*sic*) the knight of faith of *Fear and Trembling*. 'Double danger' is the *only undangerous position*: the only one, literally, that does not liberate from one dominion — for 'danger' comes etymologically from Latin, *dominus*, 'lord' — to submit to another. Anxiety of beginning and equivocation of the middle — restlessness that yet remains with both dangers — is the only way to avoid the spiritual, social and political inversions which attend any alleviation.

> And when in an elder formation the decisive moment was overcome, then the ordinary worldly government took over; but from the moment the fourth estate came into the picture it will be seen that even when the crisis has been overcome it is not possible to govern in a *worldly* way.[19]

The series in the *Journal* of explicit and remorseless reflections on the outcome of the Reformation — how feigned spiritual inwardness came to justify the outer resourcefulness and assurance of ruthless individualism — is developed and completed by the facetious representation of the inversion which might result if the atomization inherent in the epoch of 1848 is resolved by establishing communistic or communitarian Pietism.

> So soon as the fourth estate comes into the picture it is possible to rule only in a godly way, religiously.[20]

This prophecy of the end of politics, repeated twice, goes deliberately unheeded by the author who issues it. Without expanding what he means by 'religious' rule, he continues by imagining the alternative: 'Discontented, unsatisfied, with the State, with the Church and with everything related to them (art, learning, etc., etc.) the human race, if allowed to follow its own devices, would resolve itself into a world of

---

[18]   Ibid., 2543 p. 95.
[19]   *On Authority and Revelation*, p. lx.
[20]   Ibid., pp. lx–lxi.

atoms.'[21] This social and political dissolution into rampant individualism might imply spiritual progress: 'now God will himself come directly into relation with the single individuals, not through abstractions, neither through representative persons, but God will himself, so to speak, undertake to educate the countless individuals of the generation, to become himself the schoolmaster who looks after all, everyone in particular.'[22] In spite of the careful concluding distinction between 'all' and 'everyone in particular', this hypothesis of a direct relationship between God and the single individual is undermined by the image of the 'schoolmaster', with its implication of regressive, unequivocal, and unanguished authority. This implication is spelt out − but not before an explicit double warning against such spelling out is unequivocally issued: 'Here thought comes to a stop. The form of the world would be like − well, I know not with what I should liken it:'

> It would resemble an enormous version of the Christenfeld [an example of Christian communism], and so there would be present the two greatest possible contrasts, striving with one another about the interpretation of this phenomenon. On the one hand *communism*, which would say, This is the correct worldly way, there must not be the slightest difference between man and man; riches, art, learning, rule etc., etc., are of the evil one, all men ought to be equal like laborers in a factory, like cattle in a barnyard, partake of the same food, be washed in one common tub at the same stroke of the clock, be of the same dimensions etc., etc. On the other hand *pietism*, which would say, This is the right Christian way, that one make no difference between man and man, we ought to be brothers and sisters, have all in common; riches, art, learning, etc., etc., are of the evil one; all men should be equal as it was once in little Christenfeld, all dressed alike, all pray at fixed times, marry by casting lots, go to bed at the same stroke of the clock, partake of the same food, out of one dish, at the same time, etc., etc.[23]

This clockwork double representation of eternity − the community rather than the kingdom of God, depicted by the sect mentality of Christenfeld − is the facetious representation of that direct faith without works, where 'every opposition − that of power, talents, numbers − ideally viewed, is already overcome, even though *accidentally* [one]

---

[21]  Ibid., p. lxi.
[22]  Ibid., p. lxi.
[23]  Ibid., pp. lxi–lxii.

has experienced or may experience suffering for it'.[24] Such faith, an eternity posited as the end, can only be represented by turning it into its contrary — clockwork time and clockwork people. Luther's faith delivers religion to the Prince, and, in so doing, leaves the world exactly as it is, reinforcing its most divisive values. For the age to posit the end of oppositions in 1848 is to resolve its chaos, which has been inherited from the Protestant ethic, by installing the kind of authority which characterizes the Pietist sect — the tyranny of totalitarian locality which imposes both beginning and end and abolishes the middle entirely.

Under his 'own' name — which we now know to be as aporetic as any assumed or fictitious name — a heteronym rather than a pseudonym,[25] Kierkegaard employs a resentful and indignant persona to point to the dangers of *The Present Age*, 1846.

> And the ultimate difference between the modern world and antiquity is: that 'the whole' is not concrete and is therefore unable to support the individual, or to educate him as the concrete should (though without developing him absolutely), but is an abstraction which by its abstract equality repels him and thus helps him to be educated absolutely — unless he succumbs in the process.[26]

Acclamation of the advent of the 'fourth estate' to social prominence as herald of the end of politics in the 'Preface' to *The Book on Adler*, is elaborated further here as an 'either...or...or' crisis in which the meaning of 'the rule of martyrs' or 'religious rule' emerges from a dialectic of anxiety traced to the levelling or egalitarianism which transforms people into 'a public'.

> [A]n age without passion gains in *scope what it loses in intensity*. But this scope may once again become the condition of a still higher form, if a corresponding intensity assumes control of the extended field of activity which is put at its disposal.[27]

The scope opened by the abstract equality of civil society also opens dialectically two alternative fates — to be educated or to succumb. To be educated is to become ethical; but there are many ways of succumbing: envy or resentment and jejune association are two responses to

---

[24]   Ibid., p. lxii.
[25]   Compare the Portuguese poet, Fernando Pessoa, and his 'heteronyms', discussed in the 'Introduction' by Jonathan Griffin to his translation of *Selected Poems*, pp. 9–23.
[26]   *The Present Age*, p. 62.
[27]   Ibid., pp. 62–3, 68.

being repelled by abstraction, two ways of succumbing, which, together, help to intimate their third: absolute education.

Addressing people under the qualification of 'a public' is flattering and undermining: it elevates reflection and debases both passion and action, so that the response to distinctions, especially to one's distinction from oneself as abstraction, is to retreat into *ressentiment* – resentfulness towards the actuality of the pain of differences, instead of passion to recognize them, and action to aid others to recognize them.[28] Such action and passion is what is meant by 'martyr', that is, witness. Resentfulness offers instead a dangerous security and comfort: 'A selfish envy makes such demands upon the individual that by asking too much it prevents him from doing anything. It spoils him like an indulgent mother, for the envy within him prevents the individual from devoting himself to others.'[29]

Premature acts of association with others, which avoid the agony of reflection and *ressentiment* and have not learnt to transform them into anxiety of beginning, are eqully calamitous. The clockwork tyranny of an established Pietistic communism is not imagined here, but the motivation for surrendering sovereignty to such a system and anticipation of its dissolution are addressed:

> It is quite impossible for the community or the idea of association to save our age. On the contrary, association is the scepticism which is necessary in order that the development of individuality may proceed uniformly, so that the [single one] will either be lost or, disciplined by such abstractions, will find himself religiously. Nowadays the principle of association (which at the most is only valid when material interests are concerned) is not positive but negative; it is an escape, a distraction and an illusion. Dialectically the position is this: the principle of association by strengthening the individual, enervates him; it strengthens numerically, but ethically that is a weakening. It is only after the individual has acquired an ethical outlook, in face of the whole world, that there can be any suggestion of really joining together. Otherwise the association of individuals who are themselves weak, is just as disgusting and harmful as the marriage of children.[30]

This argument for an 'absolute' or ethical education which would be singular and thereby able to acknowledge the possibility of every

[28]  Ibid., pp. 51, 49.
[29]  Ibid., p. 48.
[30]  Ibid., p. 79.

other to be educated, is what is meant by 'religious' education or the rule of martyrs:

> for unless the individual learns in the reality of religion and before God to be content with himself, and learns, instead of dominating others, to dominate himself, content as priest to be his own audience, and as author his own reader . . . because it is the expression of the equality of all men before God and of our likeness to others, then he will not escape from reflection . . .[31]

> Reflection . . . cannot buy up the essentially religious and eternal view of life; on the other hand, it can tempt people astray with its dazzling brilliance, and dishearten them by reminding them of all the past. But, by leaping into the depths one learns to help oneself, learns to love others as much as oneself, even though one is accused of arrogance and pride — because one will not accept help — or of selfishness, because one will not cunningly deceive people by helping them, i.e. by helping them to escape their highest destiny.[32]

It is these passages in the work most explicitly dealing with politics, least pseudonymously dealing with the education of existence, which are *least* able to speak about politics, and which are only able to *reflect* abstractly about the individual; and this explains the limitations of the book. For only if the ethical is suspended and faith failed towards can the scope for politics be discovered in the simultaneous actuality of the political and the existential which is the possibility of the ethical: what it might yield — suspended and released — in the same instance of staking. Otherwise, as in the texts discussed here, authorship will, unwittingly, objectify and arrogate to itself the authority it seeks to explore. For, 'if you wish to be and to remain enthusiastic, then draw the silk curtains of facetiousness . . . and so hide your enthusiasm.'[33]

However, this path to rediscovering the equivocation of the ethical has revealed its specific political history. This is what one would expect, because it is what 'suspending' implies: that existential exploration should continue to acknowledge historical and legal actuality, and not abolish it by positing an origin or nature which merely smuggles it back in. 'Suspending the ethical' is now revealed to be not just a heuristic device, designed and employed to avoid a vicious circularity,

---

[31] Ibid., p. 57.
[32] Ibid., pp. 58–9.
[33] *Journals* (Dru), p. 126.

but to be an intrinsic part of the historically specific modes of equivocation it attests. To put it abstractly, Kierkegaard's authorship, Hegel's
authorship and Weber's authorship all uncover the *inversions of instituted
meaning* attendant on a culture which has *separated* religion and politics
since the origin of Christianity; which has *subordinated* religion to politics since the Reformation; which has '*emancipated*' religion into civil
society since the early nineteenth century, and has, effectively, *delivered*
politics to 'religion', dissipating both in subjectivity. Under such conditions, every meaning or representation is prone to turn into its contrary. Partial in origin yet holistic in ambition, every meaning is equally
implicated in the meaning against which it is defined; infected with
institutions it seeks to eschew: individual inwardness inverted into the
ruthlessness of social institutions, or lack of inwardness colluding in
new tyrannies.

'Equivocation of the ethical' not only figures the Janus-faces with the
aesthetic, the psychological or the religious – of the beginning and the
end; it also figures this historical fate of the inversion of intentions. Out
of this specific history of separation, subordination, 'emancipation' of
contrary institutions, the equivocation of the ethical, with its reverse
faces and inverse meanings, is accentuated and not relieved by any
danger which is not double. Agon of authorship arises out of such
new and renewed danger. Theory, therefore, does not present, as
post-modernism argues, 'grand narratives' – fictions which have the
'function' of legitimizing spurious universality by conferring on it an
arcadian beginning and a utopian end.[34] 'Fictions', theoretical and literary, are themselves facetious forms which configure the double danger
as it changes historically: *aporia* of the universal and *agape* of the singular. They configure the aporia, the difficulty, of the relation between
universal, particular and singular. This difficulty is *the* political difficulty *par excellence*: the opposition between particular and general will, to
use Rousseau's terms; or the struggle between particular and universal
class, to use Marx's terms; and the difficulty of representing this relation in terms of political institutions and aesthetic values. While arcadian and utopian universalism would reconcile and posit the unity of
particular and universal, aporetic universalism explores and experiments
with the disunity of singular and universal. Fiction and facetiousness
maintain this tension, this aporia of the universal, and prevent it, even
when personified and characterized, from succumbing to the contrary
danger: from representing the agape of the singular, the inwardly
piteous, outwardly pitiless individual, or the clockwork love-

---

[34]  Lyotard, *The Postmodern Condition: A Report on Knowledge*, esp. chs 6, 8, 9.

community set in an authoritarian locality. These two flights from the predicament of the separation of civil society and the state − to opt for individual inwardness or local community − merely reinforce what is abhorred − 'the spiritual animal kingdom [*das geistige Tierreich*]'[35] − treating oneself and others as means instead of coming to recognize oneself and others even in the struggle of misrecognition. Facetious form not 'grand narrative' sustains this double agon of authorship, which seeks to examine authority without arrogating it, to suspend the ethical and not abolish it.

*Aporia* and *agape*, marks of double danger, are themselves comparable only because they signal, not *kinds* of, but each in its own way, incomparability. Both were suppressed in the development of the Christian tradition: *aporia*, reduced to logic and ontology after Aristotle, has been traced by Edward Booth, in *Aristotelian Aporetic Ontology in Islamic and Christian Thinkers* (1983), who argues that Thomas opens the aporia again;[36] *agape*, synthesized with nomos and eros from the Early Church to the Reformation, has been traced by Anders Nygren in *Agape and Eros* (1932, 1938, 1939), who argues that Luther's Copernican Revolution reinstates 'God is Agape'.[37] Both Booth and Nygren, each of whom combines immense, dispassionate, historical scholarship with the pathos of their paradox, distinguish their term by opposition to a contrary metaphysical meaning − aporia to inclusive universal; agape to eros − *and* introduce it without *tertium comparationis* as the disturbance in the texts under discussion. Each provides in this way ironic initiation into a meaning which predates − logically rather than historically − clarity, univocity, system, aspiration, and the logic of contraries and similitude itself. For, in each case, aporia and agape have no object and are no subject. In each case the meaning is difficult, and it is difficult to state the meaning.

For Aristotle, 'the greatest of aporias' is to know the individuality of individuals, that is, individual substance, unknowable except in universal terms.[38] This aporia may be addressed; it may occur, especially when different methods are combined; and it may be indicated by 'tentative analogies', like the perception of a particular colour, and by 'homely examples' such as 'the snub nose', which 'even more in Greek than in English, freakishly gives a simultaneous connotation of nose

[35] See Hegel, *Phenomenology of Spirit*, 'The spiritual animal kingdom and deceit, or the "matter in hand" itself', under Reason: C 'Individuality which take itself to be real in and for itself', tr. Miller paras 397–418, pp. 237–252.

[36] Op. cit., chs 1 and 6.

[37] Op. cit., p. 740.

[38] Booth, *Aristotelian Aporetic Ontology*, pp. 2–3.

and its concavity. "Concave" is a mathematical conception, entailing complete regularity; "snub" has about it the toleration of every individual irregular development.'[39] 'Snub' keeps unity and difference, universal and singular (individual not the particular) aporetically together.[40] Unfortunately, Booth comments, the 'snub' in the nature even of physical things has no analogous expression; the aporia can only be manifested but not resolved in this way.[41] Manifestation, however, may be the beginning of movement, although this is not conveyed by the etymology of the Greek *aporia*, 'without a ford', nor by its customary English translation, 'difficulty'. Booth himself cites Le Corbusier to capture and convey this consequence:

> If not best understood, the aporetic of philosophy is well described by the Swiss-French architect-painter, Charles Edouard Jeanneret-Gris ('Le Corbusier'). Having submitted a mathematical relationship, which he had grasped intuitively himself, to a mathematician for his appreciation, he was told:

> '[Y]our two initial squares are not squares; one of their sides is larger by six thousandths than the other.'

> In everyday practice, six thousandths of a value are what is called a negligible quantity which does not enter into account; it is not seen with the eye.

> But in philosophy (and I have no key to that austere science), I suspect that those six thousandths of a value have an infinitely precious importance: the thing is not open and shut, it is not sealed; there is a chink to let in the air; life is there, awakened by the recurrence of a fateful equality which is not exactly, not strictly equal...

> ... And that is what creates movement.[42]

This evident difficulty in finding a description of difficulty − plundering Le Corbusier's identity of indiscernibles, with its coda concerning movement − has, however, already been explored in the movement of

---

[39] Ibid., pp. 6, 7, 8.
[40] Ibid., p. 7; see, too, p. 115.
[41] Ibid., pp. 7–8.
[42] Ibid., p. x; Le Corbusier, *The Modulor*, tr. pp. 234–5; layout and punctuation of Le Corbusier's text restored.

phenomenological experience, expounded in the 'Introduction', suffered explicitly in the first subsection 'Sense-Certainty: Or the "This" and "Meaning"', and in compound form at every subsequent moment, in Hegel's *Phenomenology of Spirit*. Similarly, while Booth is aware that 'the Aristotelian aporetic of the distance between the individual as individual and the individual as instance of a universal bears, in its human, social and political context, on a matter of undying concern',[43] he argues that 'Witness from the political thinkers would be too vast to bring forward',[44] and this *obiter dictum* is left unmoved.

The politics of 'agape' also remain uncatalogued and unmoved by Nygren, even though his account of *Agape and Eros* has the formal structure of a phenomenological philosophy of history, organized in its second part along the continuum of the 'preparation', 'completion' and 'destruction of a synthesis'. However, by distinguishing 'motif-research' from 'historical-genetic research', and subordinating the latter to the 'fundamental-motif' of the former, the 'migrations', 'origins' and 'historically demonstrable connections' of the motifs are designated 'empirical elements'.[45] This denigration of history and movement rebounds to the detriment of 'motif-research', which, impoverished by such purification, becomes an exercise in typological dogmatics, culminating in Luther.

While a considerable critical literature has elaborated *Agape and Eros*, the historical and analytical refusal by both Nygren and his critics to consider antecedent and alternative expositions from philosophy and social theory is striking.[46] Nygren introduces 'Agape' by citing with approval Troeltsch's remarks on not interpreting Christianity as class struggle, and by citing with disdain Nietzsche on Christian love as *ressentiment*,[47] but he proceeds as if they − and Hegel and Kierkegaard and Weber − have not expounded the political and sociological inversions of Luther's 'rediscovery' of agape. What Nygren calls 'Luther's Copernican Revolution' and presents as the theological dénouement of 'a tense drama'[48] is the starting point of what Nietzsche addresses under the interrogative title 'What is the Meaning of Ascetic Ideals?', the third essay of *On the Genealogy of Morals*; while the 'unintended' sociological

---

[43] Booth, p. xi.
[44] Ibid.
[45] Op. cit., pp. 34–8.
[46] Gene Outka, however, in his discussion of agape and justice argues *en passant* that Kierkegaard's *Works of Love* can in part serve as a substitute for Nygren; see *Agape: An Ethical Analysis*, p. 2, n. 1.
[47] Nygren, p. 64.
[48] Ibid., p. 55.

consequences of 'this-worldly asceticism' are the focus of the second part of Weber's *Protestant Ethic and the Spirit of Capitalism.*

However, this methodological asceticism is itself part of Nygren's theme: that agape and eros are not contraries, even though he will expound what he calls their 'symptoms' as opposed types, for *agape* means divine love while *eros* means human love. The history of agape, reconstructed in the second part of the work as an unstable synthesis, is admitted at the outset of the first part to be more correctly characterized as the perennial smothering of agape, which 'sometimes breaks out, if only at isolated points in Christian history, with all its original force'.[49] Agape, to put it in metaphysical terms, is transcendental in the Medieval sense: it precedes the division of being into categories; while Eros is within categorical thinking. Or, to put it in Maimonidean terms, all speaking of God will slip inevitably but illegitimately into anthropomorphic and anthropocentric terms. Or, to put it in existential terms, Agape is the paradox, while Eros is within the realm of aesthetic representation. To represent Agape would be to confer on it the spurious status and authority of Eros. With no relation to either metaphysics or dialectic, Nygren can only catalogue and warn against the confusing of contrary symptoms.

It is this sixfold comparison of 'the Agape-system' with 'the Eros-system' that makes this work such a serviceable *point d'appui*.[50] First, the 'Eros-system' is *demonstrational* and mystical; the 'Agape-system' is *revelational*: the former is preoccupied with man's way to God, the latter with God's way to man; the former with self-salvation by means of an ascent to the Divine, the latter with a Divine revelation which establishes communication between God and man. Second, Eros stresses '*works*' or human achievement, symbolized by the soul's ascent of the heavenly ladder; while Agape stresses *faith*, and is receptive not striving. It is not a question of working one's way up but of something offered which comes down. Third, '*Eros starts with the assumption of the Divine origin and worth of the soul; Agape, on the other hand, starts with the conviction of one's own lack of worth.*' Fourth, Eros presupposes ethical and metaphysical dualism of Spirit (good) and Matter (evil)    the soul imprisoned in the body and seeking release from bondage by otherwordly asceticism; while Agape conceives the opposition between good and evil exclusively in terms of the will and its perversion. Creation and incarnation, the world and the body (matter), are not intrinsically evil. Conversion does not mean transference of desire from a lower to a higher object, it means a transforming of selfish will to theocentric will.

---

[49]  Ibid.
[50]  Ibid.; what follows is taken from p. 84 and pp. 220–32, emphasis in original.

Fifth, Eros is converted by the beauty of the divine, by aesthetic vision; Agape cannot see God and live. Sixth, for Eros the soul is *immortal*, and, when purified from sense, will return to its Divine origin; Agape stresses the *resurrection* of the dead, body and soul, not derivable from any natural endowment of humanity but dependent on an act of God: 'Death is the judgement of God upon human life in its entirety, and resurrection is the renewal of human life, likewise in its entirety, by God's love.'[51]

Expressed as the content of an idea, taken from Plato, Eros is acquisitive love, man's way to perfection, egocentric.[52] In short, it is motivated by desire for an object, however lofty. Agape, as content, taken from the Gospels, but also Johannine and Pauline − 'God is Agape' − is spontaneous and unmotivated, not limited by any desire, or the value or lack of it of any object.[53] Hence it is creative, in a sense derived from the idea of creation *ex nihilo*. Finally, but perhaps most important of all, 'Agape is the initiator of fellowship with God'.[54] This means that the command to love the neighbour is derived from God's love for man. It does not indicate man's way to God by loving the neighbour, nor even man's love for God, but fellowship within God's love, within God's way to man.[55]

Lacking speculative proposition, pseudonym, mask, Booth's exposition of aporia tends to the academic − relieved of incipient contradiction by the cataloguing of nuance; just as Nygren's exposition of Agape tends to the dogmatic − relieved of incipient contradiction by typologies of 'symptoms' and 'motif-systems'. By abolishing the ethical instead of consecutively and simultaneously suspending and releasing it, Nygren is relieved of psychology − of the anxiety of beginning and the beginning of anxiety which would have to be explored in the historical dialectic of eros and agape;[56] just as Booth is relieved of politics − the equivocation of the ethical which would have to be explored in the historical dialectic of inclusive universal and aporia. Were the ethical to be suspended instead of abolished, the historical dialectic of Eros and Agape and of inclusive universal and aporia in the education of existence would emerge in that 'witness' of the political thinkers, 'too vast', on the discarded assumption, to be called. Such 'witnesses' are indeed thinkers: they think out of the agon of authorship that knows itself to

---

[51] Ibid., p. 225.
[52] Ibid., pp. 175–81.
[53] Ibid., pp. 146–59.
[54] Ibid., p. 80.
[55] Ibid., pp. 91–5.
[56] Anxiety is evident, however, in Nygren's concern to separate Agape from *Nomos* as much as from Eros, see pp. 254–8, 334–48.

be prone to the historical inversions it explores, when authority is object and subject of authorship.

In the context created here, thinkers may be summoned to attest the *modi* of facetious form which exposition of the *separation, subordination, 'emancipation'* of the contrary institutions of religion and politics at the origin of Christianity, at the Reformation, at the establishing of civil society by the modern state, respectively, yields in authorships alive to their consequent and constant inversion of meaning, anxiety of beginning, equivocation of the ethical and arrogation of authority. The authorships of Rousseau, Hegel, Weber and Troeltsch attest and expound the existential and political 'double danger' of this history which reaches its culmination in the authorships of Varnhagen, Luxemburg and Arendt.

In *The Social Contract* Rousseau provides the canonical statement of political aporia — the will of all and the general will: 'the latter considers only the common interest, while the former takes private interest into account, and is no more than a sum of particular wills'. The general will is the 'sum of differences' which remains when the 'pluses and minuses' of the common interest and the sum of particular interests, the will of all, have been cancelled out.[57] A footnote at this point, citing the Marquis d'Argenson, tells us that this agreement of particular wills, formed out of opposition to a third, is the 'art' of politics.[58] This art of differences intrinsic to the formation of the general will — not just restricted to the clashes of particular wills — amounts to an aporetic expression for the aporetic universal, mobile yet formed, a changing configuration of universal, particular and singular.

Yet it is only in the last substantial chapter of the work, 'Civil Religion', after, as he himself admits, laying down rules and illustrating them from the Roman Constitution,[59] that Rousseau addresses the difficulty of the singular — an historical difficulty which, taken systematically, undermines the method and the content of the whole work:

Jesus came to set up on earth a spiritual kingdom, which, by separating the theological from the political system, made the State no longer one, and brought about the internal divisions which have never ceased to trouble Christian peoples ... this double power and conflict of jurisdiction have made all good *polity* impossible in Christian states; and men have never succeeded in

---

[57]  Op. cit., in *The Social Contract and Discourses*, p. 24, tr. p. 185.
[58]  See p. 24, n. 1, tr. p. 185, n. 1.
[59]  Ibid., p. 96, tr. p. 253.

finding out whether they were bound to obey the master or the priest.[60]

Rousseau continues to develop this historical antinomy *typologically*, by distinguishing between 'the religion of man', 'the religion of the citizen' and 'the religion of the priest'. The first and third of these are not located with the historical precision evident in the general statement of how the opposition between Jesus and the state becomes the internal division of authority between master and priest, of Caesar and Christ, but are clearly designated to 'the Gospel' and to 'to-day', and are said to be equally disastrous politically. The split sovereignty of civil and religious institutions defines the religion of the priest, and such is Roman Christianity: it 'leads to a sort of mixed and anti-social code which has no name'.[61] The religion of man, a pure Gospel Christianity, 'holy, sublime and real [*veritable*]', is yet even 'more contrary to the social spirit'[62] than the institutions of the religion of the priest which 'set man in contradiction to himself'.[63] Surprisingly, in spite of Rousseau's origin in Calvinist Geneva, the theocratic second religion, the religion of the citizen, which reunites political and religious institutions, is relegated to pre-modern 'religions of early peoples', for it is defined as 'positive divine right of law'.[64] As a result, there is no conceivable religion for the citizen, even though this is a work centred on the sovereignty of the people as citizens. There is a double antinomy in the exposition of 'citizen' – analytically, religion is irrelevant or else it presupposes 'divine right of law'; historically, religion has degenerated citizenship.

Even though this examination of the consequences of split sovereignty follows from the spread of the Roman cult along with Roman imperialism, so that 'in these circumstances' Jesus first released 'a kingdom of the other world' which turns 'under a visible leader, into the most violent of earthly despotisms',[65] there is no hint that this outcome might have been inherent in the Roman institutions which provide the illustrative material of the earlier chapters. The historical predicament of religion and politics is implicitly attributed, under the types of 'religion of the priest' and 'religion of man', to both modern Catholic and modern Reformed Christianity.

---

[60] Ibid., p. 116, tr. p. 270, emphasis in French.
[61] Ibid., p. 118, tr. p. 272.
[62] Ibid., p. 119, tr. p. 273.
[63] Ibid., p. 118, tr. p. 272.
[64] Ibid.
[65] Ibid., p. 116, tr. p. 270.

This last-minute revelation of irremediably split sovereignty in a work devoted to the 'inalienable' and 'indivisible' *gravitas* of sovereignty, underlies the agon of authorship in Rousseau. It accounts for the facetiousness of form evident throughout his *oeuvre*. While anxiety of beginning, although not in those words, is well noted in 'A Discourse on the Origin of Inequality', and in 'A Discourse on the Origin of Language', as the contradiction of the state of nature which is either inconceivable or presupposes the law it aims to deduce; equivocation of the ethical makes the strategy of so many wandering beginnings 'without industry, without speech, and without home'[66] explicit: 'for the flaws which make social institutions necessary are the same as make the abuse of them unavoidable'.[67] Priority here is inadvertently conceded to institutions. 'The flaws' arise when ground is first enclosed and claimed as 'mine', which is said to be the 'real' founding of civil society. Such 'flaws', therefore, presuppose the formal institution that, it is argued paradoxically, intervenes subsequently to assuage them but instead encourages them − the law which posits and guarantees 'right of property'. This brings out the equivocation of imposing restraint and arousing transgression which the 'state of nature', here 'the flaws', tries, impossibly, to imagine but, instead, conveys anxiety of beginning − 'sly and artful in behaviour to some, and imperious and cruel to others'.[68]

I saw the manners of the times, and have published these letters.

Rousseau here justifies a different form of beginning from the middle. From one who argued that the progress of the arts 'has corrupted our morals',[69] this declaration that romances are necessary to a corrupt people, which justifies Rousseau's publishing of the letters, *Julie ou la Nouvelle Heloise* (1761),[70] indicates the facetious use of the epistolary novel form. The novel seems to address and exploit one side of the otherwise inadmissible split sovereignty of political and religious institutions − the community of love. The violent suppression of eros, leading to the even greater violence of ascetic agape in the death of Julie, shows the difference between this pair of lovers and the original pair − Abelard and Heloise − in spite of the minatory epithet in the

---

[66] 'A Discourse on the Origin of Inequality', p. 81, tr. in ibid., p. 72.
[67] Ibid., p. 119, tr. p. 99.
[68] Ibid., p. 102, tr. p. 86.
[69] 'A Discourse on the Moral Effects of the Arts and Sciences', in ibid., p. 24.
[70] Op. cit., 'Preface', p. 3, 1803 translation by William Kenrick, *Eloisa, or a Series of Original Letters*, p. i.

subtitle: la *nouvelle* Heloise.[71] The difference resides in the place of Paris: the setting for the early stages of the erotic love of Abelard and Heloise; the setting for legal marriage and, by extension, love with 'not half the power of the common contract', as opposed to the sacramental idea of marriage and love of St Preux and Julie;[72] or, the setting for the life, in the words of the 'Discourse on Inequality', where 'being' and 'seeming' are divorced by 'right of property';[73] in short, for the permeation of even personal relations by 'the spiritual animal kingdom' of civil society — so discomforting and alien to the writer of the letters that he can only report it as hearsay and caricature.[74]

Just as agon of authorship in Rousseau may be traced to the belated but *explicit* exposition of the separation of religion and politics from the time of Caesar and Christ, yet it deals *virtually* with the modern separation of state and civil society; so, *pari passu*, agon of authorship in Hegel and Weber may be traced to their *explicit* exposition of the subordination of religion to politics in the Lutheran Reformation, yet *virtually* to the 'emancipation' of religion into civil society. The crux of this agon of authorship discernible in Hegel, Kierkegaard, Nietzsche and Weber concerning the social and political implications of asceticism has been overlooked because of their — and our — preoccupation with differences of method, metaphysics and historicism: Hegel's 'system'; Kierkegaard's 'suspension of the ethical'; Nietzsche's 'genealogy'; Weber's 'unintended consequences' — a deceptively bland phrase for specific and specified *inverse* consequences. If, on the contrary, 'methodology' is considered in the context of agon of authorship attendant on anxiety of beginning, equivocation of the ethical, and the temptation of arrogation of authority, which arises from insight into historically specific inversion of meaning, then a mode of comparison which has no point of assimilation, but which is, on the contrary, the struggle for differentiation, may emerge.

The *Phenomenology of Spirit* is the quintessence of agon of authorship in Hegel's System. Only the *phenomenological* exposition of experience brings together aporetic and agapic danger, tackled separately in the

---

[71] See Abelard, *The Letters of Abelard and Heloise*. After their child was born, it was Heloise who resisted marriage with Abelard, but, later, in their letters, Abelard answers her complaints at being forced to take the veil by presenting the consolation of ascetic agape in the form of a commentary on the Song of Songs. While initially it is clear that the exclusive agapic life was a violence to Heloise, it is difficult to judge whether she found salvation later in the religious life; see p. 74 and Letter 4, p. 137.

[72] *Julie Second Partie*, Letter XXI, p. 249, tr. Letter LXXXVI. *Eloisa I*, Vol. II, p. 116.

[73] 'The Origin of Inequality', p. 101, tr. p. 86.

[74] Ibid., pp. 249–50, tr. pp. 116–17, 119.

two works of *philosophical* reconstruction — *The Philosophy of Right* and *The Philosophy of History*. The aporiae of civil society, reconstructed philosophically, from the perspective of the concept and of philosophical consciousness, in *The Philosophy of Right*, appear phenomenologically, experience of the discordance and discrepancy between concept and object to natural consciousness, as 'the spiritual animal kingdom and deceit' — the 'being' and 'seeming' to which inequality gives rise in Rousseau — in the genealogy of reason *qua* 'Individuality which takes itself to be real in and for itself'. The aporia or difficulty of legal status is dramatized as 'the spiritual animal kingdom'; universal law, which implies a kingdom of ends — 'spiritual' — is suborned to the treatment of oneself and others as means — 'animal'. The danger, twin to aporia, of agapic response, a love ethic which affirms the community and denies the world, reconstructed philosophically in *The Philosophy of History*, appears phenomenologically as 'the beautiful soul', reworked from Goethe's *schöne Seele* in *Wilhelm Meister's Apprenticeship* (just as 'the world of self-alienated Spirit' is reworked from Diderot's *Rameau's Nephew*, first published in a German translation by Goethe) in the genealogy of morality, analogous under 'Spirit' to the 'Individuality which takes itself to be real . . . ' under 'Reason'. By means of these genealogical repetitions within the unfolding configurations of consciousness, post-Lutheran Pietism and the ruthlessness of civil society can be juxtaposed regardless of chronology. By contrast, when Weber makes seventeenth- and eighteenth-century sources, such as Baxter, serve as evidence for the 'consequences' of the Protestant Reformation, his argument can seem merely anachronistic in spite of his proviso that he was interested in doctrines in 'a state of full development'.[75]

Phenomenologically, equivocation of the ethical appears as manifold inversions of meaning: from ethical substance to subjective consciousness — nobility to ignobility, spiritual to animal kingdom; and from subject to substance — pleasure to necessity, absolute freedom to terror. These inversions appear as the experience of natural consciousness, but the tracing of the configurations of natural consciousness which develop out of these determinate negations is the work and witness of philosophical consciousness. Here we find two anxieties of beginning: natural consciousness keeps trying to begin at every moment — from the ' "this" and "meaning" ' to 'forgiveness'; while philosophical consciousness is perpetually in the bad conscience of beginning — intruding and obscuring what is to occur — from the 'Preface' and 'Introduction', which begin the work by disqualifying themselves as legitimate begin-

---

[75] Max Weber, *The Protestant Ethic*, p. 193, n. 5, and see p. 195, n. 7, tr. p. 220, nn. 6 and 7.

nings, to the continuous commentary on the experience of natural consciousness throughout the work — which has to be vigilant against arrogating the authorship of natural consciousness to itself. For the very separation of natural from philosophical consciousness is itself at the heart of the ethical inversions, traced to their mutual recognition at 'Reason as law giver' and 'Reason as testing laws', and at 'the moral view of the world — conscience'. Agon of authorship emerges from this separation and convergence of natural and philosophical consciousness, failing towards and out of a third which cannot itself be posited, not because, in the general, critical Kantian sense, it is a transcendental precondition of appearance and hence cannot itself be an appearance, but precisely because it already appears in the inversions of experience which phenomenology exposits.

Preoccupation with conflicting claims to scientific credentials — Durkheim's 'Rules of Method' versus Weber's 'Ideal-typical' *Verstehen* — and with conflicting definitions of social reality and scientific object — sanctioned social facts versus orientation to typical meanings — that is, with the apparent lack of any *tertium comparationis*, has even detracted from the inversions across authorships within the *logos* or discourse of 'the social'. Weber expounds the Protestant entrepreneurial spirit as making capitalism initially possible, while Durkheim, regardless of the empirical validity of his evidence, argues that Protestant communities have the highest suicide rate and therefore display the greatest lack of social cohesion by comparison with other religions. Durkheim may not demonstrate his thesis convincingly on the basis of the rules he has set himself, yet he still deepens hermeneutically our comprehension of the causality of fate — from entrepreneurial ethic to the grave of life, from Weber's Protestant energy and initiative to Durkheim's Protestant suicide and lack of cohesion. Out of agon of authorship, these inversions of the ethical — and their scientific or philosophical anxiety of beginning — may offer a mode of comprehension not based on any common denominator, any *tertium comparationis*; not, that is, on any reduction, assimilation, or subsumption, but on evident inversion marked by aporetic and agapic dangers.

Simultaneous valorization and denigration of ethical life is the core of the equivocation of the ethical in Hegel and in Weber's expositions of the political and social inversions of the Reformation. The Reformation reconfigures the split sovereignty of religion and politics so that Lutheran religion is subordinated to politics — 'delivered to the Prince' — yet, from the *virtual exposition* of the modern state and modern politics and the aporia of civil society, politics is effectively delivered to religion, undermined by ruthless individual inwardness, and, equally, by communities or sects of agapic love.

In Hegel's exposition, the meaning of 'freedom' proclaimed by Luther turns out to be an equivocal beginning: it involves 'full recognition of the objective process as the existence of the Divine essence [and] now takes it up and follows it out in building up the edifice of secular relations'.[76] But this *immediate* realization of a potential reconciliation does 'not yet expand into a system'[77] of ethical life, for it also induces a 'brokenness of heart', a 'turn of minute and painful introspection'[78] which regards the secular as the alien dominion of malignant power. Hegel traces the effects of the repudiation of the medieval vows of poverty, chastity, obedience and the new commendation of work, marriage, and rationality of the state,[79] but he does not deduce, as Weber does, the unplanned but progressive accumulation of resources for investment and the systematic rationalizing and legitimizing of quotidian economic and official power consequent on the cultivation of inner impotence. Instead, Hegel pits modern, liberal Protestantism, which builds the institutions of reconciliation but then does not inhabit them, against modern, liberal Catholicism, which is 'disposed' towards political virtue, but fails to build the institutions to house it.[80] Like Weber, in *The Protestant Ethic*, however, agon of authorship is least evident or engaged in this most direct presentation of inversion of meaning and institutional consequence in the *Philosophy of History*. If, for Hegel, agon of authorship could only be acknowledged by the phenomenological presentation of the separation and relation of philosophical and natural consciousness throughout their changing configurations, for Weber, the crisis of authorship — its implication in the very reduction of rationality to instrument that it itself historicizes, deploys and deplores — could not be faced when considering 'the calling' in Protestantism and the vocation (*Beruf*) of Luther, but only when considering his own 'call' (*Ruf*), the vocation of science, distinguished ethically from the vocation of politics.[81]

Agon of authorship out of ethical inversion or, equally, inversion of the ethical within agon of authorship indicates and configures anxiety of beginning in Hegel and in Weber. In these authorships a triple inversion emerges characteristic of Lutheran, Calvinist and Pietist Reformations,

---

[76] Hegel, *The Philosophy of History*, p. 502, tr. p. 422.

[77] Ibid., p. 504, tr. p. 424.

[78] Ibid., pp. 504, 505, tr. p. 425.

[79] Ibid., pp. 502–4, tr. pp. 422–4.

[80] Ibid., pp. 520–40, tr. pp. 438–57.

[81] See "Politics as a Vocation" and "Science as a Vocation" in *From Max Weber*, pp. 77–156.

respectively. Religion, delivered into the hands of the Prince, delivers politics into the heart of religion. From religion to politics: first inversion, the call into the world abandons the world (Lutheranism); second inversion, the call into the world abandons the individual to a solitary, inward relation to God, to a self-relation which perdures even when its divine interlocutor has been effaced (Calvinism). From politics to religion: third inversion, in the context of civil society, effective agapic inwardness reproduces the ruthless individualism of civil society, or, collectively, produces the sect which attempts to withdraw from the world (Pietism), and by so doing reinforces it socially but denies it politically.

In Weber's exposition, following one's calling in the world was — even in Luther's original version of absolutely unmerited, bestowed grace — a 'dark and dangerous' doctrine, since emancipation from other-worldly asceticism meant, implicitly, emancipation from all social effort and institution.[82] This spiritual extreme was modified as Luther became involved in practical politics, so that passive submission to fate rather than an active commandment to work becomes the social meaning which predominates.[83] This call into the world, ambiguous from the outset, effectively abandons, even as it methodically transforms, the world. With the flourish of facetiousness:

> Christian asceticism, at first fleeing from the world into solitude, had already ruled the world which it had denounced from the monastery, and through the Church. But it had, on the whole, left the spontaneous character of *daily* life in the world untouched. Now it strode into the market-place of life, slammed the door of the monastery behind it, and undertook to penetrate just that daily routine of life with its methodicalness, to fashion it into a life *in* the world, but *neither of* nor *for* this world.[84]

Dramatizing the personified concept of 'asceticism', Weber employs a Christological facetiousness — 'in', 'of', 'for' this world — to express the implied world-denying meaning of a declaredly world-affirming ethic. Different facets of this ambiguity of Lutheran following one's calling in and the call into the world are developed by Calvinism and Pietism — the latter itself a reform of Lutheranism and Calvinism.

[82]  Weber, *The Protestant Ethic*, p. 120, tr. p. 102, inverted commas in German.
[83]  Ibid., p. 171, tr. pp. 161–2.
[84]  Ibid., p. 165, tr. p. 154, emphases in German, omitted in English.

Weber does not consider the politicizing aspects of Calvinism,[85] but solely its formation of 'that disillusioned and pessimistically inclined individualism',[86] 'the inner isolation of the individual', which 'makes labour in the service of impersonal social usefulness appear to promote the glory of God and hence willed by Him'.[87] This 'ethic' has indifference to the ethical as its inverted result: 'the complete elimination of the theodicy problem and of all those questions about the meaning of life and world'.[88] Although he makes aesthetic pseudonymity literal and overlooks the Lutheran context, Weber, aptly, adds: 'The conflict between the individual and the ethic (in Søren Kierkegaard's sense) did not exist for Calvinism.'[89] In the 'sense' of Kierkegaard's authorship, indeed, the Calvinist has abolished the ethical, and acts out of inner conviction, as anxious as it is unquestioned, to impose his rationalism on all aspects of social, political and economic life.

Pietism of the late eighteenth century is the especial interest of Kierkegaard, Hegel and Weber because it represents the attempt to reform both Lutheranism and Calvinism from within – to resist Lutheranism's submission by default to the ethical but to temper Calvinism's theocratic impulsion to abolish the ethical. 'Pietism' represents an awareness that the split sovereignty of Caesar and Christ has corrupted once again even the Reformed institutions of both; yet Pietism itself attempts a second reformation which is even more thoroughly corrupted than the first – for it is subverted by the new politics of the state and civil society as they are separated from each other.

Pietism, ascetic and romantic at the same time, provides the bridge from religion delivered into the hands of the Prince to politics delivered to the heart of religion; it reproduces inner poverty and outer ruthlessness at the collective as well as at the individual level: 'it wished to make the invisible Church of the elect visible on this earth.'[90] This is the paradox of the agapic community, which Kierkegaard sketched facetiously as clockwork Communism: the loveful communitarian withdrawal from the world leading to an authoritarian regime which

---

[85]  See Troeltsch, *The Social Teaching of the Christian Churches*, Vol. 2, pp. 688–9; and n. 94 *infra*, and Adam Seligman, "The Eucharist Sacrifice and the Changing Utopian Movement in Post Reformation Christianity", *International Journal of Comparative Sociology*, 29, 1–2 (1988), 30–43, and "Inner Worldly Individualism and the Institutionalization of Puritanism in Late Seventeenth Century England", *British Journal of Sociology*, forthcoming.

[86]  Weber, *Protestant Ethic*, p. 123, tr. p. 105.

[87]  Ibid., pp. 125, 126, tr. pp. 108, 109.

[88]  Ibid., p. 126, tr. p. 109.

[89]  Ibid.

[90]  Ibid., p. 144, tr. p. 130.

results from refusal of anxiety of beginning and equivocation of the ethical.

> [T]he desire to separate the elect from the world could, with a strong emotional intensity, lead to a sort of monastic community life of half-communistic character, as the history of Pietism, even within the Reformed Church, has shown again and again.[91]

Instead of future salvation obtainable within the everyday routine of life in a worldly calling, demonstrated by its strict methodical conduct, the emphasis on the 'visibility' of salvation for an elect separated from the world lessened the emphasis on 'restless and successful work'[92] at one's calling, and diverted concern to the 'present emotional state', and to the forgiveness of sin rather than practical sanctification.[93]

> In place of the systematic rational struggle to attain and retain certain *knowledge* of future (otherworldly) salvation comes here the need to *feel* reconciliation and community with God now.[94]

Pietism made Calvinism less ascetic, while it made Lutheranism more so: the attempt to make salvation visible induced Calvinism to moderate its abolition of the ethical, while it made Lutheranism moderate its submission to the ethical. Yet, in both cases, the agapic community suspends without *releasing* the ethical, and hence its passage to eternity and back again — the invisible community made visible — congeals in the now of temporal legality, divided from morality on the inner side, and the state on the outer.

> Only . . . the Church [can] give to the elements of Natural Law within the State a divine strength and depth; making the secular *justitia* of the legal system into the perfect *justitia* of a piety which uses the world both for renunciation and for the exercise of love.[95]

Troeltsch is here showing how the early Church hallowed natural law within the State — a perfect mutual strengthening of imperial and ecclesiastical authority — and yet it could still enjoy the equivocal exploitation of 'the world' for renunciation *and* for the exercise of love.

---

[91] Ibid., pp. 145–6, tr. p. 131.
[92] Ibid., p. 151, tr. p. 137.
[93] Ibid., p. 151, tr. pp. 137, 138.
[94] Ibid., p. 151, tr. p. 138, emphasis in German omitted in English.
[95] Troeltsch, *The Social Teaching of the Christian Churches*, Vol. 1, p. 157.

By extension, it may be said that the modern Pietist sect, too, uses 'the world' for renunciation and for works of love, and in so doing hallows the imperfect *justitia* of natural right in civil society. Unequivocal denigration of a legal system continues to be, in this modern version, compatible with an equivocal social position, expressed in cosmological terms of the 'world'; or, vice versa, what looks like the simultaneous rejection and reform of existing social institutions — a pietistic rather than a rationalistic relation to everyday life — may conceal and presuppose the specifically modern legal system based on positive individual rights.

While Weber examines the relative extent of the rationalizing of *conduct* which results from the nuances of Reformed, this-worldly soteriology, Troeltsch — in an authorship which acknowledges the restless anchoring of the latter-day mystic, who lacks religious domicile in the scholarship of comparative religion[96] — follows the opposed *missions* of world-civilizing Church and world-denying sect, and brings out, in the modern Reformed tradition, the ostensibly inverse relation between antinomian soteriology and theological and practical obsession with law, which, on closer examination, reveals the profound connection between spiritual opposition to law and sociological legalism.[97]

From early Christianity on, 'Church' and 'sect' are distinguished in terms of their paradoxical inversion of grace and law: the acceptance by 'the Church' of the objective legitimacy – the holiness – of its sacerdotal and sacramental office, its spirit of universalism, relieves it from arousing and harbouring the individual intensity experienced by every member of 'the sect', and also from the emphasis of 'the sect' on 'the Law of God', incipient 'legalism', and 'good works': 'The Church emphasizes the idea of Grace and makes it objective; the sect emphasizes and realizes the idea of subjective holiness.'[98] In the established 'Church', institutionalized law permits the spontaneity of grace; in the voluntary sect, eschatology of grace demands the legalism of life. These types, even when summarized so ahistorically and schematically, are correspondingly worldful and worldless: 'the Church', into which members are born, baptized and confirmed, an institution endowed with grace and salvation, 'adjust[s] to the world'; while 'the sect',

---

[96]  Ibid., Vol. 2, pp. 749–50.

[97]  In the notes added to the 1920 edition of *The Protestant Ethic*, Weber refers to Troeltsch's book in general terms, 'which, besides containing many things, is a very welcome confirmation of and supplement to this Essay in so far as it deals with our problem', p. 188 n. 1 (not included in German).

[98]  Troeltsch, *The Social Teaching of the Christian Churches*, Vol. 1, pp. 100–1, 336–7.

consisting of voluntary initiates who 'live apart from the world', focuses on law instead of grace, and sets up some version of the Christian order based on love and anticipation of the Kingdom.[99]

Protestantism, however, represents an historically specific hybrid: 'the transformation of the sect-type into great mass communities, the development of their freedom within the sphere of the tolerant modern State, and the adaptation of the sects to the bourgeois social order'.[100] The politics of Lutheranism are clearly distinguished, however, from the politics of Calvinism: Lutheranism's adherence to inner virtue and public, conservative endurance is opposed to Calvinism's cultivation of democracy and liberalism and the public virtues of independence, love of humanity, liberty, and Christian social reform[101] — in striking contrast with Weber's argument that Calvinism effects a cavalier and illiberal rationalizing of ethical life. Yet outside the sanctuary of Geneva, the ambivalence of Pietistic politics is seen as the intrinsic tendency of Calvinism.[102]

Opposed both to Protestant ecclesiasticism and to the State, Pietism, of all the sects, takes the most detached and disdainful stance towards 'the world', and yet most reproduces the social relations from which it actively distances itself and which it expresses in cosmological terms.[103] The withdrawal from 'the world' implies an acceptance of the bourgeois order 'as a relative Natural Law', necessitated by sin and divinely appointed.[104] Judging this a manifestation of despair,[105] Troeltsch demonstrates, not as Weber did, that Pietism tempers Lutheran submission to the ethical and Calvinist abolition of the ethical, but that Lutheran Pietism purifies and reduces the ethical while Calvinist Pietism, outside Geneva, extends its hallowing of the ethical from the holy individual to the holy community.[106] On the one hand, Pietism, both Lutheran and Calvinist, refined sectarian asceticism: co-operation, discipline, reduction of secular culture to practically useful elements, evangelizing and educating of children; on the other hand, it did not tend towards political and social radicalism.[107] 'It did not need to *become*

---

[99]   Ibid., Vol. 2, p. 993.
[100]  Ibid., p. 691.
[101]  Ibid., pp. 688–9.
[102]  Ibid., p. 677.
[103]  Ibid., pp. 741f.
[104]  Ibid., p. 726.
[105]  Ibid., p. 727.
[106]  Ibid., pp. 714–19.
[107]  Ibid., pp. 717–18.

bourgeois like the early Baptist movement, from the very beginning it *was* bourgeois and loyal [emphasis in original].'[108]

In spite of his earnest that he will examine the connection between the development of Protestant Churches and sects and the 'bourgeois social order',[109] Troeltsch reneges on making explicit this mutual conditioning — even though it clearly troubles his whole retrospection of Christian teaching and institutions from the perspective of the specifically modern predicament. Instead he relapses into summary specifications of the fate he has thoroughly historicized by employing the ideal types of 'Church' and 'sect'; a relapse necessitated by his declared, overriding concern to present the history and the possibility of actualizing the Christian Ethos in absolute opposition to any *soi-disant* Marxist position which would reduce it to class struggle and to 'ideological reflection of economic development'.[110]

Yet Troeltsch has demonstrated that there is a sect inside every Church, and that each type is weakened, spiritually and sociologically, by its strength: 'the sect' has too little social organization — 'it possesses only a strict ethic, a living Mythos, and a passionate hope for the future'; 'the Church' too much compulsion.[111] In the modern 'bourgeois' period, Troeltsch draws out a further unanticipated inversion: each Reformed type is itself reformed by what it reforms. This entanglement of antinomianism and legalism, which becomes acute in the modern period, is consistent with the implied thesis that modern positive law based on individual rights is reinforced even by cosmological abnegation and social withdrawal just as much as ancient and medieval positive law based on natural law was affirmed by cosmological abnegation and social conformity. While Troeltsch judges his method to be far removed from Marx, and, in spite of his consistent sociological pathos, can only conclude by reaffirming an abstract dialectic of Christian Ethos and 'world outlook', he has in 'the story of a constantly renewed search for this compromise, and of fresh opposition to this Spirit of compromise',[112] set out the fate of religion 'emancipated' into civil society, as civil society is expounded by Marx, and he has frozen in oppositional and dialectical 'types' his incipient speculative historicism. Troeltsch's anxiety of beginning puts him right back to his original, posited typology — when we know him to be immured in the

---

[108]   Ibid., p. 718.
[109]   Compare text to n. 100 *supra*.
[110]   Ibid., p. 1002.
[111]   Ibid., pp. 996–7.
[112]   Ibid., pp. 728, 999–1000, 1012–13.

equivocation of the ethical which he has expounded but cannot concede.

## Droits de la Femme/Droits de la citoyenne[113]

... a 'beautiful soul' does not possess the power to renounce the knowledge of itself which it keeps to itself, it cannot attain to an identity with the consciousness it has repulsed, nor therefore to a vision of the unity of itself in the other, cannot obtain to an objective existence ... The 'beautiful soul', lacking an *actual* existence, entangled in the contradiction between its pure self and the necessity of that self to externalize itself and change itself into an actual existence, and dwelling in the *immediacy* of this firmly held antithesis − an immediacy which alone is the middle term reconciling the antithesis, which has been intensified to its pure abstraction, and is pure being or empty nothingness − this 'beautiful soul', then, being conscious of this contradiction in its unreconciled immediacy, is disordered to the point of madness, wastes itself in yearning and pines away in consumption. Thereby it does in fact surrender the *being-for-self* to which it so stubbornly clings; that what it brings forth is only the non-spiritual *unity* of being.[114]

In 'The Fraternal Social Contract', Carole Pateman insists that 'The meaning of "civil society" ... is constituted through the "original" separation and opposition between the modern, public − civil − world and the modern, private or conjugal and familial sphere', and that 'Feminists are concerned with *this* division.'[115] She distinguishes this definition of civil society from the distinction of public and private 'drawn *within* "civil society"', for example, in discussions of public versus private ownership of businesses, and she attributes this meaning of civil society to Hegel, 'the social contract theorists' greatest critic, who contrasts the universal, public state with the market, classes and corporations of private, civil society'.[116] However, in spite of Hegel's rejection, *contra* Rousseau, of 'the contractarian ideal of social life' in general, and, *contra* Kant, of marriage as analogous to contractual rela-

---

[113] The title alludes to Marx's discussion of *droits de l'homme* and *droits du citoyen* in 'On the Jewish Question', *Early Writings*, p. 191f., tr. pp. 228f.

[114] Hegel, *Phenomenology of Spirit*, p. 491, tr. Miller para. 668, pp. 406–7.

[115] Op. cit., in J. Keane (ed.), *Civil Society and the State*, p. 102, emphasis in original.

[116] Ibid.

tions, Pateman argues in *The Sexual Contract* that he nevertheless insists that marriage 'originates in a contract'; he still accepts, that is, 'the sexual contract'.[117] 'In order to incorporate women into civil society while excluding them, Hegel re-enacts the contradictions of Kant's theory.'[118] Whether 'married life' according to Pateman is expounded as mutual property in persons (Kant), or as mutual recognition of lovers (Hegel), the presupposition is the same: women must be both incorporated into civil society and its major institutional bonds − the contracts of citizenship, employment and marriage − and they must be subordinated. The sexual contract 'requires' and achieves this because it takes place in the private sphere separated from 'civil public life [sic]'.[119] It follows from this argument that to opt politically for the conception of the gender-neutral individual would not be to redress the social subordination of women, for the notion of 'the individual' has been the means by which the humanity of women could be affirmed at the same time as their agency was restricted: *droits de la citoyenne* are not *droits de la femme* − to extrapolate from Marx's discussion of the distinction between *droits de l'homme* and *droits du citoyen* in 'On the Jewish Question'.

Pateman, however, leaves the sociological potentialities of her own theory underdeveloped. By attributing an opposition between private and 'civil public' to contract theory which she claims is only ever 'shifted' *within* civil society − even by 'the most profound critic of contract', Hegel,[120] she misunderstands both that the distinctions between private and public, and between civil society and the state, are themselves posited by the legality of the modern state; and that the modern state has a history, has come to be, in a way which can be reconstructed. She thus continues to conflate 'civil and public', to endorse the political theory she criticizes by positing oppositions, instead of expounding the contradictions of all contracts which arise when both women *and* men live in ostensibly separate realms of civil society − the sphere of needs, familial and economic − and the state. As a result she fails to provide the sociology she calls for by referring to Hegel's 'ethical life' and to Durkheim's proposition that not everything in the contract is contractual:[121] contract presupposes complex social and ethical relations − Nietzsche's ironic 'breeding of an animal who can make promises' − and in turn, contractual relations give rise to, or

---

[117]   Op. cit., pp. 173, 179.
[118]   Ibid., p. 173.
[119]   Ibid., pp. 180–1.
[120]   Ibid., p. 173.
[121]   Ibid., pp. 175–6.

form, internalized identities – the moralization of legal concepts.[122] No sociology, or dialectic of activity and passivity, is provided by Pateman, although it is implied by the structural framing of women as included in contract and subordinated by it – formally free and equal to enter into contracts but compelled by necessity into those contracts and submitted to the unequal terms on which they are based.

The deeper consequence of this 'sexual contract' approach is that it is blind to the ways in which the legal and social status of women, their dialectic of activity and passivity (which Pateman sets out acutely but formally by restricting herself to statements about social and sexual contract), is at the heart, or – to eschew a metaphor of the emotions – is the difficulty, *the* aporia, of the critique of Enlightenment. This critique has always related the ideal to the social consequences arising from the separation of legal and political relations by the modern state. In Lessing, Goethe, Hegel and Kierkegaard, 'woman' is the Lear of modernity: just as Lear, foil to his Fool, is an exploration of the meaning of sovereignty – subjecting and subjected, omnipotent and impotent – so modern subjectivity – sovereign and subordinated – is explored in the soul of a woman in a way that is always overlooked by any feminist reading which knows what it is looking for before it looks: 'feminists are concerned with *this* division [emphasis in original].' This is not to say that Pateman posits an original female nature,[123] but that she presupposes and posits an *-ism*, 'feminism' – albeit no more than not 'to deny political significance to womenhood', a principle that relates judicial freedom to unfreedom as the truth of the social/sexual contract 'story'.[124]

Rahel Varnhagen, Rosa Luxemburg and Hannah Arendt present and live the agon of articulation which refuses any '-ism' to cure their complaint: any reduction of unfreedom to contract, which would relieve the actress of her implication in the activity and passivity of the ethical; they eschew any danger which is not double. Anxiety of beginning, which will not settle with any locality nor with any easy universality, but which develops a reflection on the inversions and aporiae of both, is the way in which *droits de la femme* and *droits de la citoyenne* appear in their work.

If *ressentiment*, from Nietzsche's *Genealogy of Morals*, captures the plasticity of hate – reaction peopled as a townscape of animosity; and 'resignation', from Kierkegaard's *Fear and Trembling*, captures the plasticity of a lost love mummified and embellished as the inner landscape

---

[122]  See *On the Genealogy of Morals*, 'Second Essay', secs. 1 and 21.
[123]  See *The Sexual Contract*, pp. 222–5.
[124]  Ibid., p. 227.

of the beloved; repetition, *if represented*, rigidifies the ethical and suspends the political: it inverts the political and reproduces the alienated modern state as a barbarism of pure unworldly culture where the violence is turned inward and done to oneself — the violence in love without the love in violence — causing one to 'waste away in yearning'. 'Pietism' becomes the expression — from the eighteenth-century novel (Goethe), to nineteenth-century philosophy (Hegel), to twentieth-century sociology (Weber) — for this neo-reformation caught in the trails of civil society separated from the state. The love community, its violence in love, its repetition in the feast, is represented by 'the beautiful soul' — of a woman. These positions — *ressentiment*, resignation, repetition represented and spoilt by recollection, and 'the beautiful soul' are explored by a late eighteenth-century Jewish woman in her encounter with Goethe's authorship, with the novels in which women and religion are 'emancipated' into civil society. From outside civil society, before the emancipation of the Jews, Rahel Varnhagen, *née* Levin, took on an agon of authorship, which she preferred to live with rather than resolve — both 'keeping her knowledge to herself' *and* giving it away.[125]

The position and representation of women already indicated the unease of Enlightenment with its own ideals: the ideal of Liberty, the ideal of Reason and the ideal of Fraternity. 'Liberty', the statue of militant and heroic woman at the barricades in Paris during the Revolution, is the epitome of freedom, yet her image reinforces the containment from which, momentarily, she is released in order to focus the general uproar of violence.[126] 'Reason', Mary Wollstonecraft argued in 1792, divided between man and woman, is corrupt and corrupting to both men and women. Yet, while rightly insisting that both men *and* women are implicated in this corruption, she recommends the restoration of dirempted reason instead of its enlargement and transformation.[127]

'Fraternity', captured by Lessing's play *Nathan the Wise*, 1769, ostensibly a paean of praise to the brotherhood of man, is seen to imply

[125]  See opening passage to this section, p. 83 from Hegel, *Phenomenology of Spirit*, Miller para. 668, and n. 114 *supra*.

[126]  See Marcia Pointon, 'Liberty on the Barricades: Women, Politics and Sexuality in Delacroix', and Irene Coltman Brown, 'Mary Wollstonecraft and the French Revolution or Feminism and the Rights of Man', in S. Reynolds (ed.), *Women, State and Revolution*, pp. 25–43, 1–24.

[127]  *Vindication of the Rights of Woman*, p. 201, where she speculates that the authority of Reason, 'throne of prerogative', may only rest on 'a chaotic mass of prejudice', or, even, 'on an elephant, tortoise', or even 'the mighty shoulders of a son of the earth'.

evasions which cannot be contained even though – or precisely because – fraternity is figured between brother and sister, man *and* woman. At the end of the play, Recha, adopted daughter of the wise Jew Nathan, and the Christian Knight Templar renounce their great passion for each other on coming to learn that they are brother and sister, and in turn closely related to the Muslim Sultan.[128] The play celebrates the transformation of erotic love into love of humanity in spite of the evident reluctance of the lovers to participate in this transformation. The apparently smooth resolution of the play simply moves the guiding taboo from miscegenation to incest in a way which is most unconvincing, for it unveils 'fraternity' as sacrifice and loss shored up by prohibition and intrinsically unstable.

The character of Nathan, the Jewish father, was modelled on Moses Mendelssohn, the Jewish Enlightenment philosopher and close friend of Lessing. Mendelssohn had several daughters, one of whom, Brendel, left her Jewish husband for Friedrich Schlegel, changing her name to Dorothea, and she was subsequently represented by Schlegel as the heroine of his novel, *Lucinde*, which provoked considerable scandal when it was published in 1799, for it argued for a kind of free love between men and women as the criterion of humanity.[129] Since life and letters are already here conflated in fathers and daughters, it seems that Brendel/Dorothea's fate offers a commentary on the prohibition governing 'Recha', and the trangression which was enacted and then imagined in *Lucinde*. 'Recha', who remains unmarried for the sake of fraternity, becomes 'Lucinda' – just as Brendel, brought up in an enlightened home and married within its assumptions of traditional Jewish exclusivity, tempered by free inclination,[130] nevertheless breaks the bonds of civility and, taking the name Dorothea, lives openly with Schlegel, who extols their illicit conjugality and invents a new literary form for their new form of life.

Rahel Levin took up those lived and literary dilemmas as a reflection which she developed in her letters and *Journal* on love and the development of the modern 'nation'-state. She was able to see the instability arising from the conjunction of freedom and lack of freedom within civil society – contracts and their contradictions – from the extraordinary position of being simultaneously excluded from that civil society yet hostess to the birth of the modern, bureaucratic, 'nation'-

---

[128]  Lessing, *Nathan the Wise*, Act V, Scene VIII, pp. 134–40 tr. pp. 215–20.
[129]  Friedrich Schlegel, *Lucinde*, pp. 107–9.
[130]  See A. Altmann, *Moses Mendelssohn*, pp. 98–100 and 724–5. Another daughter, Reikel, was called 'Recha'.

state. Her first salon from the last decade of the eighteenth century to the first decade of the nineteenth was unlike any 'society' salon for it was outside society — in the high garret in Berlin, where this impoverished, unglamorous and, at that time, unmarried, Jewish woman lived.[131] Yet she provided a haven for the reforming tendencies of the day in all the main media: for Fichte's reform of the state, with his increasing emphasis on nationalism; for Schleiermacher's reform of religion into universalism of feeling; for the Humboldt brothers' reform of education; for the Schlegels and the Tiecks, Paul, Kleist, Fouqué, Camisso, Wolf, and Wiesel — men and women who were experimenting with form to explore the new modes of life.

However, it was in Goethe's great novel, *Wilhelm Meister's Apprenticeship*, that Rahel Levin saw the truth of the new state and new society. For, although, subsequently, Rahel Varnhagen became associated with the sentimental and romanticized Goethe cult, and *Wilhelm Meister's Apprenticeship* has become known as the classic *Bildungsroman* — novel of the formation, education or initiation of a young person into life and the world — the significant connection between Rahel Levin and *Wilhelm Meister* is far harder than this: for the book presents love — agapic and erotic — as political. It does not make politics into a question of education: it presents individual and collective development or distortion as political precondition already congealed into the character and fate of the protagonists, who, in their attempts to acknowledge or to deny the world, explore the transition from the aristocratic to the bourgeois world. Separation of love from the 'world' is repeatedly reinforced by reformations which intend and promise their affirmation and reconciliation.

At the heart of the work lies a novel within a novel, 'Confessions of a Beautiful Soul'.[132] This juxtaposition affords a contrast between the fate of Wilhelm, released from the context of aristocratic society and learning to be a bourgeois, and the fate of 'the beautiful soul'. Her story is told in the first person by the unnamed woman who withdraws herself from the bourgeois world towards the named, historical, Pietist Moravian community of Herrnhut. Both of these educations are dangerous — but they are neither of them dangerous enough; and both culminate in mysticism — Wilhelm's in the entrepreneurial ethic of the society of the tower, *die Turmgesellschaft*; 'the beautiful soul's' in the flirtation with the otherworldly community of Herrnhut.

Rahel Levin, canonized by Thomas Carlyle, translator of *Wilhelm*

[131] See Ellen Key, *Rahel Varnhagen, A Portrait*.
[132] Op. cit., Book VI, pp. 374–440, tr. pp. 6–123.

*Meister* into English, as 'a beautiful soul', in an 1838 essay,[133] and presented by Hannah Arendt as struggling to avoid the temptations of such a beatitude,[134] is reduced by both of these readings to overcoming a single danger when she knew the danger was double.

The 'boy' apprentice, Wilhelm, charged by his brother-in-law, Werner, on his father's death to take on the management of a large estate, justifies, in a reply to his brother-in-law, his remaining with the travelling theatrical troupe, learning to be an actor in the playhouse – metaphor for the world[135] – by distinguishing between the nobleman and the burgher. The nobleman 'is hampered by no limits ... whereas nothing more beseems the burgher than the quiet feeling of the limits that are drawn around him.'[136] The nobleman may ask himself 'What art thou': the burgher 'What hast thou'; the nobleman has 'a right to *seem*': the burgher 'is compelled to *be* ... the former does and makes, the latter but effects and procures.'[137]

The girl apprentice, confessed by the mature 'beautiful soul', begins the story of her life with the onset of childhood ill-health – her vision and vocation growing out of and towards a consumptive sick-bed rather than, as Hegel exposits it, solely leading to it.[138] A child of natural curiosity and a voracious reader, her concrete learning matched by a solitary, erotic God-relationship, she finds herself unfit for the frivolity of court life.[139] Sharing in its dissipation yet distanced from the class of German courtiers, she nevertheless forms a liaison with one, Narciss (*sic*), who both mocks and furthers her education, 'on all subjects, law excepted'.[140] Drawn to Narciss when he is wounded in a dual, her betrothal to him wanes as her relation to her 'Invisible Friend' waxes. Narciss, effete at court, causes her to withdraw from her engagement to him, and from all dancing and play, to extricate herself

---

[133]  Carlyle's rendering of *Bekenntnisse eine schönen Seele* as 'Confessions of a Fair Saint' has obscured Hegel's expatiation of Book VI in the *Phenomenology of Spirit*, while in his essay on 'Varnhagen von Ense's Memoirs', 1838, Carlyle's denigration by excessive praise of Rahel's (*sic*) 'true genius' and her 'in the highest degree vaporous, vague ... multifarious, confused wind–music', a 'subjective' authorship by comparison with Goethe's 'objective' authorship, prevents their deep affinity from emerging and casts her as 'secluded' and 'imprisoned', an elevated but inarticulate soul; *Critical and Miscellaneous Essays*, Vol. V, pp. 312, 313, 319–20.

[134]  See *Rahel Varnhagen, The Life of a Jewish Woman.*

[135]  *Wilhelm Meister's Apprenticeship*, Bk VIII, ch. III, pp. 454–5, tr. p. 135.

[136]  Bk V, ch. III, pp. 303–4, tr. pp. 7–9.

[137]  Ibid., Bk V, ch. III, p. 304, tr. p. 9.

[138]  Ibid., Bk VI, p. 374, tr. p. 69.

[139]  Ibid., pp. 378–80, tr. pp. 73–4.

[140]  'die Rechtsgelehrsamkeit ausgenommen', accurately translated 'jurisprudence [erudition in law] excepted', ibid., 391, tr. p. 83.

'from the calls of a world where everything was either cold indifference or hot insanity'.[141]

Nevertheless his injunction 'that a lady ought to keep the knowledge she might have more secret than the Calvinist his creed in Catholic countries'[142] will dominate the battle to come between her piety and her activity, linking as it does the secret suppression of a woman's access to knowledge, which is otherwise public and shared, part of the social world, with her access to God, to the invisible and supernatural, which is first erotic and friendly, but subsequently converted to a deeper pathos of sin, suffering and salvation.[143] The 'confession' concerns the lacking middle term – the various 'actual existences' tempted, tried, and turned away; so that the confessor matures – she is a 'beautiful soul' – but her body falls away 'as an outward object'.[144] Such resolution is not aesthetic nor ethical but, as it were, religiousness 'A', resignation with a border on despair, which would 'pine away in consumption' were it not granted the future in the form of four children, left by a dead sister, but shortly removed from the 'dangerous' education of their aunt.

The young woman who 'had valued God above her bridegroom' is both the object of idle curiosity and the subject of serious interest from families of courts and princes with similar spiritual leanings.[145] Under the guidance of a spiritual patron, she undergoes a conversion crisis from God as 'faithful invisible leader' to, as it were, 'witness at first hand', and this leads her to the literature of the Herrnhut Pietist community led by Count Zinzendorf.[146] Yet, from inclination and from force of circumstance, she remains on the periphery, 'a Herrnhut sister on my own footing',[147] the captious spirit of the members resulting in the dismissal of 'this Herrnhut doll work'.[148]

The occasion of her sister's wedding at their uncle's castle brings her into the architecture and argument of analogy between works of art and works of nature, between man and God. Her austere piety is challenged by a restrained Italianate culture. She is encouraged to see the finger of the Deity in nature as an earnest of the value of human nature and endeavour, to strive to get acquainted with the sentient man in all his comprehensiveness, and to bring about an active harmony among his

---

[141]   Ibid., p. 394, tr. p. 86, corrected.
[142]   Ibid., p. 391, tr. p. 83.
[143]   Ibid., pp. 412–13, tr. pp. 100–1.
[144]   Ibid., p. 435, tr. p. 119.
[145]   Ibid., pp. 400–1, tr. p. 91.
[146]   Ibid., pp. 407, 415, tr. pp. 96, 102–3.
[147]   Ibid., pp. 416–17, tr. p. 104.
[148]   Ibid., p. 420, tr. pp. 106–7.

powers', instead of referring all observation back to a hyperactive, inner, moral scruple.[149]

Restored to her own environment, however, she fails to learn this lesson — to change her appreciation of the external from the sensuous or merely aesthetic, to the sacramental; and, when, released by the death of her father to a singular independence, she hastens to a local Herrnhut settlement, less organized than a full community, comprising members of all social classes, she is discomfited by the spirit of subordination — which makes the group sound ecclesial rather than radically sectarian.[150]

Retaining her spiritual integrity — against eros, against marriage, against Renaissance culture, against Pietist communitarianism — her bodily integrity begins to fail her and she lapses into the childhood ailment with which her confession began. A wise physician counteracts her assertion of spiritual independence: 'the body too will fall to pieces like a vesture; but I, the well-known I, I am':[151]

> 'To be active', he would say, 'is the primary vocation of man; all the intervals in which he is obliged to rest, he should employ in gaining clearer knowledge of external things, for this will in its turn facilitate activity.'[152]

The bodily disintegration of 'the beautiful soul' is a kind of survival, whereas her unhappily married sister dies in her fourth childbed. The burgeoning active agape of the eldest girl orphan, whether occupied or at ease, is the only fruitful female counterpoint, even though this child has been educated, together with her siblings, to seclude them 'from whatever might awaken them to an acquaintance with themselves and with the invisible, sole, faithful Friend'[153] — and, equally, to seclude them from the barren piety of their dangerous aunt, who protests the efficacy of her practice even while she admits the interested impulse of her own charity.[154]

Finally, the confession fades away — declaiming increasing facility in perfection and decreasing bodily facility to rasp in a whisper the ingenuous corruption at the root of this *Bildung*: 'I can scarcely remember a

149  Ibid., p. 424, tr. p. 110.
150  Ibid., p. 433, tr. pp. 117–18.
151  Ibid., p. 435, tr. p. 118.
152  Ibid., p. 435, tr. p. 119.
153  Ibid., p. 439, tr. p. 122.
154  Ibid., p. 437, tr. pp. 120–1.

commandment; to me there is nothing that assumes the aspect of law; it is an impulse that leads me, and guides me always alright . . . '.[155]

From image of inverted aristocratic world, 'Herrnhut' subsequently somersaults into affirmation of the insecurities of the bourgeois world when the ailing Count, Lothario, affirms his will to live actively by sacrificing a small portion of his revenue, but not, as his brother, giving away his whole fortune to save his soul. He expostulates 'recovering or dying I will stand by it, and say: *Here or nowhere is Herrnhut!*' so that 'the duty which is nearest to me' — not an idea — acts to rally whatever resources are available.[156]

> I am, therefore, observing the world. Life, nature, are here for me. Calculate the *lutte* [battle, struggle — agon] of my life, therefore; the big, the small and bitter moments. With the sharpest knowledge about myself. With the opinion, that I should be a queen (no reigning one, however), or a mother: I discover that there is just *nothing* that I am. No daughter, no sister, no lover, no spouse, not even a burgheress [*keine Bürgerin*].[157]

Rahel Levin, conscious of the contradiction, intensified in this letter to its pure abstraction, between her knowledge and her lack of actual existence, was able to avoid clinging to this pure being-for-self which she seems to express in all its fatality.[158] She untangled the contradiction between her pure self and the necessity of that self to actualize itself by refusing to dwell in the immediacy of this antithesis and by taking on instead the many apprenticeships enacted in *Wilhelm Meister*, allowing the reversals of these middles, pious and civil, to culture the immediacy of her own. By listening to Goethe, who knows how to listen, his writings become her confession;[159] so that she fixes neither her own isolation outside civil society, nor the many paths through civil society, into an absolute, but knows both position and routing as mediated immediacies: knows the relation between the aporiae — the difficult paths — and what is fixed or static — the state. By not keeping this knowledge to herself, confessions become authorship; 'the beautiful

---

[155]  Ibid., p. 440, tr. p. 122.
[156]  Ibid., Bk VII, ch. III, p. 453, tr. p. 133.
[157]  Letter to Fredrick de la Motte Fouqué, 26 July 1809, in Rahel Varnhagen, *Gesammelte Werke*, Bd I, p. 436, trans. and cited in L. Weissberg, 'Turns of Emancipation: On Rahel Varnhagen's Letters', p. 9. The following discussion is deeply indebted to the work of Liliane Weissberg.
[158]  See Hegel, *Phenomenology of Spirit*, Miller para. 668, pp. 406–7 (n. 114 *supra*).
[159]  Letter to David Veit, 22 March 1795, Bd I, p. 140; Arendt, *Rahel Varnhagen*, pp. 115, 116–117; see L. Weissberg, 'Turns of Emancipation', pp. 6, 16–17.

soul' becomes the agon of that authorship — which cultivates the dangers of both paths, skirting and moving through civil society. To interpret her life and letters in terms of the 'pariah' who comes to play 'the parvenu' is to reduce her, consecutively, to one of these dangers.[160]

This agon of authorship confronts the anxiety of beginning at its birth — the birth of the modern 'nation'-state — and yet takes on fully the equivocation of the middle-to-come: the reconfigured vulnerability of the Jew, 'emancipated' into civil society. In this deeply vicarious way authorship acquires an education — it develops without the means of development — and, in so staking herself, the author remains with the broken middle. 'Listen to Goethe . . . with tears I write the name of this mediator, in memory of my extreme distress . . . Read [him] as one reads the Bible in misfortune.'[161]

Yes, if I could live outside the world, without customs [Sitte], without relationships, diligently in a village . . .[162]

By remaining a witness at first hand in the double difficulty of either being outside civil society or moving into civil society, Rahel Levin did not confuse birth with beginning. Born a Jew, yet becoming hostess to the birth of the modern 'nation'-state, her authorship, in letters, fictionalized posthumously,[163] debates and dramatizes the anxiety of how to begin when the new start seemed to welcome the Jew on equal terms. Aware that she might merely exchange one precarious privilege for another: the exceptional status of hostess for heightened bourgeois individuality — the former resting on feudal protection, the latter inse-cure on bourgeois equality — she enacts in advance the shifting meaning of 'the nation state' already evident in Fichte's lectures in Berlin which she attended.[164] To the French, the state defines the 'nation': participa-tion in universal law qualifies 'humanity' as the collective political will of a people. 'People' or 'nation' here provide a substitute for divine legitimation; 'the people' or 'nation' are identified by the general will. To the Germans — and to the French Catholic counter-Revolution — the nation defines the Republic, 'the state': participation in a common birth, inheritance, custom, provides the legitimation for a political

---

[160]  Arendt, *Rahel Varnhagen*, ch.12 'Between Pariah and Parvenu' pp. 199–215; Weiss-berg, 'Stepping Out: The Writing of Difference in Rahel Varnhagen's Letters', pp. 2–3.
[161]  Arendt, *Rahel Varnhagen*, p. 112.
[162]  Letter to David Veit, 22 March 1795, Bd I, p. 134, Weissberg, 'Stepping Out', p. 14.
[163]  See Key, *Rahel Varnhagen*, p. 135; Arendt, *Rahel Varnhagen*, pp. 127–30.
[164]  Karl August Varnhagen first published her letters as an epistolary novel in 1833; the 1834 three-volume edition was edited on the same principle: see Weissberg, 'Writing on the Wall: Letters of Rahel Varnhagen', pp. 157–8.

identity, whether universal or traditional. 'Nation' therefore veers, analytically and historically, from identification and legitimation of formal-legal representation to substantial patrimonial traditionality.[165] The paradox is that it is only *after* the development of legal-rational universality separated from the state — in form, knowable, general and reliable, but in content and effect unknown, local and insecure — that traditional, patrimonial legitimation is sentimentally rediscovered (even though in the case of Germany, it provided an initial boost to the development of a collective, political will across inherited political fragmentation) and exploited to exclude the Jews, who were *self-consciously* aware of being patrimonial and traditional before entering civil society, and who, therefore, could never pretend to such naivety, *ex post facto*.

> This week, I invented what a paradox is. A truth, that has not yet found the space to present itself; that forcefully presses into the world, and breaks out with a sprain. Unfortunately, I am like this! — *in this*, there lies my death . . . [166]

Yet, as Liliane Weissberg has traced, Rahel Levin uses the imagery of 'spraining' and 'lameness' to force the space for her difficult truth, expressed with the pain of the paradox — in subjective, phantasized, personified, negative terms. To the 'yes' of living hypothetically outside 'the world' 'without custom, without relationship' she goes on to juxtapose the 'yes' and 'no' of being lame within 'the world':

> Yes, the lame person would say, if it would not be necessary for me to walk, then I do not have to live and each step that I want to make and cannot make, does not remind me of the general calamity of men, against which I want to take steps, but I feel my special misfortune still, and twice and ten times, and one is always reminding me of the other. How ugly I am not at this; is the world clever then when it says 'Poor lame one, let's greet him with this — how hard each step is to him one can see'.[167]

Rahel Levin comments on this scenario by negating it: she affirms that the refusal to take steps, however difficult they may be, would be

---

[165] See A. Finkielkraut, *The Undoing of Thought*, pp. 15–17; Weissberg, 'Stepping Out', pp. 10–11; F. Neumann, *Behemoth*, pp. 85–9.
[166] Letter to Varnhagen, 19 February 1809, Bd I, pp. 400–1; Weissberg, 'Writing on the Wall', p. 172.
[167] Letter to David Veit, 22 March 1795, Bd I, p. 134 (tr. amended) and cited in Weissberg, 'Stepping Out', pp. 14–15.

found 'ugly' — for it would provoke no response; no effort matched by no recognition — not even recognition of lameness.[168] Not a beautiful soul, nor an ugly body, but the difficulty of moving with an impediment — when you know that each time you risk a step in order to recognize and alleviate the calamity of others and of all, you intensify your own disability. Yet your efforts do provoke a partial recognition — even though the one on whose behalf you are straining disassociates your difficulty from his and her own. But the lame one knows the connection.

Unwilling to withdraw from the world, or to acquiesce in this lame or mute condition, or to idealize the opposed and calamitous world, she turned to Goethe 'as a substitute for tradition',[169] who in his novel *Wilhelm Meister* represents acting, actors, actresses, and new authorities at the moment when tradition is transformed into the bourgeois world:

> With a stroke of magic Goethe has preserved in this book the whole prosiness of our infamous small lives... He catches and describes us at the moment we were clinging to these lives of ours; and he bids the burgher who feels his poverty and who does not want to kill himself to turn to the theatre, to art and even to deceit [*Schwindelei*].[170]

Goethe can bring into representation — by means of the therapeutic facetiousness noted here — the paradox which Rahel Levin could not express herself. This is what Hannah Arendt misses when she judges that Rahel [*sic*] 'saw either too little, or too much' in the whole novel: either only the relationships between the characters or the unrelenting darkness hanging over every single book of *Wilhelm Meister*: 'since man here on earth understands nothing because there is wanting in him that other half to which this mad game may belong.'[171] Not 'too little', nor 'too much', not a quantity at all, but a quality is intimated here: 'that other half' is the paradox which Goethe brings into representation but which he respects, too, in the facetious form of the playhouse, school of the bourgeois world, 'the mad game'. Finding that 'emancipated' characters, women and men — and their ethical adventures, marked by erotic and agapic reversals in the place of reconciliations — were incomplete, gave Rahel Levin back the richness of her own fate. She learns

[168]  Ibid., pp. 134–5.
[169]  Arendt, *Rahel Varnhagen*, p. 114.
[170]  Cited in ibid., p. 115, tr. amended; letter to Varnhagen, 20 December 1808, discussed in Käte Hamburger, 'Rahel und Goethe', p. 195; Bd IV, p. 216.
[171]  Arendt, *Rahel Varnhagen*, pp. 116–17; cf. Weissberg, 'Turns of Emancipation', p. 16.

through Goethe's pages that her own lack of position is poised on a double-danger: exclusion and emancipation; authority and authorship. This knowledge confers the integrity of the paradox on the anxiety of beginning — evident in letter after letter to Marwitz which 'deal with herself and speak about Goethe'[172] — a knowledge which she both 'renounces' by forming it and keeps to herself.

'Should Goethe with scorn [*mit Bedacht*] make all those for whom love absorbs the whole of life die? Sperata, Mariane, Mignon, Aurelie, the harpist?'[173] Not the inner emphasized at the expense of the outer, or pure subjectivity renouncing the world, is questioned here, as Hannah Arendt assumes,[174] but precisely the ambition of love to heal the world. Rahel Levin had already provided the commentary on her question when, in a earlier letter, the failure of people to meet, and their being parted when they do, itself provokes Wilhelm/Goethe's expostulation on the abundance of possibility and impossibility for humans, *and* by a reflection on the way 'the best we can *possibly* do on earth — what we think is best — may also well be fettered to pilasters which rest upon other worlds which we do not know; meanwhile, however, men move about — and this is what he shows us in his book as if it were a mirror.'[175] This moving about freely yet fettered to supports of unknown worlds — which guide the reversals of such subjective freedom — provides the link between the 'sociological' and erotic motifs which Käte Hamburger discerns in Rahel Varnhagen's appreciation of *Wilhelm Meister*, but which she seeks to keep apart.[176] For it is the modern state, 'pilaster' and 'unknown world', which is presupposed and occluded in a free 'society' of actors — civil society — and which guarantees free movement of actors and actresses and yet thwarts with its insecurities their attempts to reconcile by love the opposition between society and state which opens up their freedom; and, by thwarting again and again any such reparation, the question is raised of where or whether they may come to rest, whether the acting is ever over — in the community of Herrnhut, or in the society of the tower, *Turmgesellschaft*.

If ever life discovers what it — life — is through letters, literary and missive; if ever agon of authorship opens up biography while preserving its paradox, then it must be in this symbiosis between Rahel Levin

---

172   Ibid., p. 17.
173   Arendt, *Rahel Varnhagen*, p. 119; letter to Varnhagen, 28 March 1814, Bd II, p. 190, tr. extended.
174   Arendt, ibid., p. 118.
175   Ibid., pp. 115–16, emphasis added; letter to Varnhagen, 20 December, 1808, Bd IV, p. 217.
176   'Rahel und Goethe', Bd X, p. 195.

and Goethe – a symbiosis which, nevertheless, fostered her courage to endure an anxiety of beginning in anticipation of the equivocation of the ethical while still unequivocally being excluded from it. The further conjunction of life and letters when David Veit reports to Rahel Levin after the first of her two meetings with Goethe in Karlsbad in 1795, the year he completed Book VI, 'Confessions of a Beautiful Soul', that Goethe described her to Franz Horn as 'a beautiful soul' barely comes as a surprise.[177] However, there is no hint of Pietistic withdrawal or resignation in Goethe's reported description of her (these connotations led Schiller to object to the adjective 'beautiful' to describe what he deemed to be 'holiness' of the soul).[178] Instead Goethe emphasizes an original harmony between the strength of her perceptions and the grace of their expression – in short, she evinces faith not resignation, having learnt to convert her removal and return into plasticity of authorship in partnership with her lifelong Friend.

Like this friend, Goethe, who did not kill himself over Lotte – unlike his fiction Werther[179] – so Rahel Varnhagen – unlike 'the beautiful soul', whether in Goethe's novel or in Hegel's philosophical commentary or in Carlyle's misattributions – did not waste away in consumption.[180] She acquired the power, not possessed by 'the beautiful soul', to renounce knowledge of herself: for 'the sharpest knowledge of myself' became the agon, '*la lutte* of my life'. Lacking an actual existence, she created an interstitial one as hostess to the modern re-forming 'nation'-state. From this coign of vantage, in letters as in life, she was able to exploit and express the contradiction between her pure self: 'I *discover* that there is just *nothing* that I am [first emphasis added]', and the necessity of that self to externalize itself: 'I should be a queen ... or a mother ...' – but, without investing body and soul in that firmly held antithesis – '(no reigning one, however)'. Conscious of this contradiction, she does not allow any phantasized middle term to usurp the immediacy of the antithesis: 'no daughter, no sister, no lover, no spouse'. Able to bear this disorder, which is not 'beautiful' nor 'pure', but marked by the difficult borderline between regality and legality: 'no queen ... not even a burgheress', she does not approach the point of madness nor does she pine away in consumption.

---

[177] Ibid., pp. 201–2; Horn's report is appended to a letter to Rahel from Veit, 3 September 1795, Bd I, pp. 157–8.

[178] Hamburger, 'Rahel und Goethe', Bd X, p. 201.

[179] See nn. 112, 123, *supra*.

[180] See Carlyle's discussion of the sentimental reception of Goethe's 'tone of strength and sarcastic emphasis' as recorded in the original 'Sorrows of *Werter*', 'Translators' Preface to the First Edition of Meister's Apprenticeship', in *Wilhelm Meister*, q.v.

Instead, she sustains an agon of authorship by cultivating an extraordinarily modern Nicomachean ethic of friendship, *philia*, not eros or agape, but between the new 'just', vicarious and precarious, with the unease and paradox across Goethe's authorship. In this way, she struggles to 'give her knowledge away' without transforming it into unknowledge — without claiming *droits de la citoyenne* or *droits de la femme* — without affirming the politics of the former or the immediacy of the latter. With the additional knowledge of being a Jewess, and so able to witness the community separated ethically and collectively from political life as it is dissolved and dispersed by emancipation into the separations of civil, moral and individual life, she took on, time and time again, anxiety of beginning — the agon of this authorship occurring at that historical moment when the equivocation of the ethical was the beginning of anxiety.

While the beautiful soul which 'persists in its self-willed impotence'[181] is considered, nevertheless, as acting, its counterpart, moral conscience, it turns out, '*does not act*; it is the hypocrisy which wants its judgements to be taken for an *actual* deed'.[182] 'Dissolute freedom', the predecessor *and* successor of the beautiful soul and of this hypocritical judgement, excludes all other individuals from the entirety of the deed, and 'therefore, can produce neither a positive work nor a deed; there is left for it only *negative* action; it is merely the *fury* of self-destruction'.[183] The *Phenomenology* charts here the transition from terror to morality under the signature of the beautiful soul,[184] as, in reversible order, the omnipotence, the impotence, the hypocrisy of the political will. Rahel Levin/Varnhagen expounds the consequences of the original movement from terror to morality in the aftermath of the French Revolution, while Rosa Luxemburg expounds the implications of the subsequent temptation for pre- and post-World War I Social Democracy — to retrace the passage from bourgeois morality to the culture of terror; and while, once again, we — agonal 'we' — witness the transition from culture to morality.

Rosa Luxemburg will not be presented and judged here as 'right' or 'wrong' in the debates with Bernstein and Lenin and in Lukács' assessment of them,[185] over revisionism, imperialism, centralism and

---

[181]　Hegel, *Phenomenology of Spirit*, p. 483, Miller para. 658, p. 400.
[182]　Ibid., p. 487, Miller para. 664, p. 403.
[183]　Ibid., p. 435, Miller para. 589, p. 359.
[184]　Ibid., p. 580, Miller para. 795, p. 483.
[185]　Lukács, 'Critical Observations on Rosa Luxemburg's "Critique of the Russian Revolution"', 1922, in *History and Class Consciousness*, pp. 272–94.

nationalism, and utopianism, respectively. Rahel Levin/Varnhagen was not 'a beautiful soul', but sustained an agon of authorship in order to effect a repetition — anxiety of beginning which acknowledges the beginning of anxiety in the equivocation of the ethical (separation of civil society from new nation-state) — a repetition which does not, by advancing or embracing the new, merely perpetuate and even accentuate the old. Rosa Luxemburg, equally idealized, unlike Rahel Levin/ Varnhagen, but like Socrates and Simone Weil, sexually 'suspect', difficult authorships, awkward actors, for being 'ugly' — 'Red Rosa' — yet, subsequently, like Rahel Levin/Varnhagen in her relation to Goethe, sentimentalized and feminized as distraught lover, ardent botanist, defender of animals and *belle lettriste*,[186] sustained an agon of authorship which, equally distanced from the corruption of bourgeois morality, 'revisionism', and from the culture of terror, 'centralism', and 'nationalism', expounded these contrary barbarisms — not by appealing to a spontaneous and voluntarist revolutionary utopianism, as Lukács argues, but by attending consistently to the equivocation of the ethical — the perduring inversions of law.

But in absolute freedom [that . . . has completed the destruction of the actual organization of the world] there was no reciprocal action between a consciousness that is immersed in the complexities of existence, or that sets itself specific aims and thoughts, and a valid *external* world, whether of reality or thought . . .

The culture [*die Bildung*] to which it attains in interaction with [its] essence is, therefore, the grandest and last, is that of seeing its pure, simple reality immediately vanish and pass away into empty nothingness.[187]

Consequently, it knows that will to be itself, and knows itself to be essential being; but not essential being as an *immediate existence*, not will as revolutionary government or anarchy striving to establish anarchy, nor itself as the centre of this faction or the opposite faction . . .

There has arisen the new shape of Spirit, that of *moral* Spirit.[188]

---

[186]  See H. Arendt, 'Rosa Luxemburg: 1871–1919', in *Men in Dark Times*, pp. 42–3.
[187]  Hegel, *Phenomenology of Spirit*, p. 439, Miller para. 594, p. 362; p. 436, Miller para. 590, pp. 359–60.
[188]  Ibid., pp. 440–1, Miller para 594–5, p. 363.

For the consciousness which holds firmly to duty, the first consciousness [the one for which the certainty of itself is the essential
in fact of the universal] counts as *evil*, because of the disparity
between its *inner being* and the universal; and since, at the same
time, this first consciousness declares its actions to be in conformity with itself, to be duty and conscientiousness, it is held by the
universal consciousness to be *hypocrisy*.[189]

In denouncing hypocrisy as base, vile and so on, it [universal
consciousness] is appealing in such judgement to its *own* law, just
as the evil consciousness appeals to *its* law.[190]

It remains in the universality of *thought*, behaves as a consciousness that *apprehends*, and its first action is one of judgement . . . it is
the hypocrisy which wants its judgement to be taken for an *actual*
deed, and instead of proving its rectitude by actions, does so by
uttering fine sentiments.[191]

If 'revisionism' is a cultivation of moral judgement — collusion with
the hypocrisy of bourgeois morality; 'centralism' is a temptation of
pure culture — destruction of the actual organization of the world in the
name of the organization of the party. Rosa Luxemburg's disputes with
Bernstein and Lenin and her development of the idea of the 'mass
strike' will be reconsidered here not as alternative political strategies for
the specific historical conjuncture, but as investigations of inversions
arising from the otherwise unacknowledged equivocation of the ethical.

[Bernstein] does no more than the following: preach to the
working class the quintessence of the morality of the bourgeoisie,
that is, reconciliation with the existing social order and the transfer of the hopes of the proletariat to the limbo of ethical
simulacra.[192]

In her critique of Bernstein's *Evolutionary Socialism*, Rosa Luxemburg
demonstrates that Bernstein's arguments supporting the gradual transformation of capitalism into socialism betray a judgemental conviction

[189]   Ibid., p. 485, Miller para. 660, p. 401.
[190]   Ibid., p. 487, Miller para. 663, p. 402.
[191]   Ibid., p. 487, Miller para. 664, p. 403.
[192]   Rosa Luxemburg, 'Reform or Revolution' (1899), in *Gesammelte Werke*, Bd 1/1,
pp. 439, tr. *Rosa Luxemburg Speaks*, pp. 85–6.

that culminates explicitly in the rejection of revolutionary action and the reaffirmation of bourgeois morality. 'Reform or Revolution' succeeds where it would fail: it provides an exposition of reformism as an intelligible and predictable outcome of the social democratic position: 'Marxist doctrine cannot only refute opportunism theoretically. It alone can explain opportunism as a historic phenomenon in the development of the party.'[193] This reconstruction of the historical possibility — not the necessity — of revisionism depends not on adopting an 'overall organic view' of historical possibility, as Lukács contends,[194] but on an aporetic perspective, 'not, indeed, "so simple a thing"'.[195] 'The peculiar character of this movement resides precisely in the fact that here, for the first time in history, the popular masses themselves, *in opposition* to the ruling classes, are to impose their will, but they must effect this outside of the present society, beyond the existing society.'[196] This 'beyond' and 'outside' are not utopian: u–topia — without a place — thereby implying an idealized place, but aporetic: a–poria — without a path. It involves the 'union' of 'the daily struggle' and 'the great world transformation'. This implies disunion of the quotidian, 'day', and the cosmic, 'world'; a path only definable oppositionally: 'the social democratic movement . . . must grope on its road [*sic*] of development between the following two rocks: abandoning the mass character of the party or abandoning its final aim, falling into bourgeois reformism or into sectarianism, anarchism, or opportunism.'[197] The order of the 'fall' is here reversed, for 'sectarianism' or 'anarchism' would correspond to abandonment of the mass character of the party, while bourgeois reformism amounts to abandonment of the final aim. Both are characterized by 'opportunism' — opportunism of the 'left' and of the 'right' — for 'opportunism' is also a temporal notion. It implies seizure of the opportune, the immediate, whether of collusion (bourgeois reformism) or of violence (sectarianism, anarchism) and fixing it. This goes against the common view that Rosa Luxemburg is herself a theorist of immediacy and spontaneity, of the easy path. On the contrary, her authorship is the difficult path of the repeated recognition of mediators which prevents any fixing of the outcome of the previous 'daily struggle'. The 'daily' or quotidian is the aporia — the difficult path, 'outside' and 'beyond', which is, *qua* difficulty, temporally inside and within,

---

[193] Ibid., p. 443, tr. p. 88.
[194] See Lukács, 'Critical Observations on Rosa Luxemburg's "Critique of the Russian Revolution"', pp. 287, 278–9.
[195] Luxemburg, 'Reform or Revolution', p. 443, tr. p. 88.
[196] Ibid.
[197] Ibid., p. 426, tr. p. 75.

continual but not continuous, intermittent but never-ending as opposed to incessant but coming to a finite end.

In his book *Evolutionary Socialism*, Bernstein, as analysed by Rosa Luxemburg, provides both economic and political arguments for the gradual realization of socialism, but what he, in effect, achieves, is 'a resurrection of bourgeois democracy'.[198] His method turns on the social and political equivocation of the idea of 'socialization'; Lenin's method will turn on the equivocation of 'discipline'. In both cases, the refusal to recognize ambiguity amounts to a refusal of the equivocation of the ethical. Bernstein argues that 'the perfected means' of capitalism — credit, communication, cartels — represent an adaptation which 'socializes' production and exchange, and signals the cessation of capitalist crisis.[199] 'Socialization' conveys no more than 'the social character of production', but it is attenuated to imply the redistribution and restructing of the capital wage–labour relationship. An analogous, sociological sleight-of-hand attends the judgement that social reform, like trade union organizations, amounts to a transfer of 'social control' to labour.[200] By smuggling in functionalist notions such as 'social control', the presupposition of 'the control of society working freely in its own labour process'[201] is insinuated, and the contrary exposition of a class state founded on conflicting interests is abandoned.

This nascent functionalism emerges explicitly in connection with the relation of state and society. Bernstein capitalizes on the idea that capitalist development 'prepares, so to say, the return of the function of the state to society'.[202] The deployment of tariffs and militarism, however, demonstrate, on the contrary, that for a class state — as opposed to a universal 'society in general' — such deployment may, initially, or for a specific sector, contribute to development, but subsequently disturbs any further development: 'From a motor of capitalist development militarism has changed into a capitalist malady.'[203] The 'socialization' thesis, whether applied to reform of production, of juridical or property relations, or to political organization, attends solely to the form of such changes, not to the substantial conflict and interests out of which these forms arise. The exclusive attention to formal change and formal relations synthesizes with the translation of revolutionary activity into the form of judgement.

[198]  Ibid., p. 426, tr. p. 75.
[199]  Ibid., pp. 376, 377, tr. pp. 40, 41.
[200]  Ibid., p. 392, tr. p. 51.
[201]  Ibid.
[202]  Ibid., p. 395, tr. p. 53.
[203]  Ibid., p. 398, tr. p. 55.

In opposition to this, Rosa Luxemburg's authorship intrudes agon and aporia. 'The difference is not in the *what* but in the *how*.'[204]

> According to the present conception of the party, trade-union and parliamentary activity are important for the socialist movement because such activity prepares the proletariat, that is to say, creates the *subjective* factor of the socialist transformation for the task of realizing socialism. But according to Bernstein, trade unions and parliamentary activity gradually reduce capitalist exploitation itself. They remove from capitalist society its capitalist character. They realize *objectively* the desired social change.[205]

When 'reformism' *judges* change, it makes change impossible: it denies the contradictions and undermines comprehension of them by the working class and undermines the potential of the working class for transformative activity. But this verdict on capitalist 'adaptability' undermines not only class consciousness and class struggle, but the interests of capital itself:

> As a result of their periodic *depreciation* of capital, crises bring a fall in the prices of means of production, a paralysis of a part of active capital, and in time the increase of profits. They thus create the possibility of the renewed advance of production. Crises therefore seem to be the instruments of rekindling the fire of capitalist development. Their cessation — not temporary cessation, but their total disappearance in the world market — would not lead to the further development of capitalist economy. It would destroy capitalism.[206]

The conclusion that Bernstein's implicit aim is to affirm bourgeois morality is derived from his explicit recommendation of democracy, since democratic institutions in Germany — such as universal suffrage — are not only minimal as opposed to liberal institutions — competitive institutions of civil society — but on the retreat in the face of increased competition on world markets, and the growth of militarism in world politics which is decisive in the interior as well as in the exterior life of the great states.[207]

---

[204] Ibid., p. 400, tr. p. 57.
[205] Ibid., p. 401, tr. p. 58.
[206] Ibid., p. 407, tr. p. 62.
[207] Ibid., pp. 424–5, tr. p. 75.

He advises the proletariat to disavow its socialist aim, so that the mortally frightened liberals might come out of the mousehole of reaction.[208]

Underpinning Bernstein's approach is the assumption that judicial reform can effect fundamental social reform. This is to ignore in general the structure of legal epochs: 'in each historic period work for reforms is carried out only *in the framework* [and within the impetus] of the social form created by the last revolution.'[209] It also overlooks in particular the form of capitalist juridicality: that, unlike feudalism, legal statuses in capitalism do not correspond to status within the division of labour, the capital wage—labour relation, but, on the contrary, mask the divisions by bestowing formal legal equality on persons: 'In our juridical system there is not a single legal formula for the class domination of today.'[210] While bourgeois law 'obliges the proletariat to submit itself to the yoke of capitalism', by legal definition and dispositions, capitalist exploitation does not correspond to any explicit legal disposition, and hence it cannot be transformed by legislative reform.[211] Nor therefore can setbacks in proletarian conquest of state power be deemed evidence of a 'premature' tentative, for there is no guaranteed, mechanical development of society, and no victory for the working class '*outside* and *independent of* the class struggle'.[212]

The difficulty of the authorship emerging here stems from the insinuation of agonal and aporetic struggle which is based intellectually on a comprehension — which must not itself become, or be stated as, a judgement — of the ways in which Bernstein's position is utterly implicated in the bourgeois juridical actuality which he leaves unexplored. This legal form which, by its very formality, consolidates the capital wage–labour dependency, leads to the inversion of his avowed intentions: the argument for socialism becomes the call of bourgeois morality and the possibility of revolutionary action is dissipated in the objective judgement that action is obsolete.

Hypocritical judgement, which rejoins the morality it disdains, is one danger; the culture of terror, which substitutes its own will under the name of the collective will, is the contrary danger; yet this latter tendency will also, even though inadvertently, revitalize the corruption

---

[208]   Ibid., p. 425, tr. p. 75.
[209]   Ibid., p. 428, tr. p. 77, emphasis in German.
[210]   Ibid., p. 429, tr. p. 78.
[211]   Ibid., p. 430, tr. p. 79.
[212]   Ibid., p. 435, tr. p. 83.

it seeks to overcome. Rosa Luxemburg's agon of authorship arises out of her awareness of the double danger of these two insinuated 'authorities' – of 'judgement' (reformism) and of 'culture' (centralism). The one, reformism, by judging the beginning to be already made, and the other, centralism, by substituting for the beginning, the one, abandoning action, and the other, acting in the name of the collective will, 'over-anxious', as she says, but insufficiently anxious, collude in the equivocation of the ethical and political of an even more dangerous kind: the decomposition of bourgeois society which arouses 'the anguish, rancor and hope [*die Gegenwartschmerzen*] of this motley aggregation . . . the tumult of nonproletarian protestants'.[113] Recognized in 'Reform or Revolution' (1899),[214] this was restated in 'Organizational Question of Social Democracy' (1904), and developed further in 'The Russian Revolution' (1917–18), which was not published until 1922:

> It follows that this movement can best advance by tacking betwixt and between the two dangers by which it is constantly being threatened. One is the loss of its mass character; the other, the abandonment of its goal. One is the danger of sinking back to the condition of a sect; the other, the danger of becoming a movement of bourgeois social reform.[215]

This delineation of the double danger of the 'movement': that it tends to substitute old or new authority in the place of daily struggle and anxiety over its outcome, cannot itself become a further judgement or 'culture':

> That is why it is illusory and contrary to historic experience to hope to fix once and for always, the direction of the revolutionary socialist struggle with the aid of formal means, which are expected to secure the labour movement against all possibilities of opportunist digression.[216]

Instead, the 'unavoidable social conditions' out of which such dangers arise, and the *aporia* intrinsic to socialist activity between the daily struggle and the goal beyond the limits of that struggle, which

---

[213]  'Organizational Question of Social Democracy' (1904), *Gesammelte Werke*, Bd 1/2, p. 441, tr. *Rosa Luxemburg Speaks*, p. 128.

[214]  Op. cit., p. 443, tr. pp. 88–9.

[215]  'Organizational Question of Social Democracy', p. 442, tr. p. 129.

[216]  Ibid.

therefore cannot secure itself in advance, may be expounded – earnestly and facetiously:[217]

> It is amusing to note the strange somersaults that the respectable human 'ego' has had to perform in recent Russian history. Knocked to the ground, almost reduced to dust, by Russian absolutism, the 'ego' takes revenge by turning to revolutionary activity. In the shape of a committee of conspirators, in the name of a nonexistent Will of the People, it seats itself on a kind of throne and proclaims it is all-powerful. But the 'object' proves to be the stronger. The knout is triumphant, for czarist might seems to be the 'legitimate' expression of history.[218]

This repetition backwards is intensified when the 'legitimate' – Rosa Luxemburg's scare quotes – child of history, the Russian Labour movement, basis for the formation of a 'real people's will' is 'created in Russian history'.[219] This facetious representation continues by drawing the obvious analogy:

> But here is the 'ego' of the Russian revolutionary again! Pirouetting on its head, it once more proclaims itself to be the all-powerful director of history – this time with the title of His Excellency the Central Committee of the Social Democratic Party of Russia.[220]

Facetiousness is not cynicism – it is exposition in the prospective not the retrospective mode, anticipation of how 'the proposed means turn against the end they are supposed to serve':[221]

> In Lenin's *overanxious* desire to establish the guardianship of an omniscient and omnipotent Central Committee in order to protect so promising and rigorous a labour movement against any misstep, we recognize the symptoms of the same subjectivism that has already played more than one trick on socialist thinking in Russia. [emphasis added][222]

---

[217] While 'contradiction' is a logical term, which, applied to social structure, implies possible resolution, 'aporia' is prelogical, it refers to lack of way, and implies no exit from its condition. Both discourses are discernible in Luxemburg's writings.

[218] 'Organizational Question of Social Democracy', pp. 443–4, tr. p. 130.

[219] Ibid., p. 444, tr. p. 130, corrected.

[220] Ibid.

[221] Ibid., p. 443, tr. p. 129.

[222] Ibid., p. 443, tr. pp. 129–30.

'Subjectivism' and 'overanxiety' attempt to legislate the path of an 'unqualified centralism – the idea that the road to opportunism can be barred by means of clauses in a party constitution'.[223] What is implicitly recommended here is a more thorough-going anxiety which would not fix any path in advance of the daily struggle, but would cultivate a plasticity that is able to educate and assimilate 'the afflux of non-proletarian recruits to the party of the proletariat'.[224] This deeper sub-mission to uncertainty leads to a more inclusive activity – to cultivation of plasticity rather than culture of terror.

Agon of authorship here means in argument both to recommend struggle and to struggle daily against this culture, and discursively to comprehend it: to oppose it and to let it be. The argument turns, analogously to the argument with Bernstein, around equivocation in the meaning of 'discipline' towards socialism, in this case to justify partyist centralism not holist gradualism. Lenin 'glorifies the educative influence of the factory', which, he says, accustoms the proletariat to 'discipline and organization',[225] and qualifies it to form a centralist party organization which will act on behalf of the working class – imposing undisputed and indisputable leadership and submitting itself to the same discipline. This generalization of 'discipline' is equivocal: it extends the discipline 'being implanted in the working class not only by the factory but also by the military and the existing state bureaucracy – by the entire mechanism of the centralized bourgeois state'[226] to the idea of revolutionary practice, as if 'a Central Committee can teach the party membership in the same way as troops are instructed in their training camps'.[227]

> We misuse words and we practice self-deception when we apply the same term – discipline – to such dissimilar notions as: (1) the absence of thought and will in a body with a thousand automatically moving hands and legs, and (2) the spontaneous coordination of the conscious, political acts of a body of men. What is there in common between the regulated docility of an oppressed class and the self-discipline and organization of a class struggling for its emancipation?[228]

[223] Ibid., pp. 440–1, tr. p. 127.
[224] Ibid., p. 441, tr. p. 127.
[225] Ibid., p. 430, tr. p. 119.
[226] Ibid.
[227] Ibid., p. 428, tr. p. 118.
[228] Ibid., p. 430, tr. p. 119.

Lenin is explicitly transferring submission to the type of legal-rational domination, methodical means regardless of ends, found in factory, military, bureaucracy, to a type of social-democratic domination *as a means*, so that revolutionary action is conceived as drawing on ingrained passivity to realize a schema, but not as a schooling of struggle where ends and means are fused, which would involve: 'the possibility for workers to develop their own political activity through direct influence on public life, in a party press, and public congresses'.[229]

The development of reformist and centralist tendencies is derived from their specific historical preconditions – from German parliamentarianism and czarist Russia: 'despotic centralism [is] preferred when the revolutionary elements among the workers still lack cohesion and the movement is groping its way, as is the case now in Russia. In a later phase, under a parliamentary regime and in connection with a strong labour party, the opportunist tendencies of the intellectuals express themselves in an inclination toward "decentralization".'[230] This insight into the way revolutionary legalism reproduces the illegality it deplores, in conformism to bourgeois hypocrisy in Germany or to autocratic substitutionism in Russia, is opposed to the uninvented tactics of spontaneous class struggle 'seeking its way forward'.[231] This apparent paean of praise to 'spontaneity'[232] does not amount to antinomian ecstasy – affirmation of disorder of opportunity – but, on the contrary, to recognition of inversions which will attend any *a priori* revolutionary intent or abandonment of intent: reinstalling legal-rational domination of a bourgeois or a revolutionary kind, which, in its desire for fixity, will fertilize the germ of further instability, for it will fail to 'enclose the tumult of the non-proletarian protestants against existing society within the bounds of the revolutionary action of the proletariat. It must assimilate the elements that come to it.'[233] Social democracy 'has always contended that it represents not only the class interests of the proletariat but also the progressive aspirations of the whole of contemporary society'[234] – lest these aspirations become regressive.

---

[229] Ibid., p. 429, tr. p. 119.

[230] Ibid., pp. 439–40, tr. p. 126.

[231] Ibid., p. 432, pp. 120–1.

[232] The word 'spontaneous' does not appear in the German; it has been used to translate 'acts of experimenting, often elemental class struggle [*Akte des experimentierenden, oft elementaren Klassenkampfes*]'. In addition, much literary facetiousness is omitted. For example, the use of Goethe's Faust, 'In allen diesen Fällen war im Anfang die "Tat"', which occurs in the middle of the paragraph which has been divided into two in the English translation, is omitted: see p. 432, tr. pp. 120–1.

[233] Ibid., p. 441, tr. p. 128.

[234] Ibid., p. 441, tr. p. 127.

As Lukács points out in his essay on Rosa Luxemburg, in *The Accumulation of Capital* Luxemburg herself provides the socio-economic theoretical underpinning of the thesis that as capitalism develops it destroys those strata which are neither capitalist nor proletarian.[235] Yet Lukács, who *judges* Rosa Luxemburg's position to be 'utopian', only considers how this destructive process contributes to the success of socialism: 'they unleash movements which do not themselves proceed in the direction of socialism but which through the violence of the impact they make do hasten the realization of the preconditions of socialism: namely, the collapse of the bourgeoisie.'[236] Rosa Luxemburg, however, was aware how this incipient politicization of non-proletarian strata was equivocal – that it could lead to barbarism as well as to socialism. In 1904 she attributed this fateful decomposition of bourgeois society to German not to Russian society,[237] but by 1917–18 she saw the ways in which revolutionary terror even in a prebourgeois society might contribute to the simultaneous politicizing and corrupting of social strata which have no interest in socialism. The experience of systemic corruption in capitalist Germany is extended to outline the ways in which such corruption may be fostered in a society without bourgeois economic or political institutions. This argument takes account of the difference between a society with the equivocation of civil society and state, and one as yet without civil society and hence with non-legitimate domination by a pre-legal-rational bureaucracy which claims nevertheless to act as the 'universal' class between state and society – whether the latter is 'civil' or not. 'Draconian measures of terror are powerless. On the contrary, they cause still further corruption.'[238] This corruption is the unintended 'culture' of terror, drawn from German society, where 'the gradations between commercial profiteering, fictitious deals, adulteration of foodstuffs, cheating, official embezzlement, theft, burglary and robbery flow into one another in such fashion that the boundary line between honourable citizenship and the penitentiary has disappeared'.[239] The way in which bourgeois legality masks the immorality of mutual exploitation profoundly corrupts the mores of civil society in its mismatch of legalism with the daily experience of inequality. However, repression by martial

---

[235]  Lukács, 'Critical Observations', p. 289.
[236]  Ibid.
[237]  Luxemburg, 'Organizational Question', pp. 437–8, tr. pp. 124–5.
[238]  Luxemburg, 'The Russian Revolution', pub. 1922, *Gesammelte Werke*, Bd 4, p. 361, n. 1:3 tr. in *Rosa Luxemburg Speaks*, p. 393.
[239]  Ibid., p. 361 n. 1, tr. p. 392.

law only contributes further to the general corruption: 'for every form of arbitrariness tends to deprave society'.[240] The dictatorship employed by Lenin, even if transferred by ukase (proclamation) to society, will repress and fix public life in its poverty stricken and unfruitful condition, and will foster either arbitrary bureaucratic domination or anarchistic violence.[241]

> Decree, dictatorial force of the factory overseer, draconian penalties, rule by terror – all these things are but palliatives. The only way to a rebirth is the school of public life itself, the most unlimited, the broadest democracy and public opinion. It is rule by terror which demoralizes.[242]

Agon of authorship would display and recommend democratic struggle developed in 'public' institutions, but there is no historic or organizational anchoring for such non-authoritarian debate over authority, for such 'publicity', neither in civil society divided into 'private' and 'public', nor without civil society, without 'public' or 'private', in Germany or in Russia. What can be 'concluded', therefore, is only anxiety of beginning in the equivocation of the ethical – not a beginning without anxiety, whether 'gradual' within the ethical (Bernstein), or 'dictated' over the ethical (Lenin).

> But socialist democracy is not something which begins only in the promised land after the foundations of socialist economy are created; it does not come as some sort of Christmas present for the worthy people who, in the interim, have loyally supported a handful of socialist dictators. Socialist democracy begins simultaneously with the beginnings of the destruction of class rule and of the construction of socialism . . .[243]

Expressed facetiously – not with a 'consummate' facetiousness, but with one that, to paraphrase Antigone, admits, as it were, 'Because we are facetious, we acknowledge that we have erred',[244] with the face-

---

240 Ibid.
241 Ibid., p. 360, tr. p. 390.
242 Ibid., pp. 361–2, tr. p. 391.
243 Ibid., p. 363, tr. pp. 393–4.
244 Cf. 'The ethical consciousness must, on account of this actuality and on account of its deed, acknowledge its opposite as its own actuality, must acknowledge its guilt. "Because we suffer we acknowledge we have erred."' Hegel, *Phenomenology of Spirit*, p. 340 Miller para. 470, p. 284, citing *Antigone*, v. 1.926.

tiousness that is neither judgement nor culture but would cultivate the plasticity of aporia, Rosa Luxemburg was not 'right' or 'wrong' in relation to the disputes with Bernstein, Lenin, Trotsky or Lukács – she was consistently anxious in the equivocation of the ethical.

> But in absolute freedom there was no reciprocal action between a consciousness that is immersed in the complexities of existence, or that sets itself specific aims and thoughts, and a valid *external* world whether of reality or thought . . .[245]

The drama, facetious and earnest, of *The Mass Strike, The Political Party and The Trade Unions*, written in 1906 in the wake of the Revolution of 1905 in Russia, serves the vision of galvanizing multiple 'reciprocal action' between socialism in Russia and in Germany, between organized and unorganized workers, between trade unions and social democracy, between economic and political struggle. It remains, however, caught in the antinomy of its own dialectic: the mass strike is not an Idea, a schema, an abstract blueprint, a *Sollen*; it cannot therefore, strictly speaking, be recommended or even anticipated in any context without a 'history' of mass strike, a 'history' that is continuous only in its discontinuity. What abides, once again, is the educative experience of political freedoms: not in the relative sense of individual rights, but in a radically democratic sense of opening up public space; this space, it is admitted, will be eroded by the development of bourgeois liberal democracy, and will hence be short-lived, even in the Russian context of the mass strike, once the proletarian-led revolution against absolutism achieves bourgeois reform. The mass strike as a 'culture' – as the agon and aporia of economic and political struggle, daily and transcendent – will then be 'civilized' or decomposed into the *Sollen* of bourgeois compartmentalization and judgementalism. In the very course of drawing on Russian experience for Germany, Luxemburg disqualifies it – and thus reveals the corruption of state separated from civil society to be even stronger than her insinuated, indirect politics of reciprocal action:

> The mass strike, as the Russian Revolution shows it to us, is such a changeable phenomenon that it reflects all phases of the political and economic struggle, all stages and factors of the revolution. Its adaptability, its efficiency, the factors of its origin are constantly changing. It suddenly opens new and wide perspectives of the

---

[245] Ibid., p. 439, Miller para. 594, p. 362.

revolution when it appears to have already arrived in a narrow pass and where it is impossible for anyone to reckon upon it with any degree of certainty. It flows now like a broad billow over the whole kingdom and now divides into a gigantic network of narrow streams; now it bubbles forth from under the ground like a fresh spring and now is completely lost under the earth. Political and economic strikes, mass strikes and partial strikes, demonstrative strikes and fighting strikes, general strikes of individual branches of industry and general strikes in individual towns, peaceful wage struggles and street massacres, barricade fighting – all these run through one another, run side by side, cross one another, flow in and over one another – it is a ceaseless moving changing sea of phenomena. And the law of those phenomena is clear: it does not lie in the mass strike itself nor in its technical details, but in the political and social proportions of the forces of the revolution.[246]

This prose poem conjoining the mass strike and the revolution accentuates both the agonal 'and' of reciprocal means and the aporetic 'and' of pathless but motile end, within the law of their 'proportion'. Facetious representation of something that cannot be represented, the mass strike is differentiated from anarchism, terrorists now 'become the sign of the common thief and plunderer';[247] from an 'idea' that might be 'propagated',[248] 'the abstract schematic mass strike';[249] yet 'the mass strike has passed through a definite history in Russia, and is passing still further through it.'[250] This 'history', leading to the strikes of spring and summer, 1905, displays the strength of its defects – a general strike breaking up into local, partial strikes; a political strike breaking up into economic strikes; a strike proceeding regardless of the appeals of the social democratic leadership. It has the immense advantage of

fermenting throughout the whole of the immense empire an uninterrupted economic strike of almost the entire proletariat against capital – a struggle which caught on the one hand, all the petty bourgeois and liberal professions, commercial employees, technicians, actors and members of the artistic professions – and on the other hand, penetrated to the domestic servants, the minor police

---

[246]  Op. cit., Bd 2, p. 124, tr. in *Rosa Luxemburg Speaks*, pp. 181–2.
[247]  Ibid., p. 96, tr. pp. 157–8.
[248]  Ibid., p. 100, tr. p. 161.
[249]  Ibid., p. 103, tr. p. 163.
[250]  Ibid.

officials and even to the stratum of the lumpenproletariat, and simultaneously surged from the towns to the country districts and even knocked at the iron gate of the military barracks.[251]

'Spontaneity' is here gauged (*sic*) as a 'living political school' which, accelerating the formation of modern class divisions, educates proletarian and liberal, radical and reactionary parties against absolutism – all agonal 'ands' which both hamper and spur class maturation in incessant mutual friction between classes and within them.[252] These political and revolutionary gains are urged in contrast to the excessive and debilitating organization of German trade unions, against their overly cautious and complacently teleological approach to struggle – such 'urging', however, can only be prescriptive and self-defeating – or, it is facetious, the only non-legislative authorship: 'Dame History, from afar, smilingly hoaxes the bureaucratic lay figures who keep grim watch at the gate over the fate of German trade unions.'[253]

The attempt to draw together a general description of the mass strike, which may be extended from Russia to Germany, involves an equivocation between presenting it as law-like and presenting it as 'spontaneous': unlike law-governed phenomena, the mass strike 'alters its forms, its dimensions, its effects';[254] unlike a spontaneity, the mass strike is the 'indication, the rallying idea, of a whole period of the class struggle lasting for years, perhaps for decades'.[255] This is the 'law' of the 'proportions of the forces of the revolution'. Not engaged in setting out a method for making the proletarian struggle more effective,[256] Luxemburg claims to be merely tracing the transmission of struggle from one centre to another – political to economic, trade union to mass, organized to unorganized workers, and vice versa in each case – for struggle itself is the mediator and educator of revolution which cannot be controlled or conducted. Yet, she is, in effect, demonstrating the formation of a political will without ethical authority – willing to be 'premature', to act on faith with what knowledge it can muster, to fail even, but thereby to gain in self-knowledge and self-consciousness.[257]

The attempt to draw 'lessons' from the working-class movement in Russia that would be applicable to Germany is doomed, intellectually

[251]   Ibid., p. 111, tr. p. 170.
[252]   Ibid., p. 113, tr. p. 172.
[253]   Ibid., pp. 117, 124, tr. pp. 176, 181.
[254]   Ibid., p. 125, tr. p. 182.
[255]   Ibid.
[256]   Ibid., pp. 125f., tr. pp. 182f.
[257]   Ibid., pp. 132f., tr. pp. 188f.

and practically. Contrary to the common wisdom, the German proletariat is not economically superior to the Russian, but subsists in a
regime of economic absolutism, as it were, together with political
liberalism, the legality of trade unions: instead of 'a powerful and
restless fighting action of the industrial proletariat', which would in-
terrelate economic and political struggles, party, trade unions, and
masses, the pure political mass strike in Germany is 'a mere lifeless
theoretical plan'.[258]

As a result of this unequivocal *judgement* the three chapters concluding this discourse have the unmistakable imprint and tone of indictment, of *Sollen*: the culture of the mass strike – agonal and aporetic
conjoining – up against the intransigence of a trade union history and a
social democratic history that represents the separated spheres of economic and political struggle, and that wages those struggles, directed by
central committees, within the parameters of bourgeois parliamentarianism, bourgeois morality and civility. This dilemma can only infest
the authorship that would not abolish it.

Since the union of organized and unorganized workers, the union of
economic and political struggle, the union of trade unions and social
democracy, cannot be prescribed, it is instead contrasted with their
union in Russia, and projected, with the grammar of providential
futurity, on to Germany, a projection which nevertheless resounds
counterfactually and with circularity:

> A year of revolution has therefore given the Russian proletariat
> that 'training' which thirty years of parliamentary and trade-union
> struggle cannot artificially give to the German proletariat. Of
> course this living, active class feeling of the proletariat will con-
> siderably diminish in intensity, or rather change into a concealed
> and latent condition, after the close of the period of revolution and
> the erection of a bourgeois–parliamentary constitutional state.
>
> And just as surely, on the other hand, will the living revolu-
> tionary class feeling, capable of action, affect the widest and
> deepest layers of the proletariat in Germany in a period of strong
> political engagement, and that the more rapidly and more deeply,
> more energetically the educational work of social democracy is
> carried on amongst them.[259]

This 'prognosis' may be taken counter-suggestively as prophetic index
of the counter-revolutionary politics that are likely to emerge when

---

[258]  Ibid., p. 140, tr. pp. 194–5.
[259]  Ibid., p. 145, tr. p. 199.

non-organized workers are not rallied and do not rally to the political and economic struggle; and hence of the diremptive not aporetic 'and' evident in all the joinings this authorship wants to record: economic 'and' political, organized 'and' non-organized, trade unions 'and' masses, trade unions 'and' social democracy, and – the one it does not address explicitly but most registers – the diremptive, sociological 'and' of state and civil society.

> The consciousness that judges in this way is itself base, because it divides up the action, producing and holding fast to the disparity of the action with itself... It repels this community of nature, and is the hard heart that is *for itself*, and which rejects any continuity with the other...[260]

> The breaking of the hard heart, and the raising of it to universality, is the same movement which was expressed in the consciousness which made confession of itself... But just as the former has to surrender its one-sided, unacknowledged existence of its particular being-for-self, so too must this other set aside its one-sided unacknowledged judgement... The latter, however, renounces the divisive thought, and the hard-heartedness of the being-for-self which clings to it, because it has in fact seen itself in the first... The forgiveness which it extends to the other is the renunciation of itself...[261]

If Rosa Luxemburg's authorship not only declares 'Socialism or Barbarism' but contains the incipient insight that barbarism without 'socialism' means some variety of fascism; if, further, its emphasis on the publicity of spontaneity in order to recruit 'non-proletarian protestants' could itself result not in mobilizing the masses for socialism but for fascism; and, further still, if the internationalism of this authorship itself contributed to the failure of social democracy and, later, of Communism, to recruit both proletarian and non-proletarian 'protestants' to socialism and prepared the ground for National Socialism; and if this failure of political *judgement* finds its own correction in the economic theory of *The Accumulation of Capital* itself, then it is Arendt's authorship, witness and commentator of these diremptions, which took up the agon of prophesying radical democracy under the far

---

[260]  Hegel, *Phenomenology of Spirit*, pp. 489–90, Miller paras 666–7, p. 405, introducing 'forgiveness' as the fourth to 'the beautiful soul', n. 114 *supra*, absolute freedom and hypocrisy of moral judgement, nn. 187–191 *supra*.
[261]  Ibid., p. 492, Miller paras 669–70.

heavier burden of the diremptive 'and' of state and civil society, 'over-come' by the 'nation-state' and its decline from eighteenth-century anti-semitism to twentieth-century 'So-called Totalitarian State'.[262]

Elizabeth Young-Bruehl contends that Hannah Arendt's 'later con-cern with the founding of public realms was rooted not in any Christian philosophy, but in Greek and Roman thought'.[263] However, Arendt's agon of authorship reinsinuates anxiety of beginning which is, as a principle, how she expounds 'the meaning of revolution', 'the public realm', and 'the shared world'. The distinction drawn between the aporetic individual at the mercy of incalculable agape, contrasted with the public political world of equals, is how she presents authority and actor. All this has its source and recurring *point d'appui* in her under-standing of St Augustine, 'a Christian thinker ... the first to formulate the philosophical implications of the ancient political idea of freedom'.[264]

From her dissertation on *St. Augustine's Concept of Love* to the reading of *The City of God*, evident throughout her work, St Augustine does not cast the subtextual shadow of spirit across an otherwise political authorship. On the contrary, it is the agon to represent and defend radical democracy in Augustinian terms in *The Human Condition* (1958) that explains both the consistency and inconsistency of this authorship. For having demonstrated the historical demolition of the modern nation-state in its failure to abide with the diremption of state and civil society in *The Origins of Totalitarianism* (1951) where this is attributed to the equivocation of the ethical, Arendt fails herself to abide with this. In *The Human Condition* she separates the 'social' from the 'political', devises a genealogy of that separation, and *judges* that 'separation' in a way that ignores her own earlier insight into the diremption of state and civil society.[265] It is this deployment of aporetic and agapic Augustinianism that leads the authorship to reduce philosophy and political culture either to 'judgement', culled from Kant's third *Critique*, or to 'friendship', learnt from Lessing – friendship, however, which made Nathan unwise, and which would repeat the fate of Recha. The authorship is consistent in maintaining anxiety of beginning – critical

---

[262] It has, perhaps, been overlooked that Arendt discusses 'Totalitarianism in Power' under the subheading 'The So-called Totalitarian State', *The Origins of Totalitarianism*, pp. 392–419.

[263] *Hannah Arendt: For Love of the World*, p. 498.

[264] 'What is Freedom?', in *Between Past and Future*, p. 167.

[265] Richard Bernstein, in his essay on Arendt, 'Rethinking the Social and Political', discusses the untenability of this opposition, but he does not contrast *The Human Condition* with *The Origins of Totalitarianism*; see *Philosophical Profiles*, pp. 238–59.

independence equally of universal human rights, of public conflations, such as nationalism and racialism, and of private elevations, such as love, fraternity, community. Yet, subsequently, it judges and separates the ethical into 'the social' and 'the political' instead of suspending the ethical. To suspend the ethical would be to hold fast for the eternal moment and so instantaneously to release the historical diremption of state and civil society. Suspension of the ethical makes it possible to explore this diremption in the experience of the individual, and to explore the effect of each dirempted sphere in the realm of its contrary. But the authorship does not follow through this suspension which it itself teaches in *The Origins of Totalitarianism*.

*The Origins of Totalitarianism* was 'written against a background of both reckless optimism and reckless despair... both... articles of superstition, not of faith' – that faith, the conviction that the hidden mechanics of the disintegration of the political and spiritual world may be comprehended, which means 'the unpremeditated, attentive facing up to, and resisting of, reality – whatever it may be'.[266] 'Unpremeditated comprehension' expresses an open jurisprudence of universal and unique – not reducing the unprecedented to precedents, but, equally, not submitting 'meekly' to the burden of the century by refusing to examine it – instead it involves knowing it to be 'our' burden.

Unfortunately, *The Origins of Totalitarianism* has been received largely as a cold-war, anti-Marxist work on 'Totalitarianism', the title of the third of its three parts, each first published separately, when it will be argued here that Part One, 'Anti-Semitism', and Part Two, 'Imperialism', may be seen, respectively, as the most sustained attempt to develop Marx's account of the split between state and civil society from 'On the Jewish Question', and to develop Rosa Luxemburg's *The Accumulation of Capital*,[267] to provide a political and sociological history of the modern 'nation'-state, which – contrary to liberal history which judges the aberration of German development against the assumption of the English normality of bloodless revolution, of liberal constitutionalism[268] – demonstrates the impossibility of democratic polity in the modern nation-state, in its birth, development and disintegration, and which is organized around the changing 'split' and 'tension' between civil society and state as revealed and charted by 'the Jewish Question' and by the 'social question'.

---

[266]  Op. cit., pp. vii–viii.
[267]  Op. cit., *Gesammelte Werke*, Bd 5, see esp. chs. XXV–XXXII.
[268]  See, for example, R. Dahrendorf, *Society and Democracy in Germany*.

The 'equivocalities of emancipation', the 'deepening ... split' or 'growing tension' between state and society,[269] are the starting point of the first book and recurring *point d'appui* for the development of the nation-state itself, and, subsequently, for its racialism, imperialism and totalitarianism. The split yet mutual implication of state and society is explored in French history at the individual level, 'The Jews and Society', by examining how the political or the state enabled and circumscribed the social possibilities of 'exception Jews', Disraeli and Proust, and by examining how the 'social' circumscribed the political and legal actualities in the Dreyfus case. In both cases, formal, legal equality is shown to unleash violence based on 'natural' differentiation and on the refusal of 'groups' to grant each other basic equality, and to show up the refusal of the state to impose even formal democracy in the army.[270]

In the second part, 'Imperialism', Arendt provides, as it were, a socio-political commentary on Luxemburg's political economy of imperialism. In *The Accumulation of Capital*, Luxemburg argues, *contra* Marx, that the expanded reproduction of capital – both the realization of surplus value and the increase in variable capital (i.e. more labour) – 'is an impossible task for a society which consists solely of workers and capitalists';[271] that it requires 'third persons' or 'incessant transition from non-capitalist to capitalist conditions of a labour power that is cast off by pre-capitalist, not capitalist, modes of production in their progressive break-down and disintegration'.[272] This 'emancipation' – which is also a social disintegration – of new productive forces and new sources of consumption takes place both within Europe and beyond Europe in three phases: 'the struggle of capital against natural economy, the struggle against commodity economy, and the competitive struggle of capital on the international stage for the remaining conditions of accumulation'.[273]

> Capital needs other races to exploit territories where the white man cannot work. It must be able to mobilize world labour power without restriction in order to utilise all productive forces of the globe – up to the limits imposed by a system of producing surplus value.[274]

---

[269] *The Origins of Totalitarianism*, pp. 11, 17, 25.
[270] Ibid., pp. 54ff., 100ff.
[271] Op. cit., *Gesammelte Werke*, Bd 5, p. 299, tr. p. 350.
[272] Ibid., pp. 299, 311, tr. pp. 350, 362.
[273] Ibid., p. 316, tr. 368.
[274] Ibid., p. 311, tr. p. 362.

The motivation for this imperialism, the impossibility of realizing surplus value and of increasing variable labour within any given capital–labour ratio, means that capital eventually encounters the 'natural economic impasse' of its own creating; striving to become universal (*zur Weltform zu werden*) . . . it produces its own breakdown.[275] 'It becomes a string of political and social disasters and convulsions, and under these conditions, punctuated by periodical economic catastrophes or crises, accumulation can go on no further.'[276] In spite of this prognosis of political and social 'disaster', *The Accumulation of Capital* ends on the same page in blithe spirit – forecasting that the principles of socialist universalism will complete the contradictory course of capitalism in a 'harmonious and universal system of economy'.[277]

It is Hannah Arendt who draws together first by drawing apart this global economic logic of capital from the political logic, secondary in The *Accumulation of Capital*, but central to Luxemburg's 'Political Writings' – the ruthless 'destruction of non-capitalist strata at home' in *The Accumulation of Capital*,[278] and the 'tumult of non-proletarian protestants', in the 'Political Writings' from 1905 to 1918 – to produce a socio-political examination of such global extension of domination, which, it is demonstrated, has been the condition of world-barbarism not world-socialism.

> The fundamental contradiction between a political body based on equality before the law and a society based on the inequality of the class system prevented the development of functioning republics as well as the birth of a new political hierarchy.[279]

The end of politics brought about by this 'contradiction' of the historical diremption yet mutual implication of civil society and the state, is implicitly translated 'at the very birth of the modern nation-state' into the terms of a second 'secret conflict' – that between state and nation: 'the French revolution combined the declaration of the Rights of Man with the demand for national sovereignty.'[280] The second contradiction comes to prevail over the first for it *seems* to offer a resolution:

> The practical outcome of this contradiction [the same nation was at once declared to be subject to laws . . . *and* sovereign, that is,

---

[275]  Ibid., p. 411, tr. p. 467.
[276]  Ibid., pp. 410–11, tr. p. 467.
[277]  Ibid., p. 411, tr. p. 467.
[278]  Ibid., p. 410, tr. p. 466.
[279]  H. Arendt, *The Origins of Totalitarianism*, p. 12.
[280]  Ibid., p. 230.

bound by no universal law] was that from then on human rights
were protected and enforced only as national rights and that the
very institution of a state, whose supreme task was to protect and
guarantee man his rights as man, as citizen and as national, lost its
legal, rational appearance . . . lost its original connotation of freedom of the people and was being surrounded by a pseudomystical
aura of lawless arbitrariness.[281]

It is the working out of the social and political consequences of these
two contradictions which makes politics impossible; and it is the changing configurations of that impossibility from the French Revolution to
National Socialism and Stalinism that constitute the 'origins' of 'totalitarianism'.

The critical configuration in this series of developments is the relation
of the bourgeoisie to politics: its initial 'indifference' to politics
in general and state finance in particular changing into active engagement once the overseas accumulation and expansion of capital or
'imperialism' becomes necessary.[282] The initial 'indifference' led to 'the
full development of the nation-state and its claim to be above all classes,
completely independent of society and its particular interests, the true
and only representative of the nation as a whole. It resulted, on the
other side, in a deepening of the split between state and society upon
which the body politic of the nation rested.'[283] Under the heading
'Imperialism', Arendt follows through the political consequences of
Rosa Luxemburg's political economy of the 'unlimited expansion that
alone can fulfill the hope for unlimited accumulation of capital'. 'The
destruction of all living communities' which this entails makes the
foundation of new political bodies 'well-nigh impossible'.[284] This *soi-
disant* 'political emancipation of the bourgeoisie' amounts, therefore, to
a further destruction of polity, for imperialist rule operates on the basis
of racist ideology and bureaucratic decree. Imperialist rule, which
provides an outlet for superfluous capital but without the forms of
bourgeois constitutionalism and bourgeois rights, is conducted in the
interests of the bourgeoisie by 'the mob', class residues from all classes,
'the human debris that every crisis, following invariably upon each
period of industrial growth, eliminated permanently from producing
society'.[285]

[281]   Ibid., pp. 230–1.
[282]   Ibid., p. 15.
[283]   Ibid., p. 17.
[284]   Ibid., p. 137.
[285]   Ibid., p. 150.

Arendt is here fusing what she calls 'equivocalities' of initial bourgeois emancipation, learnt from Marx's 'On the Jewish Question', with 'equivocality' of imperialist economic and political emancipation, gleaned from, but not theorized in, Luxemburg's account of the expanded accumulation of capital, and with the 'equivocalities' of the meaning of 'nation'-state, learnt from the increased vulnerability, not security, arising out of the emancipation of the Jews. The third part of the work, 'Totalitarianism', follows through the consequences of the decline of the nation–state attendant on these three equivocalities: between civil society and state; between 'home' constitutional form and overseas racist, bureaucratic decree, which rebounds from overseas to destroy the body politic of the host society; between citizens' rights, which may be alienated without loss of human rights, with the emancipated sovereignty of the nation not the legal-state (*Rechtsstaat*) to insure them, and the actuality of absolute rightlessness. This last point refers to the elimination of people from the political and hence human community, specifically the Nazi deprivation of legal status from the Jews, who were isolated prior to collection and deportation. The shocking point here, *contra* Arendt, is not the 'rightlessness' as such, but that the Nazis thereby 'carefully tested the ground', and 'found out to their satisfaction that no country would claim these people', nor it should be added, would the people of their own country.[286] 'Totalitarianism' is attributed to ideology and propaganda but not to the seizure of power and exercising it afterwards, which is designated: 'The So-called Totalitarian State'.

The argument, as many commentators have noted, draws on German much more than Russian sources, and makes sense in terms of the depoliticization *and* politicization of class-members, 'the masses', and the displaced entrepreneurial residues of all classes, 'the mob', traced in the development of the bourgeois (French, German, British, but not Russian) nation-state, which became evident in 1914 and post-1914, and which arises from, and has the result, that 'membership in a class, its limited group obligations and traditional attitudes toward government, prevented the growth of a citizenry that felt individually and personally responsible for the rule of the country'.[287] Class division has not led to class consciousness, solidarity and conflict, and even less to individual political education. Instead, 'the class-ridden society of the nation-state' whose 'apolitical character . . . came to light only when the class system

---

[286]  Ibid., p. 296. Compare the representation of the euthanasia campaign in Christa Wolf, *A Model Childhood.*
[287]  *The Origins of Totalitarianism*, p. 314.

broke down and carried with it the whole fabric of visible and invisible threads that bound the people to the body politic',[288] and 'whose cracks had been cemented with nationalist sentiment . . . in the first helplessness of their new experience tended towards an especially violent nationalism'.[289] From the perspective of the leaders, the alliance of mob and bourgeoisie, the people were 'politicized' in the attenuated sense provided by the racist and bureaucratic experience of overseas and continental imperialism. They inherit 'albeit in a perverted form – the standards and attitudes of the dominating class, but reflect and somehow pervert the standards and attitudes toward public affairs of all classes.'[290]

From the perspective of examining the appeal of National Socialist ideology, Arendt brings together the non-synchronous political oppositions implicit in Luxemburg's thought – the corruption of imperialist political institutions and bourgeoisie and the nascent nationalism of proletarian *and* non-proletarian 'protestants' – with the twin contradiction of state and civil society *and* of universal rights protected by absolute national sovereignty. The contradiction of state and civil society is expounded by Marx in 'On the Jewish Question', but the second contradiction concerning the equivocation of the nation is *apparently* overlooked both in what Marx has to say about class polarization and the Jews in civil society and state, and in what Luxemburg has to say about the ultimately 'harmonious' internationalization of capital accumulation.

> But the perfection [*Vollendung*] of the idealism of the state was at the same time the perfection of the materialism of civil society. The shaking-off of the political yoke was at the same time the shaking off of the bonds which held in check the egoistic spirit of civil society. Political emancipation was at the same time the emancipation of civil society from politics, from even the *illusion* [*Schein*] of a 'universal content'.[291]

Marx sets out the debasing of politics to individual antagonistic interests by contrasting political 'emancipation' with the configuration of society and politics in feudalism – when guild organization excluded the individual from the state but 'transformed the *particular* relation of [the] guild to the state into [the individual's] own general relationship to the

---

[288]   Ibid.
[289]   Ibid., p. 317.
[290]   Ibid., p. 314.
[291]   Marx, 'On the Jewish Question', *Early Writings*, p. 197, tr. p. 233, corrected.

life of the people'.[292] Life in civil society was directly political, albeit in a feudal sense, as opposed to the political revolution which dissolves civil society into the individual and his or her material or spiritual interests and the 'political' realm gathered from its dispersion in feudal society and constituted 'as the sphere of the community, the *universal* concern of the people ideally independent of those *particular* elements of civil life',[293] where it is, in effect, dominated by the egoism of competing, civil interests. Arendt, however, deplores the way in which politics in the modern nation-state is increasingly determined by what she describes as private, 'social' – property and power – interests, by contrasting them, not with the preceding epoch, which would be 'absolute monarchy', but with an idealized politics attributed to Augustine. In so doing her thinking becomes judgemental, abstract and ahistorical, and unintentionally falls to that very illusion of the perfection of the idealism of the state and politics which has its Janus-face in the simultaneous perfection of the materialism of civil society – the very founding historical diremption on which *The Origins of Totalitarianism* is otherwise based. As a result, the anxiety of beginning, couched in Augustinian terms, becomes formulaic, and the equivocation of the ethical turns into a *ressentiment* of the 'social' – even though she has herself expounded the 'equivocalities' of the modern nation-state as the founding moment, the 'origin' of modern political violence.

Claiming that initially the bourgeoisie had been content with 'every type of state that could be trusted with protection of property rights', in the era of imperialism, she argues, the interests of business became the interests of statesmanship:

> The significant fact about this process of revaluation, which began at the end of the last century and is still in effect, is that it began with the application of bourgeois convictions in foreign affairs and only slowly was extended to domestic politics. Therefore, the nations concerned were hardly aware that the recklessness that had prevailed in private life, and against which the public body always had to defend itself and its individual citizens, was about to be elevated to the one publicly honoured political principle.[294]

The historicity of this exposition – apart from the question of its historical validity – is progressively, and, at significant points, aprioristically, detached from history, as exposure of the limitations of a

[292]  Ibid., p. 196, tr. p. 232.
[293]  Ibid., p. 197, tr. p. 233.
[294]  Arendt, *The Origins of Totalitarianism*, p. 138.

'liberal' polity are judged by the insinuated 'Ought' of the ideal of
radical, Augustinian democracy: 'Public life takes on the deceptive
aspect of a total of private interests as though these interests could
create a new quality through sheer addition.'[295] In opposition to
National Socialism's *Gleichschaltung* of state and society – its culture of
terror, fusing the economic, political, aesthetic – Arendt fixes and
idealizes a distinction between personal life and public affairs and
betrays her own anxiety of beginning in the origin or beginning of
anxiety: the diremption of state and civil society, and its cultures
of overcoming – nationalist, imperialist, racialist.

> [T]he irresistible appeal of the totalitarian movements' spurious
> claim to have abolished the separation between private and public
> life and to have restored a mysterious irrational wholeness in
> man . . . had nothing to do with the justified [*sic*] separation be-
> tween the personal and public spheres, but was rather the psycho-
> logical reflection of the nineteenth century struggle between
> bourgeois and citoyen, between the man who judged and used all
> public institutions by the yardstick of his private interests and the
> responsible citizen who was concerned with public affairs as the
> affairs of all.[296]

It is this insinuation of a *justified* separation of private and public as
opposed to the historical struggle between *bourgeois* and *citoyen*, and its
psychological reflections, that underpins and determines the course of
this authorship. 'Justification', 'separation' and 'judgement' come to
prevail increasingly over the historical agon between state and civil
society; anxiety of beginning becomes beginning of anxiety: exposition
of the two contradictions, state and society, universal right and
sovereign nation, is replaced by the prescribed foundation and publicity
of the new; 'equivocalities' of the ethical become the judgement and
*ressentiment* of the social. In general, exposition of the historical contradictions of state and civil society, and of universality and sovereignty is
replaced by positing the illicit encroachment of the social over the
public and political. Both the foundation of the new and the opposition
between public and private as definitive of the political are 'learnt' from
St Augustine and constitute the discipline of this agon of authorship
over authority.

The end of Book Two and of Book Three reveal the beginning:

[295] Ibid., p. 145.
[296] Ibid., p. 336.

aporetic and agapic affirmation which come to serve in this authorship as disqualification of the equivocation of the ethical instead of its suspension; as transhistorical ideal–typical alternatives, instead of a pseudonymous, masked exploration, aesthetic, ethical or religious, of aporetic and agapic potentiality within the exposition of the twin historical 'contradictions' identified as the fate of the modern nation-state.

> The human being who has lost his place in a community, his political status in the struggle of his time, and the legal personality which makes his actions and part of his destiny a consistent whole, is left with those qualities which usually can become articulate only in the sphere of private life and must remain unqualified, mere existence in all matters of public concern. This mere existence, that is, all that is mysteriously given us by birth and which includes the shape of our bodies and the talents of our minds, can be adequately dealt with only by the unpredictable hazards of friendship and sympathy, or by the great and incalculable grace of love, which says with Augustine, '*Volo ut sis* (I want you to be)', without being able to give any particular reason for such supreme and unsurpassable affirmation.[297]

This moving depiction of the vulnerability and exposure of those protected neither by natural nor by national rights relies, nevertheless, on questionable antitheses which it does not articulate. The loss of political and legal community which should leave the universal 'right of man' has instead resulted in the loss of human characteristics: 'a man who is nothing but a man has lost the very qualities which make it possible for other people to treat him as a fellow-man.'[298] Yet 'mere existence' which is affirmed by the love cited in St Augustine's quintessentially agapic words – '*Volo ut sis*' – *does not include* 'the shape of our bodies' and 'the talents of our minds', for these are socially relevant characteristics, at the hazard of erotic not agapic love, at the hazard of our specific social particularity not our unqualifiable aporetic existence as such. The dogmatic guiding distinction between 'public' and 'private' which implicitly, and later, explicitly, denigrates the social, already diminishes the meaning of aporia and agape. In this statement, Arendt has assimilated the distinction in St Augustine between the two theological origins of 'man', God and humanity, created or given and made, to her own distinction between private and public,[299] which later

---

[297]   Ibid., p. 301.
[298]   Ibid., p. 300.
[299]   See *Der Liebesbegriff bei Augustin*, Dritter Teil, *Vita Socialis*, pp. 75–90.

will be said to be obfuscated by the social rather than having its historical origin within it.

> The more highly developed a civilization, the more accomplished the world it has produced, the more at home men feel within the human artifice – the more they will resent everything they have not produced, everything that is merely and mysteriously given them . . . Since the Greeks we have known that highly developed political life breeds a deep rooted suspicion of this private sphere, a deep resentment against the disturbing miracle contained in the fact that each of us is made as he is – single, unique, unchangeable. This whole sphere of the merely given, relegated to private life in civilized society, is a permanent threat to the public sphere, because the public sphere is as consistently based on the law of equality as the private sphere is based on the law of universal difference and differentiation.[300]

The conclusion that produced political equality seeks to eliminate unchangeable and unique 'givenness' such as 'ethnic heterogeneity' for such difference 'reminds us of the limitations of human activity – which are identical with the limitations of human equality',[301] follows from this compounding of elisions: there are no 'given', 'unique', 'unchangeable' *differences* between people, for recognition of difference implies a universal. The argument conflates aporetic affirmation – the 'disturbing (*sic*) miracle' of each unique life (neither natural nor changeable nor unchangeable) – with socially developed and recognized differences: the equality *and* inequality which are historical constructions, and which 'political' institutions may equally reinforce as seek to abolish. The 'threat' is the 'artifice', not the 'givenness', of human inequality, which is socially conditioned, and which the *contradictory* 'nation'-state, split from society, reinforces by its formal equality, but which the schema of the 'justified separation' of public and private spheres mystifies as 'the fact of difference as such, of individuality as such . . . those realms in which man cannot change and cannot act and in which, therefore, he has a distinct tendency to destroy'.[302] This makes it impossible to conceptualize historical and social difference as opposed to unrepresentable existential uniqueness, and makes it necessary to posit an inherent human 'tendency to destroy' what 'cannot be changed'. The Athenian *polis*, like the modern 'nation'-state, has its

[300] *The Origins of Totalitarianism*, pp. 300–1.
[301] Ibid.
[302] Ibid.

origin in heterogeneity of people not their homogeneity as is argued here. Furthermore, in the modern 'nation'-state 'the constitution of the political state and the dissolution of civil society into independent individuals . . . are achieved in *one and the same act*':

> But man, as member of civil society, inevitably appears as un-political man, as natural man . . . Egoistic man is the *passive* and merely *given* result of the society which has been dissolved, an object of *immediate certainty*, and for that reason a *natural* object.[303]

By conflating 'private' with 'given' or 'unique', and failing to distinguish between 'social' and 'existential', Arendt endorses this historical conflation of 'given' and 'natural'. This posited distinction between private and public is imposed, at the end of Part Two and Part Three of *The Origins of Totalitarianism*, on the exposited diremption between civil society and state with which the work began. It therefore reinforces the very opposition between 'naturally' given and politically created on which the deplored social-politics of 'fraternity' is based. By separating out an ideal-typical politics, the authorship reinforces the ideal-material opposition which has been 'constituted in one and the same act', and which is the contradiction on which this work is otherwise based.

> But there remains also the truth that every end in history necessarily contains a new beginning; this beginning is the promise, the only 'message' which the end can ever produce. Beginning, before it becomes an historical event, is the supreme capacity of man; politically, it is identical with man's freedom. *Initium ut esset homo creatus est* − 'That a beginning be made man was created' said Augustine. This beginning is guaranteed by each new birth; it is indeed every man.[304]

With this reference to *De Civitate Dei*, Book 12, Chapter 20, the degeneration of the capacity to add something of one's own to the common world, which is action (*praxis*), into fabrication (*poiesis*, the making of things), and then into sheer effort of labour in isolation from common concerns, reduced itself by totalitarian terror to the effort to keep alive − 'and the relationship with the world as a human artifice is broken' − is counterbalanced by this principle of hope in each new birth.[305] This repetition of the beginning, albeit as 'message' of the end,

---

[303] Marx, 'On the Jewish Question', p. 198, tr. pp. 233–4.
[304] *The Origins of Totalitarianism*, pp. 478–9.
[305] Ibid., p. 475.

does not emerge as a determinate negation of the culture of terror, and
a return to the ever-present twin contradiction of state and civil society
and of universality and national sovereignty, which would explain why
totalitarianism is now part of our stock of political possibilities, as she
rightly asserts.[306] Instead, this repetition is couched as a theological
affirmation of the new, of birth as such, but not repetition as recollection forwards of 'what has been', which would be to end on the anxiety
of beginning. But an end on the sheer 'fact of birth', which Arendt
herself has argued, understood as the 'disturbing miracle' of givenness,
is no more politically identical with man's freedom, than 'labouring',
understood as isolation from the human world, artifice, common concerns and generalized out of this context of the camps to take the lowest
place in a threefold typology of human capacity, is politically identical
with unfreedom.

Contrary to Elizabeth Young-Bruehl's argument, Arendt's general
dismissal of Christian concern with salvation of the worldless soul as
irrelevant to the foundation of the public realm cited from *The Human
Condition*, does not mean that her 'understanding of the common
world' is 'completely non-Christian' and 'rooted' in Greek and Roman
thought.[307] Arendt reads Greek political experience – as in the passage
discussed above from the end of Part Two of *The Origins of Totalitarianism* – in terms of a defence against aporetic difference and agapic
affirmation learnt from St Augustine. And she judges that St Augustine
in *The City of God* provides the quintessential statement of the Roman
public realm – not distinguishing between 'Christian' and 'Roman'
thought as Young-Bruehl claims: 'Augustine, the only great philosopher the Romans ever had', 'a Christian thinker . . . the first to formulate the philosophical implications of the ancient political idea of
freedom.'[308] Although the doctoral dissertation on St Augustine, published in 1929, was her first major work, and therefore predates her
emergence as a political thinker, Arendt's authorship becomes more
Augustinian not less as its political focus develops. For it is increasingly
based on the opposition between the progressive, inexorable 'rise' of
the social realm, realm of economics, of household, of necessity, and
invocatory and supplicatory aporia, agape, new birth, as the possibility
of politics as such, and less on the historical 'equivocalities' of emancipation – which would call for a neo-Thomist acknowledgement of
the diremption of state and religion not neo-Augustinian projection of
sociality on to the kingdom of saints; or, in Kierkegaardian terms, it

---

[306]   Ibid., p. 478.
[307]   *Hannah Arendt*, p. 498.
[308]   'What is Authority?', p. 126, 'What is Freedom?', p. 167 in *Between Past and Future*.

would call for a suspension of the ethical and not a judgemental disqualification of the social.

To establish the origin of the transition from acting with others to collective passion, Aquinas is cited in *The Human Condition* as exemplary of the 'unconscious substitution' of the 'social' for the political (*societas*, society, Latin word, Roman institution), yet it is the Romans who, unlike the Greeks, will be said to perfect the distinction between private and public in their institutional arrangements.[309] While this indicates ambivalence concerning Roman privacy versus the origins of Latin sociality, it betrays the truth of the strange projection of the distinction between private and public realm back from Roman 'private' law on to the Greeks. Arendt is so concerned to universalize and dematerialize the idea of the 'public' as *res publica* – a public thing, contour of a shared world of debate – and to separate it equally from substance, from force and violence, and thus from risk, that the origin and character of Roman private law, legal status, and restricted political participation, as opposed to Greek *kleros*, allocated property and direct democracy, is nowhere evident. Arendt has then to argue at great length to disqualify private property, and legislation and law as significant differences between the Greek and the Roman world.[310] While *The Origins of Totalitarianism* begins by expounding the equivocalities of bourgeois emancipation, *The Human Condition* begins by denying the equivocalities of Roman 'emancipation' – of private legal status, the 'person', the separation of retributive from distributive justice, of competition from collaboration and the mutual contamination of such separated realms. When the idea of the 'public' is made into an ideal, transhistorical, discursive plurality, its origin in this equivocal emancipation of 'persons' from the collective interest is completely obscured. This fictional 'public realm' amounts to a celebration of the birth and potential emergence of each individual into its light. It becomes in effect the City of God while the City of Man is abandoned to the 'complete victory of the social'.[311]

> To be political, to live in a *polis*, meant that everything was decided through words and persuasion and not through force and violence.[312]

This opposition omits the precondition of its distinction – ethical life: where 'custom', which means legitimized relations of domination,

---

[309]   *The Human Condition* (1958), pp. 23, 59, '*homo est naturaliter politicus, id est socialis*'.
[310]   Ibid., sec. 8, pp. 58–67.
[311]   Ibid., p. 44.
[312]   Ibid., p. 26.

such as marriage and slavery, are transparent, not obscured by formal
legality which is distinct from actual relations of domination. But
instead of bringing these relations of domination into the light of
theory, they are redefined transhistorically as 'household economy',
with which the sanctity of the public realm of politics is undermined in
the modern age. This 'emergence of the social realm' which, magnified
as 'social economy', preoccupies politics, is said to coincide with 'the
emergence of the modern age'.[313] 'Emergence' is consciously or unconsciously substituted for 'equivocalities': 'modern age' for 'modern
nation state'. 'Violence', no longer 'justified' and confined to pre-
political necessity,[314] becomes, in effect, the emancipated equivocality.
Yet this emancipation of violence is not followed through in 'that
curiously hybrid realm where private interests assume public significance that we call "society"'.[315]

'Society' certainly seems 'hybrid': it covers the magnified household
which absorbs the realm of family, 'polite' society, and the realm of
equality and conformity, as opposed to agon.[316] It embraces meanings
ranging from 'sheer survival' to the idea of being unseparated and
therefore unable to unrelate, established by analogy with a spiritual
séance *sans table*.[317] The meaning of the 'public realm' is correspondingly 'hybrid': it covers concerns and things that also appear to others or
perceptions belonging to 'the outer world';[318] it also means relating to
others by means of a third when that third is an artifact of human
fabrication which assembles *and* differentiates;[319] and also an earthly
immortality which transcends the mortality of the fabrication and
fabricators.[320] Subsequently, however, although dismissing Marx's insight into the substituting of private for public interests as predating the
'submersion of both in the sphere of the social' — a distinction without
a difference for it misrepresents Marx's exposition, formerly her own,
of contradiction between, not 'submersion' of, civil society and the
state — she acknowledges a third as mediating the social: the translation
of formerly secure, because situated, private property into 'the common
denominator of money'[321] — mediator of mediation between persons
and 'common' things and of thingified persons and personified things.

---

[313]  Ibid., p. 28.
[314]  Ibid., p. 31.
[315]  Ibid., p. 35.
[316]  Ibid., pp. 46, 41.
[317]  Ibid., pp. 46, 53.
[318]  Ibid., pp. 50–1.
[319]  Ibid., pp. 52–3.
[320]  Ibid., pp. 54–5, 70–3.
[321]  Ibid., pp. 53–4, 69.

Instead of further exploration and exposition, the 'emancipation' of those who labour – 'working classes' and 'women' – is presented, without any equivocation, as indicator of the abolition, equally, of the private world of property as a secure place, and the public world where 'private' aspects of life do not come into common view.[322] A typology of 'emancipated' labour, work and action substitutes for exposition of the equivocalities of bourgeois emancipation. Instead, 'emancipation' becomes ambivalent: the progressive 'rise' of debased social realms of fabrication and of labouring versus the historically specific constitution of apparently separate yet contrary sets of institutions which presuppose and are implicated in each other – state and civil society.

The only way in which this authorship can defend its own staking of itself on 'action', a hybrid expounded as the 'unexpected', the 'now', the 'beginning', the fact of birth, from being 'worldlessness' in the way the bond of Christian charity is indicted for being unpolitic, non-public, modelled on brotherhood,[323] is by employing St Augustine's distinction between the beginning of man – *initium* – and the beginning of the world, between first birth, the sheer fact, and second birth, 'with words and deeds . . . into the human world'. Without beginners, who 'respond' to their first birth by beginning something new on their own initiative,[324] the consequences of which cannot be controlled or foretold,[325] there would be no world. This definition of having a 'world' as the capacity for action – circumscribed by Greek *polis*,[326] protected by Roman privacy, defeated by the substitutions of the modern age, quintessentially expressed as 'the unique life story of the newcomer', without any intrusive author or authority,[327] 'harbour[s] within itself certain potentialities which enable it to survive, the disabilities of non-sovereignty'.[328] 'World' and 'capacity' emerge, therefore, as action-passion of people in concert – not worldless sect but ageless city, articulated by St Augustine using Greek concepts for Roman experience – city *sans* sovereignty, without force or violence, but with perfect property or place.[329]

Sovereignty is reinstated within terms qualified by action-passion 'as

---

[322]   Ibid., pp. 72–3.
[323]   *The Human Condition*, pp. 53–4; cf. 'What is Freedom?', *Between Past and Future*, pp. 170–1.
[324]   Ibid., p. 176, cf. 'What is Freedom?', *Between Past and Future*, p. 167.
[325]   *The Human Condition*, p. 235.
[326]   Ibid.
[327]   Ibid., p. 184.
[328]   Ibid., pp. 235–6.
[329]   See 'The Concept of History', 'What is Authority?', 'What is Freedom?', in *Between Past and Future*, pp. 72–3, 126–7, 166–7.

the power to forgive', release from irreversibility, formulaic repetition backwards, as it were; and as the 'power to promise', partial release from unpredictability, formulaic repetition forwards, as it were. The 'charity' of forgiving, restricted by the erotic undertone of *caritas* even when sublated in the child, passes to love as the respect of friendship, and then to the agape of the divine Child with which 'Action' concludes: 'The miracle that saves the world, the realm of human affairs, from its normal, "natural" ruin . . . : "A child has been born unto us".'[330]

This journey from Latin *caritas*, back to Greek *agape*, via *eros* and *philia*, reveals Arendt's 'public' realm, political 'world', whether expounded as 'the human condition' or as revolutionary constitution to be the city — cosmopolis: 'World city' — of God. Birth into this city is miraculous not 'natural'; normal and natural ruin pertain to the city of man. With the existential qualification of 'forgiveness', judgement should enter this holy city by renouncing itself, and by acknowledging its identity with the action it so harshly judges — the fate of the hypocritical judgement of hypocrisy in the *Phenomenology*.[331] However, because 'forgiveness' is posited but not enacted in this authorship, such authorship retains its judgemental authority and continues to indict, to condemn, to judge the 'modern age' held against the ageless world — which is presented, alternatively, as agapic birth, charitable affirmation, respectful friendship. This dual standard for dual worlds explains how the saints may be social but men may not. St Augustine's *Socialis est vita sanctorum*, 'even the life of the saints is sociable', is cited as the distilled expression of Roman life-together-with-other-men; whereas St Thomas is said to distil the corruption of politics by social relations: *homo est naturaliter politicus, id est socialis*, 'man is by nature political, that is, social'.[332] 'Sociality', acceptable in the one axiom, indicted in the other, is 'holy' in St Augustine, conventional in St Thomas.

Although 'The Power to Forgive' and 'The Power to Promise' are offered as the redeeming finale of 'Action', the authorship does not renounce judgement; instead, it proceeds to foreground it as a culture — first, of political capacity, and, then, of mental faculty.[333] The two parts of the essay 'The Crisis in Culture' are structured according to the subtitle 'Its Social and Its Political Significance'.[334] The first part is judgemental of the 'ruin' of the social in its 'cultural' aspect, which

---

[330] *The Human Condition*, pp. 243, 244, 247.
[331] Hegel, *Phenomenology of Spirit*, pp. 490–4, Miller paras 667–71, pp. 405–9, *ad fin.*
[332] 'The Concept of History', *Between Past and Future*, p. 73; *The Human Condition*, p. 23.
[333] See R. Beiner, 'Hannah Arendt on Judging', in Hannah Arendt, *Lectures on Kant's Political Philosophy*, pp. 89–156.
[334] *Between Past and Future*, pp. 197–226.

involves the transition from 'society' to 'mass society', and from 'culture' as relatively autonomous exchange to sheer assimilated consumption.[335] The second part presents 'judgement' itself as the principle of persuasion in politics. Kant's aesthetic judgement of taste 'debarbarizes the world of the beautiful by not being overwhelmed by it; it takes care of the beautiful in its own "personal" way and thus produces a "culture" '.[336] Kant is enlisted to expand an otherwise exemplary 'Roman', non-utilitarian politics, which 'can only woo the consent of everyone else', and which eschews coercion by violence or by truth:[337] 'Culture and politics, then, belong together because it is not knowledge or truth which is at stake, but rather judgement and decision, the judicious exchange of opinion about the sphere of public life and the common world, and the decision what manner of action is to be taken in it, as well as to how it is to look henceforth, what kind of things are to appear in it.'[338] This apparently secular humanism, formalized by Kant but culled from the Roman — essentially Ciceronian — ethos, which values 'the activity of the truly cultivated mind, *cultura animi*', 'the integrity of the person as person', and friendship, above 'the primacy of an absolute truth',[339] still makes sense only as the sociality of saints. For to define politics as the culture of judgement by reference to the exchange of 'opinion' but not to the struggle for truth, and by reference to public life as 'the common world' but not to political representation, is, implicitly, to define the social, not the political; explicitly, it is to affirm the cerebral *cultura animi*, not the practical; and, generally, it is to remain with the traditional and not to risk the new. The guiding presupposition of the absence of coercion and violence, physical or mental, yet the presence of established institutions — if intelligible — can only imply a culture without risk — without struggle, pain or death. This marks the retreat of the authorship from political action to ecclesiology, completed subsequently, when the mentalist aspect of judgement increasingly prevails in the *Lectures on Kant's Political Philosophy*, *Grundrisse* for the third volume *Judging* of *The Life of the Mind*, as coenobitical — common life, *koinos-bios* — without command yet based on the solitarinesss and sociability of the aspirant saint, only imaginable at a remove from the otherwise judged and unloved 'world'.[340]

---

[335]  Ibid., pp. 209–10.
[336]  Ibid., p. 224.
[337]  Ibid., p. 222.
[338]  Ibid., p. 223.
[339]  Ibid., p. 224.
[340]  Beiner argues, in his 'Interpretative Essay', that judgement becomes progressively more solitary and isolated in Arendt's *oeuvre*; see 'Hannah Arendt on Judging', in Hannah Arendt, *Lectures on Kant's Political Philosophy*, pp. 138–40.

If judgement as a culture, nevertheless, preserves its hard heart, 'friendship' — *philia* or *philanthropia* — preserves respectful distance yet seems more willing to engage in dispute. Lessing's 'concept of friendship' is elaborated in 'On Humanity in Dark Times: Thoughts about Lessing' as an alternative to the politics of 'fraternity': severe not intimate, active not compassionate, selective not indiscriminate and egalitarian, discursive vitality not concern with objective truth, world-ful not worldless.[341] Yet here, too, love does not know the state: 'friendship', whether presented as Nathan's wisdom or Lessing's existential pathos, is defended by the explicit debasement of 'fraternity' to intimacy, which judges class struggle to be based on the *caritas* which is as available to rogues as to the just, to be without a world, to merge people but not to found political institutions, trade unions and parties. It is also defended by 'repetition in lamentation' on the one side and by the imploration and imperative, 'Be my friend', on the other — hallowed but shallow pathos with which the address resounds. The evasion of the reality of Jewish identity in Nathan's 'I am a man', stated to counter the command 'Step closer Jew', and the weakness of the humanism exemplified in fraternity, are not relieved by 'Be my friend' with which eros is stayed and truth allayed.[342] 'Friendship' does not suffice any more than 'humanity' in an exposition which denies or overlooks desire and command, law and prohibition, and coercion, and assimilates them to untoutable 'truth'.

This inhibited pathos is also attributed to Lessing's public persona, *agent provocateur* of 'the infinite number of opinions that arise when men discuss the affairs of this world'. Invested in no truth, except where it is 'humanized by discourse', Lessing is 'a completely political person'[343] without any apperception of the double oxymoron 'completely political', 'political person'. Johannes Climacus also presents Lessing 'almost like Socrates', in the second book of *Concluding Unscientific Postscript*, 'Something about Lessing', as 'excusing himself from all fellowship'.[344] Yet, unlike Arendt, Climacus' 'Lessing' serves truth not infinite opinion; he displays not respect for the finite difference of the other, but concern for the inner agon of the other — for the anxiety of beginning, not cool and sceptical in face of the 'inhumanity' of truth, but 'mingling jest and earnest' in face of the equivocation of the ethical.[345] Arendt's

---

341 *Men in Dark Times*, pp. 11–38.
342 Ibid., pp. 25, 33.
343 Ibid., pp. 33, 38.
344 *Concluding Unscientific Postscript*, p. 65.
345 'On Humanity in Dark Times: Thoughts about Lessing', *Men in Dark Times*, p. 38; *Concluding Unscientific Postscript*, p. 65.

'Lessing' is not qualified for the 'repetition in lamentation' which she proposes, quoting Goethe's 'Dedication to Faust' as tragic reconciliation not mastery of 'the past of Hitler Germany'.[346] He cannot be − for the line which is not quoted but which in the original immediately precedes the two lines which intone the lament is:

*Kommt Lieb und Freundschaft erst*
'love' and 'friendship' come first or before − not in place of −

*Der Schmerz wird neu, es wiederholt die Klage*
*Des Lebens labyrinthisch irren Lauf*
Pain arises anew, lament repeats
Life's labyrinthine, erring course.[347]

How could friendship without intimacy, but also without truth, ever approach this pathos, this repetition in lament?

Arendt's authorship moves from love as charity, St Augustine's *caritas*, to love as *agape* found in St Augustine's *Volo ut sis*, affirming new birth, miraculous precondition of the new in politics, to love as friendship presented as Greek *philia* but nearer to Latin *amicitia* in its selectivity and cunning, a social as much as a political bond.[348] Concomitantly, the barbarism *and* the culture of 'judgement' in this authorship lead it both to condemn and to found the 'social' *not* the political, as it intends. These inversions are the price of retreating from the 'equivocalities of emancipation' and anxiety of beginning which are initially elaborated as 'the twin contradictions' of state and civil society, and of natural rights and national sovereignty. While eschewing the political reconciliations of the particular in the universal − nationalism, racialism, imperialism − the authorship affirms instead a transcendent *amicitia*, social relation, when it intends a suspended agape of aporia − love of the singular. Without agon of anxiety and equivocation of the ethical, it would found a sociality of saints, but it will not endure the action-passion of the law that is always already begun. While the authorship does not suspend the ethical, it is itself nevertheless suspended − between the hard-heart of judgement and the sociality of the saint. It presents many loves and many worlds − the unloved 'social' world impinging with deleterious effect on the loved world, with its unselective agape, '*Volo ut sis*', its selective *philia*, and its cosmopolity

---

[346] *Men in Dark Times*, p. 27.
[347] Ibid., p. 28.
[348] See Cicero, 'On Friendship', in *Cicero's Offices*, pp. 180, 190, 192.

of new birth and new initiative. This city of God perpetuates these loves without law – for law belongs to the fallen, sentimental, fraternal city of Man.

The impotence of 'the beautiful soul', the 'hypocrisy of judgement', and the 'omnipotence' of 'pure culture', represent three temptations whose precondition is the triple diremption – not 'twin contradiction' – which, unresolved, recurs in the three crises of bureaucratic reform, social democratic defeat, rise and fall of Fascism, and whose structural prevalence is especially exposed in the wake of 1989. 'Contradiction' implies 'resolution', whereas 'diremption' may only be manifest as paradox; 'contradiction' is a logical term, which implies the simultaneous assertion of A and not-A, while, as a term of political economy, it implies structural and developmental opposition of social functions and interests, capital and wage-labour, which become progressively polarized and conflictual; 'diremption', on the other hand, implies 'torn halves of an integral freedom to which, however, they do not add up' – it formally implies the third, *tertium quid*, implicit in any opposition, *qua* sundered unity, without positing any substantial pre-existent 'unity', original or final, neither finitely past or future, nor absolutely, as transcendent. 'Diremption' draws attention to the trauma of separation of that which was, however, as in marriage, *not* originally united. Yet, for the child, the marriage seems an original unity, and there exists no form of return to alleviate the trauma – the persistence of the rent. This is to elaborate the structure which appears in the apparently neutral, innocuous, irenic concatenation of conjunctive 'ands': civil society and the state; 'natural' or 'human' rights and national sovereignty; gender and the state – *droits de la femme* and *droits de la citoyenne*. The cross-over between the first and third diremption is only evident in both terms in the gendered French. *Droits de l'homme*, rights of 'Man' ('natural' rights), and *droits du citoyen*, rights of the citizen, do not necessarily include rights of women or rights of 'citizenesses'; and 'rights' extended to women still represent a formal legality which presupposes and sustains systematic social inequality for both men and women. 'The Jewish Question' exposed for these three authorships – excluded, as they were, from traditional Judaism itself and from Christianity – a further diremption in the agape of Christian love, *Volo ut sis*, the cover for irreducible singularity, yet as easily expunged as abstract humanity, formal equality and national rights.

Love 'and' the state cannot be thought apart or together. 'The beautiful soul' repulses the world and retreats from it. She can give neither her knowledge nor her love away; and the sect she flirts with but fails to found or join returns her to a solipsism which wastes away the body and which is impotent in the world – unable to educate or form others. She is a *beautiful* not a 'holy' soul (as Schiller wanted her to be called) because she does not sanctify life, however reduced, but both denies it and sublimates the denial into an ethereal eros without form or contact – and hence the body is not concentrated in the soul but dispersed and dissipated in it. While the beautiful soul withdraws herself from the world by repulsing it and retreating from it, the hard-heart remains in the world but survives by retreating from and repulsing the other in judgement – judgement of hypocrisy – the self-conscious disparity between declaring universal duty yet living particular inner being, which is itself hypocritical in appealing to its own law and also failing to act – making duty a mere matter of words.[349] This judgement, exalted into a culture, would eliminate barbarism – of evil, of hypocrisy, of 'banality' of evil.[350] It affirms the 'infinity of opinions' so that 'going astray with Plato' is taken to mean opting for the charm of Plato's person in preference to whatever truth is chanced upon by his opponents.[351] This interpretation reduces the difficulty of truth to opinion, and the play of opinion to fancying persons. 'Judgement' here becomes a 'pure culture'[352] which inverts truth and opinion, universal and person – 'This judging and talking is, therefore, what is true and invincible, while *it* overpowers everything; it is solely with this alone that one has truly to do with in this actual world.'[353] If absolute freedom removes the antithesis between universal and individual will so that the world may be destroyed, absolute judgement[354] – judgement made omnipotent – would result in universal hypocrisy: for there is no truth, no universal, to be acknowledged, but only the dissolving play of opinions from which knowledge and truth and the risk of staking oneself for the sake of something transcendent and uncertain are banished. Absolute judgement would become absolute perversion as dynamic but suppressed knowledge must masquerade as opinion, and so appears as universal deception of itself and others.[355] Can this be the sociality of saints?

These three temptations – of pseudo-Pietist soul-beauty, of founding a barbarism of pure culture, and of moral judgement or founding judgement as a culture, with its hard-heart or 'friendly' heart towards

---

[349] Hegel, *Phenomenology of Spirit*, pp. 485, 487, Miller paras 660, 664, pp. 401, 403.
[350] The ontological status of evil, or *privatio boni*, is not at issue here.
[351] Arendt, 'Lessing', *Men in Dark Times*, p. 33; 'Crisis in Culture', *Between Past and Future*, p. 224.
[352] Hegel, *Phenomenology of Spirit*, p. 385, Miller para. 521, p. 316.
[353] Ibid., p. 386, Miller para. 521, p. 317.
[354] Ibid., p. 438, Miller para. 595, p. 363.
[355] Ibid., p. 386, Miller para. 521, p. 317.

unloved world or loved city – were resisted by these three authorships
whose agon consisted in finding a way to give their knowledge away
and not keep it to themselves, without substituting their authority for
the anxiety of beginning in the equivocation of the ethical. And they
succumbed to these temptations to the extent that all three were less
equivocal later in life and authorship – Rahel Varnhagen more 'beautiful' in her Second Salon; Rosa Luxemburg more judgemental in ways
she herself anticipated in her last writings on the Russian Revolution;
Hannah Arendt, who at first knew the equivocalities of emancipation
and twin contradictions, who knew truth in its equivocation, cultures
judgement, and then, in a subsequent retreat, turns the culture of
judgement back into a mental capacity in the lecture sketches for the
final volume of the *Life of the Mind*: 'Judging'.

This quantitative shift to sustaining less equivocation and anxiety and
to claiming more authority over time, is correlated to the shift in
method and in substance: between exploring an unimaginable radical
democracy in its existing historical diremptions by suspending the
ethical, or by opposing those diremptions and by cultivating their
oppositions. For the diremptions of civil society 'and' state, natural
rights 'and' national sovereignty, gender – *droits de la femme, droits de la
citoyenne* – 'and' state, may be concentrated by suspending the ethical
so that love and law are simultaneously explored as in *The Origins of
Totalitarianism*, Part One. However, if the dirempted terms of the
ethical are set in opposition to each other, so that 'love' – discursive,
friendly, saintly, agapic, aporetic, political – is opposed to 'the law' –
the world, the city of man – and made into an unworldly culture – a
city of God – this holy city will be infected with the same judgemental
banality of opinion about good and evil it would repulse. To suspend
the ethical is to acknowledge the continuing oppositions – the diremptions summarized as 'love' and 'law' – without assimilating them to a
supernal one: it is to continue acknowledging the incommensurability
of universal, particular and singular, without culturing them and, thus,
without dirempting them yet again.

## Nation-State and Violence

Generally speaking, the role of the 'heart' in politics seems to me
altogether questionable.

I have never in my life 'loved' any people or collective – neither
the German people, nor the French, nor the American, nor the
working class or anything of the sort... To clarify this, let me

tell you of a conversation I had in Israel with a prominent political personality who was defending the — in my opinion disastrous — non-separation of religion and state in Israel. What he said . . . ran something like this: 'You will understand that, as a Socialist, I, of course do not believe in God; I believe in the Jewish people'. I found this a shocking statement and, being too shocked, I did not reply at the time. But I could have answered: the greatness of this people was once that it believed in God, and believed in Him in such a way that its trust and love towards Him was greater than its fear. And now this people believes only in itself? What good can come out of that?[356]

This passage, taken from a letter by Hannah Arendt dated 24 July 1963, to Gershom Scholem concerning her book *Eichmann in Jerusalem*, contains a reflection more in tune with the original insight of the authorship into the 'twin contradictions' of civil society and the state, natural rights and national sovereignty, than with the later condemnation of the 'rise' of the social and defence of 'the public realm' by reference to 'the power to promise' and 'the power to forgive' — the miracle of new birth. For the reflection developed here implies that the 'non-separation of religion and the state', that is, the non-separation of civil society from the state, expresses and encourages nationalism, a 'love' of a specific people, which prevents the development of a just polity, without idealizing that polity as a 'public realm', and, on the other hand, without denigrating the rise of the 'social', and without idealizing civil society as the realm of voluntary association. The belief in God recalled here is not being simply opposed to the dubious belief in 'a people' — which would simply be to reproduce the *soi-disant* socialist's substitution of 'the people' for God. The latter substitutes an apparently 'natural' object for a supernatural one but really posits one abstract, absolute unity in the place of another; whereas Arendt, in effect, proposes here a repetition in lament — remembering the love and fear of God as a suspension of the ethical: a hearing open beyond any current political condition or any current realizable collective interest or will, beyond any specific finite desire or fear, love or hate, which, released to the ethical, would acknowledge not just the infinite differences of people or of opinions, but the historical difficulty of the diremption of state and civil society, and would not succumb to any 'love' or 'belief' that seeks to abolish the ethical in its equivocation or anxiety.

[356] 'Eichmann in Jerusalem', Letter to Scholem, 24 July 1963, p. 54.

This exposition of how 'the suspension of the ethical' offers access to the diremptions of 'modernity' — where 'modernity' is discovered to be diremptive and is not defined, *quasi-a priori*, as a 'project' — implies that the mode of production is neither suppressed by the generality of 'modernity', nor posited as a schema with a post-historical warranty; instead, it is rediscoverable in the diremptions and their culturing.

In the title 'Love and the State', therefore, the violence resides in the 'and'. 'Violence' is neither hypostatized nor is it ontologized, nor is it made into one term of an equation — not even an aporetic one — as in *Violence and the Sacred* or *The Nation-State and Violence*. The severe styles of Girard's anthropology and of Giddens's sociology may be contrasted with the facetious 'Love and the State'. The metaphysics of 'violence' in Girard, and the naturalization of violence as a 'resource' of the modern nation-state in its monopoly of the legitimate means of physical violence and of administrative violence, 'surveillance', in Giddens,[357] may be contrasted with the diremption of civil society and the state, natural rights and national sovereignty, *droits de la femme* and *droits de la citoyenne*. These have been explored in authorships which comprehend how 'love' can result in violence and violence in love, and which seek therefore in their authorships not to reproduce authorities which amount to the abolition or resolution of anxiety of beginning and equivocation of the ethical.

First, therefore, *love* is not opposed to 'violence', which would be to replace one pre-sociological concern with another, for 'love' is equivocal and its employment facetious; secondly, the 'and' is diremptive, not conjunctive, nor aporetic; while, thirdly, 'the state' is not the composite 'nation-state' which leads to the historical perspective of 'Nations and Nationalism',[358] with perplexity compressed in the evasive 'and' — the transition from 'nation', meaning the universalizing, liberal-democratic constitution, *la patrie*, where 'citizenship' defines the people, to 'nationalism', where divisive, 'ethnic' or 'racial' qualifications are the criteria of political membership, so that 'the people' define citizenship. Leaving 'the state' bare, without epithet or construct, makes it possible to explore the interconnected fate of all diremptions, inner and outer, civil society and the state, natural rights and national sovereignty, *droits de la femme* and *droits de la citoyenne*, and their cultures — their love and

---

[357] A. Giddens, *The Nation-State and Violence*, esp. chs 1 and 2, pp. 7–60, and also p. 121.
[358] See E. Gellner, *Nations and Nationalism*; E. J. Hobsbawm, *Nations and Nationalism Since 1780*; Giddens, *The Nation-State and Violence*, pp. 116–21, 209–21. Gellner argues that 'official' nationalism *precedes* the modern nation-state, but by 'nationalism' he means symbolic nation-building. He is then unable to distinguish this use of 'nationalism' adequately from twentieth-century Fascist and Nazi nationalism.

their violence — without presupposing the hybrid nation-state, without positing a composite of social and political and national, and without reproducing an intellectual economy of 'social and system integration' to hold against Marxism on the one hand, functionalism on the other, but which takes violence — historical, loveful, authorial — out of the account.

The severity of recent attempts to think modernity, nation and violence, historically, systematically and sociologically, is frequently premised on two misapprehensions concerning Hegel's and concerning Marx's exposition of the modern state: that they did not anticipate the importance of the nation and nationalism;[359] and that the opposition they did uncover between civil society and the state is equivalent, broadly speaking, to the opposition between the social and the political;[360] systematically speaking, to the duality of social and system integration.[361]

However, the expositions in Hegel and in Marx of the modern state uncover the 'national' problem as intrinsic to the inner fissure of the state, and, in so doing, remain consistent with the anticipation of their predecessor, Rousseau — in spite of this oversight on the part of their successors. In *The Social Contract*, Rousseau drew attention to the nation/national question as intrinsic to the original conception and definition of sovereignty:

> This public person, so formed by the union of all other persons, formerly took the name of *city*, and now takes that of *Republic* or body politic; it is called by its members *State* when passive, *Sovereign* when active, and *Power* when compared with others like itself. Those who are associated in it take collectively the name of *people*, and severally are called *citizens*, as sharing in the sovereign authority, and *subjects*, as being under the laws of the State.[362]

These sets of Janus-faced terms comprise, taken collectively, when passive 'the state', when active the 'sovereign'; taken individually, when passive 'subjects', when active 'citizens'. To its members, 'city', 'republic' or 'body politic'; 'when compared to others like itself', it is 'power'. Here 'power' is the sovereign people in relation to other sovereign people, which, in Barère's report to the Committee of Public Safety, 'in

---

[359] See, for example, Giddens, op. cit., p. 212; see Hobsbawm's historiographical 'Introduction' to *Nations and Nationalism Since 1780*, pp. 1–13.

[360] See John Keane, 'Despotism and Democracy', in Keane (ed.), *Civil Society and the State*, pp. 35–71.

[361] See D. Lockwood, 'Social Integration and System Integration"; see n. 378, *infra*.

[362] Rousseau, *The Social Contract*, ch. VI, p. 14 n. 1, tr. p. 175 and n. 1.

relation to the remainder of the human race, constituted a nation'.[363]
However, it is Rousseau's 'people' that is often taken to mean 'the
nation' and in this way an equivocation arises between 'nation' as the
'act' of political association, inner legitimacy by means of universal
membership, and 'nation' as bounded by the particularity of its
sovereignty with no reference to recognition or legitimation. This comparative 'Power' without legitimation marks an age-old dilemma with a
great future ahead of it, which may also explain why this radical
attempt to found and justify revolutionary-democratic polity by positing the distinctions between these terms, indicated by a long footnote,
appended by Rousseau to 'the name of city', is, nevertheless, cast as a
reflexive hermeneutic: 'is called by its members'; 'when compared with
others like itself'. The 'ways' of a body politic when confronted with
the ways of another give rise to a reflexive perception of the initial way
as custom, convention or law,[364] which for its members acquires an
inner validation or legitimacy not corresponding to an outer one, for it
is the confrontation with its boundary that provokes the initial, reflexive, political awareness. The ancient and medieval idea of universal
'natural law' as distinct from particular, conventional, positive laws
may be seen as an interpolitical (one hesitates to say 'international')
response to this dilemma which is not available to Rousseau as it would
presuppose to him the divinity of law. It is this old opposition between
outer resistance or impulse, 'power', and inner self-definition and legitimation which, in Rousseau's democratic formulation, is reconfigured
by the inner duality of activity and passivity which draws attention
away from the dualism which the duality presupposes: the universality
of citizen and subject, whether active or passive, depends on the autar-
chic autonomy or particularity of the sovereignty which bounds and
protects it.

   This is not to imply that modern states are 'nation'-states in their
very original constitution, but to argue, on the contrary, that these
mutual implications between inner, universal activity and passivity, and
outer sovereignty and particularity, between legitimate and non-
legitimate power, should remain explicit so that their dynamic and its
namings re-emerge. For this antinomy takes on a new virulence when,
as Hegel and Marx dissect Rousseau's schema historically, by bringing
the second Discourse *On the Origin of Inequality* to *The Social Contract*,
the definition of all citizens as universal and active, the definition of
subjects as universal and passive, can no longer be maintained. For an
inversion is evident within the inner, universal oppositions between

[363] Cited in Hobsbawm, *Nations and Nationalism Since 1780*, p. 22.
[364] See L. Strauss, *Natural Right and History*, pp. 81–119.

collective and individual, or universal and particular realms: civil society based on the realm of the particular needs of subjects and separated
from the state, which represents the universal interest of the community. As a result subjects pursuing their particular interests are active;
citizens acting in the interests of the universal become passive. For
Hegel and Marx, Rousseau's definitions, his posited meanings —
citizen-active, subject-passive — corresponding, collectively, to sovereignty and state, are experienced in terms of an opposition between
universal and particular, which is inner as well as outer. The universal,
the community, has to be generated, when its historical basis is the
separation of civil society, economy and property, from political institutions of the state.

Hegel's *Philosophy of Right* acknowledges that the abstract particularity of civil society is completed only by police and corporation; and the
transition to the universal, the state, is, in its turn, only completed by
the concluding sections on 'International Law' (*Das äussere Staatsrecht*)
and 'World History'.[365] Throughout, Hegel uses the word *Volk*, never
*Nation*, as it is consistently translated. While Fichte uses *Nation* in his
*Addresses to the German Nation*,[366] and Herder uses *Volk* to imply a
people historically united by language, yet prior to nationalist Germaniz-
ing *Nation* as *Volk* after 1875, *Volk* would have been the usual German
equivalent of Rousseau's sovereign citizen-people. It is this mix of
particularity and universality that Hegel grapples with — only able to
justify the universality he has laid out in 'The State' in relation to the
patent 'state of nature' between states in relation to each other,[367] where
'there is no Praetor to judge between states',[368] no universal will only
particular wills, by reference to the 'court of world history'.[369] This is
to appeal to a universality based not on judgement but on the movement of history, collected out of recognition of the 'stern struggle'[370]
not of 'nations' but of 'peoples' — Greek, Roman, Germanic — defined
by the oppositions and inversions generated in their one-sided attempts
to realize their sovereign law, defined, that is, by universality but infected with particularity. This 'grief of history' is enlisted to conceptualize the oppositions, inner and outer, between universal and particular
in the modern state. The *Philosophy of Right* concludes as the unre-
deemed history of right — and wrong.

[365]  Op. cit., paras 330–60, pp. 497–512, tr. pp. 212–23.
[366]  Fichte, *Reden an die deutsche Nation*.
[367]  *Philosophy of Right*, para. 333, p. 499, tr. p. 213.
[368]  Ibid., para. 333, p. 500, tr. p. 213, Remark.
[369]  Ibid., para. 341, p. 503, tr. p. 216: '[*Die Weltgeschichte*] ist ein Gericht' misleadingly
translated as 'world history is a court of judgement'.
[370]  Ibid., para. 360, p. 512, tr. p. 222.

Marx, as well as Hegel, may be read as offering an implicit analysis of the conflation of nation with state and not as failing to anticipate it. This also involves attending to the restless refusal to resolve inner and outer oppositions of universal and particular. The reference to Rousseau with which Part One of 'On the Jewish Question' concludes emphasizes how political emancipation makes political man into an abstract, artificial man, 'an *allegorical, moral* person',[371] how it reduces political life and institutions to the interests of egoistic man, the member of civil society.[372] This has been taken to mean that the state is inevitably reduced to civil society once the separation is constituted. As a result the perspective of their mutual presupposition – and the interdependence of these spheres of legality – is lost. This throws their illusory opposition into a quantitative ratio: more civil society, less state – which leads, in spite of Marx's critique of its egoism, to an idealization of civil society as a realm of free association.[373] Yet their dirempted relation is a question of configuration which is always precarious: the relative freedoms of state and civil society undermine each other – the undermining of the state appears as the freedom of civil society and the consequent violence of its members and its police; the undermining of civil society appears as the freedom of the unharmonized state and the violence of its law. Marx has the German state, with its minimal civil society, in mind as much as the French and American Constitutions and Declarations which apparently reduce the relative power of the state. The emphasis on the reduction of politics to civil society, is balanced by the emphasis that the right to freedom ceases to be a right as soon as it comes into conflict with *political* life, whereas in theory political life is simply the guarantee of the rights of man, the rights of individual man, and should be abandoned as soon as it contradicts its goal of realizing them.[374]

The problematic second part of 'On the Jewish Question' where Marx returns to the question of Jewish Emancipation may be elucidated by reading it as a commentary on the idea of Jews as a 'nationality', which is derived from the commercial role of the Jew on which civil society depends. Marx shows how the most central feature of civil society – 'money' – is personified as alien – as an alien *nation*, the Jew, whose image is preserved in the interests of civil society: 'The

---

[371]  Op. cit., p. 234, tr. p. 234.
[372]  Ibid., p. 234, tr. p. 233.
[373]  By interpreting Marx's theory as an economism, Keane treats civil society and the state as a ratio of power in order to defend civil society as 'socialist' or pluralistic – as a 'culture' – see *Democracy and Civil Society*, pp. 58, 23, 31, 61, and 'Despotism and Democracy' in Keane (ed.), *Civil Society and the State*, pp. 28, 53, 62.
[374]  'On the Jewish Question', p. 195, tr. p. 231.

*chimerical* nationality [*Die schimärische Nationalität*] of the Jew is the nationality [*die Nationalität*] of the merchant, of the man of money in general.'[375] The analysis of the separation and opposition between civil society and the state thus shows how the outer particularity — power/ nation — 'when compared with other' sovereign people-states rebounds into the inner oppositions so that an alien 'nation' is imagined out of and in the opposition of universal and particular between spheres and individuals and classes.

The judgement that Hegel and Marx had nothing to say on the nation-state has meant that speculative exposition of the unbearable tensions of modernity and their violent solutions which may, nevertheless, come to learn their own implication has been set aside. This jettisoning of speculative thinking by recent 'critical theory' of modernity has also meant the abandonment of that methodological reflexivity, which is equally substantive, and which learns by coming to know its own formation in the culture it explores. Habermas and Giddens write in the severe style, having disqualified not only Marx and Hegel, but also Weber, Horkheimer and Adorno, who are read without any attention to their difficult and facetious presentation.[376] This lack of attention to form and style leads to the functionalism of the subject: to the critical theorist who becomes a sociologist, his own authoritative voice a neutral, unimplicated discourse of its object;[377] and to the functionalism of substance, which can only be established on holistic grounds by mobilizing Lockwood's duality of 'social integration' and 'system integration',[378] and equipping it with a new operationalist terminology: 'colonization', 'juridification', 'steering media', 'resources', 'co-presence'.[379] The critical perspective is restricted to the evolutionary 'uncoupling' of life world and system, followed by the progressive rationalizing of life world by system;[380] or to the 'breaking away' of system from social integration,[381] leading to 'surveillance' as the medium of administrative power, tending to totalitarianism but 'counterbalance[d] in the form of polyarchic involvement'.[382]

---

[375] Ibid., p. 205, tr. p. 239.

[376] See, for example, Habermas, *Theory of Communicative Action*, Vol. 1, *Reason and the Rationalization of Society*.

[377] See, for example, Giddens, *Constitution of Society*, p. xx; *Nation-State and Violence*, p. 20.

[378] See, for example, Habermas, *Legitimation Crisis*, p. 4; Giddens, *Constitution of Society*, p. 28 n. 31 and p. 36 n. 32, with reference to Lockwood.

[379] See, for example, Habermas, *The Theory of Communicative Action*, Vol. 2, *Life World and System: A Critique of Functionalist Reason*, pp. 335ff.

[380] See ibid., vol. 2, ch. 2, 'The Uncoupling of System and Life World', pp. 153–97.

[381] See Giddens, *Constitution of Society*, pp. 183–4.

[382] See *Nation-State and Violence*, p. 341.

This sociology in the severe style wins the battle against the critical theory it disqualifies and claims to be receiving — but at the cost of losing the battle against functionalism. For it is grounded on posited 'dualities' — historicized backwards by Giddens in the development of the nation-state and violence, historicized forwards by Habermas in the theory of communicative action. The result is an intellectual culture in which anxiety of beginning is displaced by voluminous sociology; equivocation is replaced by 'integration'; the broken middle translated into 'steering media' or administrative and physical resources. In this culture, 'violence', objectified and tamed, would never have to confront its good intentions — no violence in love and no love in violence. And without repetition backwards, without recollection, there can be no repetition forwards . . .

# 6

# New Political Theology – Out of Holocaust and Liberation*

## Levinas, Rosenzweig and Fackenheim

### Violence and Halacha

With Girard, anthropology of violence; with Arendt, ecclesiology of violence; with Giddens, sociology of violence; with Heidegger, ontology of violence;[1] with Taylor, a/theology of violence;[2] with Levinas, eschatology of violence and violence of 'the said'.[3] The canny particle 'of' tames the violence ontologized in the dominant opposition to be found in each of these authorships which thereby infects what they would keep apart: holy middles, full of the fury against which they fulminate, transliterated into dispassion, *sine ira ac studio*.

---

* Throughout this chapter the title 'Liberation Theology' is used to include German political theology, even though 'Liberation Theology', strictly speaking, refers to its Latin-American cousin. The intention is to emphasize and criticize the idea of 'liberation' in the German tradition.

[1] See Heidegger, *An Introduction to Metaphysics*, pp. 88–149, tr. pp. 98–169.

[2] See 'Reframing Postmodernisms', in *Shadow of Spirit: Contemporary Western Thought and its Religious Subtexts*, Berry and Wernick (eds).

[3] 'Eschatology of Violence' in *Totality and Infinity*; violence of 'the said' in *Otherwise than Being*. Although Levinas subsequently disclaims his early defence of eschatology in *Totality and Infinity*, it will be argued here that it remains a significant concept for comprehending the structure and implications of this thinking throughout his authorship; see the 'Dialogue' with Richard Kearney, *Dialogues with Contemporary Continental Thinkers*, p. 59.

Derrida's essay 'Violence and Metaphysics: An Essay on the Thought of Emmanuel Levinas', *Writing and Difference*, pp. 117–228, tr. pp. 79–153, only covers Levinas' work up to *Totality and Infinity*, although Derrida has published a reply to Levinas' reply, 'God and Philosophy', *The Levinas Reader*, pp. 93–127, tr. pp. 166–89: 'En ce moment même dans cet ouvrage me voici', *Psyché Inventions de l'autre*, Paris, Galilée, 1987, pp. 159–201.

When you compare world history, where there are so many mystical thoughts and movements, so many movements and doctrines of peace and love, with the true political course of this history made up of wars, violence, conquests and the oppression of men by their fellows, then you have less cause to worry about Israel's soul and political history. Ethics will never, in any lasting way, be the good conscience of corrupt politics . . .[4]

Simultaneously acknowledging and refusing to know the inversions of love and the state, speaking of 'world history' in terms of the *eschatons* of 'peace' and 'war', Levinas exonerates not only Israel in particular but also the whole political–historical structure of repetition backwards which he evasively identifies. *A fortiori*, he exonerates his own ethics.

The other is the neighbour, who is not necessarily kin, but who can be. And in that sense, if you're for the other, you're for the neighbour. But if your neighbour attacks another neighbour or treats him unjustly, what can you do? Then alterity takes on another character, in alterity we can find an enemy, or at least then we are faced with the problem of knowing who is right and who is wrong, who is just and who is unjust. There are people who are wrong.[5]

Levinas keeps inviolate a holy middle just as he reveals that it is broken. In the 'necessity' for which he calls of 'rejoining' justice and power,[6] justice and knowledge fall further apart.

Ethics is, therefore, *against nature* because it forbids the murderousness of my natural will to put my own existence first.[7]

Ethics redefines subjectivity as this heteronomous responsibility in contrast to autonomous freedom.[8]

Stated here with exemplary clarity, this disqualification of the opposition between 'nature' and 'freedom' constitutes the fundamental

---

[4] 'Ethics and Politics', *The Levinas Reader*, p. 295; the context is the massacre in Sabra and Chatila camps, West Beirut, 1982 see the editor's introductory note, p. 289.

[5] Ibid., p. 294.

[6] 'To Love the Torah More Than God', p. 193, tr. *Judaism*, 28, 2 (1979), 220.

[7] 'Dialogue' with Richard Kearney, 1981, in Kearney, *Dialogues with Contemporary Continental Thinkers*, p. 60, emphasis in original.

[8] Ibid., p. 63.

metaphysical shift of all these irenic authorships. Treated as one of a number of arbitrary, binary myths belonging to the mêlée of metaphors inherited from 'Western metaphysics', 'nature' and 'freedom' are relegated to the post-metaphysical 'premodern', that is, the modern. Thinking, however, does not stop — it has merely exited from the struggle of universal and aporia. For instead of recognizing and comprehending the opposition between 'nature' and 'freedom' as the tension of freedom 'and' unfreedom, and bearing that tension as agon of authorship, anxiety of beginning, equivocation and suspension of the ethical, these authorships invariably proceed to invent a 'passage', a path, from violence to the holy.

> We must speak first of all, not of the relation between ethics and Halacha, but rather of the passage from the non-ethical in general to the ethical, for this is truly the necessity of our time. This question must be answered on behalf of that Jewish youth which has forgotten the Holocaust, and which sees in the rejection of all morality an end to violence, an end to repression by all forms of authority.[9]

Caught in 'the saying', his originary, Levinas' authorship here acknowledges and denies the diremption of ethics and *halacha*, ethics and law, just as in the interview cited above, it acknowledges and denies the diremption of love and the state. *Halacha* means the legal passages of the Talmud, distinguished from *Aggada*, the non-legal passages; this is also expressed as the distinction between 'law' and 'lore'. Both diremptions will show up in its 'said'. For Franz Rosenzweig's 'spanning' 'ands' — of God 'and' world 'and' man[10] — here meet their nemesis in this passage from world to God, and it will be 'dialogic' man in the middle who breaks under the burden.

Commentator and exponent of the law in his *lectures talmudiques*, who, nevertheless, stakes his authorship on divine 'an-archy', Levinas expounds subjectivity, the ego, representation, consciousness,[11] freedom as the anxiety of beginning; he offers 'trace', 'illeity', the holy,[12] as the enigma and equivocation of the ethical beyond being and he

---

[9] 'Ideology and Idealism', *The Levinas Reader*, p. 236; the introductory paragraphs from which this passage comes are not included in the French version, in *De Dieu qui vient à l'idée*, pp. 17–33.

[10] 'The New Thinking', pp. 150, 158, trans. in Glatzer (ed.), *Franz Rosenzweig, His Life and Thought*, pp. 198, 205.

[11] For example, *Otherwise than Being*, p. 210, tr. p. 165.

[12] Ibid., pp. 154–5, 216, tr. pp. 120, 170.

crowns this agon of authorship by being willing to bear the violence and betrayal of 'the said'[13] in his philosophy, which thereby fails to-wards 'saying', towards 'disengaging the holy',[14] 'called upon to conceive [*penser*] ambivalence, to conceive it several times'.[15]

While the authorship cultivates the equivocation between pre-original 'saying' and its betrayal, 'the said', its equilibrium, not 'aimed at', settles each of these 'several times' in the middle:

> An approach is not a representation . . . of a being beyond being . . . The trace of a past in a face is not the absence of a yet non-revealed, but the anarchy of what has never been present, of an infinite which commands in the face of the other, and which, like an excluded middle could not be aimed at.[16]

This analogic 'excluded middle' is the holy middle:

> Illeity [a neologism formed with *il* (he) or *ille* . . . indicates a way of concerning me without entering into conjunction with me. / This detour at a face and this detour from this detour is the enigma of a trace we have called illeity] overflows both cognition and the enigma through which the Infinite leaves a trace in cognition. Its distance from a theme, its reclusion, its holiness, is not its way to effect its being . . . but is its glory, quite different from being and knowing. It makes the word God be pronounced, without letting 'divinity' be said . . .[17]

While this de-circumscription would revert 'the said' to the utterance of the holy, it reveals the 'ambivalence' or 'ambiguity'[18] of the relation of the order of the holy or the ethical to the order of being: it reveals the Janus-face of the third party:

> The neighbour that obsesses one is already a face, both comparable and incomparable, a unique face and in relationship with faces, which are visible in the concern for justice . . . The relationship with the third party is an incessant correction of the asymmetry of

---

13  Ibid., pp. 206, 215–16, tr. pp. 162, 169–70.
14  Ibid., p. 76, tr. p. 59.
15  Ibid., p. 206, tr. p. 162.
16  Ibid., pp. 123–4, tr. p. 97.
17  Ibid., pp. 15, 206, tr. pp. 12, 162.
18  Ibid., p. 206, tr. pp. 161, 162.

proximity in which the face is looked at. There is weighing, thought, objectification, and thus a decree in which my anarchic relationship with illeity is betrayed, but in which it is conveyed before us.[19]

Passing from 'I' to 'us', the 'I' now 'counted among them', this 'itinerary' can no more be 'assembled' than it can when 'I substitute myself for him', for it marks justice at the very Janus of divesting of the order of being/investing of the ethical or freedom;[20] or passing from being comparable to being unique in the substitution, and from being unique to being comparable, 'I' now 'among them'. Yet this ' "Peace, peace to the neighbour and the one far-off" (Isaiah 57:19)', this middle, most finely tuned, relapses into the discordant coherence of 'the state', 'master' and 'medicine': 'violence or reasons of state or an approach ensures to the rationalism of logic a universality and to law its subject matter'.[21] Such 'alliance of logic with politics' leaves resistance only as 'interruptions' which occur in 'the periodic rebirth of scepticism', the wager of authorship, 'saying it to one that listens to it, and who is situated outside the said that the discourse says, outside all it includes', as witness to the *eschaton* of the *ille* – escaping the order of being of nouns, the presence of verbs.[22]

From *Totality and Infinity* to *Otherwise than Being or Beyond Essence*, and without here assembling them into an itinerary, anxiety of beginning, agon of authorship, equivocation of the ethical, hold off-centre the holy yet broken middle which, excluding the political history it evinces of love and the state, ethics and *halacha*, reverts to eschatology, to peace, at war 'with the totality of wars and empires'.[23] In *Totality and Infinity*, the terror and the violence of being are made peaceable as paternity;[24] in *Otherwise than Being*, 'illeity', made peaceable as the face of justice, is interrupted immediately in its 'just violences'.[25] Love sublated and the state deflated appear, respectively, as agon of authorship in each work where the 'passage from the non-ethical in general to the ethical' would dissemble the deeper agony which otherwise forms modern Jewish thinking – that of ethics and *halacha*.[26]

---

[19]   Ibid., p. 201, tr. p. 158.
[20]   Ibid., pp. 201, 206, 201, tr. pp. 160, 162, 158.
[21]   Ibid., pp. 200, 216, tr. pp. 157, 170.
[22]   Ibid., pp. 217, 216, 233, tr. pp. 171, 170, 185.
[23]   *Totality and Infinity*, p. xi, tr. p. 23.
[24]   Ibid., p. 283, tr. p. 306.
[25]   *Otherwise than Being*, p. 216, tr. p. 170.
[26]   'Ideology and Idealism', *The Levinas Reader*, p. 236.

To support *without* compensation, the excessive or disheartening hubbub and encumberment of the *there is* [*il y a*] is necessary to him [who is elected, assigned] [1974].[27]

The rustling of the *there is* [*il y a* ] . . . is horror. We have noted the way it insinuates itself in the night, as an undetermined menace of space itself disengaged from its function as receptacle for objects, as a means of access to beings [1947].[28]

For at times, my room, my large workroom, is so kind to me at night, so enwrapping, that I can't bring myself to leave it; I light the fire, I sit with my book, I contemplate, I delay endlessly while drinking with all my senses that indescribable silence that frightened me as a child but which loves me now, and more, is preparing me for I know not what, but I almost believe, to my purest labour [Rilke, *Letters to Merline*].[29]

The travail of Levinas' authorship without itinerary began with *beginning of anxiety*, excerpted here, as phenomenology of *il y a*, of the 'rustling' in the night, an anxiety of Being without world, developed in explicit opposition to Heidegger's anxiety of nothingness.[30] This anxiety is rediscovered in *Totality and Infinity* by the lover and the beloved,[31] and, embedded in 'the structures of justice', it reappears at the end of *Otherwise than Being*, as the *anxiety of beginning*: anxiety made over by 'the beginning'; 'the one' or subject posited and thematized 'as an ego, that is, as a present or as a beginning or as free, as a subject facing an object'. Yet beginning of anxiety continues to threaten anxiety of beginning and its bustling, until and unless, in a substitution 'before any beginning', 'initiative', 'assumption', 'correlation' or 'receptivity', 'It [the ego, the self] is consumed as an expiation for the other'.[32] This 'ethical deliverance' would seem to convey the one (the self) from the terrible *il* of *il y a* to the holy *il* of *illeity* in an aural analogy of 'the trace' – from 'the buzzing' and 'the rustling', 'the incessant murmur of terror' to the mundane neutrality and monotony of 'bustling', with which these clamorous bruits are overlaid, but through which they still

[27]  *Otherwise than Being*, p. 209, tr. p. 164, emphasis in French, translation amended.
[28]  *Existence and Existents*, p. 98, tr. p. 60, omission marks in translation.
[29]  Op. cit., 28 November 1920, trans. MacDonald, p. 57; and trans. Browner, p. 40.
[30]  Levinas, *Existence and Existents*, p. 102, tr. pp. 62–3 and note, p. 63 with reference to Maurice Blanchot, *Thomas l'obscur* (Paris, Gallimard, 1941).
[31]  *Totality and Infinity*, p. 236, tr. p. 258.
[32]  *Otherwise than Being*, pp. 207–8, 208, tr. pp. 163, 164.

pervade, silenced only by the deeper trauma which effects the ethical, 'the ultimate retraction of passivity'.[33]

These pre-ontological and ontological anxieties are separate and simultaneous: beginning of anxiety is here anxiety of existence without existents, while anxiety of beginning is the anxiety of beginning-to-be in the order of Being, as incunabula of essence or ego, assembled 'indefinitely', 'equal and indifferent to all responsibility' and 'without . . . in all equity, any instant's halt, without respite, without any possible suspension . . .'.[34] Beginning of anxiety as anxiety of existence is the prelude to this triplicity: anxiety of beginning, the subject's mounting anxiety at the inexorability of essence, still permeable and permeated by beginning of anxiety without essence, can only be surmounted by Anxiety of anxieties – by being 'consumed' in responsibility.

Philosophy, servant of both extremes, brought 'neutrality and equality' to the primeval terror, brought, that is, anxiety of beginning to ward off beginning of anxiety, now imports equity into expiation, 'into the abnegation of the one for the other', relieving Anxiety of anxiety again with mundane anxiety of beginning.[35] 'In an alternating movement . . . philosophy justifies and criticizes the laws of Being and the City.'[36] Since expiation belongs to the ethical and equity belongs to philosophy, this account excludes any conception of equity in the city, in the degraded modality of historical time, 'the indefinite time of essence, the neutrality of its historical flow',[37] and, conversely, it excludes any conception of the law of the city in anarchic responsibility. It cherishes pre-ontological violence, *il y a*, and violence of the *ille*, of being 'consumed', the ambivalent Janus-faced incomparable being-for-other of proximity or freedom, and comparable being approached in reciprocity in the order of Being.[38]

Hedged on all sides with equivocation – 'the enigma of sense and being' and 'the enigma' of the trace – subjectivity is 'ambiguous', but the phenomenal middle, neutral and monotone essence, has no intrinsic equivocation.[39] Yet as the third party, who 'counts' and who calls to account, this middle, unholy and holy, will turn out to be the most equivocal of all.[40]

---

[33]  Ibid., p. 209, tr. p. 164.
[34]  Ibid., pp. 207–8, tr. pp. 163, 164.
[35]  Ibid., pp. 209–10, tr. pp. 164–5.
[36]  Ibid., p. 210, tr. p. 165, capitals in French.
[37]  Ibid., p. 207, tr. p. 163.
[38]  Ibid., pp. 209, 201–2, tr. pp. 161, 158.
[39]  Ibid., pp. 15, 210, tr. pp. 12, 165.
[40]  *Totality and Infinity*, p. 229, tr. p. 251.

'Love . . . is *the equivocal* par excellence.'[41]

In *Totality and Infinity*, love sublated as paternity is held against the state deflated; in *Otherwise than Being*, love elevated as the *ille*, 'commandment to love', is both 'betrayed' *and* 'conveyed' as the state – and instantaneously relayed to the saving scepticism of authorship.[42] In *Totality and Infinity* 'the truth of the will' resides in the judgement of the 'invisible' – 'offense' to 'visible' history and institutions and the state,[43] yet it attains perfect peace alongside them in the patience of fecundity and family;[44] whereas in *Otherwise than Being* 'the wisdom of desire' resides in 'the incessant correction of the asymmetry of proximity' which would seem to legitimize 'justice, the state and its institutions, exchanges and works' not as the contrary of proximity, not *qua* neutral order, but as incessantly comprehensible 'out of proximity'.[45] While the ethical or responsibility would seem to be more deeply invested in the later of these two works, so that the social is incessantly suspended for the incursion of proximity and illeity, yet the 'superimposition' of justice as 'substitution', its heteronomy, means that the institutions of freedom, the order of being, remain, in both works, the degraded modality – alliance of logic and politics to suppress the equivocation of 'saying'.[46] Instead of suspending the ethical teleologically, which would be to allow the simultaneous exploration of freedom and of faith, of eros and of paternity, without denigrating or absolutizing either realm, Levinas has to police proximity as initial duo and subsequent trio with the 'incessant rumbling' of the 'there is'.[47] There can be no faith, only threat which lapses back into violent love and violent state. Authorship without irony and without aesthetic, without pseudonym, or facetiousness, modestly inscribes itself as 'sceptical', when it is alternatively herald in the heights of glory, witness of the sign given to the other, and 'passing from prophecy to philology and transcending philology towards prophetic signification'.[48]

Included above with statements from Levinas of the shrieking silence of the *il y a* was a passage from Rilke's *Letters to Merline*,[49] which brings out, implicitly, a development in the erotic from terror to faith; and, in its very affirmation of solitude, founds the fraternal without fictio-

---

[41]    Ibid., p. 233, tr. p. 255, emphasis in original.
[42]    *Otherwise than Being*, p. 201, tr. p. 158.
[43]    *Totality and Infinity*, p. 221, tr. p. 243.
[44]    Ibid., p. 283, tr. p. 306.
[45]    *Otherwise than Being*, pp. 202–3, tr. p. 159.
[46]    Ibid., pp. 205, 217, tr. pp. 161, 170.
[47]    Ibid., p. 208, tr. p. 163, *l'incessant bourdonnement*.
[48]    Ibid., pp. 190, 194, tr. pp. 148, 152.
[49]    Rilke, *Letters to Merline*, see p. 252 n. 29 *supra*.

nomy or submission. For it is the child — or adult in the state of a child — who is terrified by the nocturnal 'rustling', by fear of a 'menace' from which she cannot withdraw, and which is not that of nothingness but of 'undetermined anonymous being', a heavy atmosphere, 'anonymous rustling of being' which keeps the child — or the analogous adult — sleepless, watchful, detached from objects, yet oppressed by the universal 'there is'.[50] It is the child, or adult, who, alone at night, or even with another child in the room, cannot speak because the silence is so menacing that her very own breathing or the rustling of the sheets seem magnified, accusatory, themselves alert, poised to overwhelm her slightest movement or appeal for help, verbal or physical. What bestows such malignant power on the echoic *il y a*? It is fear of her desire, desire for her fear, exposed to such magnification and omnimobile projection because there is no Other present or proximate to receive, absorb and return such desire, such fear, and alleviate it by teaching it movement and configuration and growth. Jealousy too, perhaps, because the child has been sent to the silent, noisome night, while the 'beloved' parent continues, vivacious, to engage and be engaged not so far away — downstairs? — but infinitely removed from her fear and her desire — her desire for what she fears, her fear of what she desires.[51] Such desire and such fear is already the law — not prior to law. For there would be no desiring fear, fearing desire, if there were no commandment, no prohibition — thou shalt/thou shalt not — which first arouses capacity, being-able, and then teaches it content. Otherwise she might play *fort-da* but she is too old for the relief offered by such mime of absence, too young to create from its uncontingency. And there would be no projected menace if the little lover were able to sustain in solitude her love-ableness: to have confidence that even in the absence of the loving parent she is lovable, worthy of being loved, and, therefore, love-able, capable of loving; of being the lover who knows herself originally beloved, and so not needing the constant presence of the contingent beloved to demand that they take on the role of original lover. The adult who achieves this has faith: her love is not violent, constantly prey to the return of the menace of the *il y a*, nor does she violently insist on the attendance of the beloved. She senses and knows that 'this indescribable silence' loves her, and, should she become anxious, she is patient with her anxiety as her own lapsed love-ability, for she is beloved *and* lover. Such a one does not demand the exclusive

[50] *Existence and Existents*, pp. 95–6, 109, tr. pp. 58–9, 65.
[51] Compare the discussion *supra* of 'sympathetic antipathy' and 'antipathetic sympathy' from Kierkegaard, *Concept of Anxiety* (ch. 3, p. 93 and n. 40).

society and intimacy of the other. While enjoying the other voluptuous-
ly, the morrow is not full of the terror of the *il y a*, lying slyly in
wait,[52] and only relievable by becoming gravid,[53] or by the transcendence of 'my Desire' opening me to a command that orders 'me' to
'the undesirable'; the holiness of the *il*, he, rescuing me from the
ravages of the *il y a* — the watchfulness of sheer terror mobilized by the
wakefulness of sheer good, malignant immanence taken over by
benevolent transcendence.[54] For the solitary nocturnal one, who has
learnt, and so knows that she is beloved and lover, in and beyond every
contingency — she has faith — even when she lacks confidence — she
has faith; and her loving is not violent, not a recourse to running from
the *il y a*, and not a further recourse to running further from its
re-emergence in such forced alleviation. Such a one has faith, and she is
being prepared for she 'knows not what' but she 'almost believes' her
'purest labour'; for new labour is the purest, and the labour of love is
the commingling of eros and agape — not love of 'the undesirable', nor
charity withdrawn from the world, nor responsibility superimposed in
one's glimpses of transcendence which fleetingly alleviate and reconfirm
the intrinsic violence of the state; not anything in itself representable,
but emergent in the aesthetic, the representation of the law. For one has
learnt one's faith by failing; and the configurations of such failing have
found their way and their aporia — their lack of way — through the
universality, the imperative, which first impelled the struggle to learn.

> To proclaim the universality of God in consciousness, to think
> that everything is consummated while the peoples that tear one
> another to pieces belie this universality in fact, is not only to
> prepare the irreligion of a Voltaire, but is to shock reason itself.[55]

To turn from such 'velleity for freedom',[56] from history to eschatology, and to proclaim instead peace not 'identified with the end of
combats',[57] transcendent, always present, always absent, is to abandon
reason by refusing to undertake the labour of discovering how universality and barbarism reproduce each other, and instead to embrace a

---

[52] *Totality and Infinity*, pp. 116–17, tr. pp. 142–3.
[53] Ibid., 'Fecundity', pp. 244–7, tr. pp. 267–9; 'Transcendence and Fecundity',
pp. 251–4, tr. pp. 274–7.
[54] 'God and Philosophy', *The Levinas Reader*, p. 113, tr. p. 178.
[55] *Totality and Infinity*, p. 218, tr. p. 241.
[56] Ibid.
[57] Ibid., p. 283, tr. p. 306.

piety that separates itself from history, taking the separated 'same' of interiority beyond freedom, to a love dirempted from the state which leaves the field of Mars to the love-in-barbarism it abhors.

'Universality' was never *kerygma*, proclaimed, it was *didache*, taught as a critical criterion; and, in leaving the realm of 'freedom' altogether, both 'inner' freedom, and freedom 'cut into the real only by virtue of institutions',[58] this eschatology would debauch reason by replacing the judgement of history with 'the judgement of the invisible', judgement not of the freedom of subjectivity but of its desire for the invisible: 'the exaltation of the singularity in judgement is produced precisely in the infinite responsibility of the will to which the judgement gives rise.'[59]

'The will is under the judgement of God when its fear of death is inverted into its fear of committing murder.'[60] This new fear 'deepens' the inner life which is no longer guided by 'the evidences of history'.[61] Inner life at the mercy of such supra-singular judgement is sure to become perverse: for its only movement is from fear to fear. It may become resentful, unable fully to celebrate the greater fear; or supra-autonomous, throwing off such endless fear altogether.[62] But it will never have the chance to grow in faith or in knowledge: to come to recognize its fear and thence to acquire faith. For outside history and institutions, there can only be fear of death, there can never be the further recognition that even the substituted fear of killing someone else, for example, one's own son, could involve lack of faith: making one confront the violence in love in that exclusive love, and the love in violence in the temptation – not the judgement of God – to 'sacrifice' Isaac. Instead, for Levinas, paternal love 'conjoins' the 'instant of eroticism' and 'the infinity of paternity';[63] it provides a safe place in fecundity and the family, rather than exposing paternal love to the fear of killing someone else, to the lurking danger not of the *il y a*, but of violent exclusivity in one's desire for infinity: Abraham torn between God's command and God's prior promise – the command to sacrifice Isaac, and Isaac as the future of Israel.[64]

Levinas' insistence that the family 'does not represent a reduced model of the State', 'the anonymous universality of the State', but is to

[58]  Ibid., p. 219, tr. p. 241.
[59]  Ibid., p. 222, tr. p. 244.
[60]  Ibid.
[61]  Ibid., p. 224, tr. p. 246.
[62]  Compare Nietzsche, *On The Genealogy of Morals*, 'First Essay', *passim*, 'Second Essay', sec. 2.
[63]  *Totality and Infinity*, p. 283, tr. p. 306.
[64]  Compare Thomas Mann's exposition in *Joseph*, discussed *supra*, ch. 4, pp. 149–50.

be identified as the conjoining of subjective morality, human time, and, as guarantor of any movement from egoism to peace, infinite time,[65] places such domesticated love outside of the state, where, without knowledge and without faith, its members would become either resentful, or supra-normatively 'autonomous', or self-righteous. Such a family cannot develop beyond fear of the external command to fear of its fear: beyond its interested love limited to staving off the *il y a*; or beyond its interested obedience to the command not to kill another. Because the institution of the family has no other – no other institutions at stake against which it might discover its interests, it is more likely to reproduce the violence of the state, ontologized by Levinas as 'the order of being'. Like any parent who would protect the members of *his* family from the harshness of 'the world', Levinas will expose them to it all the more, and will produce – not responsibility – but subservience, passivity, not 'beyond' passivity but within it, the passivity of the personal within the impersonal surrounding forces – the anonymity 'of the universality of the State' and the anonymity of the *il y a*. This 'holy family' in the middle of eros and eternity will break apart – not only from each other – but within each single one – from the violence propagated in this culture of persons against 'impersons'.

Levinas cannot suspend the ethical. Instead he dirempts it – separating love and law: eros redefined as the peace of paternity, as law and commandment; 'law' redefined as freedom, being, the state. As a result, law and ethics, recurring in each of these equations, become *equivocal, par excellence*.

The ethical is not suspended – not tensed, held and released, equally time and eternity, simultaneously universal and singular, without fixing either, and without, therefore, any need to reproduce and reinforce the prevailing diremption of the institutions of Caesar and the institutes of God in order to be able to explore each – the ethical is not suspended because it is *said* to be 'transcendent'. As 'transcendent' the ethical is 'suspended' in another sense of kept apart and obscured by the institutions of 'being' – logic, politics, 'the said', or discourse itself. *Otherwise than Being or Beyond Essence* seems to have relinquished the sacralizing of the family as the transhistorical, autonomous yet institutional bearer of equivocation, of eros and eternity, *il y a* and *ille*, and would seem to attempt to lower suspended transcendence into the bustling of historical flow,[66] achieving a finer equivocation by presentations of predicaments. The *ille*, the third, is moved more into the

65    *Totality and Infinity*, p. 283, tr. p. 306.
66    *Otherwise than Being*, p. 207, tr. p. 163.

middle, 'a unique face and in relationship with faces', invisible and visible; the ego and the author, correspondingly, in the predicament of the saying and the said; none of these are contraries, for enigmatic responsibility is not a legality but remains the overriding 'centre of gravitation' for *any* positive institutions (including the family, paternity etc.).[67] The *ille* would seem to sustain its enigma as Janus-face between 'Face' and 'faces', between incomparability and comparability, to legitimize these positive institutions which preserve their *raison d'être* 'out of proximity'.[68] Yet this divine criterion of positive justice has neither been released from 'anarchic' suspension, nor, alternatively, does it yield a natural law. For it fixes its medium — positive institutions — and can only revert to judgement of them — inflexible judgement in the face of inflexible institutions. The state, allied with its reasons, is judged to be forever mending by 'just violences' the rending of its texts — thematizing the excluded middle: the trace of illeity, and recuperating it.[69] Were the ethical instead to be suspended and released, no judgement would be called for — since no politics or legality would be transhistorically fixed and demonized; and 'I' would not be alternatively conquering ego and destitute chosen one,[70] broken and mended and broken again — broken in responsibility, mended in the mundane; broken by the *il y a* and 'consumed' by expiation, mended in the coherence of the state; broken by prison and asylum, master and medicine, wielded by the violence of political 'coherence'.[71] These separated temporalities of responsibility and positive justice offer no criterion for whether the empirical is 'out of proximity', and also preclude any natural law where the deviation of human from divine law could be ascertained and hence reform or revolution of positive institutions legitimized.

In Levinas, there is neither the simultaneity of suspending the ethical, nor the radicality of transforming the political, but there resounds the brutal sincerity, 'exposedness without reserve', the said in this would-be saying, of judgement which has itself fixed what it deplores.[72] For, according to its own metaphysic, this authorship can have no aesthetic — no mask or pseudonym — nor any humour of the

---

[67]  Ibid., pp. 196, 203, tr. pp. 153–4, 159.
[68]  Ibid., p. 203, tr. p. 159.
[69]  Ibid., pp. 214–16, tr. pp. 168–70.
[70]  Ibid., pp. 195–9, tr. pp. 153, 154.
[71]  This statement of alternating breaking and mending follows the sequence in sections 3, 4 and 5 of ch. V, ibid., pp. 195–218, tr. pp. 153–71.
[72]  For example, 'God and Philosophy', *The Levinas Reader*, p. 121, tr. p. 183.

religious; even less can it draw the silk curtains of facetiousness which would be to expiate the authority that authorship arrogates. The ambivalence and equivocation of 'the saying' and 'the said' are reintroduced in the guise of perennial philosophical scepticism which punctuates reason, and, in this way, the author appeals over the top of his own text to his 'interlocutor' beyond its totalizing discourse.[73]

Why *should* we respond to this quite unequivocal call from author and authority to actor? It is not the difficult liberty – the discipline – which repulses us, but the *deep* disorder, celebrated as repetition, of *il y a* and *ille*, which would leave us terrified, alternatively, by menace, by measure and by the mendacity of the mundane; at the mercy of violence in three places – eros, eternity, everyday. Worse still, this unequivocal call is equivocal where it admits it neither as 'theme' nor as 'non-assemblable enigma': the supra-historicized opposition between 'law' *and* 'law', divine law and human law, which is presented as divine 'anarchy' opposed to positive 'law', or as ethics opposed to politics and history. In effect, commandment is separated from representation, from any aesthetic, from any struggle or relation between universal and singular – the aporia, configured and reconfigured in institutions. Instead, divine law and positive law are alienated from each other and fixed, and the war-cries of intransigent versus intransigent, infested with each other, and continually menaced by their Other in the foul womb of night, are staged with the philosopher as chorus. With God 'and' the world 'and' broken then mended then broken man, love still outside the state becomes, as in Arendt, barely disguised hate.

The equivocation of ethics and *halacha* which the authorship had deliberately set aside in order to attend to the transition from the non-ethical to the ethical has re-emerged in the very opposition which would banish it: the so-called 'non-ethical', variously defined but generally 'the order of being', covers positive law and occludes its correlated order of ethics; while the so-called 'ethical', defined as the holy, *ille*, 'trace' or 'enigma' covers divine law and occludes its specific status within Judaism as *halacha*. In this way, Levinas obscures a difficulty which modern Judaism – across the range from cultural orthodoxy to liberalism – admits: that the clash of Judaic law (*halacha*) and non-Judaic law raises issues concerning the relation of law and ethics within Judaism and between Judaic and non-Judaic judgement and institutions. This obscuring may be traced to the implication that the *soi-disant* 'orders' of 'being' are not themselves ethical when the idea of 'order' implies that they are ethical – normative, general and im-

---

[73]    *Otherwise than Being*, p. 217, tr. p. 170.

perative, immanent and transcendent, actual and ideal, even when dirempted.

In effect, the separation of 'the order of being' from 'beyond being' reveals the triple diremption of modernity collected up in the over-arching predicament of love outside the state: the diremption of civil society and state, of natural right and national sovereignty, of abstract equality and class and gender disparity. In *Totality and Infinity*, family, peace, fecundity and paternity would stabilize, respectively, the state, the nation, eros and femininity. Cast as *eschatons* of an irenic sociality, and opposed to the warfare and anxiety of the order of being, these promises produce a holy sociology which is posited in its heterono-mous agape on indifference and ignorance — want of differentiation and want of knowledge or recognition — of the politics of modern social life, the diremptions of which are thereby sacralized and become the *sacred* not the *social* relation — the contrary of what Levinas insists: that the ethical is, on his account, a social not a sacred relation.[74]

In *Otherwise than Being or Beyond Essence*, and in other places, such as the much earlier essay, 'The Ego and Totality' (1954); in one of the *lectures talmudiques*, 'The Pact' (1982);[75] and in the occasional piece 'Ideology and Idealism' (1982), equivocation of the ethical is moved into the middle and away again. Not suspended and released, equivoca-tion of the ethical has, nevertheless, changed from eschatological post-ontology to eschatological judgement of justice 'out of proximity'. The opposition of love to the state becomes much more intrinsically equivocal: judgements of their proximity are coupled with judgemental principled denials of it. Yet as specific institutions are no longer elected to bear the sacred sociality but are figured collectively as 'the state' and its discourses, further equivocation, evident neither in the said nor the saying, nowhere thematized nor assembled, of ethics and *halacha*, of ethics and law, emerges. The explicit diremption of being from ethics leads in reverse direction: 'the passage' or lack of passage from the 'ethical' to 'the non-ethical', to its implicit triple dimension.

If I recognize the wrong I did you, I can, even by my act of repentance, injure the third person.[76]

This seems to acknowledge that the meaning of confession and for-giveness may be inverted in their unintended consequences.

---

[74] *Totality and Infinity*, p. 81, tr. p. 109.
[75] 'The Ego and Totality', *Collected Philosophical Papers*, pp. 25–45; 'The Pact', *The Levinas Reader*, pp. 211–26.
[76] 'The Ego and Totality', p. 30.

> The love of the neighbour depends on chance proximity; it is hence love of one being to the detriment of another, always privilege even if it is not preference.[77]

This seems to acknowledge the potential violence in the exclusivity of love, not only love between intimates but respect for the neighbour, which 'is only a pious intention oblivious of the real evil'.[78]

> If there were only two of us in the world, I and one other, there would be no problem. The other would be completely my responsibility. But in the real world there are many others. When others enter, each of them external to myself, problems arise. Who is closest to me? Who is the Other? *Perhaps something has already occurred between them.* We must investigate carefully. Legal justice is required. There is need for a state. [emphasis added][79]

This seems to acknowledge the possible inversion of even acute responsibility for the other, neither intimate nor neighbour, out of the contingencies of history, which may, nevertheless, be comprehended, and which give rise to this perplexity in the immediacy of the face to face. It implies that historical knowledge must precede any assumption of 'responsibility'.

> But the fact is that general principles and generous principles can be inverted in the course of their application. All generous thought is threatened by its own Stalinism ... Ideology arises out of the generosity and clarity of a principle, qualities which do not take into account the betrayal which lies in wait for this general principle at the moment of its application ...[80]

This seems to acknowledge the inversion attendant on the 'missionary' universal – 'general principles' – and the 'sect' universal – 'generous principles' – imagined as Jacob's struggle with the Angel, 'the angelism or other-worldliness of pure interiority',[81] whether exhibited by Jacob or by Israel. It is overcome by the perfect casuistry of the Talmud, 'the special discipline which studies the particular case in order to identify the precise moment within it when the general principle is at risk of

[77]  Ibid., p. 31.
[78]  Ibid.
[79]  'Ideology and Idealism', *The Levinas Reader*, concluding discussion, p. 247.
[80]  'The Pact', ibid., pp. 98–9, tr. p. 220.
[81]  Ibid., p. 98, tr. p. 220.

turning into its opposite; it surveys the general from the standpoint of the particular'.[82] This seems to recognize that love, the divine commandment to love, as 'general' principle, missionary and active, may be inverted in application; and that the beautiful soul, as 'generous' principle, the sect-like purity of withdrawal from the world 'for the sake of' transcendence, even though initiatory and pedagogic, may yet be 'betrayed' as the contrary meaning.

This series of steps back from 'the ethical' to the 'non-ethical' yet effects no passage. For such a trajectory cannot protect itself from the very inversions against which it would warn, since it is invested in the diremption it posits between 'the order of being' and 'the disorder of the ethical' which disqualifies any 'knowledge' or recognition or representation of precisely 'what has already occurred',[83] of the history and repetition of the inversion of universal and particular. Without legitimate knowledge or representation, this wisdom, which would alert us to the incipient 'Stalinism' of our principled generosity and teach us instead a perfect equity, can only appear itself as a 'disengaged' prescription — holy and without any purchase on 'the real world'. *A fortiori*, it cannot undertake any reconstruction of 'what has already occurred' to fulfil the aspirations of this perfect yet dirempted jurisprudence. Indeed, in Levinas' Talmudic and Jewish writings, the presentation of such eternally vigilant equity can only be undertaken as the exact multiplication of the forty-eight modes of adherence and dimensions of the covenant by the number of people present to match the singularity of each witness, as in the Talmudic reading, 'The Pact'; or, in the essay on the 'way' (*la voie*) of Franz Rosenzweig, as the self-contained integrity of the eternal people or community of Israel, 'beyond' history and politics, beyond 'what has already occurred', as 'resistance' to the 'claimed necessities of history',[84] or as repetition of the irruption of responsibility which relegates once again 'the Being served by knowing' to the monotony of ideology.[85] Such jurisprudence can only exemplarize itself in these *modi* of singularity or holiness because it disallows the representation and knowledge that would bring to light the configuration and reconfiguration of universal and particular in institutions which cut across the diremption insisted on by Levinas between 'the order of being' and 'the disorder of responsibility'. Instead of the monolithic, violent 'coherence' of 'logic' and 'politics', contrastable with the articulated, peaceable 'coherence' of Talmudic

---

[82]   Ibid., pp. 98–9, tr. p. 220.
[83]   Translation in *The Levinas Reader*, pp. 211–26.
[84]   'Entre deux mondes (La Voie de Franz Rosenzweig)', 1959, in *Difficile Liberté*, p. 260, tr. p. 201 (translation my own).
[85]   'Ideology and Idealism', *The Levinas Reader*, p. 31, tr. p. 245.

casuistry, with its perfect jurisprudence of general and particular,[86] this evident inversion would be opened to an exposition that can acknowledge that it *does not know in advance* whether such institutions are violent or peaceful, for it is able to find out – by reconstructing the changing relation between universal, particular and singular. This is experience – the struggle to recognize: to know, and still to misknow, and yet to grow. Such virtual equivocation of the ethical is, however, banished from Levinas' 'ontology' of the order of being versus the disorder of responsibility, but, in effect, it is recast by him as 'holiness' and as 'singularity', less conveyed than betrayed in 'the said' and 'discourse' to which any knowledge or representation would be relegated. With no middle, suspended and released, there can be no nuancing of anxiety; but instead there are two unequivocal twin terrors – of the *il y a* and of the *ille*. And there can be no love where there is demonstrably so little faith.

The whole ambition to present and defend love outside the state emerges from a systematically flawed not a perfect jurisprudence, in which it reinvests by advancing the general rule to eschew the 'ideology' of general and of generous principles. This 'flawed' jurisprudence – the middle, broken between ethics and law, ethics and *halacha*, which Levinas shares with the philosophy or ontology that he intends to supersede, may be discerned in the way he delimits modern knowledge and rationality and modern Judaism – and the politics and history of modernity in which both are implicated.

> Knowledge is re-presentation, a return to presence, and nothing may remain *other* to it . . . This is a regal and as it were unconditioned activity, a sovereignty which is possible only as solitude, an unconditioned activity . . . a notion that allows a second one to be sustained, the notion of the pure *theoretic*, of its freedom, of the equivalence between wisdom and freedom . . .[87]

In his concern to disengage both theoretical and practical reason from ethics and responsibility, Levinas defines theoretical reason in terms of practical reason, 'an activity', 'unconditioned activity', and so reduces freedom to the model of the grasping and appropriating of being by cognition, to pure spontaneity. This representation of cognition, premodern and modern, as the theoretic priority of practical reason, or the practical efficacy of theoretic reason, is designed phenomenologically to effect a different 'return' – to the humble 'prior to' the hubris of

---

86    *Otherwise than Being*, p. 216, tr. p. 170; 'The Pact', *The Levinas Reader*, pp. 98–9, tr. p. 220.
87    'Ethics as First Philosophy', ibid., p. 77.

this regal and sovereign theoretic activity of freedom, which, without memory or remorse, is oriented to 'a "glittering future" where everything can be rectified'.[88] However, this accentuation of implicit remorse 'without any initiative that might refer back to an ego', analogized as the pure passivity of ageing (although it could be argued that 'ageing' is the most spiritually ambiguous effect of the history of the struggle — not the passivity — of the relation of the relation, of *psyche* and *soma*),[89] reinforces and repeats the static, oppositional model of cognition and freedom, pure activity of A = A, versus the unmasked mortality of strangers, exposed to each other; repetition of a scenario which can only be phenomenologically described, again and again, as 'murderous uprightness', ignorant of its own violent design, versus the summons into responsibility, calling me 'into question'.[90] In opposition without agon there can be no development for that, it seems, would reduce 'relationships with neighbours, with social groups, with God', to '*experiences*', that is, it would reduce the Other to the Same.[91] These assertions, explicitly *contra* Hegel, would have us believe that what is at stake is the difference between the scientific freedom of knowledge where self-consciousness is actively affirmed as '*the strength and strain of being*',[92] and the difficult freedom of the ethical summons where we find ourselves always already commanded — prior to ego, being, cognition or freedom, or any assembly into the Same. The meaning of Hegelian absolute knowing is thereby transformed into a philosophy of Being reduced to the partiality of perception; and the meaning of Hegelian 'phenomenology' is obscured — the term appropriate to both Hegel and Levinas because both present shapes of consciousness which are always already commanded. The birth of Hegelian speculative experience out of the Kantian dualisms of theoretical and practical philosophy, laws of nature and law of freedom, is the ruse designed to induce proud *Meinen*, intention, to discover that its idea of its own subjectivity and the object it seeks to grasp has been formed within the historical configuration of the commandment — the 'categorical' imperative — which turns out not to be simply conditioned, i.e. relative, but to be configured, to be the institutional inversions of just that transcendence which Levinas wants — 'love without concupiscence' or desire for the other.[93] Fear is not 'prior to' the power and sovereignty

---

[88] Ibid., pp. 81, 78.
[89] Ibid., p. 79.
[90] Ibid., p. 83.
[91] Ibid., p. 77, emphasis in original.
[92] Ibid., p. 78, emphasis in original.
[93] Ibid., p. 85.

of the ego: it exists in the constitution of the ego which – in this sense unknown to Levinas – is always already commanded, discovering that command within its perennially reconfigured oppositions of subject and object. This *tertium quid* in its equivocation without reduction makes it possible to comprehend both Levinas and Hegel through making the very difference in the place of the commandment precise, so that the struggle – not the path – between universal and singularity, between law and ethics, between that 'generous' and this flawed jurisprudence, which Levinas will not thematize, but which Hegel dramatizes, may emerge.

> We will not retain from this citation Hegel's affirmation of the provisional character of immediate evidence.[94]

Levinas here agrees with Hegel that the Same is aporetic – self-consciousness is both distinguished from and not distinguished from itself.[95] His ensuing, casual, setting aside of the provisionality of immediate evidence sets aside in effect the 'fate' of self-consciousness – its movement and instability within the changing configuration of the law. Instead, Levinas sets out 'the *way* [*la manière*] of the I': the world as 'site', not of the labile reflexivity of 'self-consciousness', but of the 'I', saved from 'monotonous tautology' by the business of 'dwelling' as 'medium', which offers resistance of a merely 'formal' kind.[96] For Hegel, the 'provisional', in the sense of the temporary or fleeting, and in the sense of 'pro-vision', orientation of sight, is 'the world'; and 'the world' is not the means or middle of the dwelling, of stability, 'home': it is the Bacchanalian revel where no member is not drunk, and, equally, it is repose; it is the incessant command *and* the ways in which it has been met, the command which has a history, which is configured – as master and slave, as 'spiritual animal kingdom', as the beautiful soul, as the hard and hypocritical heart of judgement. Levinas is preserving our purity for the Stranger – so he keeps us the same *and* the other: 'The conjunction *and* here designates neither addition nor power of one term over the other'; it preserves the relation between same and the other for language.[97] 'Language' is the language of conversation, where 'something happens', to use Rosenzweig's description of 'the new thinking' as a new method of speech to replace philosophy – which claims to be timeless and to know in advance[98] – presented by

---

94  *Totality and Infinity*, p. 7, tr. p. 37.
95  Ibid., p. 6, tr. p. 36.
96  Ibid., pp. 7, 8, tr. pp. 37, 38, emphasis in original.
97  Ibid., p. 9, tr. p. 39.
98  'The New Thinking', pp. 151–2, tr. in Glatzer, *Franz Rosenzweig*, p. 199.

Levinas as perlocutionary 'Apology, in which the I at the same time asserts itself and inclines before the transcendent'.[99] Whether offered as 'welcoming' of the other, in *Totality and Infinity*, or as 'maternity' — bearing, giving birth and being born — in *Otherwise than Being*[100] these analogies of the relation between Same and the Other leave it inscrutable how the conversion from being 'murderer' and 'usurper' to discourse with and desire for the other occurs, why freedom should begin 'to feel arbitrary and violent'.[101] Even though a mix of activity and passivity is involved in all these analogies of responsibility, however primordial their vocabulary — 'maternity' — the definition of 'the *critical essence* of ... knowing' as 'the movement of a being back to what precedes its condition'[102] means that 'knowing' can never make the movement forwards, equally hubris and humility, to risk any cognition. For without hubris there is no humility, as the example of the apology shows, nor can 'knowing' make the movement backwards and forwards which would comprehend how our 'welcoming', our 'apology', may be interested, hypocritical, harbouring not humility but harvest of disdain and pride. Such movement would risk knowing how, as a result of the changing historical and political configuration of the transcendent commandment, our responsibility may change the meaning of the law; and the law may change the meaning of our cherished ethics in a way that the general indictment of the alliance of logic and politics separated from proximity cannot capture but instead encourages. We cannot opt out of the difficulty of ethics and law, ethics and *halacha*, to rediscover 'the passage from the non-ethical to the ethical', for in so doing we discredit ethics once again by exalting it beyond the way of the world, replacing the broken with the holy middle. If we so do, we collude in the diremptions we intend to sublate.

This supernatural justification of ethical reality which takes ethics out of secular history — even if it would return perfected ethics to 'the world' — takes it out of the relation to the law and ethics of the historical world and out of the contested status of ethics and law, ethics and *halacha*, within Judaism, ancient and modern. In this respect, Levinas, like Rosenzweig from whom this was learnt, is a philosophical rather than a Jewish thinker precisely when ethics is most explicitly distinguished from ontology as the way of the world, just as Judaism is distinguished from Christianity, expounded as 'the Eternal Way through the world', in the third 'Book' of Rosenzweig's *Star of Redemption*. The meaning of Levinas' enigmatic acknowledgement of the

---

[99]   *Totality and Infinity*, p. 10, tr. p. 40.
[100]  *Otherwise than Being*, p. 95, tr. p. 75.
[101]  *Totality and Infinity*, p. 56, tr. p. 84.
[102]  Ibid.

omnipresence of the *Star* in the 'Preface' to *Totality and Infinity* is therefore not exhausted by its updating 'the opposition to the idea of totality' in previous philosophy, and the development of a 'new thinking' based on dialogue from 'Book One'; nor by its adapting the discourse of the lover and the beloved – where eros and agape are intertwined, mutually enhancing not threatening, as in Levinas – or the pathos of responding to the commandment with 'Here I am', from 'Book Two'.[103] For it is equally the oppositional political methodology of 'Book Three' of the *Star*, 'The Configuration or Eternal Hyper-Cosmos', which is implicit in Levinas' thought.

In the third book of the *Star* Rosenzweig developed a dirempted political theology in which Judaism is represented as the holy community, sociological not ecclesial, in the liturgically fulfilled year, without wars against other nations or coercion in its own; whereas Christianity is represented as the mission of world conversion.[104] Christianity is tempted in the great dualism between Church and State in historical time into three 'eschatological dangers' inherent in its way through the world: the spiritualization of God, characteristic of the Eastern Church; the apotheosis of man, characteristic of the Northern Church; and the pantheification of the world, characteristic of the Southern Church.[105] These three Christian dangers are matched by three 'eschatological dangers' of Judaism: denial of the world, disdain of the world, mortification of the world.[106] While Rosenzweig tries to equalize this comparison by way of conclusion, 'All three of these dangers are the necessary consequences of an inwardness turned away from the world, as those of Christianity are the consequence of an externalization of the self turned toward the world',[107] the different weight borne by the meaning of 'the world' – the formation or configuration of meaning and political history – makes this a comparison without a *tertium comparationis*. 'The world' for Christianity is, since its beginning, separated into Church and State, while 'the world' for Judaism has recovered since its beginning a cosmic unity: 'the Jewish people has left its holy war behind in its mythical antiquity'.[108]

However, in order to clinch this eschatological realism, there

---

[103]    Ibid., p. xvi, tr. p. 28. See Richard Cohen, 'Rosenzweig, Levinas and the Teaching of Hermeneutics', *First Workshop on Jewish Philosophy*, Jerusalem, July 1988, forthcoming; and Michael Fishbane, 'Franz Rosenzweig', *The Playground of Textuality: Modern Jewish Intellectuals and the Horizons of Interpretation*, Detroit, March 1988, forthcoming.

[104]    *The Star of Redemption*, pp. 368, 386–7, 390–2, tr. pp. 331, 348–9, 352–3.

[105]    Ibid., pp. 443–8, tr. pp. 389–402.

[106]    Ibid., pp. 452–3, tr. p. 407.

[107]    Ibid., p. 453, tr. p. 407.

[108]    Ibid., pp. 390–2, 368, tr. pp. 352–3, 331.

achievement and fulfilment, Rosenzweig can only define it against the nations, *contra gentiles*, as it were, their wars and their state: 'The Jewish people have already reached the goal towards which the nations are still moving.'[109] By having to sequester diasporic Judaism 'outside of time agitated by wars' and outside of 'law in the state', Rosenzweig reveals the diremption of ethics and law, ethics and *halacha*, with which the self-perficient irenic community will be riven.[110] 'Coercion' is the means by which the state maintains and preserves 'old law' as 'new law', so that lawfulness and coercion are inseparable in the historical time of the state; while, for the living, that is, eternal, people, customs may multiply and laws alternate without any need for the constant coercive renewal of old law by the state.[111]

This opposition between 'lawfulness' and 'coercion' in 'Book Three' corresponds to the opposition between 'commandment' and 'law' in the pathos of lover and beloved, the rewritten Song of Songs, of 'Book Two', where 'love' is presented as 'the sole commandment incapable of being law'.[112] Instead of bringing this predicament of love and the state — of law as love, 'commandment', and as coercion — out into the political history of the final 'Book', that history is dirempted into the community of the commandment — Judaism — and the ecclesiology of the *imperium* — Christianity. This dualistic philosophy of history is frozen and completed by triadic typologies of parallel eschatological 'dangers', without any historical exposition, but played off against 'the world', which once again bears the burden of the projected and un-explored diremptions of the political theology compressed into the types. While Judaism is eschatologically completed and Christianity 'on its way', 'the world', veering from the mundane to proto- and hyper-cosmic, becomes more dangerous than the typologies imply. For 'the world' bears all the equivocation of the ethical in its ambiguity: mundane as the 'cosmopolis' or imperial order, it also still implies 'the *polis*'; proto- and hyper-cosmic, it carries eschatological connotations of 'the kingdom', and utopian connotations of 'community' without *dominium*.

Damaged by these underdeveloped dangers, which appear as icon in the Davidic congress of two inverted triangles, the *Star* fuses what it refuses to expound. It thus disowns the effective magnanimity of Judaic history — the *halachic* inventiveness of historical, rabbinic Judaism.[113]

---

[109] Ibid., p. 368, tr. p. 331.
[110] Ibid., pp. 368, 369, tr. p. 332.
[111] Ibid., p. 370, tr. p. 333.
[112] Ibid., p. 197, tr. p. 177.
[113] See, for example, Ismar Schorsch, 'On the History of the Political Judgement of the Jew', *Leo Baeck Memorial Lecture*, 20, New York, 1977, 3–23.

Within the agon of ethics and *halacha*, defined, respectively, as the witness of revelation without coercion versus the renewal of 'old law' by coercive means, Rosenzweig attributes perfected, ahistorical and unworldly 'Messianic politics' to Judaism, which is to smother its Messianic impulse, its futural and universal aspiration. The question of ethical supplementation of *halacha* to pre-modern and to modern Judaism arises within any legal system in time, whether or not it is also in eternity. Judaism, contrary to Rosenzweig's and to Levinas' version, has never set its *halachic* life outside time, while, politically, it awaits the Messiah. And it has debated the question of equity without anchoring it at the pole of metaphysical multiplication as in 'The Pact'. Simultaneously within the agon of ethics and *halacha*, and within the agon of the host legality between universal and instance, whether pre-modern regality or modern legality and rights, Judaism and Jewish communities have always been more – not less – exposed to the equivocation of the ethical; the clash between meaning and configuration, the inversion of 'generous' principles into outcomes of domination, the likelihood of which has intensified within modern, formal law. Dangers, divided between Christianity and Judaism, blandly typologized, would envelop and intensify each other in the missing account of the development of specifically modern law, which is, nevertheless, pacified in the methodology of the final 'Book' of the *Star*.

It is thanks to its Hegelian structure and ruse that Rosenzweig is able to leave underdeveloped the intrastellar connections of the *Star*: the Lover and the Beloved of 'Book Two', and the eternal people and the coercive state or warring nations of 'Book Three', even though both the connections and the opposition depend on the distinction between non-coercive commandment or love and coercive law; but it is still unjustifiable that in the final 'Book' this demonstrably ineluctable predicament of commandment and law is attributed exclusively to Christian world-polity. Yet Levinas, at the end of his essay on '"Between Two Worlds" (The Way of Franz Rosenzweig) [1959]' renews the discussion of the *Star* as the question of whether 'Judaism exists any more', reducing the central tensions of Rosenzweig's great political theology to the question of Judaism's claim to be an eternal people apart from and beyond 'the political history of the world', by distinguishing it from a so-called Hegelian historicism which would reduce 'all our *Aggada* as all our *Halacha*' to sociology or psychoanalysis, to a historical subjectivity and finitude that has outlived its time.[114] It is this refusal of

---

[114]    Op. cit., *Difficile Liberté*, pp. 256, 257–9, tr. pp. 198, 199–200 (my own translation).

political history − of any knowing of 'what has occurred' − by casting such knowledge as sheer reductive relativism and not as the reconstruction of the perpetual reconfiguration of 'law', of commandment and coercion, or of divine law ('ethics') and of human law ('the order of being'), and even less of the reconfigurations specific to modernity, on which this authorship is staked in its 'passage' from the non-ethical to the ethical, in spite of the equivocation of 'the third party' − whether holy proximity or partaking allied to logic and politics. But such a refusal, which in Rosenzweig depends on the *fusing* of what it will not know, appears in Levinas as its *fissioning* − the dimensions of the law dissemble its diremption: 'These [48] dimensions [of the law] cannot be accommodated by the formalism of today's law, which is utterly anonymous; a fact which may be regarded as the origin of the crisis facing modern society.'[115]

This apparent *obiter dictum* reveals the underlying and dominant interest in restaging this particular debate between the Rabbis of the Talmud: the multiplication of the dimensions of the law which includes its pedagogy, its generality, and, notably, its particularity as well as its singularity. Every single witness is to protect it not only from any contention between commandment and coercion and from any representation or means of arbitration, that is, from what Levinas calls 'totality' and 'history' in the philosophical work, but also from the specifically modern history where the law is not total but 'formal' − anonymous. 'Anonymous' designates for Levinas any indefinable menace − the *il y a, par excellence* − but, in the context of modern law, the 'anonymous' or 'impersonal' charge is striking, because the implied contrary would be 'the personal', and modern law in fact depends on *persons* − the bearers of rights and duties − in its structure and operation. What is presented *halachically* in 'The Pact' as the people assembled on the two mountains, Mount Ebal and Mount Gerizi, to receive the law in all its dimensions, singularly, not anonymously, but also, it is stressed, in its particularity as well as its generality, is the fissioning of the legal idea of a 'person', who is general, bearer of universal rights and duties, particular by virtue of the interiorization of that legality as individual morality, and singular, as figured and fused in the name − legal surname with first, 'given', or 'Christian', singular, name. In the philosophical work, this invisible justice which befalls the singular outside the 'virile' and 'cruel' judgement of 'universal norms' is also presented as pertaining to 'irreducible singularity' − but of the 'I' − the

---

[115] 'The Pact', *The Levinas Reader*, pp. 103−4, tr. p. 224.

'I' as *morality*, not, as here, *ethics*, which is opposed to the 'formal reason' of a being equivalent to all others.[116] 'Formal reason' occupies the same position here as 'formal law' in the Talmudic reading and, once again, the summons goes to singularity, now an 'I', bypassing the universal, bypassing, that is, any 'arbitrary and partial freedom'.[117]

> In reality, justice does not include me in the equilibrium of its universality; justice summons me to go beyond the straight line of justice, and henceforth nothing can mark the end of this march; beyond the straight line of the law [*derrière la ligne droite de la loi*] the land of goodness extends infinite and unexplored, necessitating all the resources of a singular presence.[118]

'Beyond the line of the law': in Hebrew, this is *lifnim mishurat hadin*. Omitting the dimension of the general here, and relating the holy summons directly to the singular 'me', this counsel of supererogation would perfect the modern person, labouring under formal reason and formal law. That person as 'I' is not figured as the I distinguished from myself, as the duality which modern formal law deposits when rights and duties are posited, but, fusing that universality and particularity of rights and duties into a composite singularity – calling 'irreducible' the 'I' which has been most reduced – the summons is then issued to advance: *lifnim mishurat hadin* – beyond the line of the law. This summons, as cited here from *Totality and Infinity*, translated back into the Hebrew to which it alludes, explains the otherwise inscrutable conversion or 'passage' from the free and arbitrary ego to the infinite responsibility of the 'I', for it draws on the Rabbinic institution of *lifnim mishurat hadin*, an institution with a pre-modern ancestry, which has been at the forefront of Rabbinic and philosophical reflection on the relation between ethics and *halacha* in modernity. Without 'nature' and 'freedom', the temptation of singularity or holiness has yet been disciplined within Judaism by the tension of unfreedom and freedom; and this supralegal injunction has been and continues to be at the heart of the debate between orthodox and reform Judaism   the distinction within modern Judaism which itself emerges from the relation to modern formal law which is known to impinge on intra-Judaic ethics and *halacha*.

Beyond the line of the law – *lifnim mishurat hadin* – is insinuated into the agon of authorship that decries modernity as formal law, and yet

---

116   *Totality and Infinity*, pp. 221, 223, tr. pp. 243, 245.
117   Ibid., p. 222, tr. p. 245.
118   Ibid., p. 223, tr. p. 245.

would solve modernity's unspecified 'crisis' by compelling singularity
to supererogatory morality — which would mend its middle by con-
densing its persons and so breaking its men (*sic*).

Would that they would forsake Me but observe My Torah
(*Palestinian Talmud*, 'Haggigah' 1:7)[119]

*Dina de-malkhuta dina* 'the law of the kingdom is valid law'[120]
(Shmuel — third-century *amora*)

Between these two affirmations of two bodies of law — the revealed
law and the law of the nations — Judaism has wrestled with the
antinomianism they jointly imply: for adherence to the law of the
nations could impugn the allegiance to *halacha* — even if only by
spiritualizing it for the sake of a general social ethic. The relation
between these two kinds of law has been raised in Rabbinic sources as
the idea of 'natural law' — law common to uncommanded and commanded man — but natural law is invariably rejected as contrary to the
system of *halacha*. The implicit issue of the relation of *halacha* as specific
law to the law of the nations, the idea of a 'natural law' common to
peoples with different positive laws, has, therefore, not been pursued in
the way it was developed by Cicero, and, subsequently, Roman law,
or, in the early modern period, between Christian polities — *De Jure
Naturali et Gentium*, etc. The idea of 'natural morality' has been more
liberally entertained, since, historically, it is far weaker, and, focusing
on the individual, it contains no implicit or explicit comparison between *halacha* and non-*halachic* law.[121] The issue of 'natural morality' is
frequently raised as a preliminary and provisional discourse on the way
to discussion internal to the corpus of revealed and oral law, or, as
Maimonides expounds it, the written law and its interpretation — the
commandment or oral law — both revealed to Moses on Sinai.[122] What
is striking about recent formulations and disputes over the relation of
ethics and *halacha* is how, within this explicitly intra-normative and
intra-Judaic concern, the modern tension between freedom and unfreedom is discernibly at stake, yet there is no evidence of the modern

---

[119]   Cited in J. D. Bleich, 'Is There an Ethic Beyond Halacha?', in Samuelson (ed.),
*Studies in Jewish Philosophy*, p. 542.
[120]   For a recent discussion, see M. Washofsky, 'Halakhah and Political Theory: A Study
in Jewish Legal Response to Modernity', *Modern Judaism*, 9, 3 (Oct. 1989), 293.
[121]   A. Lichtenstein, 'Does Jewish Tradition Recognize an Ethic Independent of
Halacha?', from Fox (ed.), *Modern Jewish Ethics*, pp. 103–6.
[122]   See Maimonides' 'Introduction to Mishneh Torah', in Twersky (ed.), *A Maimonides
Reader*, p. 35.

metaphysic of nature and freedom on which this problematic is otherwise invariably assumed to depend.

The contrast between the different formulations of the initial question concerning the relation of ethics and *halacha* indicates the difference in the underlying ideas of the form and content of law. Underlying these divergencies in modern Judaic self-understanding, evident in the conceiving of law and ethics, lies the context within which the question of ethics and *halacha* is posed – modern legality and morality – which is itself transposed into divergent self-reflections, evident in the jurisprudence dirempted between sociology and philosophy.

Aharon Lichtenstein, in a now famous article, first published in 1975, asks 'Does Jewish Tradition Recognize an Ethic Independent of Halacha?'; while Eugene Borowitz questions 'The Authority of the Ethical Impulse in "Halakhah"'.[123] Two intrinsically different modes of address are posed here. On the basis of Weber's distinctions, it appears that Lichtenstein questions the ethical legitimation of *halacha qua* traditional authority, while Borowitz questions the ethical legitimation of *halacha qua* legal-rational authority. *Prima facie*, Lichtenstein asks whether *halacha* is *equitable* by inquiring into the *status* of equity within *halacha*, while Borowitz asks whether *halacha* is *egalitarian* by inquiring into the *flexibility* of *halacha*. Lichtenstein focuses on the ethical potential 'within' *halacha*, while Borowitz focuses on the ethical potential 'of' *halacha*. Yet, paradoxically, it is Lichtenstein who demonstrates the flexibility of *halacha*, while it is Borowitz who demands that ethics be as 'categorical' (unconditioned) as *halacha*, and not a secondary kind of imperative, 'its own way', the position he attributes to Lichtenstein, and it is Borowitz who inquires into the *status* of women.

Lichtenstein considers several preliminary definitions of ethics: *lex naturalis*, *derekh eretz*, natural morality. Although the Rabbis were opposed to natural law thinking, Lichtenstein concludes that all rationalizing of *halacha* presupposes natural morality. The contemporary concern is whether *halacha* – either *din*, specific statute, or the whole of Judaism as an ethical system – needs an additional ethical supplement. To avoid the simple equation of law with morality, which would imply that no instance of uncertainty concerning 'what ought I to do' need arise, Lichtenstein proceeds to consider *lifnim mishurat hadin*. It was transformed by Nahmanides from the negative, condemnatory judgement that destruction befell those who, within the limits of Torah, yet failed to act 'beyond the line of the law', into the suprapositive counsel

---

[123]　Lichtenstein, see n. 121 *supra*, pp. 102–23; Borowitz, op. cit. (1981), in Samuelson (ed.), *Studies in Jewish Philosophy*, pp. 489–505.

of perfection: 'Ye shall be holy' and act beyond the line, i.e. the strict demands of the law. This morality of aspiration is supralegal but not optional. Lichtenstein scours the traditional sources to bring out the range of connotations of this unique idea of 'supralegality', from an actionable, rigorous obligation to supreme idealism. *Lifnim mishurat hadin* is gradually delineated as a situational or contextual morality. By contrast with a formal ethic which is categorical and fixed, *lifnim mishurat hadin* balances universal and local factors in any specific case instead of assimilating each case to the average of the category or class under which, strictly speaking, it falls. Overall, this discussion supports Lichtenstein's defence of *halacha* as multiplanar and not deductive. The penumbral regions of *mitzvot* or *din*, specific or strict statute, are continually complemented and never completed with *lifnim mishurat hadin*.

It is with the non-categorical status of this equitable element that Borowitz takes issue. He argues that the supralegality of *lifnim mishurat hadin*, presented by Lichtenstein as 'imperative in its own way', amounts to no more than a vague species of command and is all of a piece with Judaism generally which manages to be both highly ethical as a whole, yet qualifies the ethical by leaving it unqualified. He agrees that there are varying levels of authority within Rabbinic Judaism but argues that the ethical impulse is so restricted or denied that it can provide no remedy for issues such as the status of women. The much vaunted flexibility of *halacha* is sacrificed when such an issue arises, even though a solution is crucial to its continuing legitimation and future survival. Instead the cumbersome resistance of Rabbinic Judaism proves its formal, outmoded reliance on human rather than divine authority which it shares with other fallible social institutions.

Borowitz is right to raise the changing status/role of women as a crucial test for *halacha*, according to which the category of 'woman' has always been explicit. But the remedy he proposes is bizarre: that ethics 'ought to come as a categorical or unmediated imperative',[124] even though he has argued against Schwarzschild's Cohenian fusing of legality and morality[125] and accuses contemporary Rabbinic Judaism both of excessive formality[126] and of excessive tampering with the imperative quality of the Torah's ethical behests.[127]

Instead of searching for a conception that would render both ethics *and* law more flexible, or questioning the conditions which drive them apart and rigidify them, Borowitz imports the Kantian categorical ethic

[124] Borowitz, ibid., p. 500.
[125] Ibid., p. 495.
[126] Ibid., p. 503.
[127] Ibid., p. 502.

back into Judaism; the same ethic which has itself been fundamentally questioned by modernity, and which displays the qualities of absoluteness, unconditionality, formality and imperativeness which he otherwise deplores in the idea of law. This way of enlarging the idea of *halacha* with an ethics imperative in an unquestionable sense coincides with the very mode of *halachic* judgement rejected by Lichtenstein. Furthermore, Lichtenstein does not subordinate ethics to law as 'imperative in its own way'. He sets out the universal and local jurisprudence at stake throughout the sources in a variety of carefully related expositions.

Neither Lichtenstein (on substantial grounds) nor Borowitz (on formal grounds) are able to remedy, say, the changing 'status' of women because they will not confront directly the modern problematic of freedom and unfreedom which their disagreement nevertheless implies. Judaism, with its substantial legislation of women, in the Talmudic tractates of the Third Division, *Nashim*, 'Women', cannot dissemble its assumptions and impositions. This does, indeed, constitute a significant difference from modern positing of formal legal equality which veils and perpetuates substantial ethical inequality.

The apparent coincidence of the modern question of the legal status of women with the Talmudic *Seder* on 'Women' leads, however, to an invalid comparison: for the form of law in each case offers no *tertium quid*. There is no contextual equivalent in *halacha* for modern, formal, civil law, within which the comparison between form and actuality can arise out of the observable inversion of meaning in configuration. So when Steven Schwarzschild argues, without reference to the dispute over ethics and *halacha*, that the priority of practical reason in post-Kantian philosophy shows that Judaism is qualified to lead the way in the convergence of philosophy and Judaism,[128] he overlooks the drawback evident in the dispute over ethics and *halacha*, that Judaism recognizes no formal law, while post-Kantian philosophy has inherited the diremption presupposed in Kant's priority of practical reason, of the categorical imperative, between inner morality and outer legality, which nevertheless would be imported back into Judaic self-definition by Borowitz. In short, he avoids the question as to whether there is anything on which to converge, or whether, rather, Judaism and philosophy converge on a middle broken between ethics and law.

---

[128] 'Authority and Reason contra Gadamer', 1981, in *Studies in Jewish Philosophy*, pp. 161–90; 'Modern Jewish Philosophy', in *Contemporary Jewish Religious Thought*, pp. 629–34.

The dispute reveals more than any idealization of Judaic jurisprudence will concede: that exclusive emphasis on subjective freedom insists on remaining ignorant of the inversion of intention, while exclusive defence of legal procedure as self-perficient casuistry insists on remaining ignorant of inversion of form in configuration. Once again, within *halachic* Judaism, as within philosophical presentation of Judaism from Rosenzweig to Levinas, there is *no comprehension to complement commandment*: no recognition of freedom and unfreedom. And there is also the further irony that the unresolvable, intra-normative diremption of Judaism between ethics and *halacha* should become the model, the aspiration for new political theologies winged between singularity and holiness, that would mend their broken middles at the furthest remove from the conflict of the laws.

## New Jerusalem Old Athens: The Holy Middle

This rediscovery of Judaism *at the end of the end of philosophy*, at the *tertium quid*, the middle of ethics, occurs at the deepest difficulty of both philosophy and Judaism, where they are equally cast into crisis over the conceiving of law and ethics, ethics and *halacha*. This convergence on ethics turns out to be a mutual aspiration *without* a third, a middle, on which to converge. Yet the converging proceeds apace in the form of holy middle, loveful polity − beyond nature and freedom, freedom and unfreedom − but also without law and therefore without grace. This converging by philosophy and Judaism corrupts. For, in spite of the inversion of their previous meliorist intentions into contrary configuration, they introduce no reflection on that repetition; but, claiming such unconstrued inversion to be the 'totalized' and 'totalizing' domination of Western metaphysics, and its cognates, they would enthrone the equally 'total' expiation of holy jurisprudence, refusing any recognition of their own implication in the *rearticulation* of domination.

There are two kinds of proclaimed 'end' to philosophy: the end of 'metaphysics' from Kant to Nietzsche, Rosenzweig and Heidegger, which may well found a *new thinking*; and the end of 'philosophy' from Hegel and Marx to Lukács and Adorno, which raises the question of the *realization* of philosophy. By 'the end of' the end of philosophy, I mean the discovery in the long debate between Judaism and philosophy − understood in relation to the Greek quest for the beginning − principles, causes − of the missing middle, the *tertium quid* − ethics, which finds itself always within the imperative, the commandment, and hence always already begun.

If Heidegger celebrates 'The End of Philosophy',[129] Levinas celebrates the end of the end of philosophy as ethics, presented in philosophical as well as in Judaic form – *lectures talmudiques*. Yet this is a
distinction with much less difference than Levinas claims. For Levinas'
'overcoming' of ontology depends on characterizing ontology as the
non-ethical other; while Heidegger's ethical impulse depends on the
characterization of Western metaphysics, his other, as 'onto-theology'.
To be sure, Levinas denies the ethics in the 'other' of his authorship,
while Heidegger makes no claims for the ethics in his authorship. Yet
*Ereignis*, 'the Event of appropriation', presented as playing and inter-
playing of the fourfold dimensions of time – 'pure space and ecstatic
time' – or as the four-beinged 'round dance of appropriating' by 'earth
and sky, divinities and mortals',[130] this ethical paganism, shares with its
'Judaic' counterpart of responsibility, initially domesticated and subsequently traumatized, the reintroduction of Revelation into philosophy,
the incursion of unique alterity, divine singularity. Furthermore, they
share this reintroduction of Revelation *without raising the question of
realization*; and hence without critique of the metaphysics of nature and
freedom which would make the specific history of modern freedom and
unfreedom reconstructable. The current Heidegger controversy therefore remains far too close to its quarry.[131] For the production of holy
middles, where Revelation is opposed to a totalized history of 'Western
metaphysics' – 'metaphysics' unified, thereby, since the Greeks –
continues to be licensed by the inventions of his late thinking. We are
ourselves the test-case which we would project back to 1933–4: called
by post-modern theology to the Kingdom – pagan, Judaic, Christian
– beyond 'Western' metaphysics, we are blandished away from the
very modern anxiety of polity: the opposition between morality and
legality. Instead of heeding the anxiety of beginning in the equivocation
of the ethical, we respond to new repetition in the feast – the promise
of unending angelic conviviality – new but ancient political theology.

Taylor's post-modern 'a/theology' and Milbank's post-modern
'Beyond Secular Reason' offer Christian New Jerusalem for old
Athens.[132] These authorships provide evidence of that prodigious,
omniscient, 'contemporary' 'Western' intellectuality that would

---

[129]  'The End of Philosophy and the Task of Thinking', *On Time and Being*, pp. 55–78.
[130]  'Time and Being', pp. 15–22, tr. pp. 15, 19, 21, and 'The End of Philosophy', p. 66,
*On Time and Being*; 'The Thing', *Poetry, Language, Thought*, pp. 172, 173, tr. pp. 179, 180.
See Rose, *Dialectic of Nihilism*, pp. 72–84.
[131]  See, *inter alia*, *Die Heidegger Kontroverse*, Jürg Altwegg (ed.). For elaboration, see
Rose, 'Diremption of Spirit: on Derrida's *De l'esprit*,' in *Judaism and Modernity*.
[132]  Mark C. Taylor, *Erring: A Postmodern A/theology*, 1984; *Altarity*, 1987; John Milbank,
*Theology and Social Theory: Beyond Secular Reason*, 1990.

crown post-modern theology or a/theology: 'queen of the sciences'. Each self-declaredly 'post-modern', their work is comprehensive while decrying comprehension: it disrespects and breaks down further the already lowered barriers between philosophy and literary criticism in the one case, between philosophy and social theory in the other, which are then gathered up and completed as post-modern a/theology or theology. Thereby is vindicated an old prognostication: that if we fail to teach theology — we will usurp it. Or, to cite the very words of John Henry Newman himself in 1852, *The Idea of a University*: 'supposing Theology be not taught, its province will not simply be neglected, but will be actually usurped by other sciences . . .'.[133]

In spite of their shared scope and fervent ambition for post-modern a/theology or theology — what do these two bodies of thought have in common? Nothing — where sources, style, tone and method are apparent. Working closely with Nietzsche and Derrida on that 'shifty middle ground *between* Hegel and Kierkegaard',[134] Taylor inserts Heidegger and recent French thought into the terrain: while Milbank's argument covers the development of secular politics to classic sociology from Malebranche to Durkheim and Weber, from Hegel and Marx to Catholic Liberation Theology, classical philosophy and medieval theology, all also oriented, however, by recent French thought, as *trivium* to its ultimate ecclesiology. Stylistically, they are even more diverse: Taylor offers a montage of text and illustration, accruing grammatical, phonetic and graphological juxtapositions and complications, learnt, it would seem, from *Finnegans Wake*; Milbank offers a treatise, four books in one, with sober, sustained argumentation, paced temporally and spatially from beginning to end. In tone, Taylor is masked, ironic, transgressive and extravagant; Milbank is straight, logical — in spite of his ontology of narration — severe, authoritative and original. Yet, we are explicitly offered by the one, a deconstruction of theology; by the other, a deconstruction of classical and modern secularity; by the one, a deconstructive a/theology; by the other, 'Difference of Virtue, Virtue of Difference'.

In *Erring*, Taylor deconstructs 'Death of God', 'Disappearance of Self', 'End of History', 'Closure of the Book', which are translated into deconstructive a/theology in four paratactic 'moves': 'Writing of God', 'Markings', 'Mazing Grace', 'Erring Scripture', to culminate in Dionysian 'joy in . . . suffering';[135] 'The "Yes" of anguished joy breaks the

---

[133] Op. cit., p. 74.
[134] Taylor, *Erring*, p. 99.
[135] Ibid., p. 182.

power of the law and fissures the "Notshall" of history',[136] while 'The unending erring in scripture is the eternal play of the divine milieu', for, in play, 'which is interplay', 'the entire foundation of the economy of domination crumbles'.[137] In *Altarity*, the middle ground between Hegel and Kierkegaard is no longer occupied by Nietzsche but by Heidegger and recent French thinkers. Yet the whole is framed by Hegel as 'Conception' and Kierkegaard as 'Transgression', titles of the opening and concluding chapters. Hegel is expounded as the identity of difference and identity, Kierkegaard as the Abrahamic transgression of the ethical from *Fear and Trembling*, and every other author is locked into this opposition between knowledge and faith which Taylor nevertheless knows Kierkegaard invented for his pseudonym, Johannes *de silentio*. No transgression occurs, for Abraham's arm is stayed by an angel, but the work concludes by affirming the opposition between 'the Law' and 'the Call of the Other', an erring in time, where *Erring* offers a nomadicism in space.

In *Theology and Social Theory: Beyond Secular Reason*, Milbank demonstrates, by a genetic-archeological reconstruction, that 'secular discourse' is constituted by its opposition to orthodox Christianity as 'pagan' theology or antitheology in disguise.[138] In four 'sub-treatises' the complicity of secular reason with an 'ontology of violence' is rehearsed: first, in eighteenth-century politics and political economy; second, in all nineteenth-century sociology which, including Weber, is presented as a 'Positivist Church'; third, in Hegel and in Marx, whose impulse towards the non-secular is said to be indecently recruited for secular science; this equivocation, evident to Milbank, is itself, with indecent alacrity, recruited to 'a "gnostic" plot about a historically necessary fall and reconstruction of being, with a gain achieved through violence undergone'.[139] These two treatises conclude with attempts to terminate the dialogue between theology and sociology and between theology and liberation, respectively. Fourthly and finally, at the threshold to the last great treatise, Milbank disentangles his self-declared nihilistic voice from his Greek-medieval voice to complete nihilism with Christian logos and virtue which 'recognizes no original violence'.[140] Not the difference of nihilism nor the virtue of the Greeks; not liberal, of course, but equally 'Against "Church and State" '[141] –

---

136   Ibid., p. 169.
137   Ibid., p. 134.
138   Op. cit., p. 3.
139   Ibid., p. 4.
140   Ibid., p. 5.
141   Ibid., pp. 406f.

that is, without natural rights and without natural law – 'transcendental difference' is 'encoded' as a 'harmonic peace' beyond the circumscribing power of any totalizing reason.[142] Without violence or arbitrariness, and yet with difference, non-totalization and indeterminacy, and without representation, the Augustinian 'other City' is 'advocated' as 'the continuation of ecclesial practice': it is 'the imagination in action of a peaceful, reconciled social order, beyond even the violence of legality'.[143] The active imagination of 'the *sociality* of harmonious difference'[144] (emphasis in original) sketches the peaceful donation of 'the heavenly city' where 'beyond the possibility of alteration' 'the angels and saints abide... in a fellowship [whose] virtue is not the virtue of resistance and domination, but simply of remaining in a state of self-forgetting conviviality'.[145] Between this heavenly city and the sinful city, founded on the murder of Abel, of the *saeculum*, 'the interval between fall and final return of Christ',[146] God sends a salvation city, the 'City of God on pilgrimage through this world' which does not exclude anyone but 'provides a genuine peace by its memory of all the victims, its equal concern for all its citizens and its self-exposed offering of reconciliation to enemies',[147] 'its salvation... "liberation" from political, economic and psychic *dominium*'.[148]

This explication of pilgrimage and inclusivity effectively destroys the idea of a city: its task of salvation deprives it of site; while its inclusive appeal deprives it of limit or boundary that would mark it off from any other city and their different laws: 'the city of God is in fact "a paradox, a nomad city" (one might say)'.[149] The otherwise always indicted features of Gnostic demiurgic soteriology in this messenger city, and the precondition of violence committed by sinful cities in this 'peace coterminous with all Being whatsoever' should be noted in this 'encoded narrative'.

The new Jerusalems have emerged: post-modern a/theology as nomadic ecstasy – Dionysian joy; post-modern theology as nomadic ecclesial eschatology – harmonious peace; both breaking the frame in their antinomianism, and both reinstating the frame in their dependence on law transgressed – joy that 'breaks the power of law';[150] or law

[142] Ibid., pp. 6, 5–6.
[143] Ibid., p. 6.
[144] Ibid., p. 5.
[145] Ibid., p. 391.
[146] Ibid., pp. 391–2.
[147] Ibid., p. 392, first set of inverted commas in original.
[148] Ibid., p. 391.
[149] Ibid., p. 392.
[150] Taylor, *Erring*, p. 169.

subdued – peace that is 'beyond even the violence of legality'.[151] Taylor with joy but without sociality; Milbank with sociality and glimpses of angelic conviviality; both converge on the acknowledgement of difference, but in so doing reinstate the *age-old* oppositions between law and grace, knowledge and faith, while intentionally but, it will turn out, only apparently, working without the *modern* duality of nature and freedom.

This replacing of old Athens by new Jerusalem consigns the opposition between nature and freedom to one of any number of arbitrary, binary, metaphysical conceits – instead of recognizing it as index and indicator of freedom and unfreedom – and then proceeds to complete such 'deconstruction' in holiness. This founding and consecrating of holy cities inadvertently clarifies what that discarded opposition made it possible to reflect upon; reflection which is disqualified by its disappearance. Furthermore, those two Christian holy cities – Protestant (Taylor), Catholic (Milbank) – arise on the same foundations – antinomian and ahistorical – as the Davidic cities of Leo Strauss and Levinas.

These authorships – Strauss and Levinas – also embrace the paradox in presenting Judaic theologico-political prophecy or ethics *in philosophical terms* as the end of the end of philosophy. They also claim for Judaism the solution of the theologico-political or the ethical problem without the opposition between nature and freedom: Strauss presents Judaism *contra* nature; Levinas, *contra* freedom. Consequently, both represent Judaism or Jewish history eschatologically: for Strauss, in *Philosophy and Law*, however, 'the prophet is the founder of the [ideal] Platonic state',[152] and while the 'era that believes in Revelation / is *fulfilled*', this is not because of the belief but because what is revealed is 'a simple binding Law, a divine Law, a Law with the power of right'.[153]

These philosophical presentations of Judaism which have made Judaism accessible and available for rediscovery at the end of the end of philosophy – *die Ironie der Ironie*, for the religion historically denigrated as superseded – are, nevertheless, *deeply* misleading. They misrepresent the rationalism or knowledge against which they define themselves; they misrepresent Judaism; and they misrepresent the history and modernity in which they are implicated. Strauss misrepresents Greek rationalism and ignores the connection between the birth and development of philosophy and earlier strata of pre-Olympian Greek

---

151    Milbank, *Beyond Secular Reason*, p. 6.
152    Op. cit., p. 105.
153    Ibid., pp. 110, 106.

religion.[154] If philosophy begins 'in wonder' then it is not a response to what is wonderful, but to what is awe-ful: it begins too, even apotropaically, in fear and trembling.[155] Preserving all cognition for philosophy while insisting that Judaism is always already commanded, they avoid any recognition of the struggle between universality and aporia, from Kantian judgement to Hegelian speculative experience, of the predicament of universal and local jurisprudence which characterizes modern philosophy as much as modern Judaism.

Moreover, they both misrepresent Judaism. The 'Talmudic argument' rehearses a rationalism which is constantly exploring its own limits – the oral law a never-ending commentary on the written law, according to which knowledge and responsibility are renegotiated under the historically and politically changing conditions of both. Yet Strauss and Levinas present Judaism as unchanging and without a history; internal and external, as commentary, as law, as community. Strauss gives priority to medieval Judaism, while Levinas' decision that modernity compels him to give priority not to 'the relation of ethics and halacha' 'but rather [to] the passage from the non-ethical to the ethical', arguing that the latter 'is truly the necessary of our time' when all authority and morality is 'called into question', draws attention systematically away, as demonstrated above, from the mainstream debate within modern Judaism over ethics and *halacha*, from which he nevertheless takes his terms, and which, far from being specific to Judaism, shows the mutual difficulty shared by Jewish and non-Jewish thinkers in the conceiving of law and ethics. It is this evasion which permits post-modern political theology to allude to a Judaism, taken from Rosenzweig, Buber or Levinas, as an open jurisprudence, a holy sociology, instead of confronting the configuring of conceiving of law and ethics in the shared context of modern legality and morality.

These four kinds of holy cities – pagan (Heidegger), Davidic (Levinas), nomadic Protestant (Taylor), nomadic Catholic (Milbank) – consecrated in the shifting sands of ahistoricism and antinomianism, may be compared in the terms made explicit by the last two as *post-modern political theologies*. First, they are 'political theologies' because they present a solution to the political problem: for Taylor, economies of domination will crumble;[156] for Milbank, salvation 'must mean "liberation" from political, economic and psychic *dominium*, and therefore

---

[154]   See, for example, F. M. Cornford, *From Religion to Philosophy*, ch. IV, pp. 124–53.
[155]   J. Harrison, *Prolegomena to the Study of Greek Religion*, ch. 1, pp. 1–31.
[156]   *Erring*, p. 134.

from all structures belonging to the *saeculum*'.[157] Second, they are 'post-modern' because their politics and their theology are explicitly developed without the prevalent, guiding, modern contraries of nature and freedom, critiqued as the tension of freedom and unfreedom; not therefore re-presentable, they can only be presented as 'holiness': for Taylor, 'the coincidence of opposites extends the divine milieu'; while for Milbank, ecclesial practice extends to the divine.[158] Significantly, both lay claim to the middle: Taylor joins 'the eternal play of the divine milieu' while Milbank distinguishes his ontology from Levinas' by denying that 'mediation is necessarily violent'.[159] So third, then, the agon of post-modernisms: within the holy play, the holy city, holy nomads – beyond nature and law, freedom and unfreedom – they resonate with and claim to do justice to the unequivocal middle. But where is this middle? Neither ecstatic affirmation vaunting its 'totally loving the world', nor eschatological peace vaunting its continuity with untarnished ecclesial practice, display any middle.[160] There are no in-stitutions – *dominium* – in either: Taylor offers no exteriority; Milbank offers no interiority. Without command and without revelation, Taylor's ecstatic affirmation remains exiled in an interior castle; where-as, with Milbank's latinity of 'sociality' and 'charity', how could 'peace' bequeathed as 'harmonious' arise, without acknowledging the *polis* in-truding into such vague sociality, without acknowledging eros and agape intruding into such tamed 'charity'? In both cases, without anxie-ty, how could we recognize the equivocal middle? In fact we have here middles *mended* as 'holiness' – without that examination of the *broken* middle which would show how these holy nomads arise out of and reinforce the unfreedom they prefer not to know.

This rediscovery of the holy city, pagan, nomadic, Judaic, these mended middles over broken middle, at the end of the end of philo-sophy, may be witnessed as the post-modern convergent aspiration which, in effect, disqualifies the third, the middle, on which they would converge. This very converging corrupts – for in figuring and consecrating its city, this holiness will itself be reconfigured by the resource and articulation of modern domination, knowable to these post-modern ministers only as mute and monolithic sedimentation.

Post-modernism is submodern: these holy middles of round-dance, ecstatic divine milieu, irenic other city, holy community – face to face or *halachic* – bear the marks of their unexplored precondition: the

---

157    *Beyond Secular Reason*, p. 391.
158    *Erring*, p. 169; *Beyond Secular Reason*, p. 6.
159    *Erring*, p. 134; *Beyond Secular Reason*, p. 306.
160    *Erring*, p. 169; *Beyond Secular Reason*, pp. 6, 433–4.

diremption between the moral discourse of rights and the systematic actuality of power, within and between modern states; and therefore they will destroy what they would propagate, for once substance is presented, even if it is not 'represented', however continuous with practice, it becomes procedural, formal, and its meaning will be configured and corrupted within the prevailing diremptions of morality and legality, autonomy and heteronomy, civil society and state. Mended middles betray their broken middle: antinomian yet dependent on renounced law; holy yet having renounced 'ideals'; yearning for nomadic freedom, yet having renounced nature and freedom. This thinking concurs in representing its tradition – reason and institutions – as monolithic domination, as 'totalitarian', while overlooking the *predominance* of form – abstract legal form – as the unfreedom *and* freedom of modern states, thereby falling into the trap, not of positing another 'totalitarian' ideal, but of presenting a holy middle which arises out of and will be reconfigured in the all-pervasive broken middle.

This holiness corrupts because it would sling us between ecstasy and eschatology, between a promise of touching our ownmost singularity and the irenic holy city, precisely without any disturbing middle. But this 'sensual holiness' arises out of and falls back into *a triune structure* in which we suffer and act as singular, individual and universal; or, as *particular*, as represented in institutions of the *middle*, and as the *state* – where we are singular, individual and universal *in each position*. These institutions of the middle represent and configure the relation between particular and the state: they stage the agon between the three in one, one in three of singular, individual, universal; they represent the middle, broken between morality and legality, autonomy and heteronomy, cognition and norm, activity and passivity. Yet they stand and move between the individual and the state. It has become easy to describe trade unions, local government, civil service, the learned professions: the arts, law, education, the universities, architecture and medicine as 'powers'. And then renouncing knowledge as power, too, to demand total expiation for domination, without investigation into the dynamics of configuration, of the triune relation which is our predicament – and which, either resolutely or unwittingly, we fix in some form, or with which we struggle, to know, and still to misknow and yet to grow . . . Because the middle is broken – because these institutions are systematically flawed – does not mean they should be eliminated or mended.

The holy middle corrupts because it colludes in the elimination of this broken middle – drawing attention away from the reconfiguration of singular, individual and universal at stake. Away from the ways in which under the promise of enhanced autonomy – whether for individuals or for communities – the middle is being radically undermined in a process of *Gleichschaltung* which, unlike the Nazi version, is quite compatible with the proclamation and actuality of civil society, with the proclamation and actuality of plurality, with the proclamation and actuality of post-modernity.

> This public person, so formed by the union of all other persons, formerly took the name of *city*, and now takes that of *Republic* or *body politic*; it is called by its members *State* when passive, *Sovereign* when active, and *Power* when compared with others like itself.[161]

Before we orient our theology, let us reconsider this passage, discussed above, in chapter 5, in relation to the city and philosophy. Neither politics nor reason unify or 'totalize': they arise out of diremption – out of the diversity of peoples who come together under the aporetic law of the city, and who know that their law is different from the law of other cities – what Rousseau called 'power', and which we now call 'nation'. Philosophy issues, too, out of this diremption and its provisional overcoming in the culture of an era – without 'disowning' that 'edifice', it (philosophy) steps away to inspect its limitations, especially when the diremptions fixated in the edifice have lost their living connections.[162] We should be renewing our thinking on the invention and production of edifices, that is, cities, apparently civilized within yet dominating without – not sublimating those equivocations into holy cities. For the modern city intensifies these perennial diremptions in its inner oppositions between morality and legality, society and state, and the outer opposition, so often now inner, between sovereignty and what Rousseau called 'power', and which we call 'nations and nationalism'; and which recurs, compacted and edified, in Levinas as 'war', as the spatial and temporal nomad in Taylor, as the nomadic city which 'remembers all the victims' in Milbank.

Look again at the labyrinth on Taylor's book, setting of this spatial and temporal nomadicism: on the cover of *Erring* we look down on a maze, and are placed not in joyous disempowerment but in panoptic dominion, notwithstanding that in the text, the maze is celebrated as 'the horizontality of a pure surface', and we are said to be situated 'in the midst of a labyrinth from which there is no exit'.[163] Towards the end of *Beyond Secular Reason*, we are told that the nomad city means

---

[161]  Rousseau, *The Social Contract*, p. 14, tr. p. 175; also discussed *supra*, ch. 5, pp. 241–3.
[162]  See Hegel, *The Difference between Fichte's and Schelling's System of Philosophy*, known as the *Differenzschrift*, pp. 12–13, tr. p. 89–90.
[163]  Taylor, op. cit., p. 168.

that 'space is revolutionized' and no longer defensible.[164] It is worth looking more closely at these festive vulnerabilities. Taylor has put a unicursal maze on his cover – which offers no choice of route – as opposed to a multicursal maze – with choice of route. In either case, it is the beginning and the end which give authority to the way, and meaning to being lost – especially to any conceivable relishing of being lost. If the beginning and the end are abolished, so that all is (divine) middle – *Mitte ist überall* – joyful erring would not be achieved nor would pure virtue 'without resistance'; one would be left helpless in the total domination of the maze, every point equally beginning and end. This is to encounter not pure freedom but pure power and to become its perfect victim.

Violence lurks in the labyrinth. The 'imagination in action' of holiness elevates what it would exclude as its Other: so that violence migrates into the non-legitimate authority of the labyrinth, into the unmitigated penance for 'all the victims' enacted by the city of salvation. This husbanded violence becomes explicit when Taylor moves to 'reframe' post-modernisms.[165] He summons the paintings of Anselm Kiefer[166] as witness and presentation of 'the Disaster', the central imagery of which is the pure surface of the desert and no longer of the labyrinth. Yet this pure surface, companion to the pitiless, shadowless glare of the sun, is spoilt in the texture of the canvases, with their straw detritus submerging ancient photographic shards. Alleviated enough to pass from pure silence – which would not be repetition in lamentation for new Zion, but unfigured trauma, indistinguishable from the absolute figure of the pure superficies of the labyrinth – from the shadowless surface to the shadow of spirit – figured enough to signal event, the ruined desert is still not configured enough to represent.

'Death Event'[167] is posited to rename epochality, or 'Death City' to rename modernity; 'origin' of new ontological political theologies which replace any comprehension of death's declension. The *Writing of the Disaster* (Blanchot), extended to the Painting of the Disaster (Kiefer, on Taylor's reading), the Filming of the Disaster (Andrey Tarkovsky's *Ivan's Childhood*),[168] and the Theology and Sociology of the Disaster (Metz, Fackenheim, Bauman) present old Athens, ancient *and* modern,

---

[164] Milbank, op. cit., p. 392.

[165] See Taylor, 'Reframing Postmodernisms', in *Shadow of Spirit* Berry and Wernick, (eds).

[166] Compare Mark Rosenthal, *Anselm Kiefer*, especially 'On Being German and an Artist: 1974–1980', pp. 32–75, and pp. 89–104.

[167] See Edith Wyschogrod, *Spirit in Ashes: Hegel, Heidegger, and Man-Made Mass Death.*

[168] See Andrey Tarkovsky's argument in *Sculpting in Time, Reflections on the Cinema*, especially ch. 1, 'The Beginning', pp. 15–35.

as the city of death. But, by making death the meaning of the city, they return the *polis* to the firmament – but to stars torn out: *dès-astres*,[169] to cosmic disorder, to the cosmo-polis, the 'world' of depredation and devastation. Presupposing this ontological disorder of the appropriation of being (*das Ereignis*), they invariably proceed to found a new city – New Jerusalem. This twin sacrality of overburdened polities – cosmic and holy – recreates the unknowing tumult of spirit out of which such authorship is nourished, without that agon of authorship which would fail towards anxiety of beginning, equivocation of the ethical, and towards apprehension, in its three senses of know, fear, arrest, of the diremption of ethics and law, configured in the middle, broken but locatable – in history, in polity, in institutions, in *dominium*. Instead, the ontology and sociology of the city of death prefers fondly to imagine its holy end of history – love and the state undirempted – in the new community.

> It is necessary that God unveil His face; it is necessary that justice and power be rejoined. There must be just institutions on this earth.[170]

Modality of prophecy conjoins the necessity and the *Sollen*, the 'is' and the 'ought', evident in this proclamation which concludes Levinas' short piece, 'To Love the Torah More Than God', apparently unaware, in its declamatory pathos, of all the other 'rejoinings' implicated, if this commandment is not to reinforce the diremption it presupposes but refuses to recognize.

> After Auschwitz 'the metaphysical capacity is paralysed'.[171]

As confession and as witness, this minatory teaching of Adorno has been widely broadcast. Yet it has been received with brutal sincerity as refusal of and discredit to the development of thinking; while its use as dramatic irony in the major, sustained, philosophical reflection of an authorship devoted to defending comprehension against fundamental ontology in the wake of 'Auschwitz' has been utterly overlooked. (In 1966 the term 'Holocaust' had not yet acquired its emblematic status.) Yet main works of Liberation Theology and Holocaust Theology isolate the paralysis apparently proffered by Adorno, and confer on it the nimbus of angelology:

---

[169]  See Maurice Blanchot, *The Writing of the Disaster*, e.g. pp. 2, 55.
[170]  Levinas, 'To Love the Torah More Than God', p. 193, tr. p. 220 (tr. Hand, p. 145).
[171]  Adorno, *Negative Dialectics*, p. 354, tr. p. 362; compare 'To write poetry after Auschwitz is barbaric', *Prisms*, p. 30, tr. p. 34.

A Klee painting named 'Angelus Novus' shows an angel looking as though he is about to move away from something he is fixedly contemplating. His eyes are staring, his mouth is open, his wings are spread. This is how one pictures the angel of history. His face is turned towards the past. Where we perceive a chain of events, he sees one single catastrophe which keeps piling wreckage upon wreckage and hurls it in front of his feet. The angel would like to stay, awaken the dead, and make whole what has been smashed. But a storm is blowing from Paradise; it has got caught in his wings with such violence that the angel can no longer close them. This storm irresistibly propels him into the future to which his back is turned, while the pile of debris before him grows skyward. This storm is what we call progress.[172]

Walter Benjamin wrote this in 1939–40, before 'Auschwitz', in order to shock even those historians and politicians opposed to Fascism out of their progressivist conceptions of history: '*even the dead* will not be safe from the enemy if he wins. And this enemy has not ceased to be victorious.'[173] After 'Auschwitz', this strategic Messianism has also been literalized, and has come to found political theologies, Catholic and Jewish, based on a proleptic soteriology of the dead. Political theology out of the perspective of Resurrection proclaims: all 'future' thinking must do justice to (Fackenheim), or be conducted in the darkness of (Metz) the redemption of those who have died.[174] Out of this 'source', Fackenheim's holocaust theology, *To Mend the World* (1982), and Metz's political theology, *The Emergent Church* (1980), major Jewish and Catholic works, respectively, mend the middle with holy cities, crowning Love the principle of the ethical state – yet they thereby fall further into the reconfiguration of the law, of the middle, which they render unknowable. Knowing death but not diremption, political theologies out of holocaust and liberation converge yet again towards that middle which they undermine by consecration as holy elevation.

Developed with no apparent awareness of each other,[175] the agon of authorship discernible in these works may be systematically compared and contrasted, as lamentation and threefold response: religious or

---

[172] Benjamin, 'Theses on the Philosophy of History', 1940, *Illuminations*, Bd IX, pp. 697–8, tr. pp. 259–60; see, too, '*Anmerkungen*', Bd I.3, pp. 1223–5.
[173] 'Theses on the Philosopy of History', Bd VI, p. 695, tr. p. 257.
[174] Emil Fackenheim, *To Mend the World*, 1982, pp. 23, 133. Johann Baptist Metz, *The Emergent Church*, 1980, pp. 18–19.
[175] Confirmed by Fackenheim: Conversation, Jerusalem, July 1988.

anthropological; methodological or philosophical and political or social. The lamentation of 'Auschwitz' effects a 'disruption' to Metz, a
'rupture' to Fackenheim; it calls for a turning – *Metanoia*, Greek for
'repentance' – to Metz; a turning or being turned – *Teshiva*, Hebrew for
'repentance' – to Fackenheim. To both, 'Auschwitz' is a *Novum* in
temporal and in divine history: God is powerless in the world (Metz);
God is absent or has retreated from the world (Fackenheim).[176] The
primary response in each case is 'religious', and based on the same
criterion. 'We can pray *after* "Auschwitz" because people prayed *in*
"Auschwitz"' (Metz); to hear and obey the commanding voice of
'Auschwitz' is an ontological possibility because the hearing and
obeying was already an ontic reality then and there (Fackenheim).[177] In
sum, we may resist to the extent and in the way they resisted (Fackenheim); 'We [Christians] are ... assigned to the victims of Auschwitz'
(Metz).[178]

The divine and temporal *Novum* is to be met and matched by a
methodological response which involves, first of all, renunciation of the
whole intellectual tradition on the argument that any comprehension in
itself amounts to reconciliation or assimilation (Metz); 'evasion-by-
explanation' amounts to transcendence or supersession (Fackenheim).[179]
For Metz, this entails apostasy from trinitarianism; for Fackenheim,
from Hegelian mediation. In both cases, this renunciation of the third
moment is presented as the rescinding of assured eschatological grace in
contrast to the previous triumphalism of theology and philosophy. It
involves opening up to the dangers of dialogue, to the relation to the other,
the second not the third, which Metz calls 'narration' in the place of
dogma, and which Fackenheim calls 'dialogue' where the outcome is not
known in advance.[180] It involves opening up the broken middle, formerly
closed and completed by trinitarianism as achieved eschatology and by
philosophical comprehension of mediation.

Yet, the third historical and political response proceeds, uninhibitedly, to mend the middle: the basic community or emergent church
(Metz); the Jewish nation state, 'return into history', as 'mending the
world' – *Tikkun* – the Kabbalistic eschatological image of fallen light-
splinters restored to their creator (Fackenheim).[181] Both authorships,

[176]   Metz, *The Emergent Church*, p. 2; Fackenheim, *To Mend the World*, pp. 250–2.
[177]   Metz, ibid., p. 19; Fackenheim, ibid., p. 25.
[178]   Metz, ibid., p. 20; Fackenheim, ibid., p. 25.
[179]   Metz, ibid., p. 19; Fackenheim, ibid., pp. 26–8.
[180]   Metz, ibid., p. 4, *Faith in History and Society*, pp. 205f.; Fackenheim, ibid.,
pp. 128–30.
[181]   Metz, *The Emergent Church*, pp. 62–5; Fackenheim, ibid., pp. 250f.

unembarrassed by their arrogated authority, issue a call into history. Metz starts from modernity's philosophy of the formation of the subject, and issues a call to 'the people' to become the subject of their own history in the presence of God – to be 'liberated'.[182] Fackenheim starts from modernity's philosophical idea of Judaism as the disunion of union and disunion, evidence of the special qualification of the Jewish people to return to the land as the state of Israel, actualization of the Idea and equally of Revelation, a secular repentance.[183]

In both cases, the call, modernity's unrealized idea, subject or substance, rediscovers and defines the people – not the people the call; yet what is established is a community – not a polity, for there is no law and no contest; not a society, for there is no social organization; not a religion, for there is no liturgy and no theology. The collectivity imagined is soteriological and antinomian and yet it is to be temporal. It can only set off 'the people' as 'the nation', justified against others but with the internal cohesion of the community: 'solidarity' of community (Metz); or state, actualization of the Idea and of Revelation (Fackenheim).

From the death of others, dangerous memory (Metz), from the renewal of the command to remember, *Zakhor* (Fackenheim), to these political theologies for the future, the argument is structured by three movements: from the God of the living *and* the dead, to the future in the memory of suffering, by means of dialogue to foster the opening of the middle (Fackenheim), narration not dogma as mediation (Metz), theology of communicative action (Peukert).[184] Yet the middle emerges mended: figured as an ethical, communal, collective end-point, unspecified in terms of its history, its polity, its anthropology, its sociology. Named by its soteriology, 'anamnestic solidarity': 'The dead, after all, also belong equally to the universal community of all men in solidarity with each other.'[185]

This sacralizing of the dead, the dialogue and the deed, joining by divine fiat justice and sin, justice and knowledge, as well as what Levinas called for, 'justice and power', to force anthropology, ontology and *imperium* out of the city of death into the holy city, betrays the dirempted middle it would will away.

Fackenheim and Metz argue that the memory of the dead rectifies the

---

[182]   Metz, *Faith in History and Society*, pp. 46–7.

[183]   Fackenheim, *To Mend the World*; compare pp. 127–30 with 144–6.

[184]   H. Peukert, *Science, Action and Fundamental Theology: Towards a Theology of Communicative Action.*

[185]   Metz, *Faith in History and Society*, p. 75; see, too, C. Lenhardt, 'Anamnestic Solidarity: The Proletariat and its Manes', *Telos*, 25 (Fall 1975), 133–54.

triumphalism of the tradition.[186] This sanctimonious justification draws attention away from the lack of articulation in such obeisance to 'the dead'. The 'paradox of anamnestic solidarity', expatiated by Peukert, that 'the happiness of the living exists in the expropriation of the dead', refers explicitly to owing our 'solidarity', our 'happiness', to 'the conclusive irretrievable loss of the victims of the historical process',[187] to the inverse relation between future felicity and commemoration. Apart from the psychological false note here, for perfect memory or commemoration would have to be the *precondition* for liberation, for any future felicity, the 'expropriation' at stake may be seen to refer not to the undifferentiated 'victims' of the past, nor to the equally undifferentiated unborn future, but, in Lenhardt's terms, to 'the view that the man [*sic*] of the future can be *ingenuous* in his practical appropriation of the world. The evils of prehistory may have been overcome but they will linger on in the collective *anamnesis* of liberated mankind.'[188] This almost-admitted ingenuousness in relation to the impossibility of conceiving of any non-violent 'appropriation of the world' is fudged by the quick turn to the lingering memory of pre-history. The whole enterprise of putting temporal distinctions in place of structural ones, so that both 'evil' and 'victims' belong to the past, and no differentiation, or even coincidence, between violated and violators can appear, no comprehension of the violence of the living to themselves can be learnt, falls apart. Instead, this unthought political history lingers in the unexamined guilt of angelic post-history, which bears all the marks of the unsupplied anthropology which the various expositions of redemptive solidarity, nevertheless, attest. The so-called 'aporia of redemptive solidarity'[189] will not deal with the idea of sin – the result is an evasive theology which shies away equally from taking the death of others as our sin and from investigating the solidarity in violence – pre-history – or the violence in solidarity – post-history.

Fackenheim and Metz concur that all previous thought, philosophical or theological, in both cases methodological, is fundamentally outmoded and discredited in the situation of historical and divine *Novum*. This negating position partakes of expiation; but it is not consistently maintained nor maintainable: for how could the uniqueness, the *Novum*, be recognized, and judged to be such, unless the universal and

---

[186]    See, especially, Metz on 'dangerous memories', *Faith in History and Society*, pp. 109–15. This bears comparison with Milbank's idea of a providential city of 'genuine peace by its memory of all the victims', see n. 147, *supra*.

[187]    Peukert, *Science, Action and Fundamental Theology*, pp. 208, 209.

[188]    Lenhardt, 'Anamnestic Solidarity', p. 138.

[189]    Ibid.

even absolute knowledge it insists on renouncing were available? The positive version that the renewed relation to Revelation and futurity renders the mediation of previous philosophy invalid, and renders the response of 'dialogue', of being open to the Other and to others, appropriate, rejoins Holocaust and Liberation Theology for all their 'modernity' to post-modern soteriologies that conjoin the singular and the divine in holy polity. If the trinity, the three, is said to display the self-complacent grace of 'eschatology', the two are to meet without epistemology, without any means – any middle – of recognizing or misrecognizing one another – as human or as divine, and yet, in responsibility. The violence that could never be overcome – of Revelation, of 'openness' – would be eternally guaranteed by these two locked into enmity without even formal parity, and thus without any creativity – any issue. Employing knowledge which has been disowned to name the era of the *Novum*, and opposing 'openness' of dialogue to mediation relies on the third – on absolute knowledge of the eschatological epoch, the epoch founded on 'Holocaust', and on the relative knowledge that would make the minimum recognition for dialogue to take place possible. Without irony, this implicit philosophy can only be insinuation – not a new methodology, but an old, now familiar, aspirant authority.

Betraying the broken middle in order to set about 'mending the world' involves reinventing the eschatology of the 'world' (Fackenheim), and the ecclesiology of the community, 'community church' (Metz). 'World' and 'community church' evade the *polis*, any *dominium*, yet positing the loveful state, New Jerusalem, without any investigation into the meaning and configuration of the old *imperium*, neither old Athens nor the new, the City of Death, they presuppose. The discrediting and discarding of mediation means in effect that, while claiming to take full account of modernity, each gives priority to one side of a mediation: Metz concentrates on the formation of individual and political subjectivity; Fackenheim concentrates on what he calls 'the religious dimension',[190] but translates this directly into the substance of a state – the former lacks any account of substance, the latter any account of subjectivity. Justice and power are 'rejoined' in a holy and irresponsible politics.

If the broken middle is abandoned instead of thought systematically, then the resulting evasive theology, insinuated epistemology, sacralized polity, will import the features of the City of Death remorselessly. The community, mended world, response to the travail of history, emerges

---

[190] Cf. Fackenheim, *The Religious Dimension in Hegel's Thought*.

as the simple sociology at the end of this kind of Liberation and Holocaust Theology.

While Holocaust and Liberation Theology turn into unexamined sociology, Holocaust Sociology turns into its contrary – Levinas' over-employed theology.

To venture a dialectical lyric –

I am abused and I abuse
I am the victim and I am the perpetrator
I am innocent and I am innocent
I am guilty and I am guilty

Not only abused and abuser, victim and perpetrator, but 'innocent' in both positions and 'guilty' in both positions, yields the agon of these four lines – altogether, they imply a predicament which cannot be resolved by positing or imagining the kingdom of God as a self-perficient community, for it will be pervaded with the *dominium* and *imperium* which its very terms deny and imply; nor by affirming and invoking individual 'morality', or responsibility 'beyond' the socially normative, beyond the alliance of logic and politics, for such auto-nomous and disinterested morality, precisely when resisting heter-onomy, is now known to have a history: to lead to the innocence and the innocence, the guilt and the guilt, that can be found simultaneously in setting and revering the law – auto-nomy – and in being beholden to it – hetero-nomy. The very struggle to keep one's autonomy separate from one's heteronomy robs 'morality' of the knowledge and of the politics which might reorient this predicament.

Zygmunt Bauman's challenging argument in *Modernity and the Holo-caust* follows the structure of Liberation and Holocaust Theology: pre-valent intellectual methods and assumptions, in this case, sociological, are themselves implicated in and indicted for the failure to come to terms with 'the Holocaust'; 'the Holocaust' itself is not the breakdown but the test of modernity: not 'determined' by modernity, yet the basic features of modernity – instrumental rationality and its bureaucratic institutions – made 'the Holocaust' 'not only possible, but eminently reasonable'.[191] The City of Death is interpreted in this authorship as the rational outcome of a collective order based on the technical and bureaucratic institutions, not on 'moral standards'. Finally, borrowing from Levinas, Bauman argues that the social distancing produced by rational-technical means suppresses moral proximity; that socialization

---

[191]    Bauman, *Modernity and the Holocaust*, p. 18.

itself reduces moral capacity; that 'morality' is *pre-social*, not the product of society but manipulated by it.[192] Borrowing from Arendt, Bauman articulates and insists on the '*moral responsibility for resisting socialization*'.[193]

The crucial convergence Bauman seeks to establish is between modern bureaucracy and the culture of instrumental rationality which separates judgement of ends from organization of means and produces moral indifference, and the development of the sociological enterprise itself which is premised on the assumption that to socialize is to civilize: that normative social institutions control and gradually eliminate irrational and antisocial drives at the individual level and at the collective level; which, in the latter case, amounts to the concentration and specialization of violence simultaneous with the divesting of violence from daily life.[194] Bauman does not add, however, the parallel point that the elimination of antisocial drives in the individual may also lead to the internalization and specialization of violence in the psychic economy of the socialized ego: morality. Instead he will argue that the imposition of norms divests the individual of his/her 'presocial morality' or responsibility, 'the existential condition of 'being with others'.[195]

Bauman simultaneously reduces Weber's critique of legal-rational domination for his sociological explanation, and presents a reduced version of Durkheim's account of socialization when it comes to his critique of sociological method. This permits him to overlook the agon of authorship in both; and to reduce his own approach to an opposition between 'instrumentality' and 'morality', which, however, presuppose, perpetuate, and reproduce each other. For the sociology of both Weber and Durkheim may be understood as the attempt to find a way, a method, to expose and to examine the predicament of modern moral autonomy: for Weber, the combination of outer ruthlessness and inner anguish of the Protestant Ethic; for Durkheim, the discovery that the highest suicide rate is to be found in Protestant communities which are based on the internalized norms of autonomy and morality.[196] These classic sociological studies are concerned precisely with the inner violence of morality, with its history, the reproduction of its condition. They are not proposing that 'morality is created by society', which Bauman attributes to them, but that moral autonomy *and* heteronomy, 'socialization', arise together out of an historical process which is knowable and reconstructable. The call to moral responsibility cannot prevail

[192]   Ibid., p. 183.
[193]   Ibid., pp. 177–8.
[194]   Ibid., pp. 27–8.
[195]   Ibid., p. 182.
[196]   Weber and Durkheim are discussed *supra*, ch. 5, p. 175.

over instrumental rationality and bureaucracy for they share the same political history: correlated legitimacies of the inner and outer 'violence' that reproduces modernity.

Bauman's defence of personal 'morality' can only claim an existential sacrality; for he distrusts the risk of sociological authorship: that while no knowledge or politics may be *generally* available, or correspond to its insight, sociological reconstruction is still staked on comprehension and on practice. 'Violence' is thereby not translated into any oppositional holiness – moral, ecclesial or eschatological – but related to the history of the form of law as enabler and disabler. Classic sociological authorship is not ultimately nervous about its scientific credentials but about its circularity, its foundations: how to gain a perspective on, to criticize, the law which bestows its own form (legal-rationality or normative factuality) without collusion in that rationality (law) yet without ontologizing irrationality – violence; to acknowledge the limitations of representation, yet to avoid antinomianism.

The agon of authorship is to remain with anxiety of beginning and equivocation of the ethical: not to define the broken middle as 'violence', and to translate it into holiness – moral, ecclesial, eschatological. Because the middle cannot be mended, because no politics or knowledge may be available or employable, it does not mean that no comprehension or representation is possible, or that it is in any case avoidable. For as all these holy authorships, Arendt, Levinas, Milbank, Bauman, to name a few, reveal, to refuse the agon of comprehension or representation, to see only violence in the law,[197] involves the elevation of both Author and His or Her creation to love in the heavenly state – which is to ignore the violence perpetuated both in this divine fate and in its abandoned temporal mate.

## Social Utopianism – Architectural Illusion

The alternating of *imperium* and ecclesiology, already evident in modernist Liberation and Holocaust theology and sociology, and yielding the pattern of much post-modern intellectuality, follows from the

---

[197] Where Arendt is concerned, this attribution of 'violence in the law' would seem to fly in the face of her argument in *On Violence*, where legitimate power is precisely the contrary of the violence of powerlessness. However, it was argued above (pp. 151–2, 216–17, 235–6) that the condemnation of the modern as 'the social', and the affirmation of 'the political', with its ecclesial characteristics, means that Arendt, too, characterizes the modern as violent.

disqualification of critique and of equivocation, so that all power is either completely bad or completely good – total domination or holy community.

This idea of the 'autonomous community' haunts the temporal as well as the divine state. Formerly figured as the collective interest of all, as the state as such, 'the community' now seems to leave the predicament of the boundary to the larger or smaller, unspecified, political entity, so as to guard its benignity and magnanimity – its loveful cohesion: the European 'community', the 'community' charge, the Jewish 'community', ethnic 'community', 'community' architecture, etc. This currency of 'community' avoids any immediate implication of state, nation, sovereignty, representation – of power and its legitimation – yet it insinuates and ingratiates the idea of the perfectly enhanced individual and collective life. Having lost all sureness of political discrimination, we no longer know where power resides – in all institutions, in the theoretical comprehension and critique of them, in ourselves, ontically or reflexively; even less, when it is legitimate, when illegitimate, when non-legitimate; least of all, how it is articulated and reconfigured.

Yet the more the middle is eroded, the more its illusion proliferates. Irreducibly singular and potentially universal, but never holy, the individual is the site of the agon between the particularity of civil society, the precarious legitimation or non-legitimate authority of the middle, and the moral allegory of the state. With no 'reality', we have as 'individuals' only a perpetually embattled and changing actuality.

The arguments for post-modern architecture, and for community architecture, aim to redress the faults and limitations of modernism in architecture, understood as totalizing domination, by restoring the middle, whether the 'human' – colour, scale, diversity and play – of post-modernism; or the 'public realm' or 'civic space' of community architecture. Both captivated by the pre-modern, post-modern architecture plunders it with gleeful pastiche, community architecture plunders it with brutal sincerity, for fixed styles or immediate vernaculars. Yet these attempts to restore the middle have the effect of undermining it. For, once again, they involve the projection of social utopianism on to architectural practice; the projection of a holy, a princely, middle which will again be reconfigured by the broken middle it seeks to heal. The more the illusory independence of the individual and 'the community' is figured in a middle – architecture – the more vulnerable that *topos* will become to the animus of social dystopia; while the reconfiguration of individual and state proceeds apace without recognition in its imbricated legal space.

Even the neo-modernist 'New Architecture'[198] of Foster, Rogers and Stirling, especially of their unexecuted plans, shares the declared ambition of post-modern and community architecture to recreate the public realm, to restore the commonwealth in a way which implies a classical, substantial idea of social virtue, while acknowledging the declaimed 'plurality' and 'diversity' of modern life. They share this ethical impulse with the now discredited Modern Movement and the principles of the international style. In the famous statement by Hitchcock and Johnson, in 1922, the style, defined as the 'frame of potential growth', is distinguished by three principles – volume or enclosed space, not mass or solidity; regularity, not axial symmetry or balance; and the infamous proscription of applied decoration or ornament, and the emphasis on the intrinsic elegance of materials, technical projection and fine proportions.[199] These principles, considered anti-aesthetic, were 'sanctioned' in structure and design by their affinity to Gothic and classical precedent, and by modern living, 'the proletarian superman of the future',[200] an ominous phrase, to which Le Corbusier will add 'superwoman'. The 'loss of ornament' is admitted to be ambiguous, and to refer to incidental, applied ornament which is replaced by surface itself as ornament. Such building is 'sociological': the hierarchy of functions is evident – with the universal given priority over the particular, and style over local tradition.[201]

In more metaphysical vein, the theoretical writings of Mies van de Rohe and of Le Corbusier display a comparable philosophical reflection on reinventing architecture by combining classical virtue with modern will-to-power, in both cases drawing, explicitly or implicitly, on Aquinas and Nietzsche, to produce a new architectural ethic. Reading Nietzsche's emphasis on the remorseless discipline of 'giving form' as convergent with the Thomist emphasis on the analogy between God and the world and intra-convertibility of the beautiful and the good, Mies argues for a 'super-rational' architecture in self-conscious answer and opposition to the examination of modern cultural alienation which he knew in the writings of Simmel and Guardini.[202] From Francesco Dal Co's presenting of Mies' 'Notes', it appears that he considered it the responsibility of the architect to find a *tertium quid* between non-form and excess of form, both disturbing features of modern life.[203]

---

[198]    See Deyan Sudjic, *New Architecture: Foster, Rogers, Stirling*, 1986.
[199]    Hitchcock and Johnson, *The International Style*, p. 20.
[200]    Ibid., p. 93.
[201]    Ibid.
[202]    Francesco Dal Co, 'Excellence: The Culture of Mies as Seen in his Notes and Books', in *Mies Reconsidered*, pp. 72, 76, 78, 80.
[203]    Ibid., p. 81.

Le Corbusier, by contrast, declaims and enacts a Zarathustrian neo-Thomism in his book *The Decorative Art of Today* (1925), seeking to educate by pointed paradox which restores the question of meaning to the reader.[204] Proclaiming the 'elimination of the equivocal', the text unravels the equivocality in this idea of elimination in view of the 'inexplicability of cause' yet 'explanation of the concatenation' which underpins an ethics that would provoke activity, the provisional assumption of 'mastery', yet cherish the awareness of mystery.[205] Thanking St Thomas for a rational faith – equally sense of touch and truth – Le Corbusier's declarative persona would insinuate 'productive morality', which, as it were, opposes the *ressentiment* against time, 'the cult of the souvenir',[206] and, like Zarathustra, would set up new law tables:

If some Solon imposed these two laws on our enthusiasm:

### THE LAW OF RIPOLIN
### A COAT OF WHITEWASH

We would perform a moral act: *to love purity* – !

We would improve our condition: *to have the power of judgement* . . .

*Everything is shown as it is* . . . you will be *master of yourself.*[207]

'Whitewash' can mean to clean and clarify, but it can also mean to suppress, to hide the truth; and this equivocation emerges when pre-modern 'whitewash', geared to a culture, is driven out by the culture of cities, and is prescribed to restore the criterion of rule, illustrated revealingly by the 'three black heads' of a tribesman and his two sons 'against a white background', captioned 'fit to govern, to dominate'.[208] The book concludes with the reiteration of the command 'to eliminate the equivocal', the call to activity, backed now by this inapplicable, equivocal history – the modern citizen called to activity and to mastery.[209]

These quintessential delineations of architectural modernism based on

---

204   Op. cit., pp. xxi–xxvi.
205   Ibid., pp. xxvi, 175, 180–1.
206   Ibid., pp. 167, 189.
207   Ibid., p. 188.
208   Ibid., p. 190.
209   Ibid., p. 192.

active excellence, on virtue, display an ethical impulse disturbingly analogous to that underlying neo-modernist, post-modernist, and community architecture. Mies van der Rohe and Le Corbusier aimed to solve the political problem in metaphysical terms, producing social utopianism by reproducing the illusion of architectural independence. They deliberately but unselfconsciously posited holy middle over broken middle. Yet no systematic exploration of the discrepancy between these evident ethical intentions or meanings and the resultant built form or architectural configuration has been sustained. Instead, new architecture remains caught in the same discrepant illusion of meaning convergent with configuration, and will know no reason for the inevitable repetition of their alienation.

While Gustav Landauer defined every historical event as 'an ever-renewed deliverance from a topia (existing order) by a utopia, which arises out of it',[210] this anarchist perspective, if reconstructed, inadvertently implies a general law: that one day's utopia will become the following day's dystopia. For architecture, this means that it – architecture – can never be what it is to be: called to create place, 'topia', it always also creates no-place: '*u-topos*'. Whether ideal place, utopia, or its inversion, dys-topia, architecture deals in the illusion and disillusion attendant on its responsibility for conceiving and executing an independent rational order, a responsibility which has only been enlarged when it comes to mean not only building or built form but its relation to immediate context and environment – the creation of 'place' as much as sculpture and function in space. Architecture is the form of this illusion of rational independence, and the most synaesthetic, most exposed bearer of social u-topianism. It must mend the middle – heal the split between civil law and the state, yet it is itself also the middle, and stands for, represents the middle: the built form of institutions, such as, house, school, market, corporation; and of local administration, such as, hospital, police station. Architectural form configures our cognitive activity and normative passivity, distinguishable and indistinguishable from cognitive passivity and normative activity. This omnipresent form of non-legitimate domination    some architecture, not all – has been moved into a position where it requires legitimation, and yet, this dangerous politicization has been deflected yet again by aestheticization. The princely middle elevated ostensibly to assuage the ravages of modernism ensures that the range of argument about architecture remains 'utopian'.

Karl Mannheim separated 'ideology' from 'utopia': interested and

---

[210]    Mannheim, *Ideology and Utopia*, p. 178, citing *Die Revolution*, p. 7.

unobjective, 'ideology' seeks to stabilize dominant interests, while 'utopia' is a directive for action – it seeks to transform society by exaggerating existing elements which inherently tend to negate it.[211] Mannheim conceded the difficulty of applying this distinction in practice: for the very interest it is meant to clarify may itself determine judgement.[212] But it is also true that change may stabilize pre-existing dominance, and stability may serve utopian interests. Yet the distinction conceptualizes the negations, out of which utopia in general and, *a fortiori*, architectural utopia, arise – of posited totality and of static actuality. In positing the theoretical separation of the ideological from the utopian impulse, the distinction may conceptualize the peculiar burden of architectural autonomy, its social utopianism, bearing the rational ideal aloft, while at the same time isolated from ideological reconfiguration which may be legitimized, *ex silentio*, without aesthetic or representation, in unassuming legal and social identifications.

> Religion remains the ideal, unsecular consciousness of its members because it is the ideal form of the *stage of human development* which has been reached in this state.[213]

In Marx's account of ideology, which Mannheim was attempting to neutralize, the utopian element is itself an indicator of the configuration of domination. In a Christian state, prior to the political emancipation of religion, the state itself, in order to fulfil its religious pretensions, must either become 'the bailiff of the Catholic Church', i.e. become powerless; or, true to the Holy Spirit of the Scriptures, be dissolved as a state, i.e. give up its power.[214] Whether towards Church or towards sect, the 'Christian' state as such has no future. Once religion is relegated to civil society, individuals become religious as an expression of their true but separated life – a imaginary communal sovereignty, now lived as the warring sovereignties of civil society.[215] Utopia – imagined or built – moves into the broken middle and indicates the changed relation of the individual to herself.

> Political emancipation is at the same time the *dissolution* of the old society on which there rested the power of the sovereign, the political system [*Staatswesen*] as estranged from the people. The

[211] Ibid., p. 36.
[212] Ibid., pp. 176–7.
[213] Marx, 'On the Jewish Question', *Early Writings*, p. 188, tr. p. 225.
[214] Ibid., pp. 186–7, tr. p. 1, pp. 224–5.
[215] Ibid., p. 188, tr. pp. 225–6.

political revolution is the revolution of civil society. What was the character of the old society? It can be characterized in one word: *feudalism*. The old civil society had a *directly political* character, i.e. the elements of civil life such as property, family and the mode and manner of work were elevated in the form of seignory, estate and guild to the level of elements of political life. In this form they defined the relationship of the single individual to the *state as a whole*, i.e. his *political* relationship, his relationship of separation and exclusion from the other components of society. For the feudal organization of the life of the people did not elevate property or labour to the level of social elements but rather completed their *separation* from the state as a whole and constituted them as *separate* societies within society. But the functions and conditions of life in civil society were still political, even though political in the feudal sense, i.e. they excluded the individual from the state as a whole, they transformed the *particular* relationship of his guild to the whole state into his own general relationship to the life of the people, just as they transformed his specific civil activity and situation into his general activity and situation. As a consequence of this organization, the unity of the state, together with the consciousness, the will and the activity of the unity of the state, the universal political power, likewise inevitably appears as the *special* concern of a ruler and his servants, separated from the people.

The political revolution which overthrew this rule and turned the affairs of the state into the affairs of the people, which constituted the political state as a concern of the whole people, i.e. as a real state, inevitably destroyed all the estates, corporations, guilds and privileges which expressed the separation of the people from its community. The political revolution thereby *abolished* the *political character of civil society*. It shattered civil society into its simple components – on the one hand *individuals* and on the other the *material and spiritual elements* which constitute the vital content and civil situation of these individuals. It unleashed the political spirit which had, as it were, been dissolved, dissected and dispersed in the various cul-de-sacs of feudal society; it gathered together this spirit from its state of dispersion, liberated it from the adulteration of civil life and constituted it as the sphere of the community, the *universal* concern of the people ideally independent of those *particular* elements of civil life. A person's *particular* activity and situation in life sank to the level of a purely individual significance. They no longer constitute the relationship of the individual to the state as a whole. Public affairs as such became the universal affair of each individual and the political function his universal function.[216]

The breaking of the middle is exposed here in its main configuration: the fact and fiction of the 'individual' who emerges split – naturalized as 'egoism' and allegorized as 'ethical'. For 'the perfection of the idealism of the state was at the same time the perfection of the materialism of civil society'.[217] On the one hand, political community is generally reduced to the means for the commerce of civil society yet, on the other, civil freedom will be abandoned should it conflict with political life.[218] In feudalism, statuses, privileges, guilds, formed the middle of legal estate, and determined individuals as their particulars, as *members* of the middle, which, corporatively, faced the separated state; with the dissolution of this feudal middle, the 'individual' emerges with two separate lives: merely particular existence outside any middle, and yet bearer of the universalist aspirations, of citizenship, enjoyed by each – enjoying, that is, the arbitrary fate of civil society, and 'active' in the increasingly imaginary state.

When all *dominium* or law is simply equated and indicted as 'total', the very diversity of its articulation disappears so that critique is disqualified. For there are many conceivable combinations of the 'autonomy' of civil society and the 'autonomy' of the state, and what would otherwise appear only as a change in quantity or as an inverse ratio – an increase in one balanced by a decrease in the other, e.g. more freedom of civil society, less state control – may be in effect a reconfiguration, which matches the 'increase' in individual 'autonomy' with increase in powers of the police state. Attention to the agon of the middle where individuals confront themselves and each other as particular and as universal yields the dynamics always at stake in any comprehension of diremption – the articulation and reconfiguration of activity and passivity, norm and cognition, morality and heteronomy.

Community architecture bears all the marks of ecclesiology – it seeks to reclaim and abolish the middle. The kingdom of God is presented here more uninhibitedly than in any other new political theology.

This unequivocal chart appears in a book called *Community Architecture: How People are Creating Their Own Environment*,[219] the cover of which has an image of Prince Charles, shoulder-to-shoulder

[216] Ibid., pp. 196–7, tr. pp. 232–3, emphasis in original.
[217] Ibid., p. 197, tr. p. 233. Compare the argument developed here with p. 285 *supra*.
[218] Ibid., p. 195, tr. p. 231.
[219] Wates and Knevitt, *Community Architecture*, 1987, pp. 24–5.

*What Makes Community Architecture Different*

| | Conventional architecture | Community architecture |
|---|---|---|
| Status of user | Users are passive recipients of an environment conceived, executed, managed and evaluated by others: corporate, public or private sector landowners and developers with professional 'experts'. | Users are – or are treated as – the clients. They are offered (or take) control of commissioning, designing, developing, managing and evaluating their environment, and may sometimes be physically involved in construction. |
| User/expert relationship | Remote, arm's length. Little if any direct contact. Experts – commissioned by landowners and developers – occasionally make superficial attempts to define and consult end-users, but their attitudes are mostly paternalistic and patronizing. | Creative alliance and working partnership. Experts are commissioned by, and are accountable to, users, or behave as if they are. |
| Expert's role | Provider, neutral bureaucrat, élitist, 'one of them', manipulator of people to fit the system, a professional in the institutional sense. Remote and inaccessible. | Enabler, facilitator and 'social entrepreneur', educator, 'one of us', manipulator of the system to fit the people and challenger of the status quo; a competent and efficient adviser. Locally based and accessible. |
| Scale of project | Generally large and often cumbersome. Determined by pattern of land ownership and the need for efficient mass production and simple management. | Generally small, responsive and determined by the nature of the project, the local building industry and the participants. Large sites generally broken down into manageable packages. |
| Location of project | Fashionable and wealthy existing residential, commercial and industrial areas preferred. Otherwise a green-field site with infrastructure (roads, power, water supply and drainage, etc.); i.e. no constraints. | Anywhere, but most likely to be urban, or periphery of urban areas; area of single or multiple deprivation; derelict or decaying environment. |
| Use of project | Likely to be a single function or two or three complementary activities (e.g. commercial, or housing, or industrial). | Likely to be multi-functional. |

| | | |
|---|---|---|
| Design style | Self-conscious about style; most likely 'international' or 'modern movement'. Increasingly one of the other fashionable and identifiable styles: Post-Modern, Hi-tech, Neo-vernacular or Classical Revival. Restrained and sometimes frigid; utilitarian. | Unselfconscious about style. Any 'style' may be adopted as appropriate. Most likely to be 'contextual', 'regional' (place-specific) with concern for identity. Loose and sometimes exuberant; often highly decorative, using local artists. |
| Technology/resources | Tendency towards: mass production, prefabrication, repetition, global supply of materials, machine-friendly technology, 'clean sweep' and new build, machine intensive, capital intensive. | Tendency towards: small-scale production, on-site construction, individuality, local supply of materials, user-friendly (convivial) technology, re-use, recycling and conservation, labour and time intensive. |
| End product | Static, slowly deteriorates, hard to manage and maintain, high-energy consumption. | Flexible, slowly improving, easy to manage and maintain, low-energy consumption. |
| Primary motivation | *Private sector*: return on investment (usually short-term) and narrow self-interest. *Public sector*: social welfare and party political opportunism. *Experts*: esteem from professional peers. Response to general national or regional gap in market, or social needs and opportunities. | Improvement of quality of life for individuals and communities. Better use of local resources. Social investment. Response to specific localized needs and opportunities. |
| Method of operation | Top-down, emphasis on product rather than process, bureaucratic, centralized with specialisms compartmentalized, stop-go, impersonal, anonymous, paper management, avoid setting a precedent, secretive. | Bottom-up, emphasis on process rather than product, flexible, localized, holistic and multi-disciplinary, evolutionary, continuous, personal, familiar, people management, setting precedents, open. |
| Ideology | Totalitarian, technocratic and doctrinaire (Left or Right), big is beautiful, competition, survival of the fittest. | Pragmatic, humanitarian, responsive and flexible, small is beautiful, collaboration, mutual aid. |

with a casually dressed architect whose emphatic *élan* of arm and hand
and pursed lip contrasts with the Prince's corrugated forehead and
incredulous, gaping mouth. These two gesticulating figures appear
free-standing against a background montage of framed photos – 'ordinary' women discussing over a table covered with architectural plans,
and three labouring lads in what looks like an 'ordinary' backyard.

The differences here charted between 'conventional' and community
architecture fall into simple oppositions, respectively, between passive
versus active user; imperious versus companionable expert; manipulation of people versus manipulation of the system; large versus small
scale; wealthy versus decaying location; single versus plural functions;
international style versus the regional and vernacular; cold technology
versus convivial technology; static versus flexible product; profit, finan-
cial and political, versus quality of life; hieratic versus demotic operation; and, finally, totalitarian ideology versus pragmatic mutuality.

To the community is implicitly imputed the ideal speech situation of
a small-scale democratic society, with no clash of particular and general
will. Yet, like the idea of an emergent church, this collectivity is
imagined in opposition to the political and social totality – it is regional
as opposed to national – and projects the predicament of sovereignty
and representation onto the presupposed environing body-politic.
'Community' is opposed to *imperium* as a type of non-coercive social
cohesion maintained not only without politics but without sociology –
without addressing the question of how its authority is legitimized. For
that is achieved by the opposing terms on which the idea of the
community relies: the charismatic appeal of the Prince is smuggled in
iconologically to distinguish the community from the type of legal-
rational domination exemplified by impersonality, bureaucracy, technology. The personality of the Prince stands in for the middle which is
also personified as the architect: legitimizing charisma rubs its contrap-
posto regal shoulder with its intermediary, the newly humbled expert.
Attention is thereby deflected from the inevitable reproduction of all
those oppositions charted *within* any 'community' which presupposes
the separation between civil society and the state at its base  appearing
here as the opposition between the 'needs' of 'people' and the impera-
tives of the middle, 'architecture', conceived, however, as continuous
with the interests of the bureaucratic, technological, autonomous state.

While the longed-for community is fixed and allegorized in the
Prince, monarch-to-be serving apprentice as the genie of every locality,
'the evils' of both civil society *and* dirempted polity are merged in the
figure of 'the architect', who takes on the separated life of each 'citizen'
– as a particularity, vulnerable and remorseless, and as aspirant universality, frail and self-fearing. The dirempted middle is further eroded as

its princely illusion proliferates, for the ethical root of the collectivity – its potentiality – is further torn out from civil egoism by a conceptualization and iconization which reclaims an ethical immediacy for 'the people' and yet projects its egoism, its dirempted particularity and universality, on to its Other, 'the architect'. This is to avoid any anxiety of beginning – any reconsideration of our general initiation into both sides of the equivocation, and thus to preclude any transformation or education. Instead it is the architect who is to learn, not 'the people'. Such imaginary liberation from 'total' domination amounts to legitimation of a new architectural utopianism – where the celebration of the regal middle takes place at the wake of the disenfranchised 'people'.[220]

The two new kinds of political theology – the theological 'imagination in action' and the architectural imagination 'in practice' – would resist 'domination' by solidarity in irenic community, whether configured in the mind of God or the mortar of man. They succeed, however, in legitimizing new absolute sovereignties, which reinforce the diremption left unknown but reconfigured at its source. This political theology aspires to overcome law and its charted oppositions without the labour to recognize its own formation and implication in persisting diremption. Legality, whether in theology or architecture, understood to be violent *per se*, reappears as violent in holy or royal authority.

Against the tradition from Pavel to Kant which opposes law to grace and knowledge to faith, this work has shown that the modern congregation of the disciplines – from philosophy to architecture – *loses faith* when it renounces concept, learning and law. Each discipline claims its 'other' from concept and law – by 'passivity beyond passivity', as 'victims' or as 'locality' – and then these pluralities demand to be unified and statically affirmed as 'community'. These forced reconciliations of diremption in the 'new' forms of civil immediacy and holy mediation sanctify specific violence as they seek to surpass violence in general.

The more the middle is dirempted the more it becomes sacred in ways that configure its further diremption.

---

[220] For further discussion, see Rose, 'Architecture to Philosophy – The Postmodern Complicity'.

# Preface

## Pathos of the Concept

What has been witnessed here is the *pathos of the concept*: the simultaneous denial of comprehension, of any experience of coming to learn the diremption of law and ethics, and reduction of conceptuality. Comprehension breaks into its Kantian elements, where cognition is modelled on law and separated from it, so that the laws of apprehension are both compressed into and separated from the ethical imperative, the law of freedom. The dualities issuing from this breakage beg to be 'overcome' as culmination of 'Western metaphysics', to be 'deconstructed' as 'difference' and to be celebrated as post-aesthetic sublimity or holy theopathy. The pathos of the concept is this cyclical repetition. Such overcoming, with its singular, antinomian aconceptuality, betrays the diremption it will not address. Diremption, unlearnt and unchanged, demands the gratuity of being mended in origin and in perpetuity.

In this work what appears posited, however named, as the violent and ancient origin which is destined to replace the series of oppositions inherited from 'Western metaphysics', has been engaged in Part One as the difficulty of beginning from the middle, from the diremption of law and ethics, and then, in Part Two, as the difficulty of claiming the middle from the beginning. Difficulty prolonged into this 'Preface' knows no End, no Telos, no Totality, only the ever-incipient fatality of arrogating the authority of beginning instead of returning the beginning to the middle. The agon of authorship undertaken here to circumvent such arrogation of authority is redoubled when the middle is conceived as the diremption of law and ethics. For there can be no authorship without legal and ethical tone and title. To keep this work in the middle, yet to risk comprehension of the broken middle, means returning beginnings to their middle and middles to their beginning incessantly. This alertness to implication, in its facetious and suspended presentations, yields the pathos of the concept.

This confession may now approach the beginning. The first chapter, an essay on the beginning, restages the collision of Hegel and Kierkegaard's authorships at the middle of law and ethics, while introducing and employing a conceptuality in excess of its address: agon of authorship, suspension of the ethical. The second chapter resumes the difficulty and anxiety of beginning by making the equivocation of the middle explicit as the equivocation of the ethical – the beginning which fails towards and from the middle in gender and marriage in the authorships of Kafka and Kierkegaard. The third chapter resumes the difficulty of beginning from the middle by addressing the anxiety of beginning – showing how accounts of the beginning of anxiety in Kierkegaard and in Freud can themselves only be understood from the middle, that is, from the anxiety of beginning. These three essays show how beginning falls into and emerges from the middle.

The three essays of the second part of the work show the middle repeatedly displaced; how 'violence' called 'love' has overcome the broken conceptuality of the modern state. The fourth chapter reorients colonized middles to their anxiety of beginning. It investigates the mythical middle of Thomas Mann's resistance to Fascism in *Joseph and his Brothers*, and addresses the strategy of authorial facetiousness which, in places, knows the violence in love attendant on diremption, the love to mend social disorder, but in other places joins Girard in positing original and ancient love in violence, the social order mended by violence. The fifth chapter foregrounds the middle in its modern political history, as the experience of the beginning and the fate of the dirempted modern state, in the work of three Jewish women – Varnhagen, Luxemburg and Arendt. That history cannot be reconstructed in their witness without examination of beginnings which have so far appeared beyond the middle – agape and aporia – yet are implicated in it. The three expose how 'violence', made ancient and original, comes to heal the middle – the political diremption of the modern state. But even when thus comprehended, 'violence' continues to appeal as the beginning. The sixth chapter shows how violence at the beginning persists when it is meant to be overcome by the elevation and extension of the 'divine milieu'. The middle made holy conserves the phantasy of originary violence without comprehending the political precondition for such imagination. Aiming straight for redemption, these new political theologies exalt diremption – urbane but never holy – and raze the beginning in hurried and patched beatification.

The pathos of the concept, which is displaced yet emergent in all these attempts to transcend any comprehension of the diremption of law and ethics, shows its fate in the conceptuality and configuration devised in its stead. This is to challenge the prevailing intellectual resignation; to urge comprehension of diremption in all its anxiety and equivocation; to aim – scandalously – to return philosophy from her pathos to her logos. In this way, we may resume reflexively what we always do: to know, to misknow and yet to grow. The middle will then show: rended not mended, it continues to pulsate, ancient and broken heart of modernity, old and new, West and East.

# Select Bibliography

Abelard, Peter, *The Letters of Abelard and Heloise*, trans. Betty Radice, Harmondsworth, Penguin, 1979.

Adorno, Theodor W., *Kierkegaard: Konstruktion des Asthetischen*, 3rd edn, Frankfurt am Main, Suhrkamp, 1962; trans. *Kierkegaard: Construction of the Aesthetic*, Robert Hullot-Kentor, Minneapolis, University of Minnesota, 1989.

—— *Minima Moralia: Reflexionen aus dem beschädigten Leben*, Frankfurt am Main, Suhrkamp, 1969; trans. *Minima Moralia: Reflections from Damaged Life*, 1951, E. F. N. Jephcott, London, New Left Books, 1974.

—— *Prismen*, 1955, *Gesammelte Schriften* 10.1, Frankfurt am Main, Suhrkamp, 1977; trans. *Prisms*, Samuel and Shierry Weber, London, Neville Spearman, 1967.

—— *Negative Dialektik*, 1966, *Gesammelte Schriften* 6, Frankfurt am Main, Suhrkamp, 1973; trans. *Negative Dialectics*, E. B. Ashton, London, Routledge, 1973.

Agacinski, Sylviane, *Aparté: Conceptions and Deaths of SK*, 1977, trans. Kevin Newmark, Florida State University Press, Tallahassee, 1988.

Altmann, Alexander, *Moses Mendelssohn: A Biographical Study*, London, Routledge & Kegan Paul, 1973.

Altwegg, Jürg (ed.), *Die Heidegger Kontroverse*, Frankfurt am Main, Athenäum, 1988.

Arendt, Hannah, *Der Liebesbegriff bei Augustin: Versuch einer philosophischen Interpretation*, Berlin, Julius Springer, 1929.

—— *Rahel Varnhagen, The Life of a Jewish Woman*, 1933, revised edn 1957; trans. Richard and Clara Winston, New York, Harcourt Brace Jovanovich, 1974.

—— *The Origins of Totalitarianism*, 1951, new edn 1973, New York, Harcourt Brace Jovanovich.

—— *The Human Condition*, Chicago, University of Chicago Press, 1958.

—— *On Revolution*, 1963, Harmondsworth, Penguin, 1979.

—— '"Eichmann in Jerusalem" An Exchange of Letters between Gershom Scholem and Hannah Arendt', *Encounter*, 22, 1, (Jan. 1964), pp. 51–6.

—— *Between Past and Future: Eight Exercises in Political Thought*, Harmondsworth, Penguin, 1968.

—— *On Violence*, 1969, New York, Harcourt Brace Jovanovich, 1970.

—— *Men in Dark Times*, Harmondsworth, Penguin, 1988.

—— *Lectures on Kant's Political Philosophy*, ed. Ronald Beiner, 'Hannah Arendt on Judging', pp. 89–156, Chicago, University of Chicago Press, 1989.

Attar, Farid Ud-Din, *The Conference of the Birds*, trans. Afkhan Darbandi and Dick Davis, Harmondsworth, Penguin, 1984.

Bauman, Zygmunt, *Modernity and the Holocaust*, Cambridge, Polity, 1989.

Benjamin, Walter, 'Max Brod's Book on Kafka', 1938, pp. 141–8; 'Franz Kafka', 1934, pp. 111–40; 'Theses on the Philosophy of History', 1940, pp. 255–66; all in *Gesammelte Schriften* I.2, I.3, 1978, Frankfurt am Main, Suhrkamp; trans. *Illuminations*, Harry Zohn, 1955, Hannah Arendt (ed.), London, Collins, 1973.

Berkovits, Eliezer, 'Faith and Law', in *Major Themes in Modern Philosophies of Judaism*, New York, Ktav, 1974, pp. 138–48.

Bernstein, Richard J., 'Rethinking the Social and Political', in *Philosophical Profiles: Essays in a Pragmatic Mode*, Cambridge, Polity, 1986, pp. 238–59.

Blanchot, Maurice, *Thomas l'obscur*, Paris, Gallimard, 1941, trans. *Thomas the Obscure*, Robert Lamberton, New York, Station Hill Press, 1988.

—— 'The Work's Space and Its Demand', in *The Space of Literature*, 1955; trans. Ann Smock, Lincoln, University of Nebraska Press, 1982.

—— *Ecriture du désastre*, Paris, Gallimard, 1980; trans. *The Writing of the Disaster*, Ann Smock, Lincoln, University of Nebraska Press, 1986.

Bleich, J. D., 'Is there an Ethic beyond Halacha?', 1985, in Norbert M. Samuelson (ed.), *Studies in Jewish Philosophy*, Lanham, University Press of America, 1987, pp. 527–46.

Booth, Edward, *Aristotelian Aporetic Ontology in Islamic and Christian Thinkers*, Cambridge, Cambridge University Press, 1983.

Borowitz, Eugene B., 'The Authority of the Ethical Impulse in "Halakhah"', 1981, in Norbert M. Samuelson (ed.), *Studies in Jewish Philosophy*, Lanham, University Press of America, 1987, pp. 489–505.

Brod, Max, *Franz Kafka, A Biography*, 1937, trans. G. Humphreys Roberts and Richard Winston, New York, Schocken, 1960.

Brown, Irene Coltman, 'Mary Wollstonecraft and the French Revolution or Feminism and the Rights of Man', in Sîan Reynolds (ed.), *Women, State and Revolution* (q.v.), pp. 1–24.

Buber, Martin, 'The Question to the Single One', 1936; trans. *Between Man and Man*, Ronald Gregor Smith, London, Fontana, 1979.

—— 'On the Suspension of the Ethical', in *Eclipse of God: Studies in the Relation between Religion and Philosophy*, 1952, Atlantic Highlands, Humanities Press, 1988.

Carlyle, Thomas, 'Varnhagen von Ense's Memoirs', 1838, in *Critical and Miscellaneous Essays*, Vol. V, London, Chapman & Hall, 1869, pp. 289–322.

Chestov, Léon, *Kierkegaard et la philosophie existentielle: Vox clamantis in deserto*, trans. T. Rageot and B. de Schloezer, Paris, J. Vrin, 1948.

Cicero, *Cicero's Offices, Essays on Friendship, Old Age and Select Letters*, London, Dent, 1930.

Climacus, John, *The Ladder of Divine Ascent*, intro. Kallistos Ware, trans. Colin Luibheid and Norman Russell, London, SPCK, 1982.

Cohen, Richard, 'Rosenzweig, Levinas and the Teaching of Hermeneutics', in E. Fackenheim (ed.), *First Workshop on Jewish Philosophy*, Jerusalem, July 1988 (forthcoming).

—— 'Rosenzweig versus Nietzsche', *Nietzsche-Studien*, 19 (1990), 346–66.

Corbusier, Le, *The Decorative Art of Today*, 1925, trans. James I. Durnett, London, The Architectural Press, 1987.

—— *The Modulor: A Harmonious Measure to the Human Scale Universally Applicable to Architecture and Mechanics*, 1948, trans. Petor de Francia and Anna Bostock, London, Faber & Faber, 1961.

Cornford, F. M., *From Religion to Philosophy: A Study in the Origins of Western Speculation*, 1912, Brighton, Harvester, 1980.

Dahrendorf, Ralf, *Society and Democracy in Germany*, 1965, London, Weidenfeld and Nicolson, 1968.

Dal Co, Francesco, 'Excellence: The Culture of Mies as Seen in his Notes and Books', in John Zukowsky (ed.), *Mies Reconsidered: His Career, Legacy, and Disciples*, New York, The Art Institute of Chicago, 1986, pp. 72–85.

Deleuze, Gilles, and Guarttari, Felix, *Kafka, Pour une Littérature Mineure*, Paris, Les Editions de Minuit, 1975.

Derrida, Jacques, *Glas*, Paris, Editions Galilée, 1974; trans. *Glas*, John P. Leavey Jr and Richard Rand, Lincoln, University of Nebraska Press, 1986.

—— *L'écriture et la différence*, Paris, Seuil, 1967; trans. *Writing and Difference*, Alan Bass, 1978, London, Routledge & Kegan Paul, 1981.

—— 'Préjugés, devant le loi', in J. F. Lyotard, *La Faculté de Juger*, Paris, Les Editions de Minuit, 1985, pp. 87–139.

—— 'Comment ne pas parler: Dénégations', *Psyché Inventions de l'autre*, Paris, Editions Galilée, 1987, pp. 535–95.

—— *The Post Card: From, Socrates to Freud and Beyond*, 1980, trans. Alan Bass, Chicago, University of Chicago Press, 1987.

—— *Shibboleth pour Paul Celan*, 1984, Paris, Editions Galilée, 1986.

—— 'En ce moment même dans cet ouvrage me voici', *Psyché Inventions de l'autre*, Paris, Editions Galilée, 1987, pp. 159–207.

Doolittle, Hilda, 'H. D.', *Tribute to Freud*, Manchester, Carcanet, 1985.

Dunning, Stephen N., *Kierkegaard's Dialectic of Inwardness: Structural Analysis of Stages*, Princeton, Princeton University Press, 1985.

Elias, Norbert, *The Civilizing Process*, Vol. 1: *The History of Manners*; Vol. 2: *State Formation and Civilization*, trans. Edmund Jephcott, Oxford, Blackwell, 1982.

Eliot, T. S., *The Waste Land and other poems*, London, Faber and Faber, 1985.

Elliott, John R., 'The Sacrifice of Isaac as Comedy and Tragedy', in Jerome Taylor and A. H. Nelson (eds), *Medieval English Drama*, Chicago, University of Chicago Press, 1972, pp. 157–76.

Fackenheim, Emil L., *The Religious Dimension in Hegel's Thought*, 1967, Chicago, University of Chicago Press, 1982.

—— *The Jewish Return into History: Reflections in the Age of Auschwitz and a New Jerusalem*, New York, Schocken, 1978.

—— *Encounters Between Judaism and Modern Philosophy: A Preface to Future Jewish Thought*, 1973, New York, Schocken, 1980.

—— *To Mend the World. Foundations of Future Jewish Thought*, New York, Schocken, 1982.

Fichte, J. G., *Reden an die deutsche Nation*, 1806, Bd VII, *Fichtes Werke*, ed. Immanuel Hermann Fichte, Berlin, Walter de Gruyter, 1971, pp. 257–502.

Finkielkraut, Alain, *The Undoing of Thought*, trans. Dennis O'Keeffe, London, The Claridge Press, 1988.

Fishbane, Michael, 'Franz Rosenzweig', in A. Udoff (ed.), *The Playground of Textuality; Modern Jewish Intellectuals and the Horizons of Interpretation*, Detroit, March, 1988 (forthcoming).

Freud, Sigmund, *The Pelican Freud Library* (PFL), ed. James Strachey, Harmondsworth, Penguin.

—— Vol. 1, *Introductory Lecture on Psychoanalysis*, 1974;

—— Vol. 2, *New Introductory Lectures on Psychoanalysis*, 1973;

—— Vol. 10, *On Psychopathology*, 1979;

—— Vol. 11, *On Metapsychology, The Theory of Psychoanalysis*, 1984;

—— Vol. 12, *Civilization, Society and Religion*, 1985;

—— Vol. 13, *The Origins of Religion*, 1985.

Gellner, E., *Nations and Nationalism*, Oxford, Blackwell, 1983.

Giddens, Anthony, *The Constitution of Society, Outline of a Theory of Structuration*, Cambridge, Polity, 1986.

—— *The Nation-State and Violence*, Vol. 2, *A Contemporary Critique of Historical Materialism*, Cambridge, Polity, 1987.

Girard, René, *Deceit, Desire and the Novel: Self and Other in Literary Structures*, 1961, trans. Yvonne Freccero, Baltimore, The Johns Hopkins University Press, 1988.

—— *Violence and the Sacred*, 1972, trans. Patrick Gregory, Baltimore, The Johns Hopkins University Press, 1986.

—— *Things Hidden Since the Foundation of the World*, 1978, Research undertaken with Jean-Michael Oughourlian and Guy Lefort. The text consists of a trialogue with Girard's voice at the centre. Quotations may be from any one of the three 'authors'; trans. Stephen Bann and Michael Metteer, London, Athlone, 1987.

—— 'An Interview with René Girard', '*To Double Business Bound*': *Essays on Literature, Mimesis and Anthropology*, London, Athlone, 1988, pp. 199–229.

Goethe, J. W. von, *Wilhelm Meisters Lehrjahre*, 1795–6, Munich, Goldmann, 1979; trans. *Wilhelm Meister's Apprenticeship and Travels*, Thomas Carlyle (1824), London, Chapman & Hall, undated.

Goodhart, Sandor, '"I am Joseph": René Girard and the Prophetic Law', pp. 53–74; Jean-Pierre Dupuy, 'Totalization and Misrecognition', pp. 75–100; both in *Violence and Truth, On the Work of René Girard*, London, Athlone, 1987.

Habermas, Jürgen, *Legitimation Crisis*, 1973, trans. Thomas McCarthy, London, Heinemann, 1976.

—— 'Hannah Arendt's Communications Concept of Power', *Social Research*, 44, 1 (Spring 1977), 3–24.

—— *The Theory of Communicative Action* (1981): Vol. 1, *Reason and the Rationalization of Society*, Vol. 2, *Life World and System: A Critique of Functionalist Reason*, trans. Thomas McCarthy; Vol. 1, London, Heinemann, 1984; Vol. 2, Cambridge, Polity, 1987.

Haecker, Theodor, *Soren Kierkegaard*, trans. Alexander Dru, Oxford, Oxford University Press, 1937.

Hamburger, Käte, *Thomas Manns Biblisches Werk*, Frankfurt am Main, Fischer, 1987.

—— 'Rahel und Goethe', in *Rahel Varnhagen Gesammelte Werke*, Bd X, Studien, Materialien, Register (q.v.), pp. 179–204.

Hannay, Alastair, *Kierkegaard: The Arguments of the Philosophers*, London, Routledge & Kegan Paul, 1982.

Harrison, Jane, *Prolegomena to the Study of Greek Religion*, 1903, London, Merlin, 1980.

Hegel, G. W. F., *Differenz des Fichtes'chen und Schelling'schen System der Philosophie*, 1801, Hamburg, Felix Meiner, 1962; trans. *The Difference Between Fichte's and Schelling's System of Philosophy*, H. S. Harris and Walter Cerf, Albany, State University of New York Press, 1977.

—— 'Jesu trat nicht lange . . .', in *Der Geist des Christentums Schriften 1796–1800*, Frankfurt am Main, Ullstein, 1978, pp. 421–516; trans. 'The Spirit of Christianity', 1798–9, in *Early Theological Writings*, T. M. Knox, Philadelphia, University of Pennsylvania Press, 1971.

—— *Phänomenologie des Geistes*, Frankfurt am Main, Suhrkamp, 1973; trans. *Hegel's Phenomenology of Spirit*, A. V. Miller, Oxford, Clarendon Press, 1977.

—— *Grundlinen der Philosophie des Rechts*, Werke, 7, Frankfurt am Main, Suhrkamp, 1970; trans. *Philosophy of Right*, T. M. Knox, London, Oxford University Press, 1967.

—— *Wissenschaft der Logik II*, ed. Georg Lasson, Hamburg, Meiner, 1969; trans. *Hegel's Science of Logic*, A. V. Miller, London, Allen & Unwin, 1969.

—— *Vorlesung über die Philosophie der Geschichte*, Werke, 12, Frankfurt am Main, Suhrkamp, 1973; trans. *The Philosophy of History*, J. Sibree, New York, Dover, 1956.

Heidegger, Martin, *Einführung in die Metaphysik*, 1935, 1953, Tübingen, Niemeyer, 1987; trans. *An Introduction to Metaphysics*, Ralph Mannheim, New York, Anchor, 1961.

—— *Zur Sache des Denkens*, Tübingen, Niemeyer, 1969; trans. *On Time and Being*, Joan Stambaugh, New York, Harper & Row, 1972.

—— 'The Thing', 1951, in *Vorträge und Aufsätze*, Pfullingen, Neske, (1954), 1978, pp. 157–75; trans. *Poetry, Language, Thought*, Albert Hofstadter, New York, Harper & Row, 1977.

Heller, Eric, 'The World of Franz Kafka', in Peter F. Neumeyer (ed.), *Twentieth Century Interpretations of The Castle*, New Jersey, Prentice-Hall, 1969, pp. 57–82.

Henning, Fenger, *Kierkegaard: The Myths and their Origins: Studies in the Kierkegaardian Papers and Letters*, trans. George C. Schoolfield, New Haven, Yale University Press, 1980.

Hesiod, 'Works and Days', in *The Homeric Hymns and Homerica*, trans. Hugh G. Evelyn-White, London, Heinemann, 1977.

Hitchcock, Henry-Russell and Johnson, Philip, *The International Style*, 1932, New York, W. W. Norton & Co., 1966.

Hobsbawm, E. J., *Nations and Nationalism Since 1780: Programme, Myth, Reality*, Cambridge, Cambridge University Press, 1990.

John of the Cross, *Ascent of Mount Carmel*, trans. E. Allison Peters, Tunbridge Wells, Burns & Oates, 1983.

Jonas, Hans, *The Gnostic Religion: The Message of the Alien God and the Beginnings of Christianity*, 1958; 2nd edn, Boston, Beacon Press, 1963.

Josipovici, Gabriel, *The Book of God: A Response to the Bible*, New Haven, Yale University Press, 1988.

Kafka, Franz, *Tagebücher 1910–1923*, ed. Max Brod, 1949, Frankfurt am Main, Fischer, 1983; trans. *The Diaries of Franz Kafka*, Martin Greenberg and Hannah Arendt, Harmondsworth, Penguin, 1972.

—— *Briefe an Felice*, Frankfurt am Main, Fischer, 1983; trans. *Letters to Felice*, James Stern and Elizabeth Duckworth, Harmondsworth, Penguin, 1978.

—— *Hochzeitsvorbereitungen auf den Lande und andere Prosa ans den Nachlass*, Frankfurt am Main, Fischer, 1983; trans. *Wedding Preparations in the Country and Other Posthumous Prose Writings*, Ernst Kaiser and Eithne Wilkins, London, Secker & Warburg, 1973.

—— *Briefe 1902–1924*, Frankfurt am Main, Fischer, 1975; trans. *Letters to Friends, Family and Editors*, Richard and Clara Winston, New York, Schocken, 1978.

Kant, I. *The Conflict of the Faculties*, trans. Mary J. Gregor, New York, Abaris Books, 1979.

Kaplan, Gisela T. and Kessler, Clive S. (eds), *Hannah Arendt, Thinking, Judging, Freedom*, Sydney, Allen & Unwin, 1989.

Kateb, George, *Hannah Arendt: Politics, Conscience, Evil*, Oxford, Martin Robertson, 1983.

Keane, John, *Democracy and Civil Society*, London, Verso, 1988.

—— *Civil Society and the State*, London, Verso, 1988.

Kearney, Richard, 'Levinas', in *Dialogues with Contemporary Continental Thinkers: The Phenomenological Heritage*, Manchester, Manchester University Press, 1984, pp. 47–69.

Key, Ellen, *Rahel Varnhagen, A Portrait*, 1913, trans. Arthur G. Chater, Westport, Connecticut, Hyperion, 1976.

Kierkegaard, Søren: for detailed bibliographical information, see Arbaugh, George E. and Arbaugh, George B., *Kierkegaard's Authorship: A Guide to the Writings of Kierkegaard*, London, Allen & Unwin, 1968.

—— *The Concept of Irony*, 1841, trans. Lee M. Capel, Bloomington, Indiana University Press, 1968.

—— *Either/Or*, 1843, Vols I, II, trans. Vol. I, David F. Swenson and Lillian Marvin Swenson (DFS-LMS), Vol. II, Walter Lowrie (WL), Princeton, Princeton University Press, 1971; Part I, II, trans. Howard V. Hong and Edna H. Hong, *Kierkegaard's Writings*, III and IV (HVH-EHH), Princeton, Princeton University Press, 1987.

—— *Fear and Trembling, Repetition*, 1843, *Kierkegaard's Writings*, VI, ed. and trans. Howard V. Hong and Edna H. Hong (HVH-EHH), Princeton, Princeton University Press, 1983.

—— *Repetition: An Essay in Experimental Psychology*, 1843, trans. Walter Lowrie (WL), New York, Harper, 1941.

—— *Fear and Trembling: Dialectical Lyric*, 1843, trans. Alastair Hannay (AH), Harmondsworth, Penguin, 1985.

—— *Philosophical Fragments: Johannes Climacus*, 1844, *Kierkegaard's Writings*, VII, eds. and trans. Howard V. Hong and Edna H. Hong (HVH-EHH), Princeton, Princeton University Press, 1985.

—— *The Concept of Anxiety*, 1844, *Kierkegaard's Writings*, VIII, trans. Reidar Thomas, Princeton, Princeton University Press, 1980; trans. *The Concept of Dread*, Walter Lowrie (WL), Princeton, Princeton University Press, 1973.

—— *Stages on Life's Way*, 1845, trans. Walter Lowrie (WL), New York, Schocken, 1967; *Kierkegaard's Writings*, XI, trans. Howard V. Hong and Edna H. Hong (HVH-EHH), Princeton, Princeton University Press, 1988.

—— *Concluding Unscientific Postscript*, 1846, trans. David F. Swenson and Walter Lowrie, Princeton, Princeton University Press, 1968.

—— *The Present Age and Of the Difference Between a Genius and an Apostle*, 1846, trans. Alexander Dru, New York, Harper, 1962.

—— *On Authority and Revelation: The Book on Adler, or a Cycle of Ethico-Religious Essays* (1846–7, not published by Kierkegaard), trans. Walter Lowrie, New York, Harper Torch Books, 1966.

—— *Works of Love: Some Christian Reflections in the Form of Discourses*, 1847, trans. Howard and Edna Hong, London, Collins, 1962.

—— *Christian Discourses*, 1848, trans. Walter Lowrie (WL), Princeton, Princeton University Press, 1974.

—— 'The Crisis and A Crisis in the Life of an Actress, by *Inter et Inter*' (1848), in *Crisis in the Life of an Actress and Other Essays on Drama*, trans. Stephen Crites, London, Collins, 1967.

—— *The Sickness Unto Death*, 1849, trans. Howard V. Hong and Edna H. Hong (HVH-EHH), Princeton, Princeton University Press, 1980; also trans. Walter Lowrie (WL), New York, Doubleday Anchor, 1954; also trans. Alastair Hannay (AH), London, Penguin, 1989.

—— *The Point of View for My Work as An Author. A Report to History and Related Writings*, 1848, trans. Walter Lowrie, New York, Harper, 1962.

—— *Training in Christianity*, 1850, trans. Walter Lowrie, Princeton, Princeton University Press, 1944.

—— *Journals and Papers*, Vols 1, 2, 3, 4, 7, trans. Howard V. Hong and Edna H. Hong, Bloomington, Indiana University Press, 1970, 1978.

—— *The Journals of Kierkegaard 1834–1854*, trans. Alexander Dru, London, Fontana, 1969.

*Kierkegaard vivant*, *Colloque organisé par l'Unesco à Paris du 21 au 23 avril 1964*, Paris, Gallimard, 1966.

Lacan, Jacques, 'The Circuit', in 'Introduction to the *Entwurf*', in *The Ego in Freud's Theory and in the Technique of Psychoanalysis 1954–1955*, Book II, *The Seminar of Jacques Lacan*, ed. Jacques-Alain Miller, trans. Sylvana Tomaselli, Cambridge, Cambridge University Press, 1988.

—— *L'éthique de la psychanalyse*, 1959–60, *Le Séminaire*, Livre VIII, Paris, Seuil, 1986.

Laruelle, Francois (ed.), *Textes pour Emmanuel Levinas*, Paris, Jean-Michel Place, 1980.

Lenhardt, Christian, 'Anamnestic Solidarity: The Proletariat and its Manes', *Telos*, 25 (Fall 1975), 133–54.

Lessing, G. E., *Nathan der Weise*, 1779, Stuttgart, Reclam, 1979; trans. in *Laocoon; Nathan the Wise; Mina von Barnhelm*, William A. Steel, London, Dent, 1930.

Levinas, Emmanuel, *De l'existence a l'existant*, 1947, Paris, Vrin, 1986; trans. *Existence and Existents*, Alphonso Lingis, The Hague, Martinus Nijhoff, 1978.

—— 'Aimer la Thora plus que Dieu', 1955, pp. 189–93; 'Entre deux mondes (La Voie de Franz Rosenzweig)', 1959, pp. 235–60; in *Difficile Liberté: Essais sur le judaisme*, Paris, Albin Michel, 1963; trans. *Difficult Freedom: Essays on Judaism*, Seán Hand, London, Athlone, 1990, pp. 142–5; pp. 181–201.

—— *Totalité et Infini: Essai sur l'extériorité*, 1961, The Hague Martinus Nijhoff, 1980; trans. *Totality and Infinity*, Alphonso Lingis, The Hague, Martinus Nijhoff, 1979.

—— *Autrement qu'être ou au-delà de l'essence*, 1974, The Hague Martinus Nijhoff, 1978; trans. *Otherwise than Being or Beyond Essence*, Alphonso Lingis, The Hague, Martinus Nijhoff, 1981.

—— 'To Love the Torah More Than God', trans. of 1955, Helen A. Stephenson and Richard I. Sugarman, commentary Richard I. Sugarman, *Judaism*, 28, 2 (1979), 216–23; and in *Difficult Freedom*, pp. 142–5, q.v. *supra*.

—— 'Le pacte', *L'Au-delà du verset: Lectures et discours talmudiques*, Paris, Les Editions de Minuit, 1982, pp. 87–106.

—— *De Dieu qui vient à l'idée*, Paris, Vrin, 1982: 'Ideologie et idealisme', pp. 17–33, 'Dieu et la philosophie', pp. 93–127 (trans. *Levinas Reader*, q.v.).

—— 'The Ego and Totality', 1954, in *Collected Philosophical Papers*, trans. Alphonso Lingis, Dordrecht, Martinus Nijhoff, 1987, pp. 25–45.

—— *The Levinas Reader*, trans. Seán Hand, Oxford, Blackwell, 1989: 'Ethics as First Philosophy', 1984, pp. 76–87; 'God and Philosophy', 1975, pp. 166–89; 'The Pact', 1982, pp. 211–26; 'Ideology and Idealism', 1973, pp. 235–48; 'Ethics and Politics', 1982, pp. 289–97.

Lichtenstein, Aharon, 'Does Jewish Tradition Recognize an Ethic Independent of Halacha?', reprinted from *Modern Jewish Ethics: Theory and Practice*, ed. Marvin Fox, Ohio, Ohio University Press, 1975, pp. 102–23.

Lockwood, David, 'Social Integration and System Integration', in George K. Zollschau and Walter Hirsch (eds), *Explorations in Social Change*, London, Routledge and Kegan Paul, 1964, pp. 244–57.

Lowrie, Walter, *A Short Life of Kierkegaard*, 1942, Princeton, Princeton University Press, 1974.

Lukács, Georg, 'The Foundering of Form Against Life: Soren Kierkegaard and Regine Olsen', in *Soul and Form*, 1910, trans. Anna Bostock, London, Merlin, 1974, pp. 28–41.

—— *The Theory of the Novel*, 1920, trans. Anna Bostock, London, Merlin, 1971.

—— *History and Class Consciousness: Studies in Marxist Dialectics*, 1918–1923, trans. Rodney Livingstone, London, Merlin, 1971.

Luxemburg, Rosa, *Gesammelte Werke*, Berlin, Dietz, 1982:
—— Band 1/1 1893–1905, Erster Halband;
—— Band 1/2 1893–1905 Zweiterhalband;
—— Band 2 1906 bis Juni 1911, 4 1914–1919;
—— Band 5 Ökonomische Schriften. *Die Akkumulation des Kapitels: Ein Beitrag zur Ökonomischen Erklärung des Imperialismus*.
—— *Rosa Luxemburg Speaks*, ed. Mary-Alice Waters, New York, Pathfinder, 1970.
—— *The Accumulation of Capital*, trans. Agnes Schwarzschild, London, Routledge & Kegan Paul, 1971.
—— *Comrade and Lover: Rosa Luxemburg's Letters to Leo Jogiches*, trans. Elzbieta Ettinger, London, Pluto, 1979.

Lyotard, J.-F., *The Postmodern Condition: A Report on Knowledge*, 1979, trans. Geoff Bennington and Brian Massumi, Manchester, Manchester University Press, 1984.

McIntyre, Alastair, *After Virtue: A Study in Moral Theory*, London, Duckworth, 1981.

Maimonides, 'Introduction to Mishneh Torah', in Isadore Twersky (ed.), *A Maimonides Reader*, New York, Behrman House, 1972, pp. 35–41.
—— *Introduction to the Talmud*, trans. Zvi L. Lampel, New York, Judaica Press, 1975.

Mann, Thomas, *Reflections of a Non-Political Man*, 1918, trans. Walter D. Morris, New York, Frederick Ungar, 1982.
—— 'Die Stellung Freuds in der modernen Geistesgeschichte', 1929, in *Gesammelte Werke*, Bd X *Reden und Aufsätze* (GW) 2, Frankfurt, Fischer, 1960, pp. 256–80; and in Thomas Mann, *Essays*, ed. Hermann Kurzke, Frankfurt am Main, Fischer, 1982, Bd 3, pp. 153–72.
—— 'Goethe und Tolstoi', 'Goethe's Laufbahn als Scriftsteller', in *Zwölf Essays und Reden zu Goethe*, Frankfurt am Main, Fischer, 1982, pp. 65–169; trans. *Essays* (q.v.).
—— *The Theme of the Joseph Novels*, Washington, Library of Congress, 1942.
—— 'Zum Problem des Antisemitismus', 1937, in W. A. Berendsohn (ed.), *Sieben Manifeste zur 'Jüdischen Fragen'*, *1936–1940*, Darmstadt, Melzer, 1966, No. 4, pp. 23–42.
—— *Joseph und seine Brüder*, Vols 1, 2, 3 (1933–43), Frankfurt am Main, Fischer, 1983; trans. *Joseph and His Brothers*, H. T. Lowe-Porter, Harmondsworth, Penguin, 1978.
—— *The Holy Sinner*, trans. H. T. Lowe-Porter, Harmondsworth, Penguin, 1951.
—— *Doctor Faustus, The Life of the German Composer Adrian Leverkuhn as told by a Friend*, 1947, Frankfurt am Main, Fischer, 1975; trans. H. T. Lowe-Porter, Harmondsworth, Penguin, 1971.
—— *Essays of Three Decades*, trans. H. T. Lowe-Porter, New York, Alfred A. Knopf, 1976: 'Goethe and Tolstoy' (1922), pp. 93–175; 'Freud and the Future' (1936), pp. 411–28, trans. of 'Freud und die Zukunft' in Thomas Mann,

*Essays*, ed. Hermann Kurzke, Frankfurt am Main, Fischer, 1982, Bd 3, pp. 173–92.

—— *The Letters of Thomas Mann 1889–1955*, trans. Richard and Clara Winston, Harmondsworth, Penguin, 1975.

Mannheim, Karl, *Ideology and Utopia, An Introduction to the Sociology of Knowledge*, 1929, trans. Louis Wirth and Edward Shils, London, Routledge & Kegan Paul, 1966.

Marcuse, Herbert, *Studies in Critical Philosophy*, trans. Joris de Bres, London, New Left Books, 1972.

Marx, K., *Die Frühschriften*, ed. Siegfred Landshut, Stuttgart, Kroner, 1971; trans. *Early Writings*, Rodney Livingstone and Gregor Benton, Harmondsworth, Penguin, 1977.

Metz, Johann Baptist, *Faith in History and Society: Towards a Practical Fundamental Theology*, 1977, trans. David Smith, London, Burns & Oates, 1980.

—— *The Emergent Church: The Future of Christianity in a Postbourgeois World*, 1980, trans. Peter Mann, London, SCM, 1981.

Milbank, John, *Theology and Social Theory: Beyond Secular Reason*, Oxford, Blackwell, 1990.

Moore, Sebastian, *Let This Mind Be in You: The Quest for Identity through Oedipus to Christ*, London, Darton, Longman & Todd, 1985.

Mosès, Stéphane, 'Zur Frage des Gesetzes: Gershom Scholems Kafka – Bild', in Karl Erich Grözinger, Stéphane Mosès and Hans Dieter Zimmermann (eds), *Kafka und das Judentum*, Frankfurt am Main, Athenäum, 1987, pp. 13–34.

Neumann, Franz, *Behemoth, The Structure and Practice of National Socialism*, London, Victor Gollancz, 1942.

Newman, John Henry, *The Idea of a University*, 1852, ed. Martin J. Suaglic, Indiana, University of Notre Dame, 1982.

Nietzsche, F., *Werke*, Bd I–V, ed. Karl Schlechta, Frankfurt am Main, Ullstein, 1976–9.

—— 'Homers Wettkampf', in *Werke*, III, pp. 999–1007.

—— *Human All Too Human – A Book for Free Spirits*, *Werke* I, pp. 435–1008, trans. R. J. Hollingdale, Cambridge, Cambridge University Press, 1987.

—— *On the Genealogy of Morals* and *Ecce Homo*, *Werke* III, pp. 207–346, trans. Walter Kaufmann, New York, Vintage, 1969.

—— *Twilight of the Idols*, *Werke* III, trans. R. J. Hollingdale, Harmondsworth, Penguin, 1975, pp. 384–480.

Nygren, Anders, *Agape and Eros*, Pt. I 1930, Pt. II 1938–9, trans. Philip S. Watson, SPCK, London, 1982.

Outka, Gene, *Agape: An Ethical Analysis*, New Haven, Yale University Press, 1972.

Pannenberg, Wolfhart, *Basic Questions in Theology*, Vol. I 1967, trans. George H. Kehm, London, SCM, 1970.

Pateman, Carole, *The Sexual Contract*, Oxford, Polity, 1988.

—— 'The Fraternal Social Contract' in John Keane (ed.), *Civil Society and the State*, London, Verso, 1988, pp. 101–28.

Pessoa, Fernando, *Selected Poems*, trans. Jonathan Griffin, London, Penguin, 1982.

Peukert, Helmut, *Science, Action and Fundamental Theology: Towards a Theology of Communicative Action*, 1976, trans. James Bohman, Cambridge, MIT, 1986.

Pieper, Josef, *Leisure the Basis of Culture*, trans. Alexander Dru, London, Faber & Faber, 1952.

Plato, *Lysis, Symposium, Gorgias*, trans. W. R. M. Lamb, *The Loeb Classical Library*, London, Heinemann, 1975.

Pointon, Marcia, 'Liberty on the Barricades: Women, Politics and Sexuality in Delacroix', in Sîan Reynolds (ed.), *Women, State and Revolution* (q.v.), pp. 25–43.

Reynolds, Sîan (ed.), *Women, State and Revolution: Essays on Power and Gender in Europe Since 1789*, Brighton, Wheatsheaf, 1986.

Rickels, Laurence A., *Aberrations of Mourning: Writing on German Crypts*, Detroit, Wayne State University Press, 1988.

Rilke, R. M., *Lettres francaises à Merline 1919–1922*, Paris, Seuil, 1950; *Letters to Merline, 1919–1922*, trans. Violet M. MacDonald, London, Methuen, 1951; trans. Jesse Browner, London, Robson, 1990.

Robertson, Ritchie, *Kafka, Judaism, Politics and Literature*, Oxford, Oxford University Press, 1987.

Rose, Gillian, *The Melancholy Science: An Introduction to the Thought of Theodor W. Adorno*, London, Macmillan, 1976.

—— *Hegel contra Sociology*, London, Athlone, 1981.

—— *Dialectic of Nihilism: Post-Structuralism and Law*, Oxford, Blackwell, 1984.

—— 'Architecture to Philosophy – The Postmodern Complicity' in *Theory, Culture and Society*, Vol. 5 (1988), 357–71.

—— *Judaism and Modernity*, Oxford, Blackwell Publishers (forthcoming).

Rosenthal, Mark, *Anselm Kiefer*, Chicago and Philadelphia, Prestel Verlag, 1987.

Rosenzweig, Franz, *Der Stern der Erlosung*, 1921, 2nd edn 1930, *Gesammelte Schriften II*, The Hague, Martinus Nijhoff, 1976; trans. *The Star of Redemption*, 1921, William W. Hollo, London, Routledge & Kegan Paul, 1971.

—— 'Das neue Denken', 1925, *Zweistromland Kleinere Schriften zur Glauben und Denken, Gesammelte Schriften III*, pp. 139–61, trans; 'The New Thinking', in Natum N. Glatzer (ed.), *Franz Rosenzweig, His Life and Thought*, New York, Schocken, 1961, pp. 190–207.

Rousseau, Jean-Jacques, *Julie ou la Nouvelle Héloïse*, 1748 finished, 1761 published, ed. R. Pomeau, Paris, Garnier, 1960; *Eloisa or a Series of Original Letters*, 1803, Vols I and II, trans. William Kenrick, Oxford, Woodstock, 1989.

—— 'A Discourse on the Arts and Sciences', 1750; 'Discours sur l'origine et les fondaments de l'inégalité parmi les hommes', 1755, Paris, Gallimard, 1965; trans. *The Social Contract and Discourses*, G. D. H. Cole, London, Dent, 1973.

—— *Du Contract Social, ou Principes du droit politique*, 1762, ed. C. E. Vaughan, Manchester, Manchester University Press, 1962.

Samuelson, Norbert M. (ed.), *Studies in Jewish Philosophy: Collected Essays of the Academy for Jewish Philosophy 1980–1985*, Lanham, University Press of America, 1987; contains Borowitz, E. B., 'The Authority of the Ethical Impulse in "Halakhah"', 1981, pp. 489–505; Bleich, J. D. 'Is there an Ethic beyond Halacha?', 1985, pp. 527–46.

Schlegel Friedrich, *Lucinde: Ein Roman*, 1799, Stuttgart, Reclam, 1977.

Scholem, Gershom, *Walter Benjamin – die Geschichte einer Freundschaft*, Frankfurt am Main, Suhrkamp, 1975; trans. *Walter Benjamin – the Story of a Friendship*, Harry Zohn, London, Faber & Faber, 1982.

Schorsch, Ismar, 'On the History of the Political Judgement of the Jew', *Leo Baeck Memorial Lecture*, 20, New York, 1977, pp. 3–23.

Schüssler-Fiorenza, Elisabeth, *In Memory of Her: A Feminist Theological Reconstruction of Christian Origins*, London, SCM, 1983.

Schwarzschild, Steven, 'Authority and Reason contra Gadamer', 1981, in N. M. Samuelson (ed.), *Studies in Jewish Philosophy* (q.v.) pp. 161–90.

—— 'Modern Jewish Philosophy', in Arthur A. Cohen and Paul Mendes-Flohr (eds), *Contemporary Jewish Religious Thought*, New York, The Free Press, 1988, pp. 629–34.

Seligman, Adam, 'The Eucharist Sacrifice and the Changing Utopian Movement in Post Reformation Christianity', *International Journal of Comparative Sociology*, 29, 1–2 (1988), 30–43.

—— 'Inner Worldly Individualism and the Institutionalization of Puritanism in Late Seventeenth Century England', *British Journal of Sociology* (forthcoming).

Smith, John H., *The Spirit and its Letter: Traces of Rhetoric in Hegel's Philosophy of Bildung*, Ithaca, Cornell University Press, 1988.

Spiel, Hilde, 'Rahel Varnhagen, Tragic Muse of the Romantics', in P. Quennell (ed.), *Affairs of the Mind: The Salon in Europe and America From The Eighteenth to the Twentieth Century*, Washington, D.C., New Republic Books, 1980, pp. 13–21.

Steinberger, P. J., *Logic and Politics in Hegel's Philosophy of Right*, New Haven, Yale University Press, 1988.

Strauss, Leo, *Philosophy and Law: Essays Towards the Understanding of Maimonides and his Predecessors*, 1935, trans. Fred Baumann, Philadelphia, Jewish Publication Society, 1987.

—— *Natural Right and History*, 1953, Chicago, University of Chicago Press, 1971.

Sudjic, Deyan, *New Architecture: Foster, Rogers, Stirling*, London, Royal Academy of Arts, 1986.

Taminiaux, Jacques, *Dialectic and Difference: Finitude in Modern Thought*, trans. James Decker and Robert Crease, New Jersey, Humanities, 1985.

Tarkovsky, Andrey, *Sculpting in Time: Reflections on the Cinema*, trans. Kathy Hunter-Blair, London, The Bodley Head, 1986.

Taylor, Mark C., *Journeys to Selfhood: Hegel and Kierkegaard*, Berkeley, University of California Press, 1980.

—— *Erring: A Postmodern A/theology*, Chicago, University of Chicago Press, 1984.

—— *Altarity*, Chicago, University of Chicago Press, 1987.

—— 'Reframing Postmodernisms', *Shadow of Spirit: Contemporary Western Thought and its Religious Subtexts*, Conference at King's College, Cambridge, 1990.

Theunissen, Michael and Greve, Wilfred (eds), *Materialien zur Philosophie Soren Kierkegaards*, Frankfurt am Main, Suhrkamp, 1979.

—— 'Das Kierkegaardbild in der neueren Forschung und Deutung (1945–1957)', *Deutsche Vierteljahresschrift fur Literaturwissenschaft und Geistesgeschichte*, 32, 4 (1958), 576–612.

Thulstrup, Niels, *Kierkegaard's Relation to Hegel*, 1967, trans. George L. Stegren, Princeton, Princeton University Press, 1980.

Troeltsch, Ernst, *The Social Teaching of the Christian Churches*, Vols I and II (1911), trans. Olive Wyon, Chicago, University of Chicago Press, 1981.

Udoff, Alan (ed.), *Kafka and the Contemporary Critical Performance*, Bloomington, Indiana University Press, 1987.

Van der Meulen, Jan, *Hegel Die gebrochene Mitte*, Hamburg, Felix Meiner, 1958.

Varnhagen, Rahel, *Gesammelte Werke*; eds Konrad Feilchenfeldt, Uwe Schweikert, Rahel E. Steiner, Matthes und Seitz, 1983:

—— Band I Buch des Andenkens 1;

—— Band II Buch des Andenkens 2;

—— Band IV Briefwechsel zwischen Varnhagen und Rahel, 1;

—— Band X Studien, Materialien, Register.

Washofsky, Mark, 'Halakhah and Political Theory: A Study in Jewish Legal Response to Modernity', *Modern Judaism*, 9, 3 (October 1989), 289–309.

Wates, Nick and Knevitt, Charles, *Community Architecture: How People are Creating Their Own Environment*, London, Penguin, 1987.

Weber, Max, *Die protestantische Ethik und der Geist des Kapitalismus*, 1904–5, Gütersloh, Mohn, 1981; trans. *The Protestant Ethic and the Spirit of Capitalism*, Talcott Parsons, London, Unwin, 1968.

—— *From Max Weber: Essays in Sociology*, trans. H. H. Gerth and C. Wright Mills, London, Routledge & Kegan Paul, 1967.

Weber, Samuel, *The Legend of Freud*, Minneapolis, University of Minnesota Press, 1982.

Weissberg, Liliane, 'Writing on the Wall: Letters of Rahel Varnhagen' *New German Critique*, 36 (1985), 157–73.

—— 'Stepping Out: The Writing of Difference in Rahel Varnhagen's Letters', in Sandor Gilman and Stephen Katz (eds), *Antisemitism in Times of Crisis*, New York, New York University Press (forthcoming: page numbers refer to typescript).

—— 'Turns of Emancipation: On Rahel Varnhagen's Letters', *Cultural Critique*, 15 (September, 1991) (forthcoming: page numbers refer to typescript).

Wolf, Christa, *Kindheitsmuster*, 1976, Darmstadt, Luchterhand, 1988; trans. *A Model Childhood*, Ursule Molinaro and Hedwig Rappolt, London, Virago, 1988.

Wolin, Sheldon S., *Politics and Vision: Continuity and Innovation in Western Political Thought*, Boston, Little, Brown & Co., 1960.

Wollstonecraft, Mary, *Vindication of the Rights of Woman*, 1792, ed. Miriam Brody Kramnick, Harmondsworth, Penguin, 1983.

Wyschogrod, Edith, *Spirit in Ashes: Hegel, Heidegger, and Man-Made Mass Death*, New Haven, Yale University Press, 1985.

Young-Bruehl, Elizabeth, *Hannah Arendt: For Love of the World*, New Haven, Yale University Press, 1982.

# Index